PENGUIN PLAYS

CONTEMPORARY SCENES FOR STUDENT ACTORS

Having taught acting at the Lee Strasberg Theatre Institute and at The Actors Studio, Michael Schulman now teaches at his own workshop in New York City. He has also written and directed a number of plays for the Off-Off Broadway theater. He recently established the British-American Acting Academy to promote the synthesis of British and American acting techniques. In addition to his theatrical career, he is a clinical and research psychologist who has held assistant professorships at Fordham and Rutgers universities.

Eva Mekler is both a playwright and an actress who has performed in several Off-Off Broadway productions. Trained in psychology, with a master's degree from New York University, she has worked as a clinician in private practice, a staff psychologist in a residential treatment center for adolescents, and a school psychologist for the New York City Bureau of Child Guidance.

CONTEMPORARY SCENES FOR STUDENT ACTORS

Edited by
Michael Schulman and
Eva Mekler

PENGUIN BOOKS

PENGUIN BOOKS
Published by the Penguin Group
Penguin Books USA Inc.,
375 Hudson Street, New York, New York 10014, U.S.A.
Penguin Books Ltd, 27 Wrights Lane, London W8 5TZ, England
Penguin Books Australia Ltd, Ringwood, Victoria, Australia
Penguin Books Canada Ltd, 10 Alcorn Avenue
Toronto, Ontario, Canada M4V 3B2
Penguin Books (N.Z.) Ltd, 182–190 Wairau Road, Auckland 10, New Zealand

Penguin Books Ltd, Registered Offices:
Harmondsworth, Middlesex, England

First published 1980
15   17   19   20   18   16   14
Copyright © Michael Schulman and Eva Mekler, 1980
All rights reserved

LIBRARY OF CONGRESS CATALOGING IN PUBLICATION DATA
Main entry under title:
Contemporary scenes for student actors.
Includes index.
1.   Acting.   2.   Drama—20th century.   I.   Schulman,
Michael, 1941–   II.   Mekler, Eva.
PN2080.C65   808.82'04   80-15674
ISBN 0 14 048.153 2

Printed in the United States of America
Set in Times Roman

CONTENTS

Contents   **9**

ACKNOWLEDGMENTS

PREFACE

This book is designed to provide the student actor and the professional and nonprofessional auditioner with a collection of some of the best scenes ever written for the stage. The scenes selected are all from recent plays; most are from plays written during the past twenty years, and most of our major contemporary playwrights are represented.

All the scenes are for two persons, and they are organized into three groups: scenes for a man and a woman; scenes for two women; and scenes for two men. The introduction to each scene provides background information on characters, setting, and plot so that the reader will understand what the scene is about, but it cannot be emphasized too strongly that before actually preparing a scene for class or for an audition, the entire play should be read. The introductory chapter, "How to Approach a Scene," provides a list of questions that should be answered by the actor when preparing a role. The answers can only be found by careful study of the whole script.

A number of criteria went into the selection of scenes. Of primary importance was that the scenes be highly *actable;* that is, that they provide both actors with clearly definable character objectives and obstacles (the most important acting elements). Among the other considerations were that the collection represent a full spectrum of acting modes, from farcical to tragic; that the materials call for a diversity of acting styles, from naturalistic through poetic to highly stylized; that they span a range of ages; that they be set in a variety of locales and periods (they range from the Garden of Eden to ancient Greece to Elizabethan England to modern urban and suburban settings); and that excerpts of various lengths be included.

The scenes are presented with all dialogue and stage directions reproduced exactly as they appeared when first published.

Some stage directions are written by the playwright and contain crucial information about the behavior and intentions of the characters. Descriptions of the character crossing the stage, sitting down, standing up, leaning, etc., most likely derive from the initial director's blocking notes, rather than from the playwright, and are probably best ignored. Also, many actors find that trying to fulfill stage directions as to how a line should be spoken ("tenderly," "angrily," "sympathetically") or what facial expression should be used ("puzzled," "wide eyed," "glaring") leads to mechanical and stereotyped results. They argue that such directions (which also may not have been part of the playwright's original script) intrude into the actor's domain as the creative interpreter of the character. Certainly there is not just one interpretation of a play's events and characters, to be slavishly replicated by each new cast. Our own feeling about stage directions is that we should not be unduly bound by them, but neither should we ignore on principle those that might clarify some section or ignite fresh ideas.

The preparation of this book has, we believe, extended our perspectives on the state of playwrighting during the past few decades. Of course, one finds fallow seasons and disappointments where promising new playwrights or wonderful old playwrights fall short of hopes and expectations. But as one looks down the list of selected titles (and adds to these the many fine plays that were not included for one reason or another), one has an overall sense of this having been a rich time—with an abundance of good plays by a plenitude of good playwrights (and even some great ones)—a time that can be compared favorably to any period in theater history.

We earnestly thank the playwrights, and their agents, for allowing us to share their writing with you, and we thank them most heartily for providing us over the past years with so many thrilling evenings in the theater.

HOW TO APPROACH A SCENE

Various schools of acting tend to emphasize one or another element of an actor's craft, too often at the expense of other equally important elements. Audiences, though, when they enter a theater, are not concerned about theoretical allegiances to any particular school or method. They come to witness and share fully in the experience of the actors on stage. As such, they react to many aspects of an actor's or actress's performance: They get involved with the character's desires and conflicts and are engaged by the actions and utterances through which these are revealed; they are moved and impressed by strong emotional displays; they are especially intrigued when the subtle moment-to-moment changing content of thought is made visible through facial and bodily expressions; they are engrossed by characters that are distinctive and fully defined, curious to observe the peregrinations of a unique and authentic life. The best acting provides an audience with all these elements.

There are many ingredients that go into the making of a skilled actor: learning to concentrate and to bring concentration back into focus when it has drifted away or turned into self-consciousness; being able to summon up calm and confident feelings when overwhelmed by fears; developing a fully expressive voice and body so that actions and reactions are compelling, as well as visible and audible; knowing how to bring on—and turn off—emotions, and how to create fully realized characters, some of whom will have desires and behaviors that are quite different from one's own; learning to draw upon one's own past experience and fantasy life in order to comprehend and generate the experiences and reactions of the character; and, most importantly, understanding how to use one's imagination in order to actually experience the life of the character and create authentic thoughts and behaviors that appear to be (and are actually experienced by the actor as being) spontaneous.

The job of an acting teacher is to help students achieve a sense of actually experiencing the life of the character, and to provide them with a systematic approach that will prove effective and reliable. The question list that follows was developed for that purpose. The answer to each question will add information about the past and present states and circumstances of the character, as well as about the character's expectations of the future. Each answer should ultimately affect behavior and thoughts onstage.

The questions cover the desires, thoughts, actions, conflicts, expectations, memories, fantasies, sensitivities, and emotions of a character, as well as his or her cultural background and behavioral style; and they should prove to be useful for plays of any style or period. Restoration comedy requires no less reality, in the sense of the characters actually experiencing their circumstances, than do plays written in a modern naturalistic style. The outward behavior must, of course, take a form that is appropriate to the times; but stylized behavior from any period (including our own) is ordinarily very purposeful and the Restoration character is just as fully in pursuit of an objective, beset by obstacles, affected by past circumstances, and driven by passions as any contemporary character.

An actor, like any artist, is judged in terms of his or her choices, and since no two actors playing a given role are likely to come up with precisely the same answers, the questions serve the important additional purpose of stimulating and prompting each actor's creativity.

Questions to Ask in Preparing a Scene

Questions that are extensions of, or elaborations on, a single concern are grouped together. Unless indicated otherwise, all questions are asked from the point of view of the character.

Where am I and what is my relationship to this place? What time of day is it? What aspects of the physical environment (weather, odors, etc.) affect me? What actions or reactions are elicited?

All events take place in an environment. If you create the details of the character's physical environment, you will both aid your concentration (walking across a stage often leads to self-consciousness; walking through a room or meadow does not) and gain the necessary sense of the character's reality. A character will be more sensitive to certain aspects of an environment than others, perhaps because of the extremeness of those aspects (it is very hot or cold), or because of past experience (extreme cold is likely to have a special effect on someone who almost froze to death once).

What has my past contact with this place been? What objects are significant or of interest to me? Are they pleasing or displeasing? Do I take any action with respect to an object (use it, explore it, etc.)?

You behave differently in an environment in which you have already been than in one that is strange. You may already know of its potential dangers or treasures or lack of either. Interesting behaviors may be generated, and concentration and reality further enhanced, by specifying your character's relationship to or interest in particular aspects of the environment. For example, when walking through a meadow you may feel especially fond of birches or concerned about poison ivy. By the same token, the simple and common stage business of pouring wine for a guest can become an engaging moment if you are proud of your selection of wines and eager to impress the guest.

Who is here or expected? What is my relationship to them and what past contacts have we had? What do I know or suspect about them, either from personal contact or reputation? How do I act, think, or feel differently with the various people? What do I expect them to do?

Certainly your relationships to the persons that are present or expected to be present will affect your behavior and thinking. While watching or waiting for someone you may worry about consequences, recollect incidents, plan actions, or prepare yourself (by straightening your clothes, perhaps) or an object (by loading a pistol). The very way you speak to someone or orient your body toward them (or toward the place from where they are to enter) may vary from person to person and will depend on your past contacts with them and your expectations of the future.

What do I believe the others think or expect of me? What do I think they want from me? Do they know what I want from them and the degree to which I want it?

These questions are all designed to stimulate the kind of thinking, planning, and anticipatory playing out of scenarios in our minds that we all do in life. They should affect the way you interact: the way you watch an adversary, or argue for what you want, or feign in order to hide your wants.

Am I aware of my impact on others? Does this awareness affect my behavior? Do I exploit or try to minimize my impact?

A person's appearance, language, position or social status, reputation, group affiliation, physical strength, intelligence, wit, etc., may affect how you behave in his or her presence. In life one is often aware of the impact of such characteristics and has an attitude about their effect, so they should be taken into account in the development of your character's self-concept.

What just preceded this event and how did it affect me both physically and mentally?

To live through the present circumstances of your character you need a sense of continuity with the prior circumstances: where the character just came from, what happened there, and what effect it had. The memories and images of past events must be created in sufficient detail so that as you enter the present moment of the scene, you are actually experiencing the aftereffects of the past.

What do I want? What are my objectives? *What are the obstacles to be overcome? Are they within myself, from the environment, or from other persons?*

The most important acting elements are the *objective* and the *obstacle(s)*—that is, what a character wants (e.g., Hamlet wants to convince his mother to refuse Claudius's bed; Lady Macbeth wants to incite her husband to murder the king) and what is in the way of obtaining that which is wanted. These two elements and the uncertainty they generate with regard to outcomes (will the objective be achieved or will the obstacle prevail?) constitute the basic structure of a dramatic event. A character may have more than one objective. Some will be more important than others, some will be in conflict with each other, and some will change in strength or appear or disappear as a scene progresses. Also, some objectives may be subsumed under broader objectives. For example, Lady Macbeth may want the king dead so that she can gain some otherwise unobtainable degree of respect and power (and this broader objective may also affect the way she treats her servants). To use an objective successfully you need to know not only what your character wants, but *why* he or she wants it: why your character is plotting a murder or pursuing wealth or a lover or a hearty meal. During performance you must periodically reignite your character's motivation by reminding yourself of such reasons: of the unforgivable insult that must be avenged by murder, of the humiliation of poverty, of the lover's enchanting smile and the anticipated sexual encounter, or of the pangs of hunger and the imagined taste of food. These reminders must be created (imagined) with great specificity and be integrated into the actual onstage thinking (the character's "inner monologue"). For example, the "humiliation of poverty" would have to be translated from an abstract idea into the visualization of actual humiliating events from your past life (either the character's past or your own). This is, of course, similar to the way we experience motivation in life.

Obstacles may be external, in the sense that another person or some condition in the physical environment stands in the way of someone's goals; or they may be internal, in the sense that a person may want two mutually exclusive objectives at the same time (e.g., a priest who wishes to honor his vows of chastity, but who also desires a beautiful woman). The trap for actors working with such internal obstacles is to allow the two opposing impulses to cancel each other out, culminating in total inaction. A more productive approach would be for you to alternate your focus from one goal to the other, allowing each separate impulse to instigate at least the beginnings of an action toward attaining the desired goal. In this way the inner conflict becomes visible to the audience.

Do my objectives or obstacles change ("beat" changes) as the scene or play progresses? Do my expectations about getting what I want change? What discoveries do I make? How am I changed by what I learn?

Wants and/or obstacles change as a character goes through experiences, makes discoveries, and revises expectations. These changes form the structure of a scene. Expressing the transitions by thinking as a person actually would under those changing circumstances, and making such thinking apparent through bodily and vocal changes, can be, for the audience, among the most arresting aspects of acting.

What actions do I attempt in pursuing my objective? What actions do I consider taking but reject? What observations do I make to determine if my actions are succeeding? How do my actions affect me or my self-esteem? Are there moral considerations? Am I pleased or displeased with myself?

The pursuit of objectives must be expressed in both physical actions and verbal actions (words). Characters do things to get things. Even if they do not know why they do what they do, or even if each action that is initiated is quickly aborted, some behavior must occur for the audience to understand the desires of the character and thereby be able to relate to the dramatic content of the play. Even the mental actions of trying to figure something out, for example evaluating alternatives and consequences, must be physically indicated in some way. This often produces very interesting, though subtle, behaviors. An often-neglected but important set of actions derives from the periodic need of a character to evaluate whether he or she is getting closer to or further from the goal (e.g., a salesman in the midst of a pitch periodically checks the reaction of a prospective buyer). During the course of a scene actions may be intensified, modified, or entirely abandoned depending on their effectiveness in bringing you closer to your goal as well as on the impact on your own feelings, self-concept, other goals, and so on. For example, to accomplish his objective toward his mother, Hamlet may try to shame her, frighten her, reason with her, or induce maternal guilt or love (or alternate from one to the other from moment to moment). He might also abandon an action if he himself became frightened, guilty, or ashamed.

An actor's performance is largely evaluated by the quality of his or her physical actions. This may be illustrated by a piece that is usually played with little attention to the possibilities of action. In a famous passage in *Macbeth*, Lady Macbeth receives news from her husband that the king will accompany him home. She then begins a powerful monologue, invoking the spirits to "unsex" her, to give her the strength and courage to carry through her plan to murder the king. The monologue is often played as an incantation with the actress growling her lines in a witchlike manner. If you think in terms of actions, other, more interesting (and more easily playable) possibilities arise.

This is one of many possible sequences: The news has been good news, so Lady Macbeth may begin the piece with expressions of delight. This may lead her to the awareness that proper preparations must be made, followed by going to a mirror to prepare and pretty herself for her guests. The excited preparations may be quickly cut off by the discovery that the feminine character she sees before her is too weak to carry out the intended murder. Thus the need for the spirits and the unsexing. An audience will understand these thoughts if, as they hear her petition the spirits, they see her take actions to undo the prettying and then alter her makeup or clothing in order to appear harder and more masculine. The partial accomplishment of this change may then suddenly force upon her the full realization of what she intends, and make her recoil from the cold-hearted image in the mirror with fear and guilt. (Keep in mind that this is the woman who eventually takes her own life because of her guilt.) At this point we understand her next lines, her plea for courage and hardheartedness, because we have seen the obstacles within herself that she must overcome. Her commitment will be quite clear to us if we then see her resolving to continue and complete the unsexing. All this may be accomplished in little more time than it ordinarily takes to simply speak the speech.

*What do I feel toward, and what do I need from, the other per-
son(s)? What do I want them to feel about me? In what ways am
I vulnerable to them? Why do I feel as I do toward them? What
specific aspects of them or me or our past together have generated
these feelings and needs?*

Certainly your feelings toward and needs from someone will
determine or color your objectives, obstacles, and actions with
respect to them. If Hamlet loves his mother or needs her love he
will pursue his objective quite differently than if he hates her.
Feelings are aroused by concrete stimuli. You actually *feel* love
(as opposed to knowing you love) only under certain circumstances, such as seeing a special look on someone's face or remembering a certain event shared with them. Similarly, the
actual set of reactions that we call a feeling (e.g., desire) consists
of combinations of such concrete experiences as words spoken
to ourselves ("He looks attractive"), strong attentional states
(focusing for a long time on the other person's face or body),
images or 'private behavior" (imagining kissing or touching the
other person), and bodily changes. The more concretely you,
the actor, work, the more fully you will be able to create, experience, and express feelings.

*Do I consciously know what I want? If not, what do I believe I
want? In what way do the actions arising from the real and believed wants interact or alternate?*

The concept of an unconscious motivation is based essentially
on a disagreement. A person explains to others, as well as to
him- or herself that he or she has done something for some
(usually benevolent) outcome, and an observer or a psycho-
therapist contends that it was done for some other (usually
selfish or harmful) reason. Playwrights will create this kind of
circumstance in many different ways. Some extreme characters
will simply not have the intentions and actions of one moment
carry into the next moment. They have what might be described
as two separate and alternating minds. More commonly, characters will be aware of all their actions but will provide themselves with innocent justifications for them. The actor must try
to plot out the moment-to-moment perceptions and thoughts of

the character and play them as the character would experience them.

What secrets do I know? How much of what I say is actually meant or truthful? What is left unsaid? How adept am I at expressing my thoughts?

This is another question designed to promote lots of onstage thinking: what needs to be said to obtain your objective, and what must remain private; and how effective is your manner of expression and should alternate modes be attempted?

What would I be doing or thinking now if I were alone and this particular scene were not taking place?

This is a useful device for making sure that you are really playing out your character's story and not just waiting for your cue from your acting partner. If you have done the proper work on the character's objective, prior circumstances, and relationship to the environment, you should be able to logically play out the current moment in your character's life whether or not anyone else written into the scene appears. (Be aware that the moment may turn out very differently from the one that would logically transpire in the presence of the other characters.)

What past circumstances of my character's life must I (as the actor) create and live through via fantasized "private improvisations," in order to experience the present state and circumstances of my character?

Knowledge of a character's past is not sufficient for the actor. You must "live through" that past via your imagination by creating complete fantasies about the people and incidents of the character's life. For example, in playing Hamlet remembering and mourning for his father, you will be helped if you create detailed fantasies of good times spent with the father, of lessons learned from him, of moments of affection, and of discussions of his hopes and his fears. In a classroom exercise I might prompt a student with a statement such as "Remember when your father taught you a special dueling secret," and then let the student quietly play out the fantasy of this event in his imagination.

What emotional reactions do I experience and what memories, fantasies, and plans of the character ("character stimuli") can I draw upon to create those reactions?

You can experience the character's life only if you experience the character's stimuli. Emotions are reactions to stimuli, but in order to make the stimuli of your character evocative for yourself, you must embed them in a meaningful context. Such a context is provided by living out the character's past events through fantasy (thus creating memories) and, also via fantasy, creating the character's projections and plans for the future.

What does my character say that is particularly evocative for him or her? What descriptions, memories, and anticipations of the future are mentioned that must be made into concrete and specific images so that they can affect my speech (melody, pauses, emphases) to the maximum degree that is warranted and logical?

If a character talks about a delicious meal (either already eaten or planned for later) or a horrifying battle incident, the actor must create through fantasy the details of those experiences so that his or her words and gestures are affected by the images of those events. For a simple illustration of how intrinsic imagery is to verbal expression, take a moment to describe what you ate for supper last night. You will quickly find your thoughts filled with visual, taste, textural, olfactory, and perhaps even aural imagery. In life this happens spontaneously. Sometimes it happens spontaneously to the actor onstage. But, as an actor, you must make sure that you have provided yourself with such imagery for every past event or projection of a future event described by the character, and that every single utterance is animated and particularized by such imagery. Even when making general references, as when Hamlet speaks of "the law's delay, the insolence of office . . .", the actor should precede (and thus impel) each separate phrase with a specific corresponding image.

What can I draw upon from my own life ("personal stimuli") to help me understand and create the character's wants, actions, and emotional reactions?

Reminding yourself of incidents from your own life that parallel or are similar to those of the character can make you aware of the intensity of responding that must be reached for. The actor's personal stimuli can and should be brought right onstage and integrated into the thinking of the character. This addition or substitution of personal stimuli can be accomplished in many ways. The actor playing Hamlet can create the fantasies of the past as suggested above, or he can provide himself with an instant history and powerful current stimuli by using incidents with his own father (or some other person he loves and admires), or he can combine character and personal stimuli in various ways. It is essential that all stimuli—character and personal—be integrated into the onstage thinking; that is, be included in what is called the "inner monologue."

At times you may effectively use a personal stimulus that seems quite remote from the moment being experienced by the character. An actress having difficulty playing a scene in which her character describes and relives a seduction in which she felt virtually hypnotically possessed by a man achieved the desired experience—the fear and excitement and loss of will—by imagining herself standing on the edge of a high precipice as she related the incident.

What is special, different, or urgent about this event?

Searching for the special significance of this moment for the character will often lead to a keener use of your senses onstage, to more discoveries being made (by your character), and to a heightened readiness for both physical action and emotional reaction.

How does my character use (and think of) his or her body? Is the body used consciously to affect others? Does the body provide

any obstacles (pains, fatigue, infirmities, drunkenness, etc.)? Is a
special physical style required, given the period and place of the
play?

The highest goal of acting is to create a full and unique life
for each role played. The nature of this "life" is, of course, dependent on and reflected in the body and bodily style of the
character. The playwright sets the boundaries of the character's
life; but within those boundaries it is the actor's choices that are
presented to an audience. All actors playing Richard III will
have some physical defects and all will engage in actions in pursuit of the throne. But the precise form of those defects and actions (as well as the content of such "inner" conditions as
Richard's self-concept or the presence or absence of any moral
feeling) fall within the purview of each actor playing the role.

How does my character use his or her voice or use words for
effect (the voice thus becoming an instrument for action)? Is the
voice used consciously in some special way to affect others? Is a
special style, dialect, or accent required given the period and
place of the play?

Of course, choosing an appropriate character voice and
speaking style is as crucial as choosing a suitable physique and
physical style. It is also important to be aware of whether or not
the style is cultivated and purposeful, and if so, whether it has
been cultivated to the point of appearing effortless or whether it
seems strained. Selecting the proper vocal and physical style is
particularly important in playing comedy. For example, in
many comedies some characters are purposefully witty (often
sarcastically) in the sense that they intend and expect to make
other characters laugh. The character's manner must reflect
this intention and confidence. Other comedic characters do not
at all intend to be funny (e.g., Jackie Gleason's Ralph Kram-
den), but the extraordinary intensity of their wants leads to
extreme actions that an audience finds funny.

How is my character distinctive? What are some behaviors,
habits, postures, daily activities, etc., that are particular to or car-
ried out in an idiosyncratic manner by my character? How do
these change with different people and environments? Does my

character carry personal objects (a comb, a mirror, a charm) or use objects in distinctive ways?

If a playwright has done his or her job well, the characters will not be drawn in a stock or stereotyped manner. Similarly, memorable performances are generally those in which the actor has melded the various elements of a character's behavior into a unique presence. But the elements must be appropriate to (and responsive to changes in) the time, place, and circumstances of the play, and not chosen arbitrarily just to produce novelty. Artists are in the business of structuring aspects of the environment (e.g., colors, sounds, shapes). The actor's medium is his or her self, and what he or she structures is a character; and as in any art form, the audience's interest depends on the distinctiveness (and appropriateness) of the structure created by the artist.

Am I concerned about what I wear? Does my choice of clothing reveal anything about me? Is this intentional? Am I comfortable with what I wear?

Clothing plays an important part in the lives of most people; it may be an integral aspect of how we present ourselves to others, and we are often uncomfortable if we wear clothing that we consider unflattering or that makes us appear other than we wish to appear (e.g., if it could lead someone to identify us with the wrong group). Conversely, clothes can also generate good feelings. Consideration of the character's relationship to his or her clothes, an often-neglected area, may enhance one's sense of the character's moment-to-moment reality.

What aspects of people or the environment is my character particularly responsive to? Are there special hopes, dreams, desires, fears, irritations, etc.? Are there special conditions that make my character feel angry, hurt, aroused, confident, shy, etc.?

An earlier question dealt with the character's particular reactions to the persons and environmental elements present in the scene. It may help in discovering the answers to that question and also in structuring the character's overall behavioral style, to consider broader aspects of a character—ones that are likely to be carried from situation to situation.

How does upbringing, formal training, taste, position, occupation, etc., affect my character's behavior and thinking?

In selecting a character's reactions, traits, and behavioral style, it is necessary to take into account the cultural and institutional influences that go into forming a personality, and then root these influences in the character's beliefs and expectations. The servant and the master do not usually behave the same way toward each other; nor do they usually believe that they should. Also, their expectations about each other's behavior and about the consequences of violating behavioral standards would ordinarily be quite different.

Many young American actors can play an urban street tough with some conviction, even without much preparation, because they intuitively understand that behind a particular strut lies the intention to convey "I'm cool. I'm tough. I can handle anything." The same actor, though, often fails to understand that behind a restoration character's pose and walk—which is no more or less affected than the contemporary urban swagger—lies the intention to convey "I'm powerful and cultured and beautiful." Without playing that intention, one is left only with an empty and artificial set of gestures. (Such affected characters from any period are often satirized by playwrights because the character's extreme efforts at appearances usually reveal the hollowness behind the facade.)

What people do I (the actor) know or have I observed that remind me of (aspects of) my character? Where can I go to find people from whom I might gather specific habits and behavior patterns that would be useful in developing my character?

The best source of ideas for developing a character's external style is the real world. The actor must become a keen and constant observer of people and a veritable storehouse of images of human (and animal) behavioral and vocal styles. One of the essential parts of an actor's craft is knowing how to allow a character to "take possession" of you. For example, think of someone you know—perhaps someone you find funny. Imagine him or her moving inside you, taking over your body, your postures, your facial muscles, your eyes, your rhythm, your stride, the distribution of your weight, your expectations the place from which your voice comes, its rhythm, etc. Try to understand what about this person's body and temperament leads him to move and think as he does: what compensations he makes, or aspirations he has. Soon you will feel like a different person. You will not feel as though you are imitating another person but as if you have been taken over by him.

What choices can I make so that my character's speech and physical behavior are as expressive, varied, and unpredictable as is warranted and logical?

In general (but there are certainly exceptions to this), urgent wants, difficult obstacles, clearly defined actions and reactions, significant consequences, conspicuous vulnerabilities, and large and unpredictable changes—if they can be justified by the character's circumstances and nature—tend to produce more interesting theatrical events. Keep in mind that your choices should support the overall interpretation of the central event of the scene or play. For example, *Hamlet* can be interpreted as a play about an exciting and excitable young man trapped in circumstances that destroy his ability to act; or it may be seen as a play about a contemplative and aesthetic young man forced by circumstances to take actions that are totally contrary to his will and spirit. The actor's choices must, of course, be quite different under these differing interpretations.

All an actor can show on stage (or in life, for that matter) are actions and reactions: actions in pursuit of objectives and reactions in response to stimuli. The questions are all designed to evoke or elicit these two classes of behavior.

—MICHAEL SCHULMAN

PART I

———•———

Scenes for One Man
and One Woman

LOVERS AND OTHER STRANGERS

by Renée Taylor and Joseph Bologna

———•———

SCENE 2

Lovers and Other Strangers is composed of four comic scenes. Each in its own way focuses on the age-old battle of the sexes set in the most contemporary situations.

The second scene takes place in the bedroom of Johnny and Wilma, a married couple. Wilma has become quite modern: she demands rights traditionally reserved for men—including the right to initiate lovemaking. Unfortunately, Johnny, an old-fashioned type, will not cooperate. What follows is a battle over who really wears the pants in the family.

A man is watching television in bed. A woman enters, looks at him, goes to the dressing table, perfumes herself and then goes to bed. As she crosses in front of the TV, he moves violently to see. She crawls into bed. The show that's been on ends. He yawns, turns it off, and turns the light off. After a long pause, she speaks in the dark.

SHE: Are you going to make love to me, or not? *No response, so she turns on the lamp.* Are you going to make love to me, or not?
HE: Huh? Wah? Come on, I was just falling asleep. Turn the light off. *She shakes him again.* What?
SHE: It's your turn to make love to me.
HE, *thinks:* I owe you one.
SHE: You owe me two already.
HE: How do you figure I owe you two?
SHE: Last Friday and the Wednesday before when Ron stayed over and you didn't want to make noise.

HE, *thinks:* All right, three. Leave me alone. I'm good for it.

SHE: Johnieee.

HE: Wilma! I'm just not in the mood now.

SHE: All right, if you don't want to. I don't want you to do anything you don't want to do. *She turns the light out and after a long pause in the dark we hear:* Don't you ever touch me again! *She lights a cigarette in the dark.*

HE: Put the cigarette out and go to sleep.

SHE: I can't sleep when I'm like this.

HE: It's all in your mind.

SHE: It is not. I feel sexy.

HE: It's just nerves. Have a sandwich. *His mumbles trail off and in the darkness we hear:* Wilma, cut it out. In the morning, in the morning.

SHE: I'm not interested in the morning. It's not romantic in the morning. It's romantic now.

HE: To me it's work.

SHE, *turns the light on:* Johnny, when I owe you, you pick the time. But you owe me, so I pick now.

HE: Who are you kidding? *Rising up.* I never pick the time. Last night when we were driving home from Jersey, I offered to pull off the Pulaski Skyway and get something going, and you said no.

SHE: I'm a married woman with two children. I am not going to make love in the back seat of a Volkswagen.

HE: Then don't complain to me any more about lack of variety. *Lies down again.*

SHE: Johnny, it's Saturday night. We haven't made love in ten days. We've both worked very hard to make love at least twice a week and if we don't tonight, there's going to be a lot of pressure on us to catch up.

HE: Wilma, I had an unusually upsetting week. I was dizzy at a meeting Wednesday and I didn't want to go out tonight because it was too hot and I felt flushed at the party, and I am physically— *(he goes to bathroom and gets a glass of water)* and emotionally exhausted.

SHE: Do you know, you're beginning to sound exactly like my mother complaining to my father.

HE: Oh, yeah? Well, you're beginning to sound exactly like my father making sexual demands on my mother.

SHE: That's all right with me, if he's the sexy one in your family.

HE: I am sexier than you will ever be.

SHE: So, why are you hoarding it?

HE: If you didn't nag me about it, maybe I wouldn't.

SHE: Nag? *Crosses to look in mirror.* I have done everything but nag. I have suggested, implied, rubbed against you while passing, worn provocative nightgowns, perfumed my underwear. I have tried every subtle way to reach you except showing stag films.

HE: Wilma— *(sits up)* I get the feeling you're trying to make my virility look impotent.

SHE: When did that feeling first hit you?

HE: The day I married you. I was dynamite with other women.

SHE: Well, sure. They were lucky just to be there with the holder of the world's championship three-second record in intercourse. *She brushes her hair.*

HE: Out of all the women in the world, I had to marry an equal-time orgasm fanatic! You read a couple of *Ladies Home Journal*s and all you know now is, "Me too!"

SHE: And why not me too?

HE: Look, stop trying to castrate me. There's too much man here. You and your "me too's" and your cockamamie career. Me and the children aren't enough for you. No, you need "creative fulfillment" to give meaning to your existence. We could have managed very well on one salary.

SHE: So quit your job.

HE: You really want to take over, don't you? *She turns back to mirror.* Don't think I haven't noticed your new wardrobe with the suits with the pants and the ties and—your butch haircut!

SHE, *turns to him:* Butch! . . . I'm more feminine than you'll ever be.

HE, *kneels on bed, left knee:* You want to know how feminine you are? Whenever we go out, I light your cigarette, I hold your chair, I rise when you come back from the little girls' room, so you can go, "Waiter, check!" That's feminine? Then I look for a cab in a snowstorm while you stand under an awning because "Your feet are cold" and "You don't want to get your hair wet." But if I don't get a cab in two minutes, you run out in the street and yell—*(he makes a loud whistle)* "Taxi-i-i." Whenever

I try to treat you like a lady, you respond like—Rocky Graziano.

SHE: Oh, shit. *He gets back in bed.* All I want is a little tenderness.

HE: Look who wants tenderness! ... Miss Locker Room Mouth. You better decide whether you want to be a man or a woman, and then talk tenderness to me. Do you understand, Wilma, or is it Willy?

SHE: I'll tell you what. You decide what you want to be first and I'll be what's left. *Puts brush on chest.* You think you're so masculine because whenever we have a problem you roll over and go to sleep, or you go out and get drunk with the boys, or you try to act rough with me. But I got a flash for you. Those tough Marine drill sergeants are the biggest fags in the world.

HE, *sits:* Watch what you say about the Corps!

SHE: Okay. *Crosses left to head of bed.* They're the biggest latent fags in the world, but they're not real men. A real man is warm and understanding and gentle and sweet and sensitive and kind and loving and—

HE: Oh, yeah. Then what's a woman?

SHE: A woman is strong and brave and—

HE: And what?

SHE, *trying to regain the initiative:* A woman should be brave and strong in certain situations—like—when her husband is tough toward her, then she has to be tough toward him. But otherwise, a woman should be worshipped and admired and put up on a pedestal, but she should have the freedom to come down off the pedestal because she wants to be independent, but then she could go back up on the pedestal because she is not a slave any more because a woman wants to be taken care of—

HE: Excuse me, is that taken care of up on the pedestal, or down off the pedestal?

SHE: I don't know what a woman is. I don't even see any difference between us any more. *She breaks down and cries, lying on bed.*

HE: Okay, I'll tell you what I'll do for you. Next week for your birthday I'll take you down for some hormone shots.

There's a long pause.

SHE: What you need is a major transplant!

HE, *sits:* You want to know why you're so confused? Because you forgot who I am and who you are. I'm the man and you're just the woman, and the man is the boss. You said so yourself when we got married.

SHE: I was just humoring you. I said, "If it was so important to you, I would let you be the boss."

HE: What do you mean, "Let me be the boss"? I am the boss.

SHE: Don't be juvenile. There is no boss.

HE: I am the boss and you know it.

SHE: There is no boss and that's final. I don't want to hear another word about it. We are equals. *Sits on bed.*

HE, *his frustration is building:* Oh, we're equal, huh? *Standing up on bed.*

SHE: Yes! We're equal.

HE: All right, let's just see how equal we are. *Pulls her up.* Come on, equal. Let's go a couple of rounds.

SHE: Cut it out, you big jerk! *He dazzles her with his footwork. She punches him in stomach and tries to run away from him. He catches her. He grabs her arms and holds them behind her back. She can't move. She struggles to get free, but he is too strong for her.* Let me go.

HE: You're my equal. Why don't you let yourself go?

SHE: Stop it.

HE: Who's the boss?

SHE: There's no boss.

HE: Who's the boss?

SHE: I am!

HE: Who's the boss?

SHE: Stop it. You're hurting me. You're going to wake the children.

HE, *lowers his voice but he says it more intensely:* Who's the boss?

SHE: You can torture me, but I won't say it.

HE: Who's the boss?

SHE: You are.

HE: And who won?

SHE, *meek and reluctant:* You did. *He releases her, proud of himself.* Shithead.

HE: That doesn't bother me because the fight's all over and I

won and I'm the boss. So be a good little loser and let's go to
bed. Good night, loser.
SHE: Excuse me. I'm sleeping on the couch. *She takes the pillow and covers and goes into the other room.*

A STREETCAR NAMED DESIRE

by Tennessee Williams

———•———

SCENE 10

Blanche DuBois is a relic, trapped in a time and place in which
she cannot survive. She is a romantic forced to seek shelter in
the hard-edged world of her younger sister, Stella, and Stella's
working-class husband, Stanley. She is almost thirty years old,
her delicate beauty fading more from adversity than from time.
From a wealthy young southern belle—beautiful, willful,
charming, flirtatious—to her current condition on the edge of
hysteria, she witnessed her family members die off in protracted
illnesses, the wealth disappear, and the family home and estate
lost to creditors. She sought solace in liquor and strange men,
and in lies and self-delusion. Fired from her job as a teacher,
homeless and penniless, she comes to her sister for "a visit." In
manner and sensibilities, Stanley is the antithesis of Blanche.
He is practical and direct; suspicious of and repelled by her pre-
tensions to gentility. He doubts Blanche's description of the loss
of the family property, resents her intrusion into his household,
and uncovers and confronts her with her lies.

Just before the following scene, Blanche had an ugly encounter with Mitch, Stanley's friend. Mitch had fallen in love with
her, and had fallen for all the lies and illusions. He had courted
her like a young southern gentleman (which he is not), and
hoped to marry her. After Stanley tells him about her sexual

past, Mitch comes to the house. Hurt and enraged, he demands
sex with her, and derides the idea of marriage. She screams and
he flees. She is left alone in the house. (Stella is about to have a
baby and Stanley has taken her to the hospital.)

She has dragged her wardrobe trunk into the center of the bed-
room. It hangs open with flowery dresses thrown across it. As the
drinking and packing went on, a mood of hysterical exhilaration
came into her and she has decked herself out in a somewhat
soiled and crumpled white satin evening gown and a pair of
scuffed silver slippers with brilliants set in their heels.

Now she is placing the rhinestone tiara on her head before the
mirror of the dressing-table and murmuring excitedly as if to a
group of spectral admirers.

BLANCHE: How about taking a swim, a moonlight swim at
the old rock quarry? If anyone's sober enough to drive a car!
Ha-ha! Best way in the world to stop your head buzzing! Only
you've got to be careful to dive where the deep pool is—if you
hit a rock you don't come up till tomorrow . . .

Tremblingly she lifts the hand mirror for a closer inspection. She
catches her breath and slams the mirror face down with such vio-
lence that the glass cracks. She moans a little and attempts to
rise.

Stanley appears around the corner of the building. He still has
on the vivid green silk bowling shirt. As he rounds the corner the
honky-tonk music is heard. It continues softly throughout the
scene.

He enters the kitchen, slamming the door. As he peers in
at Blanche, he gives a low whistle. He has had a few drinks on
the way and has brought some quart beer bottles home with
him.

BLANCHE: How is my sister?
STANLEY: She is doing okay.
BLANCHE: And how is the baby?
STANLEY, *grinning amiably:* The baby won't come before
morning so they told me to go home and get a little shut-eye.
BLANCHE: Does that mean we are to be alone in here?

STANLEY: Yep. Just me and you, Blanche. Unless you got somebody hid under the bed. What've you got on those fine feathers for?

BLANCHE: Oh, that's right. You left before my wire came.

STANLEY: You got a wire?

BLANCHE: I received a telegram from an old admirer of mine.

STANLEY: Anything good?

BLANCHE: I think so. An invitation.

STANLEY: What to? A fireman's ball?

BLANCHE, *throwing back her head:* A cruise of the Caribbean on a yacht!

STANLEY: Well, well. What do you know?

BLANCHE: I have never been so surprised in my life.

STANLEY: I guess not.

BLANCHE: It came like a bolt from the blue!

STANLEY: Who did you say it was from?

BLANCHE: An old beau of mine.

STANLEY: The one that give you the white fox-pieces?

BLANCHE: Mr. Shep Huntleigh. I wore his ATO pin my last year at college. I hadn't seen him again until last Christmas. I ran into him on Biscayne Boulevard. Then—just now—this wire—inviting me on a cruise of the Caribbean! The problem is clothes. I tore into my trunk to see what I have that's suitable for the tropics!

STANLEY: And come up with that—gorgeous—diamond—tiara?

BLANCHE: This old relic? Ha-ha! It's only rhinestones.

STANLEY: Gosh. I thought it was Tiffany diamonds. *He unbuttons his shirt.*

BLANCHE: Well, anyhow, I shall be entertained in style.

STANLEY: Uh-huh. It goes to show, you never know what is coming.

BLANCHE: Just when I thought my luck had begun to fail me—

STANLEY: Into the picture pops this Miami millionaire.

BLANCHE: This man is not from Miami. This man is from Dallas.

STANLEY: This man is from Dallas?

BLANCHE: Yes, this man is from Dallas where gold spouts out of the ground!

STANLEY: Well, just so he's from somewhere! *He starts removing his shirt.*

BLANCHE: Close the curtains before you undress any further.

STANLEY, *amiably:* This is all I'm going to undress right now. *He rips the sack off a quart beer bottle.* Seen a bottle-opener? *She moves slowly toward the dresser, where she stands with her hands knotted together.* I used to have a cousin who could open a beer bottle with his teeth. *Pounding the bottle cap on the corner of table:* That was his only accomplishment, all he could do—he was just a human bottle-opener. And then one time, at a wedding party, he broke his front teeth off! After that he was so ashamed of himself he used t' sneak out of the house when company came ... *The bottle cap pops off and a geyser of foam shoots up. Stanley laughs happily, holding up the bottle over his head:* Ha-ha! Rain from heaven! *He extends the bottle toward her.* Shall we bury the hatchet and make it a loving-cup? Huh?

BLANCHE: No, thank you.

STANLEY: Well, it's a red-letter night for us both. You having an oil millionaire and me having a baby. *He goes to the bureau in the bedroom and crouches to remove something from the bottom drawer.*

BLANCHE, *drawing back:* What are you doing in here?

STANLEY: Here's something I always break out on special occasions like this. The silk pyjamas I wore on my wedding night!

BLANCHE: Oh.

STANLEY: When the telephone rings and they say, "You've got a son!" I'll tear this off and wave it like a flag! *He shakes out a brilliant pyjama coat.* I guess we are both entitled to put on the dog. *He goes back to the kitchen with the coat over his arm.*

BLANCHE: When I think of how divine it is going to be to have such a thing as privacy once more—I could weep with joy!

STANLEY: This millionaire from Dallas is not going to interfere with your privacy any?

BLANCHE: It won't be the sort of thing you have in mind. This man is a gentleman and he respects me. *Improvising feverishly:* What he wants is my companionship. Having great wealth sometimes makes people lonely! A cultivated woman, a woman of intelligence and breeding, can enrich a man's life—immeasurably! I have those things to offer, and this doesn't take them away. Physical beauty is passing. A transitory possession.

But beauty of the mind and richness of the spirit and tenderness of the heart—and I have all of those things—aren't taken away, but grow! Increase with the years! How strange that I should be called a destitute woman! When I have all of these treasures locked in my heart. *A choked sob comes from her.* I think of myself as a very, very rich woman! But I have been foolish—casting my pearls before swine!

STANLEY: Swine, huh?

BLANCHE: Yes, swine! Swine! And I'm thinking not only of you but of your friend, Mr. Mitchell. He came to see me tonight. He dared to come here in his work-clothes! And to repeat slander to me, vicious stories that he had gotten from you! I gave him his walking papers . . .

STANLEY: You did, huh?

BLANCHE: But then he came back. He returned with a box of roses to beg my forgiveness! He implored my forgiveness. But some things are not forgivable. Deliberate cruelty is not forgivable. It is the one unforgivable thing in my opinion and it is the one thing of which I have never, never been guilty. And so I told him, I said to him, "Thank you," but it was foolish of me to think that we could ever adapt ourselves to each other. Our ways of life are too different. Our attitudes and our backgrounds are incompatible. We have to be realistic about such things. So farewell, my friend! And let there be no hard feelings . . .

STANLEY: Was this before or after the telegram came from the Texas oil millionaire?

BLANCHE: What telegram! No! No, after! As a matter of fact, the wire came just as—

STANLEY: As a matter of fact there wasn't no wire at all!

BLANCHE: Oh, oh!

STANLEY: There isn't no millionaire! And Mitch didn't come back with roses 'cause I know where he is—

BLANCHE: Oh!

STANLEY: There isn't a goddam thing but imagination!

BLANCHE: Oh!

STANLEY: And lies and conceit and tricks!

BLANCHE: Oh!

STANLEY: And look at yourself! Take a look at yourself in that worn-out Mardi Gras outfit, rented for fifty cents from some rag-picker! And with the crazy crown on! What queen do you think you are?

BLANCHE: Oh—God . . .

STANLEY: I've been on to you from the start! Not once did you pull any wool over this boy's eyes! You come in here and sprinkle the place with powder and spray perfume and cover the light bulb with a paper lantern, and lo and behold the place has turned into Egypt and you are the Queen of the Nile! Sitting on your throne and swilling down my liquor! I say—*Ha!—Ha!* Do you hear me? Ha—ha—ha! *(He walks into the bedroom.)*

BLANCHE: Don't come in here! *Lurid reflections appear on the wall around Blanche. The shadows are of a grotesque and menacing form. She catches her breath, crosses to the phone and jiggles the hook. Stanley goes into the bathroom and closes the door.* Operator, operator! Give me long-distance, please. . . . I want to get in touch with Mr. Shep Huntleigh of Dallas. He's so well-known he doesn't require any address. Just ask anybody who—Wait!!—No, I couldn't find it right now. . . . Please understand, I—No! No, wait! . . . One moment! Someone is—Nothing! Hold on, please!

She sets the phone down and crosses warily into the kitchen. The night is filled with inhuman voices like cries in a jungle. The shadows and lurid reflections move sinuously as flames along the wall spaces. Through the back wall of the rooms, which have become transparent, can be seen the sidewalk. A prostitute has rolled a drunkard. He pursues her along the walk, overtakes her and there is a struggle. A policeman's whistle breaks it up. The figures disappear. Some moments later the Negro Woman appears around the corner with a sequined bag which the prostitute had dropped on the walk. She is rooting excitedly through it.

BLANCHE, *presses her knuckles to her lips and returns slowly to the phone. She speaks in a hoarse whisper:* Operator! Operator! Never mind long-distance. Get Western Union. There isn't time to be—Western—Western Union! *She waits anxiously.* Western Union? Yes! I—want to—Take down this message! "In desperate, desperate circumstances! Help me! Caught in a trap. Caught in—" *Oh!*

The bathroom door is thrown open and Stanley comes out in the brilliant silk pyjamas. He grins at her as he knots the tasseled sash about his waist. She gasps and backs away from the phone. He stares at her for a count of ten. Then a clicking becomes audible from the telephone, steady and rasping.

STANLEY: You left th' phone off th' hook. *He crosses to it deliberately and sets it back on the hook. After he has replaced it, he stares at her again, his mouth slowly curving into a grin, as he weaves between Blanche and the outer door.*

The barely audible "blue piano" begins to drum up louder. The sound of it turns into the roar of an approaching locomotive. Blanche crouches, pressing her fists to her ears until it has gone by.

BLANCHE, *finally straightening:* Let me—let me get by you!
STANLEY: Get by me! Sure. Go ahead. *He moves back a pace in the doorway.*
BLANCHE: You—you stand over there! *She indicates a further position.*
STANLEY, *grinning:* You got plenty of room to walk by me now.
BLANCHE: Not with you there! But I've got to get out somehow!
STANLEY: You think I'll interfere with you? Ha-ha!

The "blue piano" goes softly. She turns confusedly and makes a faint gesture. The inhuman jungle voices rise up. He takes a step toward her, biting his tongue which protrudes between his lips.

STANLEY, *softly:* Come to think of it—maybe you wouldn't be bad to—interfere with . . .
BLANCHE, *moves backward through the door into the bedroom:* Stay back! Don't you come toward me another step or I'll—
STANLEY: What?
BLANCHE: Some awful thing will happen! It will!
STANLEY: What are you putting on now?

The are now both inside the bedroom:

BLANCHE: I warn you, don't, I'm in danger!

He takes another step. She smashes a bottle on the table and faces him, clutching the broken top.

STANLEY: What did you do that for?
BLANCHE: So I could twist the broken end in your face!
STANLEY: I bet you would do that!
BLANCHE: I would! I will if you—
STANLEY: Oh! So you want some rough-house! All right, let's have some rough-house! *He springs toward her, overturning the table. She cries out and strikes at him with the bottle top but he catches her wrist.* Tiger—tiger! Drop the bottle top! Drop it! We've had this date with each other from the beginning!

She moans. The bottle top falls. She sinks to her knees. He picks up her inert figure and carries her to the bed.

TWO FOR THE SEESAW

by William Gibson

———•———

ACT II, SCENE 3

Jerry and Gittel are a very unlikely couple. He is a poised and charming lawyer from the Midwest. She is a helter-skelter Jewish girl from the Bronx—an unemployed modern dancer with a bleeding ulcer. When Jerry's wife asked for a divorce, he ran away from a successful law practice in Nebraska and came to New York City. He has been living in a small room in virtual isolation for many months. Lonely, out of money, and resolved to reconstruct his life, he goes to a party and meets Gittel. He is won over by her genuineness and generosity, but is still haunted by the memory of his wife, Tess.

At this point in the play Gittel and Jerry have been through a number of ups and downs. Whenever they try to get closer to each other, the image of Tess comes between them: Jerry becomes distant or Gittel becomes insecure and defensive. The following scene takes place in Gittel's room. She enters from outside; she is in severe pain from her ulcer.

Then there is the sound of a key at Gittel's and the door swings open. Gittel is silhouetted in the doorway, alone and motionless, resting against the jamb from brow to pelvis; then she pushes away, and comes unsteadily in. There is a sprinkling of snow on her hair and overcoat. She lets her purse drop on the floor, weaves her way around the bed without light except from the hall, and in the kitchen gets herself a glass of water at the sink; she drinks it, fills another, brings it in, and sits on the bed, with head bowed in her hand. After a moment she reaches to click on the lamp, takes up her address book, and searches for a number. She dials it, and waits; when she speaks her voice is tired and tipsy.

GITTEL: Dr. Segen there? . . . *I'm* calling, who are you? I mean are you really there or are you one of these answering nuisances? . . . So can you reach Dr. Segen for me? . . . Yeah, it's an emergency. . . . Gittel Mosca, I used to be a patient of his, will you tell him I'm very sick? . . . Canal 6-2098. . . . Thanks. *She gets rid of the phone, and still in her overcoat, drops back onto the bed. The lamplight is in her eyes, and she puts up a fumbling hand to click it off. She lies in the dark, an arm over her face. After a second Jerry in topcoat and hat comes silently up, around the bannister in the hall, and into the doorway, where he stands. The snow has accumulated thickly on him. He sees Gittel's purse on the floor, picks it up, sees the key still in the lock, and draws it out; it is this sound that brings Gittel up on her elbow, startled, apprehensive:* Oh! Hiya, Jerry. Where'd you blow in from? *Jerry regards her, his manner is heavy and grim, and hers turns light.* How was *your* party, have a good time?
JERRY: Not as good as you. Are you drunk, at least?
GITTEL, *with a giggle:* I had a couple, yeah, I had this terrible thirst all night, you know, I didn't stop to think. I mean think to stop.

Jerry drops the key in her purse, tosses it on the bed, and closes the door; he walks to the window, silent, where he leans against the casing, not removing his hat.

JERRY, *then:* Let's get it over with, who was the wrestler?

GITTEL: What wrestler?

JERRY: The fat-necked one who brought you home just now.

GITTEL: Jake? *She sits up.* He's not a wrestler, he's a very modern painter.

JERRY: That's why you kiss him good-night, you're a patroness of the arts?

GITTEL, *staring:* Where were you?

JERRY: One jump behind you. In more ways than one.

GITTEL: I didn't kiss him, he kissed me. Didn't you go to Frank Taubman's party— *(She pushes herself to her feet, changes her mind, and sits again, shivering.)* Light the gas, will you, honey, I'm awful cold.

Jerry after a moment takes out matches, and kneels to the gas heater. When it comes on, it illuminates Gittel drinking the glass of water in one gulp; Jerry, rising, sees her, and comes over to grip her wrist.

JERRY: You've drunk enough.

GITTEL: It's water! *Jerry pries her fingers loose, and tastes it. He gives it back.*

GITTEL *grins:* What's the matter, you don't trust me?

JERRY: Trust you. You were in his cellar in Bleecker Street for an hour.

GITTEL, *staring:* How do you know?

JERRY: What was he showing you, great paintings, great wrestling holds, what? *(Gittel does not answer, and Jerry yanks on the lamp, sits opposite her on the bed, and turns her face into the light.)* What? *(She only reads his eyes and Jerry reads hers, a long moment in which she might almost cry on his shoulder, but she ends it with a rueful little snigger.)*

GITTEL: So what do you see, your fortune?

JERRY: Yours. And not one I want to see. You look trampled, is that what you're in training to be?

GITTEL, *irked:* Ye gods, I had about six drinks, you think I'm ruined for life?

JERRY: I don't mean anything so wholesome as drink. You slept with him, didn't you?

GITTEL: Whyn't you take off your hat and stay awhile? *She* *pushes his hat back from his eyes, then touches his temple and cheek.* Poor Jerry, you—

JERRY: *puts her hand down:* You slept with him.

GITTEL: You want to cry? I want to cry.

JERRY, *grimly:* Differences aren't soluble in tears, this city would be one flat mud pie. *Did* you sleep with him?

But Gittel rolls away into a pillow, her back to him.

GITTEL: We both know I'm dumb, whyn't you talk plain words a normal dumb person could understand?

JERRY: How plain, one syllable?

GITTEL: Yeah.

JERRY: Fine. Did he lay you? *Gittel lies averted in silence, her eyes open.* I asked did he—

GITTEL: So what if he did, that's the end of the world? *Now she does rise, to get away from him, though she is wobbly, and soon drops into a chair. Jerry puts his fingers to his eyes, and remains on the bed; it takes him time to come to terms with this.*

JERRY: Maybe. Of this world. *But he can't hold the anger in, he smacks the glass off the night table and is on his feet, bewildered and savage, to confront her.* Why? *Why?*

GITTEL, *wearily:* What's it matter?

JERRY: It matters because I'm at a crossroads and which way I send my life packing turns on you! And so are you, you want to watch *your* life float down the sewer out to sea? You care so little?

GITTEL: I don't know, I—

JERRY: For me?

GITTEL: Oh, Jerry, I—

JERRY: For yourself?

GITTEL: Myself, I got other things to worry—

JERRY: Why did you *want* to?

GITTEL: I don't *know* why! Anyway who said I did?

JERRY, *glaring at her:* You'll drive *me* to drink. *Did you or didn't you?*

GITTEL: Well, he may of slept with me, but I didn't sleep with him.

Jerry stares at her, tight-lipped for patience.

JERRY: All right, let's go back. Why did you go home with him?

GITTEL: It's a long story, I used to go with Jake two three years ago—

JERRY: Not that far back. Get to tonight.

GITTEL: So tonight I had a couple of drinks too many, I guess it was—just a case of old lang syne.

JERRY: Old lang syne—

GITTEL: *You* know.

JERRY: Yes, I'm an expert in it, especially tonight. Why did you drink?

GITTEL, *bored:* You're supposed to be at the Taubmans' having a good time.

JERRY: Is that why?

GITTEL: Nah, who wants to go there, for God's sake.

JERRY: I went about this trouble with the affidavits. I left as soon as I could to pick you up at Sophie's, you were just coming out with him, giggling like a pony.

GITTEL, *indignantly:* I was plastered, I said so, you want a *written* confession?

JERRY: You don't get plastered and flush us down the drain for no reason, and Taubman's party isn't it. I'm after the— *(She gets up wearily, again to move away from him.)* Don't walk away from me! I'm talking to you.

GITTEL: So go ahead, talk. Lawyers, boy.

JERRY: Because when something happens to me *twice* I like to know why. I'm after the reason, what did I do this time, what's your complaint?

GITTEL: Who's complaining? *You* are!

JERRY: My God, I have no right?

GITTEL: Don't get off the subject.

JERRY: It's the subject, I'm talking about you and me.

GITTEL: Well, I'm talking about your wife!

A silence. Gittel walks, rubbing her stomach with the heel of her hand.

JERRY, *quiets down, then:* All right, let's talk about her. She's interested in you too, I feel like an intercom. What about her?

GITTEL: I saw your last month's phone bill. Omaha Neb 9.81, Omaha Neb 12.63—Whyn't you tell me you were the world's champion talkers?

JERRY: I like to keep in touch, Gittel, she's having a very rough time.

GITTEL: So who isn't? I got a headache, lemme alone.

JERRY: What's your case, I'm unfaithful to you with my wife over the phone, it's the phone bill pushes you into bed with this what's his name jerk?

GITTEL: Jake.

JERRY: Jerk! It could be you're pushing me into Grand Central for a ticket back, has that thought struck you? Is that what you want, to cut me loose? So you can try anything in pants in New York you've overlook— *(But Gittel has flopped across the bed, face down, and lies still and miserable. Jerry contemplates her, his anger going, compassion coming, until he resigns himself with a sigh.)* All right. All right, it can wait till tomorrow. We'll battle it out when you're on your feet. *He drops his hat on a chair, comes over to the bed, kneels and begins untying her shoes. This kindness sends Gittel off into a misery, her shoulders quiver, and she whimpers.*

GITTEL: Oh, Jerry—

JERRY: What's the matter?

GITTEL: You don't like me any more.

JERRY: I hate you, isn't that passionate enough? Turn over. *Gittel turns over, and he starts to unbutton her overcoat; her hands come up, his ignore them.*

GITTEL: I can do it.

JERRY: It's a huge favor, have the grace not to, hm?

GITTEL, *desisting:* You don't hate me.

JERRY: I wouldn't say so.

GITTEL: You just feel sorry for me.

JERRY: What makes you think you're so pathetic? Pull.

GITTEL, *freeing one arm:* Ever saw me dancing around that loft, boy, you'd think I was pathetic. I been sitting on that goddam floor so many hours I'm getting a callus, I wait for ideas to show up like I'm—*marooned* or something. So the dawn came, after all these years, you know what's wrong?

JERRY, *pausing, gently:* You're not a dancer?

GITTEL, *staring:* How'd you know?

JERRY: I didn't. I meant that loft as a help, not just to puncture a bubble.

GITTEL: So if I'm not a dancer, what am I?

JERRY: Is that why you got crocked? *Turn over. Gittel turns back over and he slips the coat from her other arm and off; he begins to unbutton her blouse in back.* Will you drink coffee if I make some?

GITTEL, *shuddering:* No.

JERRY: Or an emetic? Get the stuff off your stomach?

GITTEL: You mean vomit?

JERRY: Yes.

Gittel now, breaking away from his fingers in sudden vexation, rolls up to glare at his face.

GITTEL: Why we always talking about my stomach? I got no other charms? *Jerry reaches again.* Get away! *She pulls the still-buttoned blouse over her head, gets stuck, and struggles blindly.*

JERRY, *compassionately:* Gittel. *His hands come again, but when she feels them she kicks out fiercely at him.*

GITTEL, *muffled:* I don't want your goddam favors! *One of her kicks lands in his thigh, and stops him. Gittel then yanks the blouse off with a rip, slings it anywhere, which happens to be at him, drags the coat over her head on her way down, and lies still. A silence.*

JERRY, *then:* I'm sorry you don't. I could use it. *He retrieves the blouse, draws the sleeves right side out, and hangs it over a chair, then stands regarding her.* That's how you intend to sleep it off? *Gittel under the coat neither moves nor answers.* Gittel? *Again no answer.* You want me to stay or go? *After a wait Jerry walks to his hat, picks it up.* Go. *He looks at the gas heater, pauses.* Shall I leave the gas on? *No response from under Gittel's coat.* Yes. You need me for anything? *He waits.* No. Of course not. *Presently he puts the lamp out, walks around the bed to the door, and opens it. But he stands. Then he bangs it shut again, throws his hat back at the chair and walks in again after it. Gittel then sits up to see the closed door, and gives a wail of abandonment.*

GITTEL: Jerry—Jerry—

GEMINI

by Albert Innaurato

———————•———————

ACT I, SCENE 2

Francis Geminiani is about to be twenty-one years old. He is a Harvard student who has returned home on vacation to the South Philadelphia house of his father, Fran. He is paid an unexpected visit by two friends from college, Judith and Randy Hastings. Their family background is wealthy and Waspy, while Francis's is decidedly working-class Italian-American. This situation proves to be embarrassing for the young man when his visitors try to socialize with Francis's eccentric, boisterous neighbors. Adding to his discomfort is the fact that Judith is in love with him, while he has (or thinks he has) a crush on her brother Randy.

The following scene takes place in the backyard of Francis's house. Judith is trying to find out why Francis is no longer interested in her. By way of explanation, he confides his attraction to a young man. She does not know he is referring to her brother. (The "Bunny" referred to near the end of the scene is a neighbor whose kitchen window faces the backyard.)

JUDITH: Lucille and your father are—well, you know, aren't they?
FRANCIS: I don't know, they drink an awful lot of coffee.
JUDITH: Stimulates the gonads— *(She embraces Francis and kisses him. He looks uncomfortable.)* What's the matter?
FRANCIS: I'm sorry.
JUDITH: Sorry about what? *He looks away.* You know, I think you are an eternal adolescent, a German Adolescent, a German Romantic Adolescent. You were born out of context, you'd have been much happier in the forties of the last century when it was eternally twilight.
FRANCIS: Do I detect a veiled reference to *Zwielicht* by Eichendorf?

JUDITH: I took Basic European Literature also, and did better than you did.

FRANCIS: You did not.

JUDITH: I got the highest mark on the objective test: 98! What did you get? *She laughs.*

FRANCIS, *bantering with her:* My SAT verbal and achievement tests were higher than yours.

JUDITH: How do you know?

FRANCIS: I looked them up in the office. I pretended to go faint, and while the registrar ran for water, I looked at your file.

JUDITH, *entering into his game:* I find that hard to believe; I had the highest score in the verbal at St. Paul's and also in the English Achievement Test.

FRANCIS: That's what it said alongside your IQ.

JUDITH, *taken aback in spite of herself:* My IQ?

FRANCIS: Very interesting that IQ. It was recorded in bright red ink. There was also a parenthesis, in which someone had written: Poor girl but she has great determination.

JUDITH: I find jokes about IQ's in poor taste.

FRANCIS: Then you are an adolescent, a German Adolescent, a German Romantic Adolescent.

JUDITH: And before this edifying discussion you were about to say: "Fuck you, Judith."

FRANCIS: Don't put it that way . . .

JUDITH: But more or less it was get lost, see you later, oh yes, have a nice summer—and maybe, just maybe, I'll tell you why later. You seem to want to skip that part, the why. *She picks up the end of a garden hose, and points it at Francis like a machine gun, and with a Humphrey Bogart voice, says:* Look, I came to see you, that's ballsy, now you've got to reciprocate and tell me why . . . *She puts down the hose, and the accent.* Do I bore you? Do you think I'm ugly? Do I have bad breath?

FRANCIS: Oh, come on!

JUDITH: Hey, Francis, we're just alike, can't you see that?

FRANCIS, *indicates the house and yard:* Oh yeah.

JUDITH: Two over achievers. Really. I know my family is better off than yours; but we're just alike, and there was something last winter and now you're telling me . . .

FRANCIS: Look, I'm going to be twenty-one tomorrow. Well . . . I don't know what to say.

JUDITH: Is there a reason?

FRANCIS: I don't think I can say.

JUDITH: That doesn't make any sense.

FRANCIS: I think I'm queer.

JUDITH: Why don't we back up a bit. I said: "We're just alike etcetera," and you said you were going to be twenty-one tomorrow, and I looked at you with deep set, sea blue eyes, and you said . . .

FRANCIS: I think I'm queer.

JUDITH, *laughs:* Well, I guess we can't get around it. Do you want to amplify? I mean this seems like quite a leap from what I remember of those long sweet ecstatic nights, naked in each other's young arms, clinging to . . .

FRANCIS: We fucked. Big deal. That's what kids are supposed to do. And be serious.

JUDITH: I am serious. Is there a particular boy?

FRANCIS: Yes.

JUDITH: An adolescent, a German Adolescent . . .

FRANCIS: Not German, no.

JUDITH: Do I know him? *Francis doesn't answer.* Reciprocal?

FRANCIS: It was just this spring. He began to haunt me. We became friends. We talked a lot—late in my room when you were studying. Well, I don't know, and you see—I've had well, crushes before. I dreamed of him. It's not reciprocal, no, he doesn't know, but it became more and more obvious to me. I mean, I'd look at him, and then some other boy would catch my eye and I'd think—you see?

JUDITH: Well, I suppose I could start teaching you the secrets of make up. *Francis turns away, annoyed.* Well, how do you expect me to react? You seem to think I ought to leap out the window because of it. But it's like you're suddenly turning to me and saying you are from Mars. Well, you might be, but I don't see much evidence and I can't see what difference it makes. I'm talking about you and me, I and thou and all that. All right, maybe you do have an eye for the boys, well so do I, but you . . . you are special to me. I wouldn't throw you over just because a hockey player looked good, why do you have to give me up?

FRANCIS: I don't think that makes any sense, Judith. I mean, if I were from Mars, it would make a difference, I'd have seven legs and talk a different language and that's how I feel now. *Judith embraces him.* Don't touch me so much Judith, and don't look at me . . .

JUDITH: Then you're afraid. That explains that fat and ugly nonsense and this sudden homosexual panic. You're afraid that anyone who responds to you will make demands you can't meet. You're afraid you'll fail . . .

FRANCIS: Good Evening Ladies and Gentlemen, Texaco Presents: "Banality on Parade!"

JUDITH: You're afraid to venture. That's why you've enshrined someone who doesn't respond to you, probably doesn't even know you're interested. If the relationship never happens you are never put to the test and can't fail. The Over Achiever's Great Nightmare!

FRANCIS: That's crazy!

JUDITH: I bet this boy who draws you is some Harvard sprite, a dew touched Freshman . . .

FRANCIS: He was a Freshman.

JUDITH: In Randy's class and that proves it. Look at Randy—what kind of response could someone like that have but the giggles? And you know that. You're afraid of commitment. And remember what Dante says about those who refuse to make commitments. They're not even in Hell, but are condemned to run about the outskirts for eternity. *Francis, who has heard enough, has stuck his head inside Bunny's kitchen window, and brought it down over his neck like a guillotine. Judith now runs over to the fence, and starts climbing to the top.* Ed io che reguardai vidi una insegna che girando correva tanta ratta, che d'ogni posa me parea indegna . . . ! *She leaps off the fence. Francis runs to her aid.*

FRANCIS: Judith! Jesus Christ!

JUDITH, *as he helps her up:* You see? I ventured, I made the great leap and remained unscathed.

I NEVER SANG FOR MY FATHER

by Robert Anderson

———————•———————

ACT II

Gene Garrison is a forty-year-old widower who is about to re-marry and move to California when his elderly mother dies and leaves him with the problem of caring for his father. The father, Tom Garrison, is a self-made man, well respected in his small Westchester community. But his possessive and penurious nature have alienated his children from him. When his daughter Alice defied him and married a Jew, he refused to see her again. Now, with his doting wife gone, Tom makes constant demands on his son; and Gene is torn between the desire to help his father and earn his love, and the need to lead his own life apart from the tyrannical old man.

In the following scene, Alice, the exiled daughter, has come home for her mother's funeral. She advises Gene to plan his own future and accept the practical alternatives (a full-time housekeeper or an old-age home) available to their father. The lights come up on Gene and Alice in the garden.

ALICE: I don't know how you feel, but I'd like to figure out some kind of memorial for Mother. . . . Use some of the money she left.
GENE: Yes, definitely.
ALICE: Maybe some shelves of books for the Children's Library. Christmas books with the stories she liked to tell.
GENE: That's a good idea. *There is a long and awkward pause.*
ALICE: Well, Gene . . . what are we going to do?
GENE, *frowns:* Mother always said put her in an old people's home. She had one all picked out.
ALICE: Sidney's Mother and Father saw it coming and ar-ranged to be in one of those cottage colonies for old people.
GENE: Mother and Dad didn't.

ALICE: I think you should go ahead and get married and move to California. . . . But . . . I might as well get this off my chest, it would be murder if he came to live with us. In the first place, he wouldn't do it, feeling as he does about Sid, and the kids can't stand how he tells them how to do everything.

GENE: I think you're right. That would never work. *There is a pause. Gene looks out at the garden.* I can't tell you what it does to me as a man . . . to see someone like that . . . a man who was distinguished, remarkable . . . just become a nuisance.

ALICE, *disturbed at what her brother may be thinking:* I know I sound hard, but he's had his life . . . and as long as we can be assured that he's taken care of. . . . Oh, I'll feel some guilt, and you, maybe more. But my responsibility is to my husband and my children.

GENE: Yes. That's *your* responsibility.

ALICE: And your responsibility is to yourself . . . to get married again, to get away from memories of Carol . . . and her whole world. Have you called California?

GENE, *frowns:* No.

ALICE: If I were the girl you were planning to marry, and you didn't call me to tell me your Mother had died . . .

GENE, *gets up, disturbed:* I just haven't wanted to go into it all with her . . .

ALICE, *understanding . . . but worried:* Gene, my friend . . . my brother . . . Get out of here!

GENE: Look, Alice . . . your situation is quite different. Mine is very complex. You fortunately see things very clearly, but it's not so easy for me. . . . *Alice looks at Gene, troubled by what his thinking seems to be leading to. After a moment . . . reflective:* We always remember the terrible things about Dad. I've been trying to remember some of the others. . . . How much he *did* do for us.

ALICE: I'm doing a lot for my kids. I don't expect them to pay me back at the other end. *Gene wanders around, thinking, scuffing the grass.* I'm sure we could find a full-time housekeeper. He can afford it.

GENE: He'd never agree.

ALICE: It's that or finding a Home. *Gene frowns.* Sidney's folks like where they are. Also, we might as well face it, his mind's going. Sooner or later we'll have to think about Powers of Attorney, perhaps committing him to an Institution.

GENE: God, it's all so ugly.

ALICE, *smiling:* Yes, my gentle Gene . . . a lot of life is.

GENE: Now, look, don't go trying to make me out some soft-hearted . . . *He can't find the word.* I know life is ugly.

ALICE: Yes, I think you know it. You've lived through a great deal of ugliness. But you work like a Trojan to deny it, to make it not so. *After a moment* . . . *not arguing:* He kicked me out. He said he never wanted to see me again. He broke Mother's heart over that for years. He was mean . . . unloving. . . . He beat the Hell out of you when you were a kid. . . . You've hated and feared him all your adult life . . .

GENE, *cutting in:* Still he's my Father, and a man. And what's happening to him appalls me as a man.

ALICE: We have a practical problem here.

GENE: It's not as simple as all that.

ALICE: To me it is. I don't understand this mystical haze you're casting over it. I'm going to talk to him tomorrow, after the session with the lawyer, about a housekeeper. *Gene reacts but says nothing.* Just let me handle it. He can visit us, and we can take turns coming to visit him. Now, I'll do the dirty work. Only when he turns to you, don't give in.

GENE: I can't tell you how ashamed I feel . . . not to say with open arms, "Poppa, come live with me . . . I love you, Poppa, and I want to take care of you." . . . I need to love him. I've always wanted to love him.

SEXUAL PERVERSITY IN CHICAGO

by David Mamet

———————•———————

David Mamet's four-character comedy explores contemporary sexual relationships through a series of witty vignettes that are written in a style that might be called superreal. This scene is from the last half of the play.

Deborah has recently moved into Danny's apartment. The "affair" is now giving way to the mundane tasks of "living together." It is morning and they are getting ready for work.

DANNY: Do we have any shampoo?
DEBORAH: I don't know.
DANNY: You wash your hair at least twice a day. Shampoo is a staple item of your existence. Of course you know.
DEBORAH: All right. I *do*. Know.
DANNY: Do we have any shampoo?
DEBORAH: I don't know. Is your hair dirty?
DANNY: Does my hair look dirty?
DEBORAH: Does it feel dirty? *Pause.* It looks dirty.
DANNY: It feels greasy. I hate it when my hair feels greasy.
DEBORAH: Well, I'm not going to look. If you want to know if there's any shampoo, you go look for it.
DANNY: You don't have to look. You know very well if there's any shampoo or not. You're making me be ridiculous about this. *Pause.* You wash yourself too much anyway. If you really *used* all that shit they tell you in *Cosmopolitan* (and you *do*) you'd be washing yourself from morning 'til night. Pouring derivatives on yourself all day long.
DEBORAH: Will you love me when I'm old?
DANNY: If you can manage to look eighteen, yes.
DEBORAH: Now, that's very telling.
DANNY: You think so?
DEBORAH: Yes.
DANNY: I'm going to wash my hair. Is there any shampoo?
DEBORAH: Yes. And no.
DANNY: Now what's that supposed to mean?
DEBORAH: Everything. And nothing. *Pause.* Would you get my hose?
DANNY: No. Where does this come from? This whole fucking behavior. You're making it up. "Get my hose." You want your hose, I'll get your hose. Here's your fucking hose. *Rummages in dresser.* Where's your hose? *Pause.* What do they call them, anyway? Nobody says 'hose.'
DEBORAH: Pantyhose.
DANNY: Where are they?

DEBORAH: Get some out of the laundry bag.
DANNY: You're going to wear dirty hose?
DEBORAH: I think I'm out of clean ones.
DANNY: So you're going downtown in dirty hose?
DEBORAH: Do you want me walking around with a naked la-la?
DANNY: If it makes you happy, Deb. I'm on the side of whatever makes you happy.

Deborah retrieves dirty hose from bag and starts changing into them.

DANNY: You make me very horny.
DEBORAH: It's the idea of the dirty panties, Dan. You're sick.
DANNY: I love your breasts.
DEBORAH: "Thank you." *Pause.* Is that right?
DANNY: Fuck you.
DEBORAH: No hard feelings.
DANNY: Who said there were?
DEBORAH: You know there are.
DANNY: Then why say there aren't?

THE LION IN WINTER

by James Goldman

———————◆———————

ACT I, SCENE 2

The time is Christmas, 1183. The place is the court of Henry II of England. His queen, Eleanor of Aquitaine, has been summoned from her fortress (where she has been held prisoner by Henry) to join the family for the holidays.

Initially a love match, the relationship between Eleanor and Henry has turned into a battle of wits and a struggle for power, land, and the allegiance of their three sons. The most recent conflict has focused on the succession to the throne. Henry favors his youngest, John, while Eleanor continues to scheme in favor of Richard, the eldest. Their middle son, Geoffrey, hopes to play both brothers against each other and come out the sole heir.

In the opening scene of the play we find Henry with his young mistress, Alais. Alais came to court as a child when she was betrothed to Richard in exchange for a valuable piece of French land, the Vexin. Alais is in love with Henry and does not wish to marry any of his sons, but, while Henry loves her, he does not want to return the property to her brother, the king of France.

In this scene, Alais has just left. Henry and Eleanor begin discussing their children and reminiscing about the past in a manner to which both have become very accustomed: taunting, treacherous, and full of deception at every turn. This is the facade that characterizes their relationship and often masks the mutual respect and admiration they have for each other.

HENRY, *rises, crosses to right of Eleanor:* She is lovely, isn't she?

ELEANOR: Yes, very.

HENRY: If I'd chosen, who could I have picked to love to gall you more?

ELEANOR: There's no one. *Moving to the holly boughs:* Come on; let's finish Christmassing the place.

HENRY, *following her:* Time hasn't done a thing but wrinkle you.

ELEANOR: It hasn't even done that. I have borne six girls, five boys and thirty-one connubial years of you. How am I possible? *Picks up three bunches of holly.*

HENRY: There are moments when I miss you.

ELEANOR, *gives Henry two bunches of holly:* Many?

HENRY: Do you doubt it?

ELEANOR, *rumpling his hair:* That's my wooly sheep dog. *Crosses left.* So wee Johnny gets the crown.

HENRY, *following her:* I've heard it rumored but I don't believe it.

ELEANOR, *turns to Henry:* Losing Alais will be hard, for you do love her.

HENRY: It's an old man's last attachment; nothing more. How hard do you find living in your castle?

ELEANOR, *placing holly on column downstage of left arch:* It was difficult in the beginning but that's past. I find I've seen the world enough. I have my maids and menials in my courtyard and I hold my little court. It suits me now. *Takes bunch of holly from Henry and places on column upstage of left arch.*

HENRY: I'll never let you loose. You led too many civil wars against me.

ELEANOR, *crossing back to Henry:* And I damn near won the last one. *Takes last bunch of holly from him and places it on column upstage left center.* Still, as long as I get trotted out for Christmas Courts and state occasions now and then—for I do like to see you—it's enough. *Crossing downstage right:* Do you still need the Vexin, Henry?

HENRY, *following her:* Need you ask?

ELEANOR: My strategy is ten years old. *Eleanor picks up last bunch of holly and places it on downstage right column.*

HENRY: It is as crucial as it ever was. My troops there are a day away from Paris, just a march of twenty miles. I must keep it.

ELEANOR, *surveying the holly:* I'd say that's all the jollying this room can stand. I'm famished. Let's go in to dinner.

HENRY, *at right center, extending his arm:* Arm in arm.

ELEANOR, *taking it, smiling at him:* And hand in hand. You're still a marvel of a man.

HENRY: And you're my lady. *She crosses below Henry; they start to exit.*

ELEANOR, *stops:* Henry, dear, if Alais doesn't marry Richard, I will see you lose the Vexin.

HENRY: Well, I thought you'd never say it.

ELEANOR: I can do it.

HENRY: You can try.

ELEANOR: My Richard is the next king, not your John. I know you, Henry. I know every twist and bend you've got and I'll be waiting round each corner for you.

HENRY: Do you truly care who's king?

ELEANOR: I care because you care so much.

HENRY: I might surprise you. *Moves right; sits downstage edge of table:* Eleanor, I've fought and bargained all these years as if the only thing I lived for was what happened after I was dead. I've something else to live for now. I've blundered onto peace.

ELEANOR: On Christmas Eve.

HENRY: Since Louis died, while Philip grew, I've had no France to fight. And in that lull, I've found how good it is to write a law or make a tax more fair or sit in judgment to decide which peasant gets a cow. There is, I tell you, nothing more important in the world. And now the French boy's big enough and I am sick of war.

ELEANOR: Come to your question, Henry; make the plea. What would you have me do? Give out, give up, give in?

HENRY: Give me a little peace.

ELEANOR: A little? Why so modest? How about eternal peace? Now, there's a thought.

HENRY: If you oppose me, I will strike you any way I can.

ELEANOR: Of course you will.

HENRY, *extending his arm as before:* We have a hundred barons we should look the loving couple for. *They stand regally side by side.*

ELEANOR, *smiling a terrible smile at him:* Can you read love in that?

HENRY, *nodding, smiling back:* And permanent affection.

ELEANOR, *as they start, grand and stately, for the left arch:* Henry?

HENRY: Madam?

ELEANOR; Did you ever love me?

HENRY: No.

ELEANOR: Good. That will make this pleasanter. *They exit.*

THE CRUCIBLE

by Arthur Miller

———•———

ACT II

Arthur Miller's play is about the Salem witch trials. Written in
reaction to the McCarthy investigations, it is also a powerful
parable for our own time. Salem in 1692 was a place of political
factions and struggles for land, wealth, and power; and religion
became an expedient tool in this struggle. Young girls, one of
them the daughter of a reverend, the other his niece, were
caught dancing in the moonlight in the woods. In order to protect his shaky position in the community, the reverend declares
that the girls were bewitched. The girls, to protect themselves
from threats of punishment, confess their bewitchment and begin a series of accusations that shortly sends a score of citizens
to the gallows.

The leader of the young girls is Abigail Williams, seventeen
years old, headstrong, beautiful, sensual, and in love with John
Proctor. Abigail worked on the Proctor farm, and she and
Proctor had sexual relations. Elizabeth, Proctor's wife, learned
of their activities and the girl was sent from the farm. In the
seven months since the incident Elizabeth's suspicions and
Proctor's guilt have not been dispelled.

At the time of the following scene the accusations of witchcraft have already begun. The scene takes place in the Proctors'
home. John enters from outside, carrying his gun. He leans the
gun against a bench, pours water from a pitcher into a wash-
stand and begins to wash. Elizabeth enters.

ELIZABETH: What keeps you so late? It's almost dark.
PROCTOR: I were planting far out to the forest edge.
ELIZABETH: Oh, you're done then.
PROCTOR: Aye, the farm is seeded. The boys asleep? *Dips
hands in water, wipes them.*

ELIZABETH, *removes water and towel, goes out left, and returns with dish of stew:* They will be soon. *Serves stew in a dish.*

PROCTOR: Pray now for a fair summer.

ELIZABETH, *goes out left, returns with another dish:* Aye.

PROCTOR: Are you well today?

ELIZABETH: I am. It is a rabbit.

PROCTOR: Oh, is it! In Jonathan's trap?

ELIZABETH: , No, she walked into the house this afternoon; I found her sittin' in the corner like she come to visit.

PROCTOR: Oh, that's a good sign walkin' in.

ELIZABETH: Pray God. It hurt my heart to strip her, poor rabbit.

PROCTOR: Oh, it is well seasoned.

ELIZABETH: I took great care. She's tender?

PROCTOR: Aye. I think we'll see green fields soon. It's warm as blood beneath the clods.

ELIZABETH: That's well.

PROCTOR: If the crop is good I'll buy George Jacobs' heifer. How would that please you?

ELIZABETH: Aye, it would.

PROCTOR: I mean to please you, Elizabeth.

ELIZABETH, *it is hard to say:* I know it, John.

PROCTOR, *as gently as he can:* Cider?

ELIZABETH, *a sense of her reprimanding herself for having forgot:* Aye! *Gets jug from off left, pours drink into pewter mug, brings it to him.*

PROCTOR: This farm's a continent when you go foot by foot droppin' seeds in it.

ELIZABETH: It must be.

PROCTOR: On Sunday let you come with me and we'll walk the farm together; I never see such a load of flowers on the earth. Massachusetts is a beauty in the spring!

ELIZABETH: Aye, it is.

PROCTOR: I think you're sad again. Are you?

ELIZABETH: You come so late I thought you'd gone to Salem this afternoon.

PROCTOR: Why? I have no business in Salem.

ELIZABETH: You did speak of goin', earlier this week.

PROCTOR: I thought better of it, since.

ELIZABETH: Mary Warren's there today.

PROCTOR: Why'd you let her? You heard me forbid her go to Salem any more!

ELIZABETH: I couldn't stop her.

PROCTOR: It is a fault, it is a fault, Elizabeth—you're the mistress here, not Mary Warren.

ELIZABETH: She frightened all my strength away. . . .

PROCTOR: How may that mouse frighten you, Elizabeth? You . . .

ELIZABETH: It is no mouse no *more*. I forbid her go, and she raises up her chin like the daughter of a prince, and says to me, "I must go to Salem, Goody Proctor, I am an official of the court!"

PROCTOR: Court! What court?

ELIZABETH: Ay, it is a proper court they have now. They've sent four judges out of Boston, she says, weighty magistrates of the General Court, and at the head sits the Deputy Governor of the Province.

PROCTOR, *astonished:* Why, she's mad.

ELIZABETH: I would to God she were. There be fourteen people in the jail now, she says. And they'll be tried, and the court have power to hang them too, she says.

PROCTOR: Ah, they'd never hang. . . .

ELIZABETH: The Deputy Governor promise hangin' if they'll not confess, John. The town's gone wild, I think—Mary Warren speak of Abigail as though she were a saint, to hear her. She brings the other girls into the court, and where she walks the crowd will part like the sea for Israel. And folks are brought before them, and if Abigail scream and howl and fall to the floor—the person's clapped in the jail for bewitchin' her. *He can't look at her.*

PROCTOR: Oh, it is a black mischief.

ELIZABETH: I think you must go to Salem, John. I think so. You must tell them it is a fraud.

PROCTOR: Aye, it is, it is surely.

ELIZABETH: Let you go to Ezekiel Cheever—he knows you well. And tell him what she said to you last week in her uncle's house. She said it had naught to do with witchcraft, did she not?

PROCTOR, *in thought, sighing:* Aye, she did, she did.

ELIZABETH, *quietly, fearing to anger him by prodding. A step* *left:* God forbid you keep that from the court, John; I think they must be told.

PROCTOR: Ay, they must, they must. . . . It is a wonder that they do believe her.

ELIZABETH: I would go to Salem now, John . . . let you go tonight.

PROCTOR: I'll think on it.

ELIZABETH, *with her courage now:* You cannot keep it, John.

PROCTOR, *angering:* I know I cannot keep it. I say I will think on it!

ELIZABETH, *hurt, and very coldly:* Good then, let you think on it.

PROCTOR, *defensively:* I am only wondering how I may prove what she told me, Elizabeth. If the girl's a saint now, I think it is not easy to prove she's fraud, and the town gone so silly. She told it to me in a room alone—I have no proof for it.

ELIZABETH: You were alone with her?

PROCTOR: For a moment alone, aye.

ELIZABETH: Why, then, it is not as you told me.

PROCTOR: For a moment, I say. The others come in soon after.

ELIZABETH: Do as you wish, then.

PROCTOR: Woman. I'll not have your suspicion any more.

ELIZABETH, *a little loftily:* I have no . . .

PROCTOR: I'll not have it!

ELIZABETH: Then let you not earn it.

PROCTOR, *with a violent undertone:* You doubt me yet?!

ELIZABETH: John, if it were not Abigail that you must go to hurt, would you falter now? I think not.

PROCTOR: Now look you . . .

ELIZABETH: I see what I see, John.

PROCTOR: You will not judge me more, Elizabeth. I have good reason to think before I charge fraud on Abigail, and I will think on it. Let you look to your own improvement before you go to judge your husband any more. I have forgot Abigail, and . . .

ELIZABETH: And I.

PROCTOR: Spare me! You forget nothing and forgive nothing. Learn charity, woman. I have gone tiptoe in this house all seven month since she is gone; I have not moved from there to there

without I think to please you, and still a . . . an everlasting funeral marches round your heart. I cannot speak but I am doubt-
ed; every moment judged for lies as though I come into a court
when I come into this house!

ELIZABETH, *firmly:* John, you are not open with me. You
saw her with a crowd, you said. Now, you . . .

PROCTOR: I'll plead my honesty no more, Elizabeth.

ELIZABETH, *now she would justify herself:* John, I am
only . . .

PROCTOR, *in outburst:* No more! I should have roared you
down when first you told me your suspicion. But I wilted, and
like a Christian, I confessed. Some dream I had must have mistaken you for God that day, but you're not, you're not. Let you
remember it. Let you look sometimes for the goodness in me,
and judge me not.

ELIZABETH: I do not judge you. The magistrate sits in your
heart that judges you. I never thought you but a good man,
John, only somewhat bewildered.

PROCTOR: Oh, Elizabeth, your justice would freeze beer.

THE OWL AND THE PUSSYCAT

by Bill Manhoff

ACT I

Bill Manhoff's comedy is about a colorful San Francisco hooker
and a conservative would-be novelist. Late one night Felix
Sherman is hoodwinked into letting his neighbor, Doris, into
his home. She has been evicted from her apartment after her
landlord received phone calls from Felix reporting on her activ-
ites with men. After a barrage of insults and revengeful threats
Doris settles in for the night since she has no money and no
place to go. Felix is too frightened to make her leave and des-

perately wants to get some sleep. What ensues is the beginning of an unlikely love affair.

The scene opens with Doris alone on Felix's livingroom couch, trying to get her radio to work. After being bullied into letting her stay the night, Felix has crawled into his bedroom to sleep. (The "knock" mentioned in the stage directions is from a neighbor trying to quiet the goings-on in Felix's apartment.)

DORIS, *shouts:* God damn it! Hey fink, fink!

Felix enters.

FELIX: Now what?
DORIS: My radio won't work. I must have banged it coming up the stairs!
FELIX: Do you really have to—?
DORIS: It's the only way I can go to sleep. You got a radio?
FELIX: No.
DORIS: What'll I do now? Why did I have to come up here?
FELIX: Why not correct your mistake? Leave!
DORIS: I should have just given a certain friend of mine a dollar to beat you up.
FELIX: A dollar? Can't be much of a beating.
DORIS: He's a friend. He would do it for nothing, but I make him take a dollar.
FELIX: I see.
DORIS, *calls:* What's so goddam funny? I'll send him around tomorrow. I guarantee you won't think it's so funny. Now I'll never get to sleep.
FELIX: Why can't you sleep?
DORIS: I'm very high-strung.
FELIX: I don't have any sleeping pills or I'd—
DORIS: I don't take sleeping pills. I never take them. They're enervating.
FELIX: How about a hot bath? That'll relax you.
DORIS, *talking in a compulsive rush:* I never take baths. They're enervating too. You know that word—"enervating"? Most people think it means just the opposite of what it really means. *Felix walks back toward the bedroom in the middle of her speech, yawning, yearning for sleep. Doris raises her voice to a*

shout. Felix stops. Another word that kills me is naive—I always thought it was "nave" you know. How do you pronounce it?

FELIX: I never use it.

DORIS: I mean I heard the word na'ive, but—

The knock is heard again

FELIX: What's the matter with you? What are you trying to do? I got up at five-thirty this morning.

DORIS: Listen, I know this sounds crazy, but will you sit here for a little while and talk to me?

FELIX: You act as though you were afraid to be alone.

DORIS: I usually fall asleep with the television on or the radio—but now my radio's on the fritz and it's too late for TV.

FELIX: It's too late for me, too. I'm signing off. *Sings:*
  Oh say can you see by the dawn's early light—
  This is Channel Sherman signing off for the night.

DORIS, *laughing much too hard:* That's pretty funny. I never would have thought you had a sense of humor.

FELIX: I'm a funny fink.

DORIS: Just goes to show you never can tell about people. *As she talks Felix turns and makes another try for the bedroom. Without a pause and without changing her tone or her volume, Doris goes on:* If you take one more step I'm gonna scream at the top of my lungs.

FELIX: For God's sake—

DORIS: I can't help it. Do you think I can help it? I can't fall asleep unless I'm listening to something. Read me something—you got any magazines?

FELIX: Isn't there any other way for you to get to sleep?

DORIS: There's only one other way.

FELIX: That wouldn't interest me.

DORIS: That is not what I meant—evil-minded!

FELIX: Listen—I must get some sleep.

DORIS: So must I—which I would if not for some dirty rotten bastard who you and I both know. Pardon my language.

FELIX, *humoring a child:* All right—all right. What do you want?

DORIS: Read to me. Read me anything and I'll fall asleep. Nothing with big words. I hate big words. *Felix looks around the room, looks at Doris, looks at his books; looks back at Doris, obviously decides he has nothing suitable.* Well?

FELIX: We're out of bedtime stories. What was the other way you have of falling asleep?

DORIS: Huh? Oh—that's only in the winter when it's real cold—I huddle myself down in bed under about a million blankets—it's a wonder I don't suffocate—come on read to me—anything.

Felix picks up a small bronze bust, for a second considers hitting her with it.

FELIX: I could put you to sleep with Shakespeare.

DORIS: Shakespeare gives me a headache.

FELIX: I don't have anything you'd like. I don't have any comic books, movie magazines or any other literature of that nature!

DORIS, *yawning:* Don't stop—your voice is very enervating. You know what that means? Oh yeah—I told you before. Come on—keep talking—

FELIX, *looking about desperately, picks up the box of breakfast food, reads the label:* Ingredients: oat flour—wheat starch—sugar, salt, cinnamon, sodium phosphate, calcium carbonate, artificial coloring, iron, niacin, thiamine and riboflavin, caramel, vegetable oil with freshness preserved by Butylated Hydroxelene and—

DORIS: No—that's no good—I'm getting hungry. Hey—read me one of your stories. Read me your latest one.

FELIX: You wouldn't like it. *Remembering:* Four score and seven years ago our fathers brought forth on this continent a new nation—conceived in liberty and dedicated to the proposition that all men were created equal—equal— *(Stops, stuck; he sits on the end of the sofa, exhausted.)*

DORIS: Don't stop—that's nice—the Declaration of Independence—right?

FELIX: No. Custer's farewell address to the Indians.

DORIS: Oh, yes—that's right—why'd you stop?

FELIX: I don't remember anymore. Listen—I'm exhausted—

DORIS: Why wouldn't I like your story?

FELIX: It has no rape scene, no beautiful people, and no happy ending.

DORIS: Let's hear it. Maybe I can spot where you went wrong.

FELIX: You ought to be ashamed of yourself. A big girl like you afraid to be alone— *(He yawns.)*

DORIS: Isn't that ridiculous! Ever since I was a kid—I tell you it's not being alone that's scary—I wouldn't mind being alone—but there's somebody there—I can hear him breathing—he just stands there breathing and it just panics me—I had this analysis you know for six months and the doctor told me— *(Stops.)* Hey— *(He's dozed off.)*

FELIX: Oh—what were you saying?

DORIS: About being alone—my analyst said—

FELIX: You were analyzed?

DORIS: Of course.

FELIX: Really?

DORIS: There's a brain in there—honest!

FELIX: What kind of a doctor?

DORIS: Jewish.

FELIX: No. I mean—never mind. What did he say?

DORIS: Oh, I hate that!

FELIX: What?

DORIS: "Never mind" like "forget it, you're too dumb to understand."

FELIX: Oh no—it was just a foolish question on my part.

DORIS: Really?

FELIX: Sure. That's why I said "never mind." What did he tell you?

DORIS: He said I was afraid to be alone because of unconscious guilt.

FELIX: Guilt is very bad.

DORIS: It's enervating.

FELIX: If you don't let me go to sleep you're gonna be completely enervated by guilt feelings tomorrow.

DORIS: Never mind, wise guy! Read me your story.

FELIX, *picks up typewriter script:* You won't like it.

DORIS: If it puts me to sleep I'll love it.

FELIX, *reading:* Scream—

DORIS: "Scream." That's the title, right—"Scream."

FELIX: Yes.

DORIS: That's a wild title.

FELIX: Thank you. *Reads:* The sun spit morning into Werner's face—one eyelid fluttered—dragging the soul back screaming from its stealthy flight to death—

DORIS, *sitting up:* The sun spit morning into this guy's face?

FELIX: Yes.

DORIS: You were right.

FELIX: When?

DORIS: I don't like it. I hate it.

FELIX: It wasn't written for you to like.

DORIS: Why wasn't it written for me to like? I'm the public—

FELIX: You're raising your voice.

DORIS: The sun spit morning into his face!

FELIX: Shh! What are you getting angry about?

DORIS: What right do you have to put down a terrible thing like that in a story—"The sun spit morning in a man's face."

FELIX: All right—you don't like it—but calm down.

DORIS: Yeah—look at me! I always get mad at stuff like that.

FELIX: Just because you don't understand it?

DORIS: It makes me feel shut out—you know? It makes me mad as hell! You know once I threw a clock at the TV.

SAME TIME, NEXT YEAR

by Bernard Slade

———•———

ACT II, SCENE 1

Same Time, Next Year is the story of a love affair that spans twenty-five years. Doris and George are happily married—to other people. Beginning with a chance pickup in 1951, they continue to meet once a year at the same California inn. During the course of the play we witness, through the changes in both characters, a quarter-century of changes in American mores and political and social attitudes.

When the play begins, George is a conservative accountant.

Through the years he makes the transition from middle- to upper-class income bracket, goes through analysis, temporarily becomes a hippie, and ends up a loyal member of the establishment. Doris starts out as a naive, uneducated young woman who becomes, in turn, a dissatisfied housewife, a college student, a flower child, and, finally, a successful career woman.

The scene below takes place in 1965. The Vietnam War is in progress and political and social beliefs have polarized the nation. Doris enters wearing the standard costume of the 1960s: jeans, sandals, and a headband. She has returned to school and is now a student at Berkeley. George is supporting Goldwater.

George is just finishing his unpacking. The last thing he takes out of his bag is a bottle of Chivas Regal, which he takes to the tray on the piano and pours himself a drink. Drink in hand he crosses to the dressing table and takes his comb, keys, and a prescription bottle out of his pocket and places them on the table. Doris enters in jeans, turtleneck, Indian necklace, headband, long hair, and sandals. George is taken aback. They meet in an embrace.

DORIS: Hey, man! What do you say? So, you wanta fuck?
GEORGE: What?
DORIS: You didn't understand the question?
GEORGE: Of course I did. I just think it's a damned odd way to start a conversation.
DORIS: Yeah? I thought it would be a great little ice breaker. Aren't you horny after your long flight?
GEORGE: I didn't fly, I drove.
DORIS: From Connecticut?
GEORGE: From Los Angeles. We moved to Beverly Hills about six months ago.
DORIS: How come?
GEORGE: Oh, a lot of reasons. I got fed up standing kneedeep in snow trying to scrape the ice off my windshield with a credit card. Besides, there are a lot of people out here with a lot of money who don't know what to do with it.
DORIS: And you tell them?
GEORGE: I'm what they call a Business Manager.

DORIS: How's it going?

GEORGE: I can't complain. Why?

DORIS: You look kinda shitty. Are you all right?

GEORGE: I'm fine.

DORIS: You sure?

GEORGE: When did you start dressing like an Indian? You look like a refugee from the Sunset Strip.

DORIS: I've gone back to school. Berkeley.

GEORGE: Why?

DORIS: You mean what do I want to be when I grow up?

GEORGE: Well, you have to admit it's a bit odd becoming a schoolgirl at your age.

DORIS: Listen, you think it's easy being the only one in the class with clear skin.

GEORGE: What made you do it?

DORIS: It was a dinner party that made me decide. Harry's boss invited us over for dinner and I just freaked.

GEORGE: Why?

DORIS: I'd spent so much time with kids I didn't know if I was capable of carrying on an intelligent conversation with anyone over the age of five. Anyway, I went and was seated next to the boss. Well, I surprised myself. He talked—then I talked—you know, just like a real conversation. Everything was cool until I noticed him looking at me in a weird way. I looked down at his plate and realized that all the time we'd been talking I'd been cutting up his meat for him. That's when I decided I'd better get out of the house.

GEORGE: But why school?

DORIS: I felt restless and undirected and I thought school might give me some answers.

GEORGE: What sort of answers?

DORIS: Like where it's really at.

GEORGE: Jesus.

DORIS: What's the matter?

GEORGE: That expression.

DORIS: Okay. To find out who the hell I am.

GEORGE: You don't get those sort of answers from a classroom.

DORIS: I'm not in the classroom all the time. The protests and demonstrations are a learning experience in themselves.

GEORGE: Protests against what?

DORIS: The war of course. Didn't you hear about it? It was in all the papers.

GEORGE: Demonstrations aren't going to stop the war.

DORIS: You have a better idea?

GEORGE: Look, I didn't come up here to discuss politics.

DORIS: Well, so far you've turned down sex and politics. You want to try religion?

GEORGE: I think I'll try a Librium.

DORIS: How come you're so uptight?

GEORGE: That's another expression I hate.

DORIS: Uptight?

GEORGE: There's no such word.

DORIS: You remind me of my mother when I was nine years old. I asked her what "fuck" meant and do you know what she said? "There's no such word."

GEORGE: And now you've found out there is you feel compelled to use it in every other sentence?

DORIS: George, what's bugging you?

GEORGE: Bugging me? I'll tell you what's "bugging" me. The blacks are burning down the cities, there's a Harvard professor telling my kids the only way to happiness is to become doped up zombies, and I have a teenage son with hair so long that from the back he looks exactly like Yvonne deCarlo.

DORIS: That's right, honey. Let it all hang out.

GEORGE: I wish people would stop letting it "all hang out." Especially my daughter. It's amazing she hasn't been arrested for indecent exposure.

DORIS: That's a sign of age, George.

GEORGE: What is?

DORIS: Being worried about the declining morality of the young. Besides, there's nothing you can do about it.

GEORGE: We could start by setting some examples.

DORIS: What do you want to do, George? Bring back public flogging?

GEORGE: It might not be a bad idea. We could start with the movie producers. My God, have you seen the movies lately? Half the time the audience achieves a climax before the movie does!

DORIS: It's natural for people to be interested in sex. You can't kid the body, George.

GEORGE: Maybe not but you can damn well be firm with it.

DORIS: As I recall when you were younger you weren't exactly a monk about that sort of thing.

GEORGE: That was different! Our relationship was not based upon a casual one night stand!

DORIS: No, it's been *fifteen* one night stands.

GEORGE: No it has not. We've shared things. My God, I helped deliver your child, remember?

DORIS: Remember? I consider it our finest hour.

GEORGE: How is she?

DORIS: Very healthy, very noisy, and very spoiled.

GEORGE: You don't feel guilty about leaving her alone while you're at school?

DORIS: Harry's home a lot. The insurance business hasn't been too good lately.

GEORGE: How does he feel about all this?

DORIS: When I told him I wanted to go back to school because I wanted some identity he said, "You want identity? Go build a bridge! Invent penicillin but get off my back!"

GEORGE: Harry always had a good head on his shoulders.

DORIS: George, that was supposed to be the *bad* story about him. How's Helen?

GEORGE: Helen's fine. Just fine.

DORIS: Tell me a story that shows how really rotten she can be.

GEORGE: That's not like you.

DORIS: It seems like we need something to bring us together. Maybe a bad story about Helen will make you appreciate me more.

GEORGE: Okay. Helen . . . As you know, she has this funny sense of humor.

DORIS: By funny I take it you mean peculiar?

GEORGE: Right. And it comes out at the most inappropriate times. I had signed this client—very proper, very old money. Helen and I were invited out to his house for cocktails to get acquainted with him and his wife. Well, it was all pretty awkward but we managed to get through the drinks all right. Then as we went to leave, instead of walking out the front door I walked into the hall closet. Now that's no big deal, right? I mean anybody can do that. The mistake I made was that I *stayed* in there.

DORIS: You stayed in the closet?

GEORGE: I wasn't sure they'd seen me go in. I thought I'd stay there until they'd gone away—okay? I was in there for about a minute before I realized I'd—well—misjudged the situation. When I came out the three of them were just staring at me. All right, it was an embarrassing situation but I probably could have carried it off. Except for what Helen did. You know what she did?

DORIS: What?

GEORGE: She peed on the carpet.

DORIS: She did *what?*

GEORGE: Oh, not right away. First, she started to laugh. Tears started to roll down her face. She held her sides. Then she peed all over their Persian carpet.

KINGDOM OF EARTH

by Tennessee Williams

———————•———————

SCENE 6

The setting is a Mississippi Delta farmhouse. It "has the mood of a blues-song whose subject is loneliness." The levees are overflowing and a major flood is imminent. The residents of this house are two half-brothers filled with hate for each other. They are Chicken, in his thirties, strong and gruff; and Lot, "a frail, delicately—you might say exotically—pretty youth of about twenty." The house belongs to Lot, left to him by his mother.

Lot is dying of tuberculosis. He has been away, and at the beginning of the play he brings home his new wife, Myrtle. She "is a rather fleshy young woman, amiably loud-voiced," a former show girl with dyed blonde hair that "suggests an imitation of a Hollywood glamor-girl which doesn't succeed. . . ." She is robust, good natured, and, since her baptism, "scared to death of deep water."

Lot and Myrtle met and married on a TV show just days before. For her it was romance, somehow being affected by this strange, delicate young man, wanting to care for him and cure him of his illness. Lot's reason for marrying was not so benign. He regrets having signed a paper (a contract) that, upon his death, leaves the house and farm to Chicken. The house is filled with objects and furnishings that belonged to Lot's deceased mother. During the play we learn of Lot's strange relationship to her, and he explains that "it will haunt me to my grave and my mother in hers if this place went to Chicken."

His plan is to disinherit Chicken, and Myrtle is his ruse. Anticipating that his sex-starved brother will try to seduce Myrtle, Lot asks her to get Chicken drunk and try to steal the paper from his wallet—ostensibly to protect her own future in the house when she is left a widow.

As the following scene opens Chicken is alone in the kitchen. Myrtle enters with her marriage license, trying desperately (lying, in fact) to convince Chicken that her marriage to Lot was a fake. In the previous scene Chicken told her of his fear that, regardless of his contract, as Lot's wife, Myrtle, rather than he, will inherit the farm. He threatened to let her drown when the floodwaters fill the house. (He will perch on the roof with the chickens, as he has done before—earning him his nickname.)

MYRTLE: Here it is, this is it. *Hands him license:* You can see it's no good.

CHICKEN: —It's got signatures on it.

MYRTLE: Sure, they put signatures on 'em to make 'em look real, but—

CHICKEN: This looks like a genuine license to me.

MYRTLE: I give you my right hand to God!—That thing is fake!

CHICKEN: Don't give me your right hand to God. I don't want it and he don't want it neither. Nobody wants your right or left hand to nothing. However, I'll keep this thing. I'll put it with my legal agreement with Lot. *He folds the license into his wallet. Studies her somberly.* Are you able to write?

MYRTLE: Why, uh—yais!

CHICKEN: I don't mean just your name.

MYRTLE: No! Yais, I mean yais! —I been through four grades of school.

CHICKEN: Take a seat at this table. I'm gonna give you a little test in writing. *He tears a sheet from a writing tablet: sets it before her with a pen and ink bottle.* You say you are able to write and I am able to read. You see this pen an' paper I set befo' you?

MYRTLE: Yais! Perfectly! Plainly!

CHICKEN: Do you write standing up?

MYRTLE: Yais! No, I mean no! *Scrambles into chair.*

CHICKEN: Now take this pen and write out on this paper what I tell you to write.

MYRTLE: What do you—?

CHICKEN: Shut up. I'm gonna dictate to you a letter that you will write an' sign and this letter will be to me.

MYRTLE: Why should I write you a letter when, when— you're right here?

CHICKEN: You'll understand why when you write it and write it out plain enough so anybody can read it.

MYRTLE: —My hand is—

CHICKEN: What?

MYRTLE: Shakin'!

CHICKEN: Control it.

MYRTLE: It's hard to control it with my nerves so unstrung.

CHICKEN: Which hand do you write with, with the left or the right?

MYRTLE: Oh, with the right, I'm right-handed.

CHICKEN: Well, give me that shaky right hand.

MYRTLE: What do you want with my hand?

CHICKEN: Stop it shakin'. *He takes hold of her hand in both of his.*

MYRTLE: What big hands you got, Chicken.

CHICKEN: Feel the calluses on 'em? I got those calluses on my hands from a life of hard work on this fuckin' place, worked on it like a nigger and got nothin' for it but bed and board and the bed was a cot in the kitchen and the board was no better than slops in the trough of a sow. However, things do change, they do gradually change, you just got to wait and be patient till the time comes to strike and then strike hard. *He is rubbing her* *hand between his.* Now it's comin', that time. This place is gonna be mine when the house is flooded an' I won't be unhappy sittin' on the roof of it till the flood goes down.

MYRTLE: No. Me neither. I'll be—pleased and—relieved!

CHICKEN: You mean if you are still in the land of the livin'.

MYRTLE: Don't make my hand shake again.

CHICKEN: I guess you think that I'm hard.

MYRTLE: I don't think a man should be soft.

CHICKEN: You know what life is made out of?

MYRTLE: Evil, I think it's evil.

CHICKEN: I think that life just plain don't care for the weak. Or the soft. A man and his life. A man and his life both got to be made out of the same stuff or one or the other will break and the one that breaks won't be life. Because life's rock. Man's got to be rock, too. Life, rock. Man, rock. Both rock. Because if they both ain't rock the one that's not rock won't be life. Life's always rock. The one that's not rock will be man so man's got to be rock, too. Because the soft one is broke when the two things come together, the soft one breaks. And life is never the soft one. IS it? NEVER!—If one is soft the one that is soft will be man. Not life, no, not life ever! Now then. Your hand ain't shakin'.

MYRTLE: No. My hand has stopped shaking because.

CHICKEN: —What?

MYRTLE: I know in my heart that you don't hate Myrtle.

CHICKEN: I hate nobody and I love nobody. Now pick up that pen, hold it steady, and write down what I tell you. *She picks up the pen, grips it.* Dip it in the ink, it don't write dry. *She wets the pen.* Ready?

MYRTLE: Ready, my hand is steady.

CHICKEN: I got to be careful how I word this thing, it's too important for me to bugger it up.

MYRTLE: Let's make two copies of it, one for, for—practice and the other—final.

CHICKEN: Won't be necessary. I got it now. Now write down what I tell you in big letters or print. "Me, Mrs. Lot Ravenstock, if I had a claim on this place called Raven Roost or anything on this place, give up and deny all claims when my husband is dead. Because this place goes to Chicken. I known about this setup before my TV marriage and the paper which

Chicken holds with notary seal, two names of witnesses on it, still holds good. I declare this. The place and all on it will be Chicken's, all Chicken's, when Lot Ravenstock dies and also if I die too because of river in flood, a natural act of God."

MYRTLE, *who has been scribbling frantically:* "All Chicken's when Lot dies."

CHICKEN: Now put in the punctuation and dot all the i's an' cross all the t's and sign your name plain at the bottom.

MYRTLE: Yais, yais, I did, I already did that, Chicken.

CHICKEN: Give it here. *He takes the paper from her.* Huh. I bet they never give you no spelling or handwriting prize when you went to school, but anyhow it's possible to read it if the question comes up in case of you being alive when the flood goes down. There's still one question, though. Where's the witnesses and the notary seal so this would hold up in court?

MYRTLE: Oh, we could get them later, we—!

CHICKEN: You wrote this thing because you're scared of drowning. How do I know you wouldn't back out of it when the flood's over with?

MYRTLE: I swear I wouldn't.

CHICKEN: Well, anyhow it's something and somethin's better than nothing. It's worth putting in my wallet with Lot's witnessed letter and the true or false license.

MYRTLE: Chicken, trust my word. I've given you my word and never gone back on my word in all my life.

CHICKEN: I'm not counting on your word, but something else about you.

MYRTLE: What? Else? About me?

CHICKEN: —You're weak.

MYRTLE: I've always been weak compared to men, to a man. I think that's natural, don't you? *They have been sitting in chairs on opposite sides of the small, square kitchen table, chairs angled toward the audience. Now Chicken rises and crosses close to her.*

CHICKEN: Look me straight in the eyes and answer a question.

MYRTLE: What? Question?

CHICKEN: Can you kiss and like kissin' a man that's been accused of having some black blood in him?

MYRTLE: No! Yes! It would make no diff'rence to me.

CHICKEN: Let's try it out. Put your arms about me an' give me a kiss on the mouth. Mouth open. *She complies nervously, gingerly to this request. During the kiss, he puts a hand on her hips. Releasing her:* —Well? How did it feel? Disgusting?

MYRTLE: No, not a bit. I was pleased an' relieved that you wanted to kiss me, Chicken.

CHICKEN: That kiss was just a beginning. You know that. Does that please and relieve you?

MYRTLE: I'm a warm-natured woman. You might say passionate, even. A Memphis doctor prescribed me a bottle of pills to keep down the heat of my nature, but those pills are worthless. Have no effect, I'm through with them. —Don't you know I would never back down on that letter you dictated to me? Not if I could, never would!

CHICKEN: No, I reckon you wouldn't. *Chicken hoists himself onto the kitchen table, directly in front of her, legs spread wide.*

MYRTLE: Wouldn' you be more comf'table in a chair?

CHICKEN: I wouldn' be as close to you. —I'm right in front of you now.

MYRTLE: That's a —high—table. I have to strain my neck to look in your face.

CHICKEN, *with a slow, savage grin:* You don't have to look in my face, my face ain't all they is to me, not by a long shot, honey.... *She begins suddenly to cry like a child.* Why're you cryin'? You don't have to cry fo' it, it's what you want and it's yours! *He snatches up the lamp and blows it out.*

THIEVES

by Herb Gardner

———————•———————

ACT I

The twelve-year-old marriage of Sally and Martin Cramer is on the rocks. From teen-age sweethearts on the streets of the Lower East Side of New York to a successful middle-class couple living in a modern high-rise apartment building, they found their marriage deteriorating in close step with their growing affluence and with the ever-increasing height of each new apartment building into which they moved. The scene opens in the bedroom of their newest apartment—located on a high floor of an even newer and taller building on the Upper East Side of New York. It is late at night. Martin has been playing his flute on the terrace. (For scene-study purposes the actors may ignore the reference to the "Street Lady" in the stage directions.)

SALLY: Can I ask you a question?
MARTIN: Yes.
SALLY: Who are you?
MARTIN: Martin.
SALLY, *thoughtfully:* Martin, Martin . . .
MARTIN: Martin Cramer.
SALLY: Martin Cramer. Right. *After a moment:* And where do I know you from?
MARTIN: I'm your husband. You know me from marriage.
SALLY, *nodding:* Right, right . . .
MARTIN, *opening his eyes:* Sally, the forgetting game. I hate it. You have no idea how much I hate it.
SALLY: O.K., O.K., I—
MARTIN, *sitting up at edge of bed:* Sally, at least once a week now you wake me up in the middle of the night and ask me who I am. I hate it.
SALLY: You used to think it was charming.

MARTIN: I thought a lot of things were charming.

SALLY, *nodding thoughtfully:* Dr. Mathew Spengler talks about this in his book, in "Marriage and Modern Society," he calls it "the inevitable decline from charm to nightmare . . ."

MARTIN: Sally, there is no such book and there is no Dr. Spengler.

SALLY: I know.

MARTIN: Sally, why do you keep—

SALLY: I do the best I can to class up the conversation.

MARTIN: But you don't just do it with me, you do it with everybody. Last month with my mother you made up a whole country. A whole country that doesn't exist.

SALLY: I thought she'd be happy there.

MARTIN: But there *is* none. There is no Hungarian West Indies.

SALLY: My countries, my books; you used to think they were funny . . .

MARTIN: I thought a lot of things were funny.

SALLY: What happened? We—

MARTIN: O.K., Sally. *He rises decisively, goes to center of room.* I was going to wait till morning, but why wait . . .

SALLY: Let's wait.

MARTIN: First, Sally . . . First, I want you to know how much I appreciate the wonderful work you've done on our apartment here. How you've managed to capture, in only five short weeks, the subtle, elusive, yet classic mood previously found only in the Port Authority Bus Terminal. *Pacing about the room:* In addition, Sally, you have, somewhat mystically, lost or forgotten the name of the moving and storage company with whom you placed nearly fifty-five thousand dollars worth of our furniture.

SALLY: It's an Italian name, I know that. I'm working on that . . .

MARTIN: This, coupled with the fact that you disappeared eight days ago on what was ostensibly a trip to Gristede Brothers to buy some strawberry yogurt, and did not return until this evening, has led to a certain amount of confusion for me . . .

SALLY: I went to Gloria's place to think things out, to—

MARTIN, *opens crumpled letter:* All confusion, of course, vanished with the arrival last week of this simple, touching, yet concise note from the Misters Morris, Klein, Fishback, and

Fishback ... *Reads, only the slightest tremor in his voice:* "We
have been retained by your wife, Sally Jane Cramer, hereinafter
referred to as 'Wife,' to represent her in the matter of your divorce. Said wife having requested that her whereabouts remain
unknown to you at present, we therefore ..." *Carefully folding
letter into paper airplane:* After eight days of staring into the air
conditioner, wondering which Santini Brother had my furniture, which Gristede Brother had my wife, and which Fishback
owned my soul, a light began to dawn ... or maybe one went
out ... and I realized that nobody was hiding you from me,
that your whereabouts, said wife, have been unknown to me for
years ... that you make a fine letter-writer, a great decorator,
and a perfect stranger. *Going to terrace doorway:* You said you
came back tonight to talk about the divorce. You didn't mention it. Neither did I. And the habit, the habit of being together,
began again. *Turns to her.* But I couldn't sleep. I couldn't sleep
and I thought about it and tonight, Sally, I have decided to re-
tire from the games. The Olympics are over, lady, the torch is
out ... and you are free. *He tosses the paper airplane through
the terrace doorway, it sails into the street.* Said husband, hereinafter referred to as "gone," has had it. *Martin goes out onto the
terrace. Below, the Street Lady scurries out of the shadows to
pick up the paper airplane, disappears again.*

SALLY, *after a moment, quietly:* Marty, I came back tonight
because I'm pregnant and I'm terrified.

MARTIN: Can't hear you from out here.

SALLY: I know. *Rises from bed, wearing robe, going to terrace
doorway.* Marty, I came back tonight ... *At doorway, after a
moment:* Did I buy you that sweatshirt? *No reply.* It's a size too
big. If we're getting a divorce why did we make love tonight?

MARTIN: Goddamn wine ... why'd you bring a Goddamn
bottle of wine to discuss a divorce?

SALLY: Why'd you light a candle?

MARTIN: It goes with the wine.

SALLY, *she smiles. Remains in doorway, quietly:* Marty, it was
lovely tonight. Like a surprise party. Like a lovely party with
two hosts ... *After a moment:* If you've got any material of
your own on this I'd be glad to hear it.

MARTIN: Look, it goes without saying—

SALLY: No, *don't* let it go, *not* without saying— *(grabs his
arm)* Come on, keep me company, show an emotion! Emotions,

Marty, *you* remember. Come on, scream at me for walking out!
Holler, or cry, or—Christ, how many years since I've seen a
tear outa ya!? *Shaking him:* Come on, Marty-baby, you can do
it, break something, throw a plate at me—
MARTIN: I *can't* . . . They're all packed. *He goes sadly back
into the room.* This beautiful place, you never moved in . . .
SALLY, *following him:* You keep *moving* us, another room, a
higher floor—
MARTIN: This beautiful place . . .
SALLY: Poor shmuck, we'd just be back up to our ass in
French Provincial—
MARTIN: Do you have to talk like that, are you *compelled*—
SALLY: That's how I *always*—
MARTIN: When we're out with people, I cringe, I literally—
SALLY: I've seen ya, you go off in a corner and pretend you're
an onion dip—
MARTIN: All these years, that loud, embarrassing—
SALLY: That's how I talk to everybody—
MARTIN: What about at school, what about those little—
SALLY: P.S. Twenty-*Nine,* Marty, have you forgotten what
those kids *sound* like down there? Canal Street, where you came
from, you and the embarrassing lady here— *(He walks away.)*
Dummy, you bought yourself a new mouth and kept the same
old wife. *She follows him.* It's *me,* Sally Jane Kaminsky, I know
ya from before fellah. I know ya from coppin' goodies off of every open counter in the neighborhood, I know ya from knockin'
over DeSapio's Grocery with the Golden Avengers, I—
MARTIN: Sally, I was sixteen years old—
SALLY, *laughing:* I remember your jacket, the red one with the
big pockets sewn inside. You'd come draggin' outa Wool-
worth's, the only Jewish pelican in New York. . . . *Silence for a
moment. He turns to her.*
MARTIN, *quietly:* I didn't think you even noticed me in those
days.
SALLY: Sure I noticed you.
MARTIN: I mean, I thought it was years later that you . . .
SALLY: I was crazy about ya.
MARTIN: I always thought it was at Marilyn Krasney's party
that you first—*(She shakes her head.)* All this time, how come
you never talked about—
SALLY: Who talks? We don't talk, we move. We're movers.

Goes toward him. I also saw ya following me home all the time.

MARTIN: I didn't.

SALLY: I saw ya.

MARTIN: You couldn't have. I cut in and outa doorways. *He smiles:* Peter Lorre taught me how.

SALLY: Woulda stopped and talked to you except I was scared of all you guys from the Golden Avengers. I mean, you weren't as tough as Whitey Arkish, but still I was scared. *She puts her arms around him.* Coulda had me at fifteen. How about that? We coulda been divorced by now.

MARTIN, *his arms around her:* Whitey Arkish wasn't so tough . . .

SALLY, *tenderly:* First real date we had was four years later . . . we broke into Loew's Delancy with a crowbar . . .

MARTIN: Take Whitey's knife away he fell apart . . .

SALLY: We pried open the fire door at three in the morning, you put me in the middle of the eighth row . . . and then you got up on the stage and played your flute for me, "Blue-Tail Fly" and "The Streets of Laredo," fantastic repertoire . . . and over your head on the curtain, it said . . .

MARTIN, s*oftly:* "Loew's Delancy, Home Of The Stars . . ."

SALLY: And then the cops came— *(holds him tightly, inspired)* Jesus, sirens . . . sirens and everything . . . runnin' through alleys, all those alleys, halfway across town, outa breath, gettin' away with it, gettin' away clean. . . . *Tenderly:* Oh, Marty, how'd you do it?

MARTIN: What?

SALLY: Get to be so boring. *He walks away, she pursues him.* You had a knife and a flute and you wanted to be a teacher, you were a Goddamn interesting person.

OTHERWISE ENGAGED

by Simon Gray

———————•———————

ACT II

Simon has a simple desire today. He has taken the day off from
his publishing firm in order to listen to his newly purchased recording of *Parsifal*. But today there is no peace for Simon. He is
besieged by intruders: his young boarder who is behind on the
rent and constantly pops in to borrow things; his complaining
brother, Stephen; a shallow and supercilious newspaper critic;
the critic's girlfriend who tries to seduce Simon into publishing
a book that she is writing; an old schoolmate whose daughter
Simon has seduced; and finally, his wife, Beth.

The following dialogue is between Simon and Beth. She has
just returned from a trip intent on telling Simon that she has
been having a secret affair and wishes to marry her lover. Simon, who knows about the affair, is trying to avoid an open discussion. Stephen has recently left the room, and Beth believes
that Stephen has already told Simon about her relationship.

BETH: What did Stephen tell you, please Simon.
SIMON: Nothing. Nothing, except for the odd detail, that I
haven't known for a long time. So you see it's all right. Noth-
ing's changed for the worst, though it might if we assume we
have to talk about it.
BETH, *long pause:* How long have you known for?
SIMON: Oh— *(sighs)* about ten months it would be roughly.
Pause. How long has it been going on for?
BETH: For about ten months, it would be. *Pause.* How did you
know?
SIMON: There's no point, Beth—
BETH: Yes, there is. Yes, there is. How did you know?
SIMON: Well, frankly, your sudden habit, after years of admir-
able conversational economy on such day-to-day matters as
what you'd done today, of becoming a trifle prolix.

BETH: You mean you knew I was having an affair because I became boring?

SIMON: No, no, overdetailed, that's all, darling. And quite naturally, as you were anxious to account for stretches of time in which you assumed I *would* be interested if I knew how you'd *actually* filled them, if you see, so you sweetly devoted considerable effort and paradoxically imaginative skill to rendering them—for my sake I know—totally uninteresting. My eyes may have been glazed but my heart was touched.

BETH: Thank you. And is that all you had to go on?

SIMON: Well, you have doubled your bath routine. Time was, you took one immediately before going out for the day. These last ten months you've taken one immediately on return too. *Pause.* And once or twice you've addressed me, when in the twilight zone, with an unfamiliar endearment.

BETH: What was it?

SIMON: Foxy. *Little pause.* At least, I took it to be an endearment. Is it?

BETH: Yes. I'm sorry.

SIMON: No, no, it's quite all right.

BETH: You haven't felt it's interfered with your sex life then?

SIMON: On the contrary. *Quite* the contrary. In fact there seems to have been an increased intensity in your— *(gestures)* which I suppose in itself was something of a sign.

BETH: In what way?

SIMON: Well, guilt, would it be? A desire to make up—

BETH, *after a pause:* And did you know it was Ned, too?

SIMON: Ned *too?* Oh, did I also know it was Ned? No, that was the little detail I mentioned Stephen did provide. Ned. There I *was* surprised.

BETH: Why?

SIMON: Oh, I don't know. Perhaps because—well, no offense to Ned, whom I've *always* as you know thought of as a very engaging chap, in his way, no offense to *you* either, come to think of it, I'd just imagined when you did have an affair it would be with someone of more—more—

BETH: What?

SIMON: Consequence. *Overt* consequence.

BETH: He's of consequence to me.

SIMON: And *that's* what matters, quite.

BETH: What did you mean, when?

SIMON: Mmmm?

BETH: *When* I had an affair, you said.

SIMON: A grammatical slip, that's all. And since the hypothesis is now a fact—

BETH: But you used the emphatic form—when I *did* have an affair—which implies that you positively assumed I'd have an affair. Didn't you?

SIMON: Well, given your nature, darling, and the fact that so many people do have them these days, I can't see any reason for being bouleversé now that you're having one, even with Ned, can I put it that way?

BETH: Given what about my nature?

SIMON: It's marvelously responsive—warm, a warm, responsive nature. And then I realized once we'd taken the decision not to have children—and the fact that you work every day and therefore meet chaps—and pretty exotic ones too, from lithe young Spanish counts to experienced Japanese businessmen—not forgetting old Ned himself—it was only realistic—

BETH: From boredom, you mean. You know I'm having an affair because I'm boring, and you assumed I'd have one from boredom. That's why I'm in love with Ned, is it?

SIMON: I'm absolutely prepared to think of Ned as a very, very lovable fellow. I'm sure *his* wife loves him, why shouldn't mine.

BETH: You are being astonishingly hurtful.

SIMON: I don't want to be, I don't want to be! That's why I tried to avoid this conversation, darling.

BETH: You'd like to go back, would you, to where I came in, and pretend that I'd simply caught the early train from Salisbury, and here I was, old unfaithful Beth, back home and about to take her bath, as usual?

SIMON: Yes, I'd love to. *Little pause.* I thought it was Canterbury.

BETH: It was neither. We spent the night in a hotel in Euston, and the morning in Ned's poky little office at the school, agonizing.

SIMON: Agonizing? Good God, did you really?

BETH: About whether we should give up everything to live together properly.

SIMON: Properly?

BETH: We want, you see, to be husband and wife to each other.

SIMON: Husband *and* wife to each other? Is Ned up to such double duty? And what did you decide?

BETH: Do you care?

SIMON: Yes.

BETH: His wife isn't well. She's been under psychiatric treatment for years. And his daughter is autistic.

SIMON: Oh, I'm sorry. I can quite see why he wants to leave them.

BETH: But I could still leave you.

SIMON: Yes.

BETH: But you don't think I will. Do you?

SIMON: No.

BETH: And why not?

SIMON: Because I hope you'd rather live with me than anybody else, except Ned of course. And I know you'd rather live with almost anyone than live alone.

BETH: You think I am that pathetic?

SIMON: I don't think it's pathetic. I'd rather live with you than anyone else, including Ned. And I don't want to live alone either.

BETH: But do you want to live at all?

SIMON: What?

BETH: As you hold such a deeply contemptuous view of human life. That's Ned's diagnosis of you.

SIMON: But the description of my symptoms came from you, did it?

BETH: He says you're one of those men who only give permission to little bits of life to get through to you. He says that while we may envy you your serenity, we should be revolted by the rot from which it stems. Your sanity is of the kind that causes people to go quietly mad around you.

SIMON: What an elegant paraphrase. Tell me, did you take notes?

BETH: I didn't have to. Every word rang true.

SIMON: But if it's all true, why do you need to keep referring it back to Ned?

BETH: It's a way of keeping in touch with him. If I forgot in the middle of a sentence that he's there and mine, I might begin to scream at you and claw at you and punch at you.

SIMON: But why should you want to do that?

BETH: Because I hate you.

The telephone rings. Simon makes a move toward it. After the fourth ring, it stops.

SIMON: Oh, of course. I've put on the machine. *Pause.*

BETH, *quietly:* You know the most insulting thing, that you let me go on and on being unfaithful without altering your manner or your behavior one—one—you don't care about me, or my being in love with somebody else, or my betraying you, good God! least of all that! But you do wish I hadn't actually *mentioned* it, because then we could have gone on, at least *you* could, pretending that everything was all right, no, not even pretending, as far as *you* were concerned, everything was all right, you probably still think it *is* all right—and—and—you've—you've—all those times we've made love, sometimes the very same evening as Ned and I—and yet you took me—in your usual considerate fashion, just as you take your third of a bottle of wine with dinner or your carefully measured brandy and your cigar after it, *and* enjoyed it all the more because I felt guilty, God help me *guilty*—and so tried harder for your sake—and you *admit* that, no, not admit it, simply state it as if on the difference made by an extra voice or something in your bloody Wagner—don't you see, don't you see that that makes you a freak! You're—you're—oh, damn! Damn. Damn you. *Pause.* Oh, damn. *There is a silence.* So you might as well listen to your Wagner.

SIMON: I must say you've quite warmed me up for it. And what are *you* going to do, have your cleansing bath?

BETH: No, go to Ned for a couple of hours.

SIMON: Oh dear, more agonizing in his poky little office. Or is that a euphemism for Ned's brand of loveplay? Excuse me, but what precisely has all this been about? You complain of my reticence over the last ten months, but what good has all this exposition served, what's it been for Beth? Ned's not going to leave his wife, I don't want you to leave me, you don't even think you're going to leave me—we have a perfectly sensible arrangement, we are happy enough together you and I, insultingly so if you like but still happy. We could go on and on, with Ned, until you've gone off him, why, why did you have to muck it up between you with your infantile agonizings.

BETH: Because there's a problem.

SIMON: What problem?

BETH: I'm going to have a baby.

SIMON, *stares at her for a long moment:* What? *Another moment.* Whose?

BETH: *That* is the problem. *Goes out.*

GOLDEN BOY

by Clifford Odets

———————•———————

ACT II, SCENE 2

Joe Bonaparte has a talent for the violin—and for boxing. Violinists stay poor. Boxers can get rich; they can buy respect, fast cars, and beautiful women. Driven by unquenchable ambition, and against his father's wishes, Joe becomes a professional boxer. His speedy ascendance through the boxing ranks is matched by an equally rapid swelling of his self-importance and a decline in his ability to care about anyone else. Ultimately, he kills another boxer in the ring, and then kills himself in an automobile crash.

The following scene takes place on a park bench. It is still early in Joe's career, but he shows extraordinary promise. Joe's manager, Tom Moody, has asked his girl friend, Lorna Moon, to spend time with Joe, to keep him away from his father, and to prevent him from racing cars. Moody doesn't know that Joe and Lorna have already developed strong feelings for each other. Those feelings are finally expressed in this scene.

JOE: Some nights I wake up—my heart's beating a mile a minute! Before I open my eyes I know what it is—the feeling that someone's standing at my bed. Then I open my eyes ... it's gone—ran away!

LORNA: Maybe it's that old fiddle of yours.

JOE: Lorna, maybe it's you. . . .

LORNA: Don't you ever think of it anymore—music?

JOE: What're you trying to remind me of? A kid with a Buster Brown collar and a violin case tucked under his arm? Does that sound appetizing to you?

LORNA: Not when you say it that way. You said it different once. . . .

JOE: What's on your mind, Lorna?

LORNA: What's on yours?

JOE, *simply:* You. . . . You're real for me—the way music was real.

LORNA: You've got your car, your career—what do you want with me?

JOE: I develop the ability to knock down anyone my weight. But what point have I made? Don't you think I know that? I went off to the wars 'cause someone called me a name—because I wanted to be two other guys. Now it's happening. . . . I'm not sure I like it.

LORNA: Moody's against that car of yours.

JOE: I'm against Moody, so we're even.

LORNA: Why don't you like him?

JOE: He's a manager! He treats me like a possession! I'm just a little silver mine for him—he bangs me around with a shovel!

LORNA: He's helped you—

JOE: No, Tokio's helped me. Why don't you give him up? It's terrible to have just a Tuesday-night girl. Why don't you belong to me every night in the week? Why don't you teach me love? . . . Or am I being a fool?

LORNA: You're not a fool, Joe.

JOE: I want you to be my family, my life—Why don't you do it, Lorna, why?

LORNA: He loves me.

JOE: I love you!

LORNA, *treading delicately:* Well. . . . Anyway, the early bird got the worm. Anyway, I can't give him anguish. I . . . I know what it's like. You shouldn't kick Moody around. He's poor compared to you. You're alive, you've got yourself—I can't feel sorry for you!

JOE: But you don't love him!

LORNA: I'm not much interested in myself. But the thing I like best about you . . . you still feel like a flop. It's mysterious, Joe. It makes me put my hand out. *She gives him her hand and he grasps it.*

JOE: I feel very close to you, Lorna.

LORNA: I know. . . .

JOE: And you feel close to me. But you're afraid—

LORNA: Of what?

JOE: To take a chance! Lorna darling, you won't let me wake you up! I feel it all the time—you're half dead, and you don't know it!

LORNA, *half smiling:* Maybe I do. . . .

JOE: Don't smile—don't be hard-boiled!

LORNA, *sincerely:* I'm not.

JOE: Don't you trust me?

LORNA, *evasively:* Why start what we can't finish?

JOE, *fiercely:* Oh, Lorna, deep as my voice will reach—*listen!* Why can't you leave him? Why?

LORNA: Don't pull my dress off—I hear you.

JOE: Why?

LORNA: Because he needs me and you don't—

JOE: That's not true!

LORNA: Because he's a desperate guy who always starts out with two strikes against him. Because he's a kid at forty-two and you're a man at twenty-two.

JOE: You're sorry for him?

LORNA: What's wrong with that?

JOE: But what do *you* get?

LORNA: I told you before I don't care.

JOE: I don't believe it!

LORNA: I can't help that!

JOE: What did he ever do for you?

LORNA, *with sudden verve:* Would you like to know? He loved me in a world of enemies, of stags and bulls! . . . and I loved him for that. He picked me up in Friskin's hotel on 39th Street. I was nine weeks behind in rent. I hadn't hit the gutter yet, but I was near. He washed my face and combed my hair. He stiffened the space between my shoulder blades. Misery reached out to misery—

JOE: And now you're dead.

LORNA, *lashing out:* I don't know what the hell you're talking about!

JOE: Yes, you do. . . .

LORNA, *withdrawing:* Ho hum. . . . *There is silence. The soft park music plays in the distance. The traffic lights change. Lorna is trying to appear impassive. Joe begins to whistle softly. Finally Lorna picks up his last note and continues, he stops. He picks up her note, and after he whistles a few phrases she picks him up again. This whistling duet continues for almost a minute. Then the traffic lights change again. Lorna, beginning in a low voice:* You make me feel too human, Joe. All I want is peace and quiet, not love. I'm a tired old lady, Joe, and I don't mind being what you call "half dead." In fact it's what I like. *Her voice mounting higher:* The twice I was in love I took an awful beating and I don't want it again! *Now half crying:* I want you to stop it! Don't devil me, Joe. I beg you, don't devil me . . . let me alone. . . . *She cries softly. Joe reaches out and takes her hand, he gives her a handkerchief, which she uses. Lorna, finally:* That's the third time I cried in my life. . . .

JOE: Now I know you love me.

LORNA, *bitterly:* Well . . .

JOE: I'll tell Moody.

LORNA: Not yet. Maybe he'd kill you if he knew.

JOE: Maybe.

LORNA: Then Fuseli'd kill him. . . . I guess I'd be left to kill myself. I'll tell him. . . .

JOE: When?

LORNA: Not tonight.

JOE: Swiftly, do it swiftly—

LORNA: Not tonight.

JOE: Everything's easy if you do it swiftly.

LORNA: He went up there tonight with six hundred bucks to bribe her into divorce.

JOE: Oh . . .

LORNA, *sadly:* He's a good guy, neat all over—sweet. I'll tell him tomorrow. I'd like a drink.

JOE: Let's drive over the Washington Bridge.

LORNA, *standing:* No, I'd like a drink.

JOE, *standing and facing her:* Lorna, when I talk to you . . . something moves in my heart. Gee, it's the beginning of a wonderful life! A man and his girl! A warm living girl who shares your room. . . .

LORNA: Take me home with you.

JOE: Yes.

LORNA: But how do I know you love me?

JOE: Lorna . . .

LORNA: How do I know it's true? You'll get to be the champ. They'll all want you, all the girls! But I don't care! I've been undersea a long time! When they'd put their hands on me I used to say, "This isn't it! This isn't what I mean!" It's been a mysterious world for me! But, Joe, I think you're it! I don't know why, I think you're it! Take me home with you.

JOE: Lorna!

LORNA: Poor Tom . . .

JOE: Poor Lorna! *The rest is embrace and kiss and clutching each other.*

THE GREAT WHITE HOPE

by Howard Sackler

———•———

ACT III, SCENE 3

The play is based on the life of the boxer Jack Johnson (Jack Jefferson in the play), the first black heavyweight champion. It takes place prior to and during the First World War. The story traces Jack's rise to the championship; his love affair with Ellie Bachman, a white woman; the various attempts by the boxing promoters, the government, and the public to destroy him; and finally, his capitulation to his enemies.

Jack's flamboyant, irreverent lifestyle, and the fact that he, a

black man, handily defeats each new "white hope," offends and
enrages the powerbrokers in both boxing and government. A
conspiracy is formed, false charges are brought against him,
and Jack is forced to flee the country as a fugitive from the law.
Frustrated at every attempt to earn a living, and threatened
with a long imprisonment, Jack finally agrees to throw a championship fight for the promise of money and freedom.

The scene that follows is between Jack and Ellie. During the
play we have seen them driven farther apart—by the poverty,
by the need to constantly relocate, by her increasing weariness
and Jack's increasing bitterness. They are now in Juárez, Mexico. Jack still has hope that he will receive a legitimate offer to
fight. Ellie, all strength and hope gone, wants Jack to accept the
bribe. The scene takes place in a barn, crudely set up as a training room for Jack.

ELLIE: Let them go ahead, Jack.

JACK: Take dem specs off. Ah cain hardly see ya.

ELLIE, *doing so:* I didn't think you wanted to.

JACK: You readin mah mine now?

ELLIE: Jack—

JACK: Ah toleya keep outa dis, din Ah?

ELLIE: I can't. Please, let them, you have to.

JACK: Finely battin fo do home team, huh?

ELLIE: Cable them tonight, please—

JACK: *Finely come roun to it—*

ELLIE: Jack, don't bitch me now—

JACK: Ah toleya—

ELLIE, *rises, goes center to bag:* No, I don't care! Forget what
you told me! Say yes and get it over with for God's sake! You're
letting them do this to you, it's worse—

JACK: Worse fo you, mebbe—

ELLIE: Jack, it's slow poison here, there's nothing else to wait
for, just more of it. You've had enough, please, you're being
paralyzed—

JACK: Wid you mebbe—

ELLIE, *hits bag, then goes to left end of table.* All right, yes,
with me too, with everything but hammering that stupid bag
there! You're not your own man any more—

JACK: Now you rollin—

ELLIE: How can you be your own man? They have you! They do and you know it, you're theirs. At least you can buy yourself back from them—

JACK: Sold—*one buck nigger fo de lady!*

ELLIE: Let it sound the way it is! Run when they push you and back when they pull you, work yourself sick in this hell hole for nothing, and tell me you're not theirs—Here, look at the grease you swallow for them, look at the bedbug bites on your arms, and the change in your pockets and the blotches in your eyes—

JACK: Doan leave de smell out—

ELLIE: The two of us smell! Whatever turns people into niggers—there—*Shows her neck.* It's happening to both of us—

JACK: Wish comin true, huh—

ELLIE: No, never this, it wasn't this—

JACK: Sing it, sistah!

ELLIE: I want you there fighting them again, that's what I wish now. I want to watch when you're knocking them down for this, dozens of them. God help them, wipe it off on all of them—

JACK: How bout rooster-fightin? Plenty right here—

ELLIE, *moves right to Jack:* Listen to me, please—

JACK: Oughta look inta dat—

ELLIE: You'd fight them and you'd be with your friends and you'd—

Jack crows like a rooster.

JACK: *Somebody wanna sign me?*

ELLIE: Maybe we could live then, damn you!

JACK: Lil frame house, tree in front?

ELLIE: Anything!

JACK: Nice quiet street?

ELLIE: Anywhere! A place!

JACK: Lil cozy—

ELLIE: A kitchen!

JACK: Put de cat out? Tuck in de kids?

ELLIE: Oh, you're just hateful!

JACK, *grabs her from behind on the neck, swings her around and pushes her against downstage end of table:* Well, Ah gonna tellya whut de livin like, baby, far as Ah concern—

ELLIE: Get away from me—

JACK, *center:* Yeah, Ah put you straight on it—an alla you, too. Ah wen inta a fair once and dere wuz dis old pug, see, give anybody two bucks who stan up a roun widdim—perfessional set-up, reggerlation ring an all, cep dey had rope juss on 3 sides, dass right, de back side wuz de tent. So Ah watches a couple git laid out real quick in dere, but he doan look dat red hot ta me, see, so Ah climbs in widdim. An Ah doin awright fo a youngster, when all it once he bulls me up gainss dat tent-side a de ring an SLAM, WHAM, somebody behine dere conks me, right through de canvas, musta use a 2 by 4, an evvy time Ah stans up he shove me back agin, an SLAM, dere's anudder, down she come—good story, huh?

ELLIE: Jack—

JACK, *going around left end of table to above it:* Dass how it go like Ah knows it, baby—

ELLIE: Sometimes, sometimes—

JACK: All de way now! dass where Ah is and dass whut Ahm gittin, gonna git it de same sayin Yessuh, Nossuh, doan mattah whut Ah does—Ah in dere, unnerstan? An Ah doan wan you watchin, or helpin, or waitin, or askin, or hannin me you jive bout livin or anythin fromya but OUT, Ah mean OUT—

ELLIE: What—

JACK, *going around right end of table, left to chair:* How goddam plain Ah gotta make it for you!

ELLIE: Jack—if you want other girls—

JACK: Git you stuff ready, train out 10 aclock.

ELLIE: No, no, I won't, no—

JACK, *comes back center:* When Tick come Ah sen him ovah—

ELLIE: Jack—

JACK: Bettah start moving—

ELLIE: Stop it—

JACK: Ah pologize actin so yellah up ta—

ELLIE: Wait, you have to stop it—

JACK: All Ah has to is be black an die, lady—

ELLIE, *goes toward him:* I want to stay, even if we—

JACK: Stay wid you own, lady—

ELLIE: What are you doing!

JACK: Quit dat, quit it, short an sweet—

ELLIE: I won't go—

JACK, *goes downstage right:* You knowed it comin, start movin—

ELLIE: Wait—

JACK: Doan cross me now—

ELLIE, *following:* Jack, I thought we'd save something, please—

JACK: Ah said MOVE—

ELLIE: Please, I only—

JACK: Move! You through widdit now—

ELLIE, *kneeling, downstage right end of table:* Jack—

JACK: No mo lousy grub you gotta puke up, no more a ya lookin like a wash out rag here, wid you eye twitchin alla—

ELLIE: Don't—I don't care—

JACK: Juss MOVE—

ELLIE, *rises:* I'll take better—

JACK: Hangin on me, dead weight—

ELLIE: No, not for you—

JACK: Start—

ELLIE: Jack, I'll find a job, please—

JACK: Ah toleya when mah momma die, Ah toleya leave me be a while, now—

ELLIE, *goes to Jack:* Jack, I can't run anymore, not by myself—

JACK: You got you people an you a—

ELLIE: No, listen—

JACK: You a young woman an you gonna—

ELLIE: Please, I'd never—

JACK: Gonna fine—

ELLIE: No one else, I'd—

JACK: Tough titty—

ELLIE: Just—

JACK: Move, or goddam you—

ELLIE: Why can't you wait at least! Wait till you've given me a chance to make you happy—one chance, only one—*I swear I've never had one*—

JACK: Too big a order all aroun!

ELLIE: No, I won't go—

JACK: Wanna drag it out, huh—

ELLIE: I won't, I can't—

JACK: Den Ah gonna wise you up good now, you gray bitch—

(Leaps onto table, grabs towel and jumps to floor, whipping Ellie with towel. Pushes her against table and steps back center.)

ELLIE: You can't make me go, stop doing this—

JACK: Why you think Ah ain't put a han to ya for how long, why ya think it turn me off juss lookin atya—

ELLIE: Stop it—

JACK: You stayin, stay fo it all—ya know why? Does ya, honeybunch? Cause evvy time you pushes dat pinch up face in fronna me, Ah sees where it done got me, dass whut Ah lookin at, the why, the wherefore an de Numbah One Who, right down de line, girl, an Ah mean YOU, and Ah doan wanna give you NOTHIN, unnerstan? Ah cut it off firss!

ELLIE: Oh, I despise you—

JACK: Right, like alla resta ya— *(moves upstage left)*

ELLIE: Oh, I'd like to smash you—

JACK, *comes back:* Me an evvy udder dumb nigger who'd letya! Now go on home an hustle one up who doan know it yet, plenty for ya, score em up—*watch out, brudders!* Oughta hang a bell on so dey hear you comin.

ELLIE: You mean this?

JACK: Look in mah purple eyes.

ELLIE: You win, daddy. *Turns and goes off left.*

A CRY OF PLAYERS

by William Gibson

———◆———

ACT II, SCENE 1

Young Will Shakespeare is a man in conflict. He is torn between his responsibilities to his wife, Anne, and their children, and his unquenchable passion for other women. He is under pressure to take a dull, steady position as a schoolteacher; yet his very soul is ignited by the fantasy world of plays and traveling players. Anne, some years older than Will, wants to climb out of the life of poverty they have lived. She wants to secure a home for herself and her children. Most of all, she does not want to lose Will.

The confrontation between Anne and Will in the following scene was preceded by a number of incidents: A company of traveling players arrived in town; the offer to teach school was made; Anne caught Will with one of the neighborhood "wenches"; Will promised to come home early to discuss the position, but instead went to see a play—indeed, he brought home a script to read. As the scene begins Anne and Will are sitting at the table. He is reading and she is darning, waiting for him to begin the conversation. The dialogue is written in a style that captures some of the rhythms and patterns of Elizabethan English.

ANNE: Ye said talk.
WILL, *reading:* Yes.
ANNE: Are ye taking it?
WILL, *reading:* It?
ANNE: The teaching. *She waits.* Will ye put that away and— *(she sweeps the pages away)* —mind me, if ye're sober? *Will gathers them up again.*
WILL: Of course. I'm drunk only on this play, which you disrupted there too, it tells me to pillage cities to come at my desire: and what I'm asked is walk behind our schoolmaster—that sheaf of dutiful bones—
ANNE: Are ye taking it?
WILL: —into Sir Thomas's palm. It's not enough, no, it's—
ANNE: Then why talk, ye liar.
WILL: Don't— *(Anne bites the thread off, rises, slaps the darning down)* —call me liar, and—
ANNE: Damn liar.
WILL: —sit down!
ANNE, *dangerous:* Mind it, lad, I'm not ye little wench—
WILL: I didn't say lie down. *Anne stands inarticulate, then wheels to leave. He tosses a mug, she catches it, for a moment she is tempted.*
ANNE: I don't throw things, sweet.
WILL: Not when a ladylike fit of fingernails will do. I admired the two of you, such gentle blood I saw. Will you join me? *He*

puts the text aside, Anne is moveless. I said it's not enough, not that I wouldn't, sit or not. *Anne brings the mug back, sits opposite him.* Nor that I would, either.

ANNE: Oh, God help me.

WILL: Now we can patch up our differences again—

ANNE: If I made a fool of myself there it's my doing, but ye, ye damn peacock—

WILL: —over a pleasant conversation—

ANNE: —ye make such a fool of me every time—

WILL: —that leads nowhere, or—

ANNE: —ye say a word! *She strikes the needle into his wrist, he writhes away.*

WILL: God—damn—

ANNE: Don't lose the needle, please.

WILL: Certainly not, I'm deeply imbedded to you.

ANNE, *ironic:* I'm sorry if I give ye pain.

WILL: Oh, pain is always a pleasure, it reminds me we're not the—compliant vapors that drift in and out of my daydreams, now how much of it can you bear?

ANNE: Give me it. *She catches at the needle, rises.*

WILL: I mean I've been pondering a different compact with you, a conversation we can get our teeth into.

ANNE, *turns:* What?

WILL: Truth, all or nothing, no lies, no question evaded, no mercies or delicacies, go down in the slop as—honest as pigs, and look at what each of us is married to. *He waits.* No?

ANNE: Why?

WILL: To see if it's enough. *He waits.* No?

ANNE, *a pause:* Yes.

WILL: Then sit. *Anne lifts the darning off the stool, sits.*

ANNE: I'm sitting. Start.

WILL: You.

ANNE: How many times did ye lay with her?

WILL: Fifteen. Twenty.

ANNE: Why?

WILL: Is that a question? I was agog for her—dumplings, my hands itched.

ANNE: Is she the only one?

WILL: Well, that's no answer. No, she's not the only one, I was—

ANNE: Who else?

WILL: Tumble and tell?

ANNE: Ye said everything.

WILL: Yes. You don't know them though, one at Snitterfield, one—

ANNE: How many?

WILL, *recalling:* —five, six—

ANNE: I'll kill ye! *She comes at him, he slips around the table.*

WILL: No more questions?

ANNE, *grittily:* Oh, I have questions, pet, yes—

WILL: Then don't kill the goose that laid—Et cetera.

ANNE: Six is it, ha?

WILL: Seven.

ANNE, *hits the table:* Why, ye think ye're a great bull down there, ye're not—

WILL: Is that a complaint?

ANNE: No—yes, if that's all I thought about, now answer me—

WILL, *a knife:* Compared to what?

ANNE, *stopped:* Ye know what, I told ye, the—one before we—

WILL: Compared to—ancient history, it grows longer with time. Who since?

ANNE: Since we—?

WILL: Since we. *Anne sits, half averted, very reluctant.*

ANNE: One.

WILL: Who?

ANNE: Once.

WILL: Who?

ANNE: Sandy.

WILL: Sandells! *He spins in disbelief, stops.* Compared to Sandells?

ANNE: Oh, yes. *Will is dumb, her eye now taunts him.* Ye daren't ask?

WILL: How—bully is—old friend Sandells? *Anne shows with her palms apart.* Needn't kill me, I'll kill myself—

ANNE: Starts there. *She inches her palms apart, wider, wider, until she laughs.* Oh God, ye're a baby—

WILL: It's all foreskin, was there a once? *Anne no longer laughs; she then nods.* When?

ANNE: This summer.

WILL: How?

ANNE: He—he—put my hand on it, I—was—

WILL: Captured.

ANNE: Yes.

WILL: Womanly compassion.

ANNE: No.

WILL: Higgledy piggledy, two in the stew, now don't be so cleanly with me, please?

ANNE: It's not the same. Did I have a husband so—glad to do it, or able?

WILL, *terse:* I'm able, ask.

ANNE: Which one? Anyone but me, so many ye—No, why, why did—

WILL: Curiosity?

ANNE: I wasn't enough?

WILL: No, half the world is female—parts, I didn't think I should go to my grave in ignorance.

ANNE: Ignorance.

WILL: Of all others. Well, that's also no answer—

ANNE, *scornful:* Ye find such a goggle of difference?

WILL: Some.

ANNE: What's so darling damn different? *Will looks at her, glinty.* Tell me, tell me—

WILL: Size, degree of—lubricity, color—taste— *(Anne closes her eyes)* —grip, friskiness—So on.

ANNE: And theirs is—better?

WILL: Different.

ANNE: Better?

WILL: Some. *Anne puts a hand over her face, sits, without a move or sound, till Will repents.* Anne, Anne—

ANNE: Never mind!

WILL, *bitey:* Yes, don't cry.

ANNE: Is that ye plan, now?

WILL: What?

ANNE: Half the world?

WILL: It's why we're talking. *A pause.* Was it very—exciting?

ANNE: Sandy? *Will nods.* Shall I tell ye the truth?

WILL: No.

ANNE: I didn't come, lad.

WILL, *a pause:* Thank you.

ANNE: I kept seeing ye ugly face, I turned like a clam, then. *Will now comes, sits opposite her, he pokes at the text.*

WILL, *then:* I said died of complications, didn't I.

ANNE: Ye didn't tell her it was seven, twenty times each—

WILL: Not with all.

ANNE: Why not, they didn't think much of ye?

WILL: Gets boring.

ANNE: For a boy I been feeling sorry for, ye—have a grand gift to surprise me—

WILL: But God gives each of us a fruit, and one way or another I mean to eat it, before I die, before I die.

ANNE: When did ye start on them, I didn't guess one?

WILL: While you were—I'm sorry—carrying the— *(He indicates upstairs.)*

ANNE: Twins. *She nods.* Yes, that I knew, I had them all by myself, yes. And if ye hands itched for me ye'd—get the milk keeps them alive, not too pleasing to a lover, lad, is it.

WILL: It's not that.

ANNE: And I'm running around here with diapers and dishrags, nobody's picture of a—doxy ye can't keep ye hands off—

WILL: Not that.

ANNE: Ye couldn't wait, what?

WILL: Oh, I could wait, yes, but—Not take a wife any longer who suckles and swaddles and wipes me like a babe in public, no. *A wait.*

ANNE: Ye liked it, lad.

WILL: Don't call me that. I'm not always seventeen. I'm not—yours, you said I was, I'm mine, and out of whatever love you stalked in as mother tigress tonight, your tongue licks me with contempt. I like it: I loathe it. Be strong, be strong with—others, you're throttling a lover to death. And that I think is the answer.

A silence, their eyes on each other across the table.

ANNE: Is that—the worst ye have to say? *Will gazes at her.* It's a question, la—love.

WILL: No.

ANNE: What else? *Will picks up the text, stands up.*

WILL: No, the game is over.

ANNE: No it isn't, not till both of us say, and I have to know. *Will is silent.* Tell me, ye—milksop, what's the worst ye think, ye'll leave me?

WILL: I think, she's older, she'll die first.

Anne hides her face in a hand, and this time does cry, it begins with a jerky breath, she keeps the crying in her gut, but at last it breaks her open. Will comes back, tosses the text on the table, stands behind her racked figure, to finger her nape.

ANNE: Don't—touch—

WILL: Anne, nothing's impossible—the schoolteaching, family and fidelity, even Gilbert is possible—if I can— *(with both hands he caresses her hair, ears, eyes)* —ripen with it, that's all I mean by enough. Your cheek is wet. Is that the only thing? *He draws her body back against his groin, she stiffens, slowly moves against him.*

ANNE: None of—ye business—

WILL: Oh, I think it is. *His hands come down over her, bosom, belly, then he twists to the candle, he sees the marigolds, picks a few, sits beside her, and puts a flower in her hair.* That's for the dishrags. *She bites at his hand, he puts another into her bodice.* For the diapers. Yes, he— *(a last flower in his fingers, he twists to blow out the candle)* —did kiss her. You have no idea where I mean to put this one— *(Anne begins to laugh, in the dark, it is a marvelous laugh, also up out of her gut, hearty and prolonged, but it ends presently in a little gasp.)*

ANNE: Not here—

WILL: Here.

BUTTERFLIES ARE FREE

by Leonard Gershe

———— ◆ ————

ACT I, SCENE 1

Don Baker is an attractive young musician living in his own apartment, in New York City, for the first time. Jill Tanner is an attractive young woman who, by happy coincidence, happens to live in the apartment next door. Not only is she attractive, but she is also very forward, and after hearing Don's voice through the door that separates their apartments, she invites herself in for a cup of coffee. All the pieces are thus neatly set up for a lovely romance to ensue, except that Jill (and the audience) soon discovers that Don is blind. But love does emerge and the rest of the play concerns the trials and tribulations of these young lovers who eventually overcome all obstacles, including Don's very meddlesome mother.

The scene below takes place shortly after the first meeting. They have been talking for a while—about blindness, about Don's former girl friend, Linda, and about Jill's intolerably long six-day marriage. Jill then suggests to Don that a locked door separating their apartments be opened so that they can have access to each other's rooms without going into the hall. Don accepts the suggestion. As the excerpt begins, Jill, who has been going at the lock with a knife, is about to give up on getting the door open.

DON: Let me try. *Jill places the knife in Don's hand. He feels for the lock and maneuvers the knife around in it. He takes the knife from the lock and, delicately, works it between the door and the lock.* I felt something. *Suddenly the door opens. Jill crosses below Don and into doorway.*

JILL: You did it! It's open! *We can see part of Jill's bedroom with a lot of her things strewn about, untidily. Quickly, embarrassed:* Oh, don't look! It's an absolute pigsty!

DON, *covering his eyes:* I won't.

JILL, *sinking; crosses downstage left and sits downstage end of coffee table on rug:* I'm sorry. I'm sorry. I'm sorry.

DON: Stop being sorry.

JILL: I'll get the hang of it. I just don't know when. *Don closes the door.* Let's leave it open.

DON, *opens the door again, then crosses to kitchen to put the knife away:* Okay, but tell me if you close it again. I don't want to break my nose on it. *Don crosses above table to right of downstage left post.*

JILL: Do you wish it were Linda living there instead of me?

DON: I never even thought about it. Why do you ask?

JILL, *crosses left of Don:* I was wondering if you're still in love with her.

DON: Did I say I was in love with her?

JILL, *crosses around to right of Don:* If I get too personal, just tell me to shut up. I get carried away. *Left hand on his chest, slinks across him.* Were you in love with her? Are you?

DON, *crosses to sofa, sits center:* Every man should have some mystery. That'll be mine.

JILL, *crosses above table to upstage end of sofa:* What's she like?

DON: She's very pretty.

JILL: How do you know?

DON: I can feel someone's face and get a good idea of what they look like. I can tell from shapes and textures.

JILL, *crosses to upstage of him:* Do you wonder what I look like?

DON: Yes.

JILL, *kneels:* I'm gorgeous.

DON: Really?

JILL: I wouldn't lie about something like that.

DON: You know, I've always thought if I could see for just half a minute—I'd like to see how I look.

JILL, *leans in to him:* I'll tell you. Cute . . . and very sexy.

Don smiles and reaches a hand to Jill's face. Gently, he runs his finger up the side of her face, exploring. He runs his hand over the top of her head and takes hold of her long hair, lightly pulling it through his fingers.

DON: Your hair is very soft . . . and very long. *Suddenly, Jill's long hair, which is a fall, comes off in Don's hand, revealing her own hair underneath. Don is startled as he feels the limp hair in his hand.* Oh, Jesus! *He falls back on the sofa.*

JILL: Don't be frightened.

DON, *dropping the fall like a hot potato:* What happened?

JILL, *picks up the fall and puts it on the coffee table:* It's just a fall. It's a long piece of hair that you attach to your head.

DON: It's not *your* hair?

JILL: It's not even my fall. I borrowed it from Susan Potter. I have hair of my own. See? I mean feel? *Places his hand on her head. Don takes in the shape of her head, then moves his hand along her face, over her eyes. A false eyelash comes off in his hand.*

DON, *rises, backs up onto platform, grabs downstage left post:* God! Now what?!

JILL: Oh damn—a false eyelash. *Takes the eyelash from him and puts it in her pocket.*

DON: Don't you have eyelashes?

JILL, *kneels downstage arm of sofa:* Of course, but these are longer than mine. They make my eyes look bigger. Didn't Linda wear them?

DON: No.

JILL: She probably has naturally long lashes. I hate her. *Placing his hand on her cheek:* Go on.

DON: This is scaring hell out of me.

JILL: It's all right. Everything's real from now on. *Don runs his fingers across Jill's mouth.* Am I not the image of Elizabeth Taylor?

DON: I've never felt Elizabeth Taylor.

JILL: We look exactly alike. Especially if you can't see. *Jill smiles at Don, oddly, as his fingers explore her throat. She takes his hand and places it on her breast.* That's my breast. All mine. Both of them. *Gently, she pushes him down on the table. She kisses him full on the mouth. Don twists his head away from her and gets off table. Suddenly, anguished, crosses above upstage end of sofa.* What's the matter?

DON: What do you think is the matter?

JILL, *between sofa and coffee table:* If I knew, I wouldn't ask.

DON: Why are you doing this? Is it Be Kind to the Handicapped Week or something? Don't patronize me! And don't feel sorry for me!

JILL, *hotly:* I'm doing it because I want to do it! And I'll be God damned if I feel sorry for any guy who's going to have sex with me!!

They kiss and sink onto the sofa.

THE DARK AT THE TOP OF THE STAIRS

by William Inge

———————•———————

ACT I

The setting for Inge's family drama is the home of Rubin Flood, his wife, Cora, and their two children. The time is the early 1920s and the place is a small Oklahoma town. The Floods' daughter, Reenie, is an overly shy teenage girl who spends more time practicing the piano than socializing with her friends. Her mother, Cora, is worried about her. Without telling her husband, Cora has purchased an expensive dress for Reenie to wear to a local dance. When Rubin is told about the dress by a gossiping shopkeeper, he is furious. He enters the house and confronts Cora just as she is trying to encourage Reenie to attend the dance. The ensuing argument between the couple snowballs into an airing of grievances that ends with Rubin threatening to leave and Cora accusing him of adultery. (Reenie's brief entrance and Cora's response to her at the beginning of the scene may be omitted for scene-study purposes, as may the later entrance of her brother Sonny.)

RUBIN, *bursting into the house:* What the hell's been goin' on behind my back? *Sees the innocent dress lying on a chair:* There it is!

CORA: Rubin!

RUBIN, *displaying the dress as evidence:* So this is what ya wanted the extra money for. Fine feathers! Fine feathers! And ya buy 'em when my back is turned.

CORA: Rubin, we were going to tell you....

RUBIN: A man has to go downtown and talk with some of his pals before he knows what's goin' on in his own family.

CORA: Who told you?

RUBIN: That's all right who told me. I got my own ways a findin' out what goes on when my back is turned.

CORA: You didn't leave town at all. You've been down to that dirty old pool hall.

RUBIN: I got a right to go to the pool hall whenever I damn please.

CORA: I thought you were in such a hurry to get out of town. Oh, yes, you had to get to Muskogee tonight.

RUBIN: I can still make it to Muskogee. *Finds the price tag on the dress.* $19.75! Lord have mercy! $19.75.

CORA, *approaching Rubin:* Did Loren Delman come into the pool hall while you were there? Did he? Did he tell you? If he did I'll never buy anything in that store again.

RUBIN: That'd suit me just fine.

CORA: Oh, why couldn't he have kept his mouth shut? I was going to pay for the dress a little at a time, and . . .

RUBIN: "The finest dress I had in the store," he says, walking into the arcade with a big cigar stuck in his mouth, wearin' a suit of fine tailored clothes. "I just sold your wife the finest dress I had in the store."

CORA: Oh, that makes me furious.

RUBIN: Jesus Christ woman, whatta you take me for, one of those millionaire oil men? Is that what you think you're married to?

REENIE, *pokes her head in through parlor door, speaking with tears and anxiety:* I told you he'd be mad, Mom. Let's take the dress back, Mom. I don't want to go to the party anyhow.

CORA, *angrily impatient:* Get back in that parlor, Reenie, and don't come in here until I tell you to. *Slams parlor doors shut.*

RUBIN: See there! That girl don't even want the dress. It's *you,* puttin' all these high-fallutin' ideas in her head about parties, and dresses and nonsense.

CORA: Rubin, of course Reenie doesn't want to go to the party. She never wants to go any place. All she wants to do is lock herself in the parlor and practice at the piano, or go to the library and hide her nose in a book. After all, she's going to want to get married one of these days, isn't she? And where's she going to look for a husband? In the public library? *Rubin goes to his corner, downstage left, sits in his big leather chair, and draws a pint of whiskey out of his desk drawer.*

RUBIN: I bought her a fine dress . . . just a little while back.

CORA: Oh, you did?

RUBIN: Yes, I did.

CORA: That's news to me, when?

RUBIN: Just a few months ago. Sure I did.

CORA: I certainly never saw it. What'd it look like?

RUBIN: It was white.

CORA: Rubin Flood, that was the dress you bought her three years ago when she graduated from the eighth grade. And she hasn't had a new dress since then, except for a few school clothes.

RUBIN: Why couldn't she wear the white dress to the party?

CORA: Because she's grown three inches since you got her that dress, and besides I cut it up two years ago and dyed it black and made her a skirt out of it to wear with a middy.

RUBIN: Just the same, I ain't got money to throw away on no party togs. I just ain't got it.

CORA: Oh no. You don't have money when we need something here at home, do you?

RUBIN: I'm tellin' ya, right now I don't.

CORA: But you always have money for a bottle of bootleg whiskey when you want it, don't you? And I daresay, you've got money for a few other things, too, that I needn't mention just at present.

RUBIN: What're ya talkin' about?

CORA: *You* know what I'm talking about.

RUBIN: The hell I do.

CORA: I know what goes on when you go out on the road. You may tell me you spruce up for your customers, but I happen to know better. Do you think I'm a fool?

RUBIN: I don't know what you're talkin' about.

CORA: I happen to have friends, decent, self-respecting people, who tell me a few things that happen when you visit Ponca City.

RUBIN: You mean the Werpel sisters!

CORA: It's all right, who I mean. I have friends over there. That's all I need to say.

RUBIN: Those nosey old maids, the Werpel sisters? God damn? Have they been runnin' to you with stories?

CORA: Maybe you don't have money to buy your daughter a

new dress, but it seems you have money to take Mavis Pruitt to dinner whenever you're over there, and to a movie afterwards, and give her presents.

RUBIN: I've known Mavis ... Pruitt ever since I was a boy! What harm is there if I take her to a movie?

CORA: You're always too tired to take *me* to a movie when you come home.

RUBIN: Life's different out on the road.

CORA: I bet it is.

RUBIN: Besides, I din ask her. She came into the Gibson House one night when I was havin' my dinner. What could I do but ask her to join me?

CORA: She went to the Gibson House because she knew *you* were there. I know what kind of woman she is.

RUBIN She's not as bad as she's painted. The poor woman's had a hard time of it, too.

CORA: Oh, she has!

RUBIN: Yes she has. I feel sorry for her.

CORA: Oh, you do!

RUBIN: Yes, I do. Is there any law that says I can't feel sorry for Mavis Pruitt?

CORA: She's had her eye on you ever since I can remember.

RUBIN: Oh, shoot!

CORA: What happened to the man she left town with after we were married?

RUBIN: He run off and left her.

CORA: For good reason, too, I bet. I also heard that she was seen sporting a pair of black-bottom hose shortly after you left town, and that you were seen buying such a pair of hose at the Globe Dry Goods Store.

RUBIN: By God, you got yourself a real detective service goin', haven't you?

CORA: I don't ask people to tell me these things. I wish to God they didn't.

RUBIN: All right, I bought her a pair of hose. I admit it. It was her birthday. The hose cost me sixty-eight cents. They made that poor woman happy. After all, I've known her ever since I was a boy. Besides, I was a li'l more flush then.

CORA: How do you think it makes me feel when people tell me things like that?

RUBIN: Ya oughtn'ta listen.

CORA: How can I help it?

RUBIN, *he has to think to call her by her full name, to keep Cora from presuming too much familiarity between them:* There's nothing 'tween me and Mavis ... Pruitt ... Mavis Pruitt, nothin' for you to worry about.

CORA: There's probably a woman like her in every town you visit. That's why you want to get out of town, to go frisking over the country like a young stallion.

RUBIN: You just hush your mouth. The daughter'll hear you.

CORA, *indulging a little self-pity:* A lot you care about your daughter. A lot you care about any of us.

RUBIN: You don't think I care for ya unless I set ya on my knee and nuzzle ya.

CORA: What you need for a wife is a squaw. Why didn't you marry one of those Indian women out on the reservation? Yes. She'd make you rich now, too, wouldn't she? And you wouldn't have to pay any attention to her at all. *Sonny is seen coming onto porch, right.*

RUBIN: All right. Maybe that's what I *shoulda* done.

CORA: Oh. So you want to throw it up to me!

RUBIN: Throw what? *Sonny quietly enters room carrying a sack of groceries. Cora and Rubin are too far into battle to notice him.*

CORA: You know what, Rubin Flood.

RUBIN: I don't know nothin'.

CORA: You never *wanted* to marry me.

RUBIN: I never said that.

CORA: It's true, isn't it?

RUBIN: I'm tellin' ya, it ain't.

CORA: It is. I've felt it all these years. *Sonny crosses and enters parlor, upstage center, still unobserved by Rubin and Cora.*

RUBIN: All right, If you're so determined to think it, then go ahead. I admit, in some ways I din wanna marry nobody. Can't ya understand how a man feels, givin' up his freedom?

CORA: And how does a woman feel, knowing her husband married her only because ... because he ... *(Cora now spots Reenie spying between the parlor doors, upstage center. She screams at her.)* Reenie, get away from there!

RUBIN: None of this is what we was arguin' about in the first place. We was arguin' about the dress. Ya gotta take it back.

CORA: *I won't.*

RUBIN: *Ya will.*

CORA: Reenie's going to wear her new dress to the party, or you'll have to bury me.

RUBIN: You'll take that dress back to Loren Delman, or I'm leavin' this house for good and never comin' back.

CORA: Go on. You're only home half the time as it is. We can get along without you the rest of the time.

RUBIN: Then that's what you're gonna do. There'll be ice cream parlors in hell before I come back to this place and listen to your jaw. *Bolts into the hallway now, far right.*

CORA: Get out! Get out and go to Ponca City. Mavis Pruitt is waiting. She's probably getting lonesome without you. *Sonny enters quietly from dining room upstage left and watches.*

RUBIN: By God, Cora, it's all I can do to keep from hittin' you when you talk like that.

CORA, *following him into hallway right, taunting him. Here they are both unseen by audience:* Go on and hit me! You wouldn't dare! *But he does dare. We hear the sound of his blow which sends Cora reeling back into parlor.* Rubin! *Reenie watches from parlor.*

RUBIN: I'll go to Ponca City, and drink booze and take Mavis to the movies, and raise every kind of hell I can think of. T'hell with you! *He bolts outside.*

CORA, *running to the door:* Don't you ever set foot in this house again, Rubin Flood. I'll never forget what you've said. Never! Don't you ever come back inside this house again!

THE TENTH MAN

by Paddy Chayefsky

———•———

ACT II, SCENE 1

The Tenth Man, loosely based on Sholom Aleichem's *The Dybbuk,* is the story of an exorcism through love. It takes place in a rundown storefront synagogue in Mineola, Long Island—a synagogue whose congregation consists of a handful of old men who rarely are able to muster the quorum of ten needed for the traditional religious service.

Evelyn (referred to in the script as "The Girl"), eighteen years old and diagnosed as schizophrenic, has been kidnapped by her grandfather just before she was to be returned to a sanitarium. His own diagnosis is quite different: "She is possessed. She has a dybbuk in her. A demon!" He has brought her to the synagogue for an exorcism so that she might be released from the possession of the angry and homeless soul that has invaded her body.

Enter Arthur Brooks—a man for whom "life is utterly meaningless." He had had the American dream life: success as an attorney, a proper wife, proper children, and "a handsome home only three blocks from the Scarsdale Country Club." Yet the loneliness and boredom that had always plagued his life persisted. He sought escape from despair and disillusionment in liquor, sordid affairs, and unsuccessful suicide attempts. Soon his wife and children were gone and his practice was failing; all that remained of his "American nirvana" was his perpetual psychoanalysis.

This morning, on the tail end of his latest binge, Arthur found himself banging on the front door of his ex-wife's home in Mineola. As he sought his way back to the railroad station, he was stopped on the street by one of the old Jews in search of a tenth man to complete the quorum. When asked if he was Jewish, he answered yes, and was immediately shuffled off into the synagogue. Against both his will and his finely honed cynicism, Arthur gets caught up in the magic of the exorcism and the plight of the young girl. Through her he discovers a compassion he thought was unattainable and a reason to continue living.

In the scene that follows the congregation is at prayer. Arthur watches them, leaning against a wall near the rabbi's office where the girl has been hidden. He has already seen the girl and become aware of her strange behavior. She comes out of the office and speaks to him. Her manner is normal now.

THE GIRL, *she frowns:* Did my grandfather say when he would be back or where he was going? *She starts from her seat, frightened again.*

ARTHUR: I understand he'll be back soon.

THE GIRL: Are you the doctor?

ARTHUR: No. You don't have to be the least bit afraid of me.

THE GIRL, *she brightens:* My grandfather and I are very close. I'm much closer to him than I am to my own father. I'd rather not talk about my father, if you don't mind. It's a danger spot for me. You know, when I was nine years old, I shaved all the hair off my head because that is the practice of really orthodox Jewish women. I mean, if you want to be a rabbi's wife, you must shear your hair and wear a wig. That's one of my compulsive dreams. I keep dreaming of myself as the wife of a handsome young rabbi with a fine beard down to his waist and a very stern face and prematurely grey forelocks on his brow. I have discovered through many unsuccessful years of psychiatric treatment that religion has a profound sexual connotation for me. Oh, dear, I'm afraid I'm being tiresome again about my psychiatric history. Really, being insane is like being fat. You can talk about nothing else. Please forgive me. I am sure I am boring you to death.

ARTHUR: No, not at all. It's nice to hear somebody talk with passion about anything, even their insanity.

THE GIRL, *staring at him:* The word doesn't bother you?

ARTHUR: What word?

THE GIRL: Insanity.

ARTHUR: Good heavens, no. I'm a lawyer. Insanity in one form or another is what fills my anteroom. Besides I'm being psychoanalyzed myself and I'm something of a bore about that too. You are a bright young thing. How old are you?

THE GIRL: Eighteen.

ARTHUR, *staring at her:* My God, you're a pretty kid! I can hardly believe you are psychopathic. Are you very advanced?

THE GIRL: Pretty bad. I'm being institutionalized again. Dr. Molineaux's Sanitarium in Long Island. I'm a little paranoid and hallucinate a great deal and have very little sense of reality, except for brief interludes like this, and I might slip off any minute in the middle of a sentence—into some incoherency. If that should happen, you must be very realistic with me. Harsh reality is the most efficacious way to deal with schizophrenics.

ARTHUR: You seem well-read on the matter.

THE GIRL: I'm a voracious reader. I have so little else to do with myself. Will you come and visit me at Dr. Molineaux's Hospital? I am awfully fond of you.

ARTHUR: Yes, of course, I will.

THE GIRL: It won't be as depressing an experience as you might think. If I am not in the violent ward, I will probably be allowed to go to the commissary and have an ice cream soda with you. The worst of an insane asylum is really how poorly dressed the inmates are. They all wear old cable-stitched sweaters. I do like to look pretty. *A vacuous, atrophied look is beginning to come across her face.* They ask me to be in a lot of movies, you know, when I have time. Did you see "David and Bathsheba" with Susan Hayward? That was really me. I don't tell anybody that. They don't want me to make movies. My mother, I mean. She doesn't even go to synagogue on Saturday. You're the new rabbi, you know. Sometimes, I'm the rabbi, but they're all afraid of me. The temple is sixty cubits long and made of cypress and overlaid with gold. The burnished Roman legions clank outside the gates, you know. Did you see "The Ten Commandments"? I saw that Tuesday, Wednesday. I was in that. I was the girl who danced. I was in that. Mr. Hirschman is here, too, you know, and my grandfather. Everybody's here. Do you see that boy over there? Go away. Leave us alone. He's insane. He's really Mr. Hirschman the Cabalist. He's making a golem. You ought to come here, Rabbi.

ARTHUR, *who has been listening, fascinated, now says firmly:* I am not the rabbi, Evelyn.

THE GIRL, *she regards him briefly:* Well, we're making a golem and—

ARTHUR: You are not making a golem, Marilyn.

THE GIRL, *she pauses, stares down at the floor at her feet. A grimace of pain winces quickly across her face and then leaves it. After a moment, she mumbles:* Thank you. *Suddenly she begins to cry and she throws herself upon Arthur's breast, clinging to him, and he holds her gently, caressing her as he would a child.* Oh, I can't bear being insane.

ARTHUR, *gently:* I always thought that since the insane made their own world it was more pleasurable than this one that is made for us.

THE GIRL, *moving away:* Oh, no, it is unbearably painful. It is the most indescribable desolation. You are all alone in deserted streets. You cannot possibly imagine it.

ARTHUR: I'm afraid I can. I have tried to commit suicide so many times now it has become something of a family joke. Once, before I was divorced, my wife stopped in to tell a neighbor before she went out to shop: "Oh, by the way, if you smell gas, don't worry about it. It's only Arthur killing himself again." Suicides, you know, kill themselves a thousand times, but one day I'll slash my wrists and I will forget to make a last-minute telephone call and there will be no stomach pumping samaritans to run up the stairs and smash my bedroom door down and rush me off to Bellevue. I'll make it some day—I assure you of that.

THE GIRL, *regarding him with sweet interest:* You don't look as sad as all that.

ARTHUR: Oh, I have made a profession of ironic detachment. It depresses me to hear that insanity is as forlorn as anything else. I had always hoped to go crazy myself some day since I have apparently no talent for suicide.

THE GIRL: I always thought life would be wonderful if I were only sane.

ARTHUR: Life is merely dreary if you're sane, and unbearable if you are sensitive. I cannot think of a more meaningless sham than my own life. My parents were very poor so I spent the first twenty years of my life condemning the rich for my childhood nightmares. Oh, I was quite a Bernard Barricade when I was in college. I left the Communist Party when I discovered there were easier ways to seduce girls. I turned from reproaching society for my loneliness to reproaching my mother, and stormed out of her house to take a room for myself on the East Side. Then I fell in love—that is to say, I found living alone so unbearable I was willing to marry. She married me because all her friends were marrying somebody. Needless to say, we told each other how deeply in love we were. We wanted very much to be happy. Americans, you know, are frantic about being happy. The American nirvana is a man and his wife watching television amiably and then turning off the lights and effortlessly making the most ardent love to each other. Television unfortunately is a bore and ardent love is an immense drain on one's energy. I began to work day and night at my law office, and besides becoming very successful, I managed to avoid my wife entirely. For this deceit, I was called ambitious and was respected by everyone including my wife who was quite as bored with me as I was with her. We decided to have children because we couldn't possibly believe we were that miserable together. All this while I drove myself mercilessly for fear that if I paused for just one moment, the whole slim, trembling sanity of my life would come crashing down about my feet without the slightest sound. I went to a psychoanalyst who wanted to know about my childhood when I could barely remember whether I took a taxi or a bus to his office that day. I began to drink myself into stupors, pursuing other men's wives, and generally behaving badly. One morning, I stared into the mirror and could barely make out my features. Life is utterly meaningless. I have had everything a man can get out of life—prestige, power, money, women, children, and a handsome home only three blocks from the Scarsdale Country Club, and all I can think of is I want to get out of this as fast as I can. *He has become quite upset by now and has to avert his face to hide a sudden welling of tears. He takes a moment to get a good grip on himself, readopts his sardonic air and says:* As you see, I have quite a theatrical way when I want to.

THE GIRL, *brightly:* Oh, I think you are wonderfully wise.

ARTHUR: Oh, it was said best by your very own King Solomon, the wisest man who ever lived, when he wrote Ecclesiastes.

THE GIRL: Oh, King Solomon didn't write Ecclesiastes. That was written by an anonymous Jewish scholar in Alexandria. I wouldn't put too much stock in it. Weariness was all the rage among the Hellenized Jews.

ARTHUR, *staring at her:* You are an amazing kid.

WHEN YOU COMIN' BACK, RED RYDER?

by Mark Medoff

———————•———————

ACT I

The setting is a diner in the desert in southern New Mexico.
The period is the end of the 1960s. This is the opening scene of
the play. Stephen Ryder—who prefers the nickname Red—is
alone reading a newspaper. It is 6:05 A.M. and he has just
finished working the night shift at the all-night diner. He waits
impatiently for his replacement, Angel. Stephen is nineteen. In
manner and dress he is "an unconscious parody . . . of the
midfifties"—slick hair combed straight back, shirt buttons
opened half way down his chest, a tattoo that says "Born
Dead." The dialogue begins with Angel's entrance. She is overweight and unattractive and, as revealed during the play, cares
for Stephen. Later in the play this sleepy diner erupts into a
scene of senseless violence where each character is forced to
confront the hypocrisy of his or her life.

ANGEL: I'm sorry I'm late. My mom and me, our daily fight
was a little off schedule today. *Stephen loudly shuffles the paper,
sucks his teeth.* I said I'm sorry, Stephen. God. I'm only six
minutes late.
STEPHEN: Only six minutes, huh? I got six minutes to just
hang around this joint when my shift's up, right? This is really
the kinda dump I'm gonna hang around in my spare time, ain't
it?
ANGEL: Stephen, that's a paper cup you got your coffee in.
Stephen is entrenched behind his newspaper.
STEPHEN: Clark can afford it, believe me.
ANGEL: That's not the point, Stephen.
STEPHEN: Oh no? You're gonna tell me the point though,
right? Hold it—lemme get a pencil.
ANGEL: The point is that if you're drinkin your coffee here,
you're supposed to use a glass cup, and if it's to go, you're sup-

posed to get charged fifteen instead of ten and ya get one of those five cent paper cups to take it with you with. That's the point, Stephen.

STEPHEN: Yeah, well I'm takin it with me, so where's the problem? *Stephen has taken the last cigarette from a pack, slipped the coupon into his shirt pocket and crumpled the pack. He basketball shoots it across the service area.*

ANGEL: Stephen. *She retrieves the pack and begins her morning routine: filling salt and pepper shakers, the sugar dispensers, setting out place mats, and cleaning up the mess Stephen evidently leaves for her each morning. Stephen reaches over and underneath the counter and pulls up a half empty carton of Raleighs and slides out a fresh pack. He returns the carton and slaps the new pack down on the counter.* What're ya gonna get with your cigarette coupons, Stephen? *Stephen reads his paper, smokes, sips his coffee.* Stephen? *Stephen lowers the newspaper.*

STEPHEN: How many times I gotta tell ya to don't call me Stephen.

ANGEL: I don't like callin ya Red. It's stupid—callin somebody with brown hair Red.

STEPHEN: It's my name, ain't it? I don't like Stephen. I like Red. When I was a kid I had red hair.

ANGEL: But ya don't now. Now ya got brown hair.

STEPHEN, *exasperated:* But *then* I did, and then's when counts.

ANGEL: Who says *then's* when counts?

STEPHEN: The person that's doin the *countin!* Namely yours truly! I don't call you . . . Caroline or . . . *Madge,* do I?

ANGEL: Because those aren't my name. My name's Angel, so—

STEPHEN: Yeah, well ya don't look like no angel to me.

ANGEL: I can't help that, Stephen. At least I was named my name at birth. Nobody asked me if I'd mind bein named Angel, but at least—

STEPHEN: You could change it, couldn't ya?

ANGEL: What for? To what?

STEPHEN, *thinking a moment, setting her up:* To Mabel.

ANGEL: How come Mabel?

STEPHEN: Yeah . . . Mabel.

ANGEL: How come? You like Mabel?

STEPHEN: I *hate* Mabel. *Stephen stares at her, sucks his teeth.*

ANGEL: Look, Stephen, if you're in such a big hurry to get outta here, how come you're just sittin around cleaning your teeth?

STEPHEN: Hey, look, I'll be gone in a minute. I mean if it's too much to ask if I have a cigarette and a cup of coffee in peace, for chrissake, just say so. A person's supposed to unwind for two minutes a day, in case you ain't read the latest medical report. If it's too much to ask to just lemme sit here in *peace* for two minutes, then say so. I wouldn't wanna take up a stool somebody was waitin for or anything. *Looking around him:* Christ, will ya look at the waitin line to get on this stool.

ANGEL, *pause:* Did you notice what's playing at the films?

STEPHEN: Buncha crap, whudduya think?

ANGEL, *pause:* I saw ya circle somethin in the gift book the other mornin.

STEPHEN: What *gift* book?

ANGEL: The Raleigh *coupon* gift book.

STEPHEN: Hey—com'ere. *Angel advances close to him. He snatches the pencil from behind her ear and draws a circle on the newspaper.* There. Now I just drew a circle on the newspaper. That mean I'm gonna get me that car?

ANGEL: Come on, Stephen, tell me. What're ya gonna get?

STEPHEN: Christ, whudduyou care what I'm gonna get?

ANGEL: God, Stephen, I'm not the FBI or somebody. What are you so upset about? Just tell me what you're gonna get.

STEPHEN, *mumbling irascibly:* Back pack.

ANGEL: What?

STEPHEN: Whuddya, got home fries in your ears?

ANGEL: Just that I didn't hear what you said is all.

STEPHEN: *Back. Pack.*

ANGEL: Who's gettin a back pack?

STEPHEN: The guy down the enda the counter. Chingado the Chicano. He's hitchin to Guatamala.

ANGEL: You're getting a back pack? How come?

STEPHEN: Whuddo people usually get a back pack for?

ANGEL: Ya gonna go campin.

STEPHEN: No I ain't gonna go *campin.* I'm gonna go gettin the hell outta this lousy little town is where I'm gonna go *campin.*

ANGEL: When? I mean . . . when?

STEPHEN: When? Just as soon as I get somethin taken care of.

ANGEL: When will that be?

STEPHEN: When will that be? When I get it taken care of—when d'ya think. Lemme have a donut.

ANGEL, *getting him a donut:* Where ya gonna go?

STEPHEN: Where am I gonna go? I'm gonna go hitchin that way *(pointing left)* or I'm gonna go hitchin that way *(pointing right)* and when I get to some place that don't still smella Turdville here I'm gonna get me a decent job and I'm gonna make me some bread. *He picks up the donut and bites into it.*

ANGEL: Rye or whole wheat, Stephen?

STEPHEN: This is some donut. I think they glued the crumbs together with Elmer's.

ANGEL: Rye or whole wheat, Stephen?

STEPHEN, *with his mouth full:* Believe me, that ain't funny.

ANGEL: Don't talk with your mouth full.

STEPHEN: Christ, my coffee's cold. How d'ya like that? *He looks at her. She pours him a fresh cup of coffee in a mug. She sets it down by him. He looks at it a minute, then pours the coffee from the mug into his paper cup.* I told ya, I'm leavin in less'n two minutes.

ANGEL: That's right, I forgot.

STEPHEN: Yeah, yeah.

ANGEL: You better let your hair grow and get some different clothes if you're gonna hitch somewhere, Stephen. You're outta style. Nobody's gonna pick up a boy dressed like you with his hair like yours. And with a tattoo on his arm that says "Born Dead." People wear tattoos now that say "Love" and "Peace," Stephen, not "Born Dead."

STEPHEN: Love and peace my Aunt Fanny's butt! And who says I want *them* to pick me, for chrissake? You think I'm dyin for a case a the clap, or what? I got a coupla hundred truck drivers come through here in the middle of the night that said they'd all gimme a ride anytime anywhere they was goin. You think I'm gonna lower myself to ride with those other morons—you're outta your mind.

ANGEL: Two hundred truck drivers? Uh-uh, I'm sorry, I have to call you on that one, Stephen, If it wasn't for Lyle's station and his motel, Lyle'd be our *only* customer.

STEPHEN: You know, right? Cause you're here all night while I'm home sacked out on my rear, so you know how many truck drivers still stop in here, now ain't that right?

ANGEL: In the three weeks since the by-pass opened, Stephen, you know exactly how many customers you had in the nights? You wanna know exactly how many, Stephen?

STEPHEN: No Christ, I don't wanna know how many. I wanna have two minutes of peace to read my damn newspaper—if that's not askin too much! Is that askin too much? If it is, just say the word and I'll get the hell outta here and go to the goddamn cemetery or somewhere.

27 WAGONS FULL OF COTTON

by Tennessee Williams

———•———

SCENE 2

The play takes place on the front porch of the residence of Jake and Flora Meighan, situated in a Mississippi cotton-farm region. Jake owns a cotton gin. During the night before this scene takes place, he set fire to the cotton gin of Silva Vicarro ("of the dark Latin looks and nature"). Vicarro had just received an order to process twenty-seven wagons full of cotton. Jake, needing money, set the fire anticipating that Vicarro would be forced to bring the cotton to his mill. Flora, described as "a woman not (just) large but tremendous," knows that Jake started the fire, and has been drilled by Jake the previous night on what to say if questioned about his whereabouts at the time of the fire.

The scene takes place at midday, the day after the fire. Vicarro has just signed a contract with Jake; but, before he goes off to do the ginning, Jake instructs Flora to "keep Mr. Vicarro comfo'table," and refers to "Th' good-neighbor policy ... you do me a good turn an' I'll do you a good one!" Vicarro bitterly repeats Jake's phrase as the scene begins.

VICARRO: The good-neighbor policy! *He sits on the porch steps.*

FLORA, *sitting on the swing:* Izzen he out-*ray*-juss! *She laughs foolishly and puts the purse in her lap. Vicarro stares gloomily across the dancing brilliance of the fields. His lip sticks out like a pouting child's. A rooster crows in the distance.*

FLORA: I would'n' dare to expose myself like that.

VICARRO: Expose? To what?

FLORA: The sun. I take a terrible burn. I'll never forget the burn I took one time. It was on Moon Lake one Sunday before I was married. I never did like t' go fishin' but this young fellow, one of the Peterson boys, insisted that we go fishin'. Well, he didn't catch nothin' but jus' kep' fishin' an' fishin' an' I set there in th' boat with all that hot sun on me. I said, Stay under the willows. But he would'n' lissen to me, an' sure enough I took such an awful burn I had t' sleep on m' stummick th' nex' three nights.

VICARRO, *absently:* What did you say? You got sunburned?

FLORA: Yes. One time on Moon Lake.

VICARRO: That's too bad. You got over it all right?

FLORA: Oh, yes. Finally. Yes.

VICARRO: That must've been pretty bad.

FLORA: I fell in the lake once, too. Also with one of the Peterson boys. On another fishing trip. That was a wild bunch of boys, those Peterson boys. I never went out with 'em but something happened which made me wish I hadn't. One time, sunburned. One time, nearly drowned. One time—poison ivy! Well, lookin' back on it, now, we had a good deal of fun in spite of it, though.

VICARRO: The good-neighbor policy, huh? *He slaps his boot with the riding crop. Then he rises from steps.*

FLORA: You might as well come up on th' po'ch an' make you'self as comfo'table as you can.

VICARRO: Uh-huh.

FLORA: I'm not much good at—makin' conversation.

VICARRO, *finally noticing her:* Now don't you bother to make conversation for my benefit, Mrs. Meighan. I'm the type that prefers a quiet understanding. *Flora laughs uncertainly.* One thing I always notice about you ladies . . .

FLORA: What's that, Mr. Vicarro?

VICARRO: You always have something in your hands—to hold onto. Now that kid purse . . .

FLORA: My purse?

VICARRO: You have no reason to keep that purse in your hands. You're certainly not afraid that I'm going to snatch it!

FLORA: Oh, God, no! I wassen afraid of that!

VICARRO: That wouldn't be the good-neighbor policy, would it? But you hold onto that purse because it gives you something to get a grip on. Isn't that right?

FLORA: Yes. I always like to have something in my hands.

VICARRO: Sure you do. You feel what a lot of uncertain things there are. Gins burn down. The volunteer fire department don't have decent equipment. Nothing is any protection. The afternoon sun is hot. It's no protection. The trees are back of the house. They're no protection. The goods that dress is made of—is no protection. So what do you do, Mrs. Meighan? You pick up the white kid purse. It's solid. It's sure. It's certain. It's something to hold *on* to. You get what I mean?

FLORA: Yeah, I think I do.

VICARRO: It gives you a feeling of being attached to something. The mother protects the baby? No, no, no—the baby protects the mother! From being lost and empty and having nothing but lifeless things in her hands! Maybe you think there isn't much connection!

FLORA: You'll have to excuse me from thinking. I'm too lazy.

VICARRO: What's your name, Mrs. Meighan?

FLORA: Flora.

VICARRO: Mine is Silva. Something not gold but—Silva!

FLORA: Like a silver dollar?

VICARRO: No, like a silver dime! It's an Italian name. I'm a native of New Orleans.

FLORA: Then it's not sunburn. You're natcherally dark.

VICARRO, *raising his undershirt from his belly:* Look at this!

FLORA: Mr. Vicarro!

VICARRO: Just as dark as my arm is!

FLORA: You don't have to show me! I'm not from Missouri!

VICARRO, *grinning:* Excuse me.

FLORA, *she laughs nervously:* Whew! I'm sorry to say we don't have a Coke in the house. We meant to get a case of Cokes las' night, but what with all the excitement going on—

VICARRO: What excitement was that?

FLORA: Oh, the fire and all.

VICARRO, *lighting a cigarette:* I shouldn't think you all would of been excited about the fire.

FLORA: A fire is always exciting. After a fire, dogs an' chickens don't sleep. I don't think our chickens got to sleep all night.

VICARRO: No?

FLORA: They cackled an' fussed an' flopped around on the roost—took on something awful! Myself, I couldn't sleep neither. I jus' lay there an' sweated all night long.

VICARRO: On account of th' fire?

FLORA: An' the heat an' mosquitoes. And I was mad at Jake.

VICARRO: Mad at Mr. Meighan? What about?

FLORA: Oh, he went off an' left me settin' here on this ole po'ch last night without a Coca-Cola on the place.

VICARRO: Went off an' left you, did he?

FLORA: Yep. Right after supper. An' when he got back the fire'd already broke out an' instead of drivin' in to town like he said, he decided to go an' take a look at your burnt-down cotton gin. I got smoke in my eyes an' my nose an' throat. It hurt my sinus an' I was in such a wo'n out, nervous condition, it made me cry. I cried like a baby. Finally took two teaspoons of paregoric. Enough to put an elephant to sleep. But still I stayed awake an' heard them chickens carryin' on out there!

VICARRO: It sounds like you passed a very uncomfortable night.

FLORA: Sounds like? Well, it *was.*

VICARRO: So Mr. Meighan—you say—disappeared after supper? *There is a pause while Flora looks at him blankly.*

FLORA: Huh?

VICARRO: You say Mr. Meighan was out of the house for a while after supper? *Something in his tone makes her aware of her indiscretion.*

FLORA: Oh—uh—just for a moment.

VICARRO: Just for a moment, huh? How long a moment? *He stares at her very hard.*

FLORA: What are you driving at, Mr. Vicarro?

VICARRO: Driving at? Nothing.

FLORA: You're looking at me so funny.

VICARRO: He disappeared for a moment! Is that what he did? How long a moment did he disappear for? Can you remember, Mrs. Meighan?

FLORA: What difference does that make? What's it to you, anyhow?

VICARRO: Why should you mind me asking?

FLORA: You make this sound like I was on trial for something!

VICARRO: Don't you like to pretend like you're a witness?

FLORA: Witness of what, Mr. Vicarro?

VICARRO: Why—for instance—say—a case of arson!

FLORA, *wetting her lips:* Case of—? What is—arson?

VICARRO: The willful destruction of property by fire. *He slaps his boots sharply with the riding crop.*

FLORA, *startled:* Oh! *She nervously fingers the purse.* Well, now, don't you go and be getting any—funny ideas.

VICARRO: Ideas about what, Mrs. Meighan?

FLORA: My husband's disappearin'—after supper. I can explain that.

VICARRO: Can you?

FLORA: Sure I can.

VICARRO: Good! How do you explain it? *He stares at her. She looks down.* What's the matter? Can't you collect your thoughts, Mrs. Meighan?

FLORA: No, but—

VICARRO: Your mind's a blank on the subject?

FLORA: Look here, now—*(She squirms on the swing.)*

VICARRO: You find it impossible to remember just what your husband disappeared for after supper? You can't imagine what kind of errand it was that he went out on, can you?

FLORA: No! No, I can't!

VICARRO: But when he returned—let's see . . . The fire had just broken out at the Syndicate Plantation?

FLORA: Mr. Vicarro, I don't have the slightest idea what you could be driving at.

VICARRO: You're a very unsatisfactory witness, Mrs. Meighan.

FLORA: I never can think when people—stare straight at me.

VICARRO: Okay. I'll look away, then. *He turns his back to her.* Now does that improve your memory any? Now are you able to concentrate on the question?

FLORA: Huh . . .

VICARRO: No? You're not? *He turns around again, grinning evilly.* Well . . . shall we drop the subject?

FLORA: I sure do wish you would.

VICARRO: It's no use crying over a burnt-down gin. This world is built on the principle of tit for tat.

FLORA: What do you mean?

VICARRO: Nothing at all specific. Mind if I . . . ?

FLORA: What?

VICARRO: You want to move over a little an' make some room? *Flora edges aside on the swing. He sits down with her.* I like a swing. I've always liked to sit an' rock on a swing. Relaxes you . . . You relaxed?

FLORA: Sure.

VICARRO: No, you're not. Your nerves are all tied up.

FLORA: Well, you made me feel kind of nervous. All of them questions you ast me about the fire.

VICARRO: I didn' ask you questions about the fire. I only asked you about your husband's leaving the house after supper.

FLORA: I explained that to you.

VICARRO: Sure. That's right. You did. The good-neighbor policy. That was a lovely remark your husband made about the good-neighbor policy. I see what he means by that now.

FLORA: He was thinking about President Roosevelt's speech. We sat up an' lissened to it one night last week.

VICARRO: No, I think that he was talking about something closer to home, Mrs. Meighan. You do me a good turn and I'll do you one, that was the way that he put it. You have a piece of cotton on your face. Hold still—I'll pick it off. *He delicately removes the lint.* There now.

HELLO OUT THERE

by William Saroyan

———————•———————

A young man has been arrested in a small town in Texas and thrown in jail. He has been accused falsely of raping a married woman who picked him up and then wanted money from him. He is a gambler, traveling from town to town, and he hasn't "had any luck in years." Lonely and frightened in his cell, he calls out, "Hello out there." The jail is apparently empty. He calls out over and over and finally he gets an answer: a soft "Hello." A young girl (he comes to call her Katey—his favorite name) who cooks and cleans in the jail has stayed behind. She took care of him the night before when he was brought in unconscious (he had been hit on the head). She tells him that he was talking in his sleep and says, "You liked me." She adds, "I didn't think you'd like me when you woke up, though." She is shy and awkward and is laughed at by the young men in the town. A touching and ultimately tragic love affair ensues between these two lonely people.

Prior to the following excerpt the young man has told "Katey" that meeting her has changed his luck and that he will marry her and take her away with him.

YOUNG MAN, *suddenly:* See if you can get that fellow with the keys to come down and let me out.

THE GIRL: Oh, I couldn't.

YOUNG MAN: Why not?

THE GIRL: I'm nobody here—why, all they give me is fifty cents every day I work here—sometimes twelve hours. I'm nobody here.

YOUNG MAN: Get me out of here, Katey. I'm scared.

THE GIRL: I don't know what to do. Maybe I could break the door down.

YOUNG MAN: No, you couldn't do that. Is there a hammer there or anything?

THE GIRL: Only a broom. Maybe they've locked the broom up, too.

YOUNG MAN: Go and see if you can find anything.

THE GIRL: All right. *She goes.*

THE GIRL, *returning:* There isn't a thing out there. They've locked everything up for the night.

YOUNG MAN: Any cigarettes?

THE GIRL: Everything's locked up—all the drawers of the desk—all the closet doors—everything.

YOUNG MAN: I ought to have a cigarette.

THE GIRL: I could get you a package maybe, somewhere. I guess the drugstore's open. It's about a mile.

YOUNG MAN: A mile? I don't want to be alone that long.

THE GIRL: I could run all the way, and all the way back.

YOUNG MAN: You're the sweetest girl that ever lived.

THE GIRL: What kind do you want?

YOUNG MAN: Oh, any kind—Chesterfields or Camels or Lucky Strikes—any kind at all.

THE GIRL: I'll go get a package. *She turns to go.*

YOUNG MAN: What about the money?

THE GIRL: I've got some money. I've got a quarter I been saving. I'll run all the way. *She is about to go.*

YOUNG MAN: Come here.

THE GIRL, *going to him:* What?

YOUNG MAN: Give me your hand. *He takes her hand and looks at it, smiling. He lifts it and kisses it.* I'm scared to death.

THE GIRL: I am, too.

YOUNG MAN: I'm scared nobody will ever come out here to this God-forsaken broken-down town and find you. I'm scared you'll get used to it and not mind. I'm scared you'll never get to San Francisco and have 'em all turning to look at you. Listen— go get me a gun.

THE GIRL: I could get my father's gun. I know where he hides it.

YOUNG MAN: Go get it. Never mind the cigarettes. Run all the way.

The Girl turns and runs. The Young Man stands at the center of the cell a long time. The Girl comes running back in.

THE GIRL, *almost crying:* I'm afraid. I'm afraid I won't see you again. If I come back and you're not here, I—It's so lonely in this town. I'll stay *here*. I won't *let* them take you away.

YOUNG MAN: Listen, Katey. Do what I tell you. Go get that gun and come back. Maybe they won't come tonight. Maybe they won't come at all. I'll hide the gun and when they let me out you can take it back and put it where you found it. And then we'll go away. Now, hurry—

THE GIRL: All right. *Pause.* I want to tell you something.

YOUNG MAN: O.K.

THE GIRL, *very softly:* If you're not here when I come back, well, I'll have the gun and I'll know what to do with it.

YOUNG MAN: You know how to handle a gun?

THE GIRL: I know how.

YOUNG MAN: Don't be a fool. *Takes off his shoe, brings out some currency:* Don't be a fool, see? Here's some money. Eighty dollars. Take it and go to San Francisco. Look around and find somebody. Find somebody alive and halfway human, see? Promise me—if I'm not here when you come back, just throw the gun away and go to San Francisco. Look around and find somebody.

THE GIRL: I don't *want* to find anybody.

YOUNG MAN, *swiftly, desperately:* Now, do what I tell you. I'll meet you in San Francisco. I've got a couple of dollars in my other shoe. I'll see you in San Francisco.

THE GIRL, *with wonder:* San Francisco?

YOUNG MAN: That's right—San Francisco. That's where you and me belong.

THE GIRL: I've always wanted to go to someplace like San Francisco—but how could I go alone?

YOUNG MAN: Well, you're not alone anymore, see?

THE GIRL: Tell me a little what it's like.

YOUNG MAN, *very swiftly, almost impatiently at first, but gradually slower and with remembrance, smiling and The Girl moving closer to him as he speaks:* Well, it's on the Pacific to begin with—ocean all around. Cool fog and sea gulls. Ships from all over the world. It's got seven hills. The little streets go up and down, around and all over. Every night the foghorns bawl. But they won't be bawling for you and me.

THE GIRL: Are people different in San Francisco?

YOUNG MAN: People are the same everywhere. They're different only when they love somebody. That's the only thing that makes 'em different. More people in San Francisco love somebody, that's all.
THE GIRL: Nobody anywhere loves anybody as much as I love you.
YOUNG MAN, *whispering:* Hearing you say that, a man could die and still be ahead of the game. Now, hurry. And don't forget, if I'm not here when you come back, I'll meet you in San Francisco. *The Girl stands a moment looking at him, then backs away, turns and runs.*

THE HOUSE OF BLUE LEAVES

by John Guare

———•———

ACT I

This is the opening scene of the play. It is five o'clock in the morning, and Bunny Flingus is knocking at the door of her boyfriend, Artie Shaughnessy. Artie is a would-be song writer who works as a zoo attendant. Bunny wants Artie to join her in witnessing the momentous first visit of a Pope to New York. She is equipped with two Brownie cameras and a sense of history. Artie is not in a hurry to leave the warmth of his sleeping bag or his Queens apartment. The ensuing conversation (begun after Artie has unlocked the door and jumped back into his sleeping bag) alternates between Bunny's plans for the Pope to marry them and Artie's attempts at coaxing her to cook something for him. (For scene-study purposes, the entrance of the "sick woman" may be ignored. The Billy referred to is an old friend of Artie's who has become a successful Hollywood filmmaker.)

ARTIE, *angry:* What I want to know is who the hell is paying for this wop's trip over here anyway—

BUNNY, *shocked:* Artie! *Reaches through the bars to close the window.* Ssshhh—they'll hear you—

ARTIE: I don't put my nickels and dimes in Sunday collections to pay for any dago holiday—flying over here with his robes and geegaws and bringing his buddies over when I can't even afford a trip to Staten Island—

BUNNY, *puzzled:* What's in Staten Island?

ARTIE: Nothing! But I couldn't even afford a nickel ferryboat ride. I known you two months and can't even afford a present for you—a ring—

BUNNY: I don't need a ring—

ARTIE: At least a friendship ring— *(reaches in his sleeping bag and gets out a cigarette and matches and an ashtray)*

BUNNY, *rubbing his head:* I'd only lose it—

ARTIE, *pulling away:* And this guy's flying over here—not tourist—oh no—

BUNNY, *suspicious of his bitterness:* Where'd you go last night?

ARTIE, *back into his bag:* You go see the Pope. Tell him hello for me.

BUNNY: You went to that amateur night, didn't you—

ARTIE, *signaling into the other room:* Shut up—she's inside—

BUNNY: You went to the El Dorado Bar Amateur Night, didn't you? I spent two months building you up to be something and you throw yourself away on that drivel—

ARTIE: They talked all the way through it—

BUNNY: Did you play them "Where's the Devil in Evelyn"?

ARTIE: They talked and walked around all through it—

BUNNY: I wish I'd been there with you. You know what I would've said to them? *Out front:* The first time I heard "Mairzy Doats" I realized I am listening to a classic. I picked off "Old Black Magic" and "I Could've Danced All Night" as classics the minute I heard them. *Recites:* "Where is the devil in Evelyn? What's it doing in Angela's eyes?" I didn't work in Macy's Music Department for nix. I know what I'm talking about. *To Artie:* That song is a classic. You've written yourself a classic.

ARTIE: I even had to pay for my own beers.

BUNNY: Pearls before swine. Chalk it up to experience.

ARTIE: The blackboard's getting kind of filled up. I am too old to be a young talent.

BUNNY, *opens the window through the bars:* Smell the bread—

ARTIE: Shut the window—it's freezing and you're letting all the dirt in—

BUNNY: Miss Henshaw's saving us this divine place right by the cemetery so the Pope will have to slow down—

ARTIE: Nothing worse than cold dirt—

The other bedroom door opens and a sick woman in a nightgown looks at them. They don't see her.

BUNNY, *ecstatically:* And when he passes by in his limousine, I'll call out, "Your Holiness, marry us—the hell with peace to the world—bring peace to us." And he won't hear me because bands will be playing and the whole city yelling, but he'll see me because I been eyed by the best of them, and he'll nod and I'll grab your hand and say, "Marry us, Pope," and he'll wave his holy hand and all the emeralds and rubies on his fingers will send Yes beams. In a way, today's my wedding day. I should have something white at my throat! Our whole life is beginning—my life—our life—and we'll be married and go out to California and Billy will help you. You'll be out there with the big shots—out where you belong—not in any amateur nights in bars on Queens Boulevard. Billy will get your songs in movies. It's not too late to start. With me behind you! Oh, Artie, the El Dorado Bar will stick up a huge neon sign flashing onto Queens Boulevard, in a couple of years flashing "Artie Shaughnessy Got Started Here." And nobody'll believe it. Oh, Artie, tables turn.

The sick woman closes the door. Artie gets out of his bag.

ARTIE, *thoughtfully, sings:*
  Bridges are for burning,
  Tables are for turning—
He turns on all the lights. He pulls Bunny by the pudgy arm over to the kitchen. I'll go see the Pope—

BUNNY, *hugging him:* Oh, I love you!

ARTIE: I'll come if—

BUNNY: You said you'll come. That is tantamount to a promise.

ARTIE: I will if—

BUNNY: Tantamount. Tantamount. You hear that? I didn't work in a law office for nix. I could sue you for breach.

ARTIE, *seductively:* Bunny?

BUNNY, *near tears:* I know what you're going to say—

ARTIE, *opening a ketchup bottle under her nose:* Cook for me?

BUNNY, *in a passionate heat:* I knew it. I knew it.

ARTIE: Just breakfast.

BUNNY: You bend my arm and twist my heart but I got to be strong.

ARTIE: I'm not asking any ten-course dinner.

BUNNY, *runs over to the piano where his clothes are draped, to get away from his plea. They are the green clothes, the pants and suit of a city employee:* Just put your clothes on over the ski p.j.'s I bought you. It's thirty-eight degrees and I don't want you getting your pneumonia back—

ARTIE, *holding up two eggs:* Eggs, baby. Eggs right here.

BUNNY, *holding out his jingling trousers:* Rinse your mouth out to freshen up and come on, let's go?

ARTIE, *seductively:* You boil the eggs and pour lemon sauce over—

BUNNY, *shaking the trousers at him:* Hollandaise. I know Hollandaise. *Plopping down with the weight of the temptation, glum:* It's really cold out so dress warm—look, I stuffed the *New York Post* in my booties—plastic just ain't as warm as it used to be.

ARTIE: And you pour the Hollandaise over the eggs on English muffins—and then you put the grilled ham on top—I'm making a scrapbook of all the foods you tell me you know how to cook and then I go through the magazines and cut out pictures of what it must look like. *Gets the scrapbook:* Look—veal parmigeena—eggplant meringue.

BUNNY: I cooked that for me last night. It was so good I almost died.

ARTIE, *sings as Bunny takes the book and looks through it with such despair:*

If you cooked my words
Like they was veal
I'd say I love you
For every meal.
Take my words,

Garlic and oil them,
Butter and broil them,
Sauté and boil them.
Bunny, let me eat you!
Speaks: Cook for me?
BUNNY: Not 'til after we're married.
ARTIE: You couldn't give me a little sample right now?
BUNNY: I'm not that kind of girl. I'll sleep with you anytime you want. Anywhere. In two months I've known you, did I refuse you once? Not once! You want me to climb in the bag with you now? Unzip it—go on—unzip it—Give your fingers a smack and I'm flat on my back. I'll sew those words into a sampler for you in our new home in California. We'll hang it right by the front door. Because, Artie, I'm a rotten lay and I know it and you know it and everybody knows it—
ARTIE: What do you mean, everybody knows it?
BUNNY: I'm not good in bed. It's no insult. I took that sex test in the *Reader's Digest* two weeks ago and I scored twelve. Twelve, Artie! I ran out of that dentist office with tears gushing out of my face. But I face up to the truth about myself. So if I cooked for you now and said I won't sleep with you till we're married, you'd look forward to sleeping with me so much that by the time we did get to that motel near Hollywood, I'd be such a disappointment, you'd never forgive me. My cooking is the only thing I got to lure you on with and hold you with. Artie, we got to keep some magic for the honeymoon. It's my first honeymoon and I want it to be so good, I'm aiming for two million calories. I want to cook for you so bad I walk by the A&P, I get all hot jabs of chili powder inside my thighs . . . but I can't till we get those tickets to California safe in my purse, till Billy knows we're coming, till I got that ring right on my cooking finger. . . . Don't tempt me. . . . I love you. . . .

THE SEA HORSE

by Edward J. Moore

———————•———————

ACT I

The "Sea Horse" is a bar in a California seaport owned by Gertrude Blum. She is a large, rowdy, seemingly unsentimental woman who uses her tough facade to keep a distance between the world and her vulnerable core. Harry Bales is a seaman who enjoys a physical relationship with Gertrude whenever he is on shore leave. On this visit, Harry surprises Gertrude with new plans to buy a charter fishing boat and settle down to married life with her.

In the scene below, Harry, somewhat drunk, confesses that he loves her and asks her to "run away" with him. Because of her own fear of being hurt, Gertrude deliberately misinterprets his proposal and bullies Harry into an argument that ends in a physical confrontation.

GERTRUDE: Ya know . . . I wish I could have been a dancer . . . *(She puts phonograph on bar. Plugs it in. Harry leans across the table, resting his head on his arms. Concentrated on what she's doing, she doesn't notice this.)* they seem so graceful . . . they kind of float, ya know . . . *(puts on the record)* like their feet don't touch . . . it just fascinates me . . . *(The music plays; it is: Cajita de Musica, "Little Music Box." She adjusts the volume.)* come on, dance with me . . . *(Now, sees him slumped over on the table. A moment, then before she can turn the phonograph off, the music moves in on her. She listens, lost a little in the gentleness of the chords. Then she sways and lifts her arms, doing little dance steps as a child might. Unseen by Gertrude, Harry has opened his eyes and is watching her. She turns slowly as a figure on a music box, until she sees him looking at her. Embarrassed, she laughs, curtsies.)* Dance with me.

HARRY, *lifts his head. Moved at seeing this sensitive side of*

Gertrude, says warmly: That was beautiful ... that was just beautiful ...

GERTRUDE, *smiles, crosses to him, takes his hand:* Come on, let's dance!

HARRY, *gently:* In a minute, okay? ... Sit down first ... *She sits next to him. He gets up, crosses to phonograph, turns it off. A beat, then:* I'm a dummy, right? ... I'm a dummy! I mean what do I know?

GERTRUDE, *compassionately:* A lot of things! ... You're a good carpenter, a good engineer ... *(smiles)* and you're about to be a good roof-fixer, right?

HARRY, *crosses back to her:* No, I mean other stuff! ... *you!* ... I'm dumb about you! ... over a year I've been staying with ya now, and I don't know ya ... you never tell me nothing!

GERTRUDE, *a moment, then:* Well ... I was born ... right here. In the Sea Horse ...

HARRY: Oh, yeah?!

GERTRUDE: Tending bar! *Laughs.* There I was, just toddling around in my diapers, pourin' 'em out and kickin' 'em out!

HARRY, *laughs:* Oh yeah! ... well I ain't that dumb ... I know you was married once ...

GERTRUDE, *a moment, then:* Who told you that?

HARRY, *hoping she will take this lead and talk about herself:* One of the guys said ya was hitched a long time ago.

GERTRUDE, *quiet warning:* Ya *hear* ... a lot of things.

HARRY, *disappointed, but not wanting to press it:* ... Naw ... that was all. *Finishes his whisky. A beat, then:* Remember the first day I came in this place? *Sits next to her.* I had this babe with me ... you said "Leave the bitch outside, Handsome, and come on in!" My babe says "Honey, let's get out of here, that woman scares me!" You said "It's a house rule sailor, nothing through that door without balls, come back without the whore sometime, and the first drink'll be on me!" *Laughs:* ... What a way to talk ...

GERTRUDE, *smiles, gets up, moves behind him:* You came back all right ... that same night!

HARRY: I never had that much fun in my life!

GERTRUDE, *rubs his neck:* Everyone sure took to you ...

HARRY: How could they miss! ... You said it was a rule for me to buy everyone a first drink ... you nearly broke me!

GERTRUDE: Well, they took to ya, didn't they?!? *(smiles, puts her arms around him)* ... You know ... that was the first time I brought anyone upstairs, the same night I met 'em.

HARRY: Yeah?

GERTRUDE: Uh-huh.

HARRY: It was kind of funny ... I mean you wasn't my type!

GERTRUDE, *chuckles:* I'll bet!

HARRY: I remember I said to myself ... "Harry ... you don't do it right, you could get killed."

GERTRUDE, *laughs:* ... You did it right!

HARRY: Yeah, lucky for me I did it right! *He takes her hand:* Gertrude? ... do you ever hear things talk? ... Not people, *things* ... machines 'n' water 'n' wind 'n' stuff. *She realizes that he's been drinking again, sniffs his coffee cup.* Ya know what a shaft alley is?

GERTRUDE: I told you, no more booze!! *Crosses, goes behind bar, puts cup in sink.*

HARRY: Ya know what a shaft alley is?! *Disgusted, as she takes his wet cigar out of sink, throws it in garbage pail. He gets up, crosses to her:* I go down this ladder, see ... *(although a little high, he is still articulate, not slurring his words)* Way down below the water line ... *(Gertrude goes to refrigerator, pours a glass of soda)* and there's the shaft ... it turns the screw ... the propeller. *Sits center bar.* And I go down there to check the bearings ... and it's quiet down there ... and I like to sit for a bit, alone, and think. I like to listen to the shaft ... it talks.

GERTRUDE, *she has taken off the record and unplugged the phonograph, winds up the cord:* It does what?

HARRY, *smiles:* It talks! ... I mean it rumbles ... It's rusty in places and it squeaks ... and it kinda says stuff ... like ... *(gesturing with his hand, indicating the turning shaft and making a squeaking sound)* "I'm old ... I'm old" and I'd answer 'n' say "Oh, yeah ... oh, yeah." *(Gertrude, leaning on stage left end of bar, drinks some soda, begins to get caught up in what he's saying)* ... then she'd speed up 'n' say other things, like ... *(again gestures)* "I'm so long at sea, I'm so long at sea" and I'd answer, 'n' say "Your bearings'll be fine, your bearings'll be fine" ... and then, that strange night, you know, the one I told ya about, the glass ocean ... well, later that same night, I went down to the shaft alley, to think about it. And that old shaft is rumbling away again, and this time she's saying "Gertrude Blum . . . Gertrude Blum" . . . and I started saying it "Gertrude Blum . . . Gertrude Blum" . . . but then she starts speeding up, and my saying "Gertrude Blum" . . . doesn't fit the rumble . . . and it started saying . . . *(indicates the speed of the shaft, spinning his arm rapidly, and talking with compulsive intensity)* "I love Gertrude Blum, I love Gertrude Blum" and I started sayin' it— *(moving toward her)*

HARRY:	**GERTRUDE:**
"I love Gertrude Blum,	Shut up!!
I love Gertrude Blum,	You drunken damn fool, shut
I love Gertrude Blum,	up!!!
I love Gertrude Blum"	I SAID SHUT UP!!!!!
	Throws the soda in his face.

GERTRUDE: You *are* a crazy man!! The guys hear you spouting that love stuff at me they'll laugh you off the pier!

HARRY, *angry, wiping his face, with the blanket:* They won't hear it! . . . none of 'em will hear it! . . . We'll be way up the coast, where nobody knows us! They can't laugh at me!!! *A moment, then he smiles:* You see . . . I figured it all . . . How in the hell can they possibly laugh at me, if we ain't here!

GERTRUDE, *trying to make sense out of what he's saying:* Vallejo?!

HARRY, *makes his way to downstage center table:* You got it!

GERTRUDE: Is that what this is all about? . . . You wanna run away with me?

HARRY, *happy she understands it:* That's it! *Sits.*

GERTRUDE: Why?

HARRY: Because I love you!! *She stares at him incredulously.* I know! . . . I couldn't believe it myself! . . . But it all fits don't ya see . . .

GERTRUDE: . . . The machine's been telling ya!

HARRY, *realization:* . . . yeah . . . kinda . . .

GERTRUDE: . . . The still ocean . . . and the pumps . . . the shaft . . .

HARRY, *fondly:* Ahhh, the shaft . . .

GERTRUDE, *crosses to him:* And your buddies won't know . . .

HARRY: That's right, they won't know!

GERTRUDE: You wanna hide me! *Both roar with laughter.*

HARRY: Yeah!! *Realizing what he said:* I mean no . . . I mean . . .

GERTRUDE: You mean I'm a blubberball and you wanna hide me! *Both laugh. During the following she moves from his left side to his right, back and forth.*

HARRY: . . . It's just that . . .

GERTRUDE: I been sleeping around so you wanna hide me . . .

HARRY: No, that's . . .

GERTRUDE: And all your buddies know!

HARRY, *still laughing:* They won't find out! . . . I mean . . . you're mixing me up . . .

GERTRUDE: You wanna hide me!!

HARRY, *suddenly explodes, jumps up, his fist clenched:* Quit making fun of me!!!

GERTRUDE, *glares at him:* You don't have any balls, Harry, you belong in a dress! Who'd wanna run away with you! *She turns, goes behind bar.*

HARRY, *infuriated, goes after her. Slams his fist on the bar:* YOU DAMN LARD ASS!!!!! SHUT UP!!!!! . . . You're right! I was just kidding ya!! . . . I been using ya, my buddies all know it!!! . . . Staying here free!! . . . Drinking your booze!! . . . Banging ya when I get the notion!! Who'd wanna run away with a fat pig like you!!!!! *Gertrude has moved right end of bar. Slowly he moves toward her now as:* You're a lard ass full of hate!! . . . You hate everything!!! Ohhhh, you hate my son! Ya hate little kids!! *Right up to her:* . . . You are so full of hate!! *Gertrude attacks him viciously with her fists. Harry, forced back, near downstage center table, drops to his knees, tries to protect himself. Covers his head.*

HARRY: Stop it!!! Stop it!!!! Damn you!! Stop hitting me!!! Quit hitting!!!

GERTRUDE: You damn son of a bitch!!! Who the hell do you think you are!!! You bastard!! You damn bastard!!!!!

HARRY: *swings wildly, hitting Gertrude with a tremendous blow to the stomach:* QUIT HITTING!!!!! *She falls to the floor in agony, her breath knocked out by Harry's punch. She clutches her stomach, desperately trying to breathe. Harry, hands over head, confused, not knowing or seeing what he has done, has crawled away from her. Realizing she has stopped hitting him:* What ya trying to do?! Knock my head off?!! You crazy woman . . . (Seeing her now, writhing on the floor . . . Starting to get her breath back, she moans in pain. He shakily gets up, moves to-

ward her.) Hey ... what's the matter ... *(bending over her, seeing she is in terrible agony)* what happened! ... I hit ya?!

GERTRUDE: ... My belly ... oh, my belly ... you hurt my belly ...

HARRY, *distressed, he tries to comfort her:* Oh ... I'm sorry I'm so sorry ... It was an accident ...

GERTRUDE, *gaining a little vocal strength:* You hurt me ... you hurt me ...

HARRY: I'm sorry ... I never hit a woman before! ...

GERTRUDE, *clutches her stomach:* Is there blood on me?!?

HARRY: What ...

GERTRUDE: Blood!! Is there blood on me?!! Am I bleeding?!?!

HARRY, *on his knees, next to her now, he sees there is no blood:* ... No! ... there's no blood! ... I just knocked the wind ...

GERTRUDE, *panicked, she screams:* You hurt me! I'm bleeding ... you hurt me!! *She starts swinging wildly.*

HARRY, *trying desperately to hold her down:* What's the matter!?! Hey !!! Take it easy!!!

GERTRUDE, *screams:* YOU HURT ME!! GET AWAY FROM ME!!! YOU HURT ME!! SOMEBODY HELP ME!!! YOU HURT ME!!!

HARRY, *panicked:* I WON'T HIDE YA!! I'M NOT GONNA HIDE YA!!! I LOVE YA!!! YOU'RE NOT A LARD ASS!!!

HARRY: I'M NOT GONNA HIDE YA!!! I WON'T HIDE YA!!! I'M NOT GONNA HIDE YA!!!

SERENADING LOUIE

by Lanford Wilson

ACT II

The play deals with two suburban couples who have been friends for years. Both have reached a crisis in their marriages: Carl loves Mary, but she is having an affair with his accountant; Alex has become distant from Gabby (he is also having an affair), and Gabby is having strange mood swings. The play traces the deterioration of both relationships as Carl and Mary try to cope with her adultery and Gabby and Alex confront their dissatisfactions with each other.

The following scene between Mary and Carl takes place in their living room. It begins with an innocuous conversation about Alex's new political career and evolves into Carl forcing Mary to admit that she is having an affair. (Their daughter, Ellen, is asleep in the bedroom.)

The play employs a number of theatrical devices such as having both couples use the same environment simultaneously, and, at times, having a character talk directly to the audience.

MARY, *enters from Ellie's room. To a very preoccupied Carl:* I'm sorry, darling. I got embroiled in a drunken question and answer session. She went back to sleep. Ellen takes more and more after you—she lacks all coherency. *Crosses to desk.* What do you make of Alex's career?
CARL: Has he decided . . . ?
MARY: Impending then. I can't decide if he isn't just seeing himself carrying a charger, advancing into battle—in which case—
CARL: Honey, you don't carry a charger into battle—the charger is the horse.
MARY, *crosses to fireplace:* I thought you carried a charger—like a lance. Well, that makes sense. Right then: charging in *à cheval*—with plumes—
CARL: He might fool us.

MARY, *Alex crosses to desk, sits:* If he's not political he'll be eaten alive and if he is political, then I've no interest in him. Why the hell doesn't he just quit and go to work for the Civil Liberties Union if he has such an overpowering social conscience? I know Gabby's confused— *(crosses to hall)*

CARL, *crosses to fireplace:* I'd think so. *As Mary starts to go:* You know I had to make a lot of quick phone-call confirmations and I knocked them off this afternoon in about ten minutes flat.

MARY: Good.

CARL, *opens curtain, gets poker:* And without even skipping a beat I called Donald and asked him how about knocking it off with my wife. *Freeze. Long pause. Alex dials a number. Looks at his watch.*

MARY: And what did he say?

CARL, *turns to Mary:* I wasn't even sure I could call him; I didn't actually know I was going to until I hung up.

MARY: Whatever gave you the idea there was anything to knock off?

CARL: No, we won't do that—

MARY: Won't do what?

CARL: Pretend. We won't pretend. Of course I'd know. I've known for months. Every Wednesday.

MARY: You're being awfully circuitous for someone with a degree—

CARL: No, Mary—

MARY: I go into town—I've been seeing Mom almost every week—she's no spring—

CARL: I'm not talking about your mother.

MARY: Well, then I haven't—

CARL: No, Mary, don't, Mary. I go by the apartment at the Commodore every Wednesday afternoon to check up and see if he's showed up. To watch the blinds turn. You turn them up and he turns them down. I told you I'd been spending lunch-hours around the Hancock Building and you never even heard me. Doubtless your mind was somewhere else; we know how one-tracked you get. We won't pretend. *Puts poker away.*

MARY, *crosses to living room:* When was that?

CARL, *closes curtain:* Months ago—three months at least; I don't know when.

MARY: Well, why on earth didn't you say something.

CARL: I didn't know *(Alex hangs up, Carl looks to him and back)* what to say. And I kept thinking it'd break off; you'd give it up.

MARY: When did—?

CARL, *without hearing:* I did try. I wrote it out once at work, what I'd say.

MARY, *sits upstage on sofa:* My god, you poor darling—

CARL: Oh, come on, now.

MARY: No, Carl, if—

CARL, *crosses right, puts lights on:* Mary goddamn it, I do not intend to discuss this rationally! I'll be damned if I will. You said what did he say. He said sure, OK, fine, and rather briefly and I hung up. And thought. Quite a lot. I thought I'm twice again his size. *To the audience:* I am, I'm about twice the man's size. *Back to Mary:* I could beat the shit out of the guy and you. And that might make me feel a little better. I'd tell Ellen mommy fell down the stairs. *Beat. Crosses to fireplace.* I just assumed, whatever he felt about you, that you managed to be in love and that it'd pass—

MARY: Oh, god, Carl couldn't I have seen him just because—

CARL: No, I don't like seen, that's too easy, say screwed, say—

MARY: All right, then, just because I enjoyed it? Without dragging romance through it? Because I dug him?

CARL: OK, it was hot stuff—better than—

MARY: —My responsibility to you hasn't altered in the least degree—

CARL: Yeah, yeah, and Ellen, I know, I know, I know, and with all this great guilt we should be even closer now; hell, I guess I should thank him, huh? No, just call it off. That's it. It's over. From now. Finis. And that's all. That's all I have to say. *A long pause.* Mary?

MARY: I couldn't do that Carl. *Carl sits with his head in his hands.* Carl?

CARL, *without looking up:* I'm here.

THE TRIP BACK DOWN

by John Bishop

———————•———————

ACT I

The play opens with Bobby Horvath returning to his hometown in the Midwest after eight years. For some of those eight years, Bobby had been a successful stock-car racer. His dream was "to be the best"; to have people recognize him and say, "That's Bobby Horvath." But after a bright start the wins came less and less often. Soon the dream turned into the reality of "havin' to race in every little Podunk that's got a track just to keep goin'. Not ever winnin' enough to really get set up right ... knowin' ... that for the rest of your life ... this is goin' be it." So Bobby comes back home hoping to find some direction for his life, some meaning, perhaps from the wife and daughter he left behind, perhaps from his father and brother, perhaps from old friends or old landscapes. But no such answers are available. Finally Bobby comes to terms with himself and his ambitions, and returns to car racing.

The following excerpt is a flashback on the last argument Bobby had with his wife, Joann, before he left home. They had been married for seven years, and by this time their relationship deteriorated to the point where both harbored strong resentments but neither could communicate their feelings. Joann had just walked out in the middle of an argument about Bobby going off to race. As Bobby is about to walk out with his duffel bag, Joann reenters.

JOANN: Wait a minute Bobby! We can't keep doing this over and over. I do want to talk ... but you don't listen.

BOBBY: You don't want me to go?

JOANN: No. You're my husband. I want you to be here. I want you to be with us. I want something solid for us all. Something solid and worthwhile.

BOBBY: Like what?

JOANN: I am saying that there is a growth to things. You plant something and wait for . . . *(Bobby moves upstage, throws duffel bag on floor and crosses to downstage right.)*

BOBBY, *interrupting:* Bullshit!

JOANN, *trying to continue:* There's an order . . . you want everyone to go racing around gambling on some strange kind of quick fortune? You think that makes sense?

BOBBY: For me.

JOANN: For you. Everything for you. What about everybody else?

BOBBY: I ain't everybody.

JOANN: Well, I am.

BOBBY: What?

JOANN: Jesus Christ, will you stop being so damn selfish?

BOBBY: Selfish . . . You wanna come with me, is that it? What do you want, Joann, what? *Crosses above table to bar.* You want me to take a job at Westinghouse? You want that for me? Well that ain't me. Never was.

JOANN: Who are you Bobby? You'll never find out by racing. It'll change ev'ry weekend ev'ry race. Don't you see that?

BOBBY: You know what . . . you're scared. You are scared to move. Scared of anything different. You didn't used to be that way but now something is scaring you. If you had your way you'd never move your butt out of this house. *He crosses to downstage right.*

JOANN, *hit hard by this:* That's not true.

BOBBY: The thing I don't understand is, where the hell was all this hate for racin' when we got married? *Joann sits left of table.* What were you gonna do . . . try and change me or something? I don't change.

JOANN, *tired, suddenly:* That was seven years ago, Bobby. A lot of things were different then.

BOBBY: You can say that again.

JOANN: You never really wanted me to share anything with you anyhow. Most of the time when I'd ask about your car or a race, you just mumble back at me. When I did go out to the track, you act like I didn't belong to you. Like you were ashamed of me. Were you Bobby?

BOBBY: I just asked you to come along?

JOANN: This is before.

BOBBY: Fuck before! I'm talking about now.

JOANN, *rises:* And I'm talking about how you made me feel. You made me feel out of place and inadequate. You cut me out of your life, Bobby. I have never turned my back on you.

BOBBY: Except in bed.

JOANN: What?

BOBBY: You turn your back in bed, don't you? You sure as hell turn your back there.

JOANN: What? *Bobby crosses above table to upstage center.*

BOBBY: You're like that joke . . . "You know how to stop an Irish-Catholic from fuckin'? Ya marry her." That's you.

JOANN: You bastard! Oh, you bastard! *Joann exits downstage right.*

BOBBY, *crossing to downstage right and yelling after her:* It's the truth ain't it? . . . Hey, come back here . . . I'm asking you a question . . . It's the truth ain't it?

JOANN, *offstage yelling back:* No it's not the truth! It's not all me. What about you? You . . .

BOBBY: No, oh no. I know about me. You were never the hottest thing comin' down the pike you know. Christ, I never knew a woman got wet until . . . *(Realizing what he is saying, he stops, and crosses to center. Joann rushes back to below table.)*

JOANN: Until what? Goddam you until what? Until you made it with one of those twitchy-assed teenyboppers that hang around the track?

BOBBY: I said . . . a woman.

JOANN, *goes crazy:* You son of a bitch . . . You son of a bitch . . . just get out of here . . . just get the hell out of here.

BOBBY: Take it easy lady. Take it goddam easy, you hear? Or someday I'll go out that door for good. *She sinks into chair and sweeps clothes off table.*

JOANN: Then go! . . . Oh damn! Damn! Damn! *Bobby crosses up for duffel bag, returns downstage, hesitates, then puts duffel bag on counter.*

BOBBY: Listen, Joann . . . Listen. *He grabs her arm, she pulls away from him, rises and crosses to downstage right.*

JOANN: No. No more. Just leave me alone get out.

BOBBY, *as he grabs her again:* Wait . . . Goddammit wait. *She pushes her hand into his face. His reaction is immediate. He*

*swings her around as they struggle, and when she is upstage,
slaps her. She collapses onto table.*
JOANN, *crying:* Goddam you ... you son of a bitch ... goddam you.

MOONY'S KID DON'T CRY

by Tennessee Williams

———————•———————

The scene takes place in the kitchen of a cheap three-room flat
in the industrial section of a large American city. The room is
unkempt. There are diapers and work shirts hung on a clothes-
line. There is a small artificial Christmas tree and a brand new
hobbyhorse. This is the apartment of Moony, a laborer who
dreams of a better life, his wife Jane, who has given up all
dreaming, and their sickly infant. The play begins with the
sounds of creaking bedsprings and voices from the offstage bedroom.

JANE, *offstage:* Quit that floppin' around. It keeps me awake.
MOONY: Think I'm gettin' any sleep, do you?!

Sound: more rattling.

JANE: Quiet! You'll wake the kid up.
MOONY: The kid, the kid! What's more important, him sleep-
ing or me? Who brings home the paycheck, me or the kid?
Pause.
JANE: I'll get up an' fix you a cup of hot milk. That'll quiet
you down maybe.

*Moony grumbles incoherently. Jane pads softly onstage, into the
kitchen. She is amazingly slight, like a tiny mandarin, enveloped*

*in the ruins of a once gorgeously flowered Japanese silk kimono.
As she prepares the hot milk for Moony, she pads about the kitch-
en in a pair of men's felt bedroom slippers which she has a hard
time keeping on her small feet. She squeezes the kimono tight
about her chest, and shivers. Coughs once or twice. Glances irritably at the alarm clock on windowsill, which says nearly four
o'clock in the morning. Jane is still young, but her pretty, small-
featured face has a yellowish, unhealthy look. Her temples and
nostrils are greased with Vick's Vap-o-Rub and her dark hair is
tousled.*

JANE, *strident whisper:* What for? I'll bring yer milk in.
Sound: scraping of furniture and heavy footsteps. That's it, be
sure you wake the kid up—clumsy ox! *Moony appears in the
doorway, a strongly built young workingman about twenty-five
years old. He blinks his eyes and scowls irritably as he draws on
his flannel shirt and stuffs it under the belt of his corduroy pants.*
It's that beer-drinkin'. Makes gas on yer stomach an' keeps yuh
from sleepin'.
MOONY: Aw, I had two glasses right after dinner.
JANE: Two a them twenty-six ounces!—Quit that trampin'
around, for Christ's sake! Can't you set still a minute?
MOONY: Naw, I feel like I got to be moving.
JANE: Maybe you got high blood pressure.
MOONY: Naw, I got a wild hair. This place's give me the jit-
ters. You know it's too damn close in here. Can't take more'n
six steps in any direction without coming smack up against another wall. *Half grinning:* I'd like to pick up my ax and swing
into this wall—Bet I could smash clean through it in a couple of
licks!
JANE: Moony! Why didn't I marry an ape an' go live in the
zoo?
MOONY: I don't know. *Jane pours the steaming milk into a
blue cup.*
JANE: Set down an' drink that. Know what time it is? Four
o'clock in the morning!
MOONY: Four o'clock, huh? *He continues to move restlessly
about.* Yeah. Soon ole fact'ry whistle be blowin'. Come on, you
sonovaguns! Git to work!—Old Dutchman be standin' there
with his hands on his little potbelly, watchin' 'em punch in their

cards. "Hi, dere, Moony," he says. "Late agin, huh? Vot you tink dis iss maybe, an afderноon tea?" That's his joke. You know a Dutchman always has one joke that he keeps pluggin' at. An' that's his. Ev'ry morning the same damn thing—

JANE: Yeah? Well—

MOONY: "Ha, ha, Moony," he says, "you been out star-gazin' las' night! How many vas dere, Moony? How man stars vas dere out las' night? Ha, ha, *ha!*"— *(strides over to the window—flings it up)*

JANE: Put that back down! I ain't got a stitch a clothes on under this.

MOONY: I'll say to him, "Sure, I seen 'em las' night. But not like they was in Ontario, not by a long shot, Mister." Greasebubbles! That's what they look most like from here. Why, up in the North Woods at night—

JANE, *impatiently:* The North Woods! Put that thing down!

MOONY: Okay. *Obeys.*

JANE: Here. Drink yer milk. You act like a crazy man, honest to Jesus you do!

MOONY: Okay. Would that give the Dutchman a laugh!

JANE: What would? You better be careful.

MOONY: He'll go all over the plant—tell the boys what Moony said this morning—said he'd seen the stars las' night but not like they was in Ontario when he was choppin down the big timber.

JANE: Yes, you'll give him a swell impression with talk of that kind. I'm dog-tired. *Pours herself some of the steaming milk.*

MOONY: Ever seen the St. Lawrence River?

JANE: Naw, I've seen wet diapers, that's all, for so long that—!

MOONY: That's what I'll ask the Dutchman. I'll ask him if he's ever seen the St. Lawrence River.

JANE, *glancing at him suspiciously:* What would you ask him that for?

MOONY: She's big. See? She's nearly as big and blue as the sky is, an' the way she flows is straight north. You ever heard of that, Jane? A river that flowed straight north?

JANE, *indifferently, as she sips her hot milk:* No.

MOONY: Only river I ever know of that flowed north!

JANE: Emma says a drop of paregoric would keep his bowels from runnin' off like that. I think I'll try it next time.

MOONY: We was talkin' about it one day an' Spook says it's because the earth is curved down that way toward the Arctic Circle! *Grins.*

JANE: What?

MOONY: He said that's why she flows north—

JANE: Who cares?

MOONY: Naw, the Dutchman don't, neither. That's why I tell him. Makes it funny, see? I'll tell him she's big, damn big, an' they call her the Lake of a Thousand Islands!

JANE: He'll say you're crazy. He'll tell you to go an' jump in it!

MOONY: Sure he will. That's what makes it funny. I'll tell him she's big an' blue as the sky is, with firs an' pines an' tamaracks on both sides of her fillin' the whole God-beautiful air with— the smell of— Hot milk, huh? Wouldn't that give the Dutchman a laugh!—Hot milk at four o'clock in the morning!—He'd go all over the plant an' tell the boys that Moony must have his liddle hot milk at night when he goes bye-bye with the Sandman.

JANE: Louise Krause's husband commenced sayin' such things an' they called out the ambulance squad. Right now he's in a straitjacket in the psychopathic ward an' when Louise went up to see him he didn't remember who she was even! Demen-shuh pre-cox they called it! *Moony seizes cup and dashes milk to floor.* Moony!—What d'yuh think yuh're doin', yuh big lug? Sloppin' good milk on the floor!

MOONY: Hot milk, huh?

JANE: Oh, dear Christ! You an' your kid, what a mess you both are! No wonder they all make fun of you down at the plant. The way that you act there's only one word for it—crazy! *Moony snorts indignantly.* Yes, crazy! Crazy is the only word for your actions!

MOONY: Crazy, huh? Sure them apes think I'm nuts. I'll tell you why; it's because I got some original ideas about some things.

JANE: Original, yeah, you're so stinkin' original it ain't even funny! Believe me If I'd a-known—

MOONY: I look at things diff'runt— *(struggling for self-justification)* —that's all. Other guys—you know how it is—they don't care. They eat, they drink, they sleep with their women. What the hell do they care? The sun keeps rising and Saturday night they get paid!—Okay, okay, okay! Some day they kick off. What of it? They got kids to grow up an' take their places. Work in the plant. Eat, drink, sleep with their women—an' get paid Saturday night!—But me—*(he laughs bitterly)* My God, Jane, I want something more than just that!

JANE: What more do you want, you poor fool? There *ain't* nothing more than just that—Of course if you was rich and could afford a big house and a couple of limoozines—

MOONY, *disgustedly:* Aw, you—you don't even get what I'm aimin' at, Jane! *He sinks wearily down on checkered linoleum and winds arms about his knees.* You never could get it. It's something that ain't contagious.

JANE: Well, I'm glad for that. I'd rather have smallpox.

MOONY: I found a guy once that did. An old duck up on the river. He got his back hurt, couldn't work, was waiting to be shipped home—We got drunk one night an' I spilled how I felt about things. He said, "Sure. You ain't satisfied. Me neither. We want something more than what life ever gives to us, kid."

JANE: It gives you what you can get.

MOONY: Oh, I dunno. I look at my hands sometimes, I look an' I look at 'em. God, but they look so damn funny!

JANE: You look at your hands! Such crap!

MOONY: They're so kind of empty an' useless! You get what I mean! I feel like I oughta be doin' something with these two han's of mine besides what I'm doin' now—runnin' bolts through an everlastin' chain!

JANE: Here's something. *Flings him a dish rag.* Try holdin' this for a change in them wonderful hands—Mop that milk up off the floor!

MOONY, *idly twisting the cloth:* An' then sometimes I think it ain't my han's that're empty. It's something else inside me that is.

JANE: Yeh, it's probably yer brain. Will you get that milk swabbed up?

MOONY: It's already swabbed! *Rises and stretches.* Moony's a free agent. He don't give a damn what anyone thinks. Live an' die, says Moony, that's all there is to it! *He tosses the wet rag back to the sink.*

JANE, *straightening things in a lifeless, ineffectual way:* Believe me, if I'd a-known you was gonna turn out this way, I'd a-kept

my old job. I'd-a-said to Mr. O'Connor, "Sure thing! Go ahead an' get me that chinchilla coat."
MOONY: Sure you would. I know it, sweetheart.

6 RMS RIV VU

by Bob Randall

———————•———————

ACT I, SCENE I

The setting is a vacant six-room apartment on Riverside Drive. Two strangers, Paul Friedman and Anne Miller, have come to see this desirable New York residence. Both are young, attractive, married to other people, and have become a little bored with the present state of their lives. While they are investigating a back room, Eddie, the superintendent, inadvertently locks them in. They soon discover that they cannot leave. The following events alternate between fear and amusement, efforts to get out and to get better acquainted.

As the scene begins, Anne is alone in the apartment. She is pacing out the size of the rooms and singing "Don't Fence Me In." Paul enters while she is in the dining room (offstage). She reenters singing.

PAUL: Sing it, baby.
ANNE: Excuse me.
PAUL: I'm sorry. I was just kidding. *She exits into bedrooms.* Three, six, nine, twelve . . .
ANNE, *Reenters:* It's twenty by twenty-three.
PAUL: Thanks.
ANNE: Look, I'm not one of your West Side schizophrenics.
PAUL: I didn't think you were.
ANNE: The apartment's so big, it got to me. I didn't know anybody else was in here.

PAUL: You don't have to explain.

ANNE: Ohh . . . did Schneider/Steinbrunner send you?

PAUL: Yeah.

ANNE, *upset:* God! They told me they wouldn't send anybody else over today.

PAUL: Yeah, that's what they told me! Can you believe those two? *Pause.* We've been looking for a bigger place for over a year.

ANNE: Next month is my second anniversary.

PAUL: We have a three and a half.

ANNE: We have one bedroom and an alcove.

PAUL: Any kids?

ANNE: Two.

PAUL: Relax. I'm only the envoy. My wife has the final say.

ANNE: Is she out of town, I hope? Go look at the dining room. *Paul goes into the dining area, Anne into the bedroom. Eddie enters and exits with the trash basket, leaving the front door open. Paul and Anne enter separately and examine the window again.*

PAUL: Tell me, where's the river?

ANNE: If you lean out the second bathroom, it's to the left.

PAUL, *looking around:* Well, anyway, it's big.

ANNE: Yeah.

PAUL: And a nice room, huh?

ANNE: I hate to admit it in front of you, but yes, it is. You put a couch over there and a few big overstuffed chairs here, by the window, facing *in* . . .

PAUL: My wife and I are more the caning and spindly-legs type.

ANNE: How eighteenth century of you.

PAUL: I like club chairs, but Janet doesn't. Do you have any club chairs at home?

ANNE: No, we have leather and chrome. My husband likes to sit up straight. *She is peering into the closet by now.*

PAUL: Not straighter than my wife. Hey, would you do me a favor? The second bedroom has no closet. I guess I could build one. Would you give me your opinion?

ANNE: Sure. My God, a strange man is inviting me into a bedroom. At last, something to tell the checker at the Daitch. *They exit. Eddie enters, eating a butter cookie, and removes the door-*

knob and exits, slamming the door. Anne and Paul reenter. I
never knew you could just build a closet. I thought it took an
architect.
PAUL: Nothing to it. Do you like club chairs?
ANNE: Yes, I do.
PAUL: That's very significant. A woman who likes club chairs
likes men.
ANNE: Erich Fromm?
PAUL: It's a man's chair. My father had a club chair.
ANNE: Everybody's did.
PAUL: What's a Morris chair?
ANNE: Search me. Look, I think I'd better get down to the
agent's and wrestle with Eva Braun.
PAUL: Mrs. Schneider or Mrs. Steinbrunner?
ANNE: Schneider.
PAUL, *in a Nazi accent:* Und tell me, Madame, vhy do you vish
to rent this apartment? Speak. Ve haff vays of making you talk.
ANNE: Notice their initials are S.S.?
PAUL: Right. It's always nice to meet a fellow bigot. My
name's Paul Friedman.
ANNE: Anne Miller.
PAUL: Really?
ANNE: You want to call Ripley?
PAUL: Didn't your parents go to the movies?
ANNE: They named me Delaney. The Miller was my hus-
band's idea.
PAUL: My God, I just met Ann Miller. Hey, I'll ride down in
the elevator with you. *He reaches for the doorknob.* What hap-
pened here?
ANNE: Where's the doorknob?
PAUL, *after trying to open the door:* No use.
ANNE, *banging on door:* Hello out there. We're stuck!
PAUL, *looking out peephole:* There's nobody there. *Calls:* Hel-
lo? Hello? This is 4B calling 4A. *Beat:* They must be out.
ANNE: Hello, there's a young mother of two in distress in here!
PAUL: Is that how you see yourself? A young mother?
ANNE: When I want sympathy. *Calls again:* Hello, there's a
college-educated person locked in here! Better?
PAUL: Which college?
ANNE: Barnard.

PAUL: Did you know Beverly Strauss?

ANNE: Not well.

PAUL: Maybe they're walking the dog.

ANNE, *calling into hole:* And I'm a dog lover! *Beat:* You want to play Simon Says?

PAUL: Shall we try the window?

ANNE: Why not? I've always loved shrieking.

PAUL: Hey, ma, throw me a nickel. *He tries to open the window. It is stuck.* Would you lend me a hand?

ANNE: Sure.

PAUL: When I count three?

ANNE: On the three or four?

PAUL: What?

ANNE: One-two tug or one-two-three tug?

PAUL: Care for the extra count for preparation?

ANNE: Whatever you say.

PAUL: One-two-three tug.

ANNE: Roger. *They tug. Nothing happens. Continues.*

PAUL: Once more. One-two-three tug! *Again nothing.* Wait a minute. *He takes off his jacket, gets on his knees on the radiator and tries mightily to open it. Meanwhile, Anne goes to the other window and opens it easily.* It's coming. It's coming. *He opens it about an inch. Then he sees the other window:* Why didn't you tell me?

ANNE: I thought it might be a matter of machismo.

PAUL, *good-naturedly:* You're a crazy lady. *Indicating the open window:* Shall I?

ANNE: Please.

PAUL: Hello! Hello! There's a woman in the kitchen downstairs. Hello!

ANNE: Hello, miss! Madam!

PAUL: You! The lady in the half-slip! Damn, she ran out of the room.

ANNE: People of New York! There's a nice young couple trapped in apartment 4B, six rooms, still rent-controlled, three twenty-five a month! Get us out and we'll give you the agent's name! *Beat:* Do you think we'll come to hate each other after a few months?

PAUL: Permit a master. *Calls out window:* Ladies and gentlemen, I see a parking space!

DIRTY HANDS

by Jean-Paul Sartre,
translated by Lionel Abel

———•———

ACT III

The play is set during World War II in the fictitious European country of Illyria. The German army is in occupation. They are opposed by an underground proletarian party (as well as by the Russians). Within the party, an assassination is planned against one of its own members, Hoederer. Hugo, the central character in the play, is a young party member. He is an intellectual from a wealthy family; an ineffectual idealist. He yearns for an assignment in which he can prove his dedication. He insists on being allowed to carry out the mission to kill Hoederer. It is arranged for him to become Hoederer's secretary so that he may gain his confidence and get past his bodyguards.

In the following scene Hugo and his wife, Jessica, are at Hoederer's quarters, a summerhouse in the country. They have recently arrived and are arranging their room and unpacking. Jessica has opened a suitcase that she was not supposed to open. In it, she found a revolver.

JESSICA: What's that revolver doing here?

HUGO: I always have one with me.

JESSICA: That's not so. You never had one before we came here. And you never had that suitcase either. You bought them both at the same time. Why did you get a revolver?

HUGO: Do you really want to know?

JESSICA: Yes, and be serious. You have no right to keep things like this from me.

HUGO: You won't tell anybody?

JESSICA: I won't tell a soul.

HUGO: It's to kill Hoederer.

JESSICA: Don't tease me, Hugo. I tell you I'm not playing now.

HUGO, *he laughs:* Am I playing? Or am I being serious? There's a mystery for you. Jessica, you are going to be the wife of an assassin!

JESSICA: But you could never do it, my poor little lamb; would you like me to kill him for you? I'll go offer myself to him and then—

HUGO: Thanks, and anyhow you would fail! I shall act for myself.

JESSICA: But why do you want to kill him? You don't even know the man.

HUGO: So that my wife will take me seriously. Wouldn't you take me seriously then?

JESSICA: Me? I would admire you, hide you, feed you, and entertain you in your hideaway. And when the neighbors turned us in I would throw myself on you despite the police, and I would take you in my arms crying: "I love you."

HUGO: Tell it to me now.

JESSICA: What?

HUGO: That you love me.

JESSICA: I love you.

HUGO: But mean it.

JESSICA: I love you.

HUGO: But you don't really mean it.

JESSICA: What's got into you? Are you playing?

HUGO: No, I'm not playing.

JESSICA: Then why did you ask me that? That's not like you.

HUGO: I don't know. I need to think that you love me. I have a right to that. Come on, say it. Say it as if you meant it.

JESSICA: I love you. I love you. No: I love you. Oh, go to the devil! Let's hear you say it.

HUGO: I love you.

JESSICA: You see, you don't say it any better than I.

HUGO: Jessica, you don't believe what I told you.

JESSICA: That you love me?

HUGO: That I'm going to kill Hoederer.

JESSICA: Of course I believe it.

HUGO: Try hard, Jessica. Be serious.

JESSICA: Why do I have to be serious?

HUGO: Because we can't always be playing.

JESSICA: I don't like to be serious, but I'll do the best I can: I'll play at being serious.

HUGO: Look me in the eyes. No. Don't laugh. Listen to me: it's true about Hoederer. That's why the party sent me here.

JESSICA: I believe you. But why didn't you tell me sooner?

HUGO: Perhaps you would have refused to come here with me.

JESSICA: Why should I refuse? It's a man's job and has nothing to do with me.

HUGO: This is going to be no joke, you know. He seems to be a hard guy.

JESSICA: Oh well, we'll chloroform him and tie him across a cannon's mouth.

HUGO: Jessica! I'm serious.

JESSICA: Me too.

HUGO: You are playing at being serious. You told me so yourself.

JESSICA: No. That's what you're doing.

HUGO: You've got to believe me, I beg you.

JESSICA: I'll believe you when you believe that I'm serious.

HUGO: All right, I believe you.

JESSICA: No. You're playing at believing me.

HUGO: This can go on forever!

THE GOODBYE PEOPLE

by Herb Gardner

———————•———————

Act I

If plays had mottoes, the motto of *The Goodbye People* would probably be Dreamers of the World Unite! And unite they do in this funny and touching play by Herb Gardner. Dreamer number one is Max, seventy years old, who "decided *not* to die" of a heart attack so that he could resurrect his once-successful but long-defunct Coney Island restaurant (Max's Hawaiian Ecstasies). His reason: "I gotta leave something you should know I been around, somethin' says I was alive, somethin' terrific, somethin' classy . . . somethin' beautiful." Dreamer number two is Arthur, an artist who loves beauty (even to the point of going out to the Coney Island beach at 6 A.M. in February to watch the sunrise) but hates his job as a Christmas-display designer, and who, at the age of forty-one, realizes that "I can't remember what I'd meant to do with it . . . my, y'know, life." Dreamer number three is Nancy, Max's daughter, who a year ago left her husband, changed her name (from Shirley), fixed her nose, dyed her hair, got a therapist and a theatrical agent, and rode off on her ten-speed Peugeot bicycle to discover her life. Unfortunately, the search was taking her somewhat longer than she had anticipated.

The following scene takes place on the beach in front of Max's boarded up restaurant. A few moments earlier Arthur and Max met and talked. During their conversation, and before the sunrise, Arthur fell asleep on his beach chair. Max went off to raise money for his business and Nancy came riding up. Arthur muttered something in his sleep about wanting to quit his job; so when Arthur's boss telephoned for him at the nearby telephone booth (the call was prearranged by Arthur on the hope that while watching a magnificent sunrise he would find the courage to quit his job), Nancy, answering the phone but unable to wake Arthur, told the boss that Arthur was quitting. She then sat on the sand near Arthur and fell asleep. The scene opens with Arthur awakening, startled at finding a strange girl sleeping at his side.

ARTHUR: Oh . . .
NANCY, *opens her eyes, also startled:* Oh . . .
ARTHUR: Hello. Hello there . . .
NANCY: Arthur, you're awake.
ARTHUR: Yes, Yes, I am. Yes.
NANCY, *rising:* Hello.
ARTHUR: Hello. How are ya? *Rising:* Good morning. *Stumbling over the bicycle:* Your bike?
NANCY: Yes.
ARTHUR: Nice bike.
NANCY: Ten-speed Peugeot with handle brakes.
ARTHUR: Hey, the old guy . . . the old guy, Silverman; where's—?
NANCY: It's a curse. All night long I'm an old Jewish man and

in the morning I turn into the beautiful girl you see before you.

ARTHUR, *to horizon:* Oh, God. Oh, my God—

NANCY: What—

ARTHUR: The sun! Looka that! It's up! It's up already! God-damn sunrise, they slipped another one right past me . . . *(slumps defeated in beach chair)* Looka that. Six mornings in a row . . . *(jumps out of his chair)* Excuse me. You wanna sit down? Forget it, stranger on the beach; who knows, right? I don't blame you. I'm Arthur Korman, I'm harmless, how-are-ya? *Holds out his hand—withdraws it before she can respond.* Right. Watch out, I could be anybody. A nut. This city; I know how you feel. *She sits down on the beach chair.* Beautiful. Look, you sat down. I'm Arthur Korman; I'm completely, completely harmless. *Shakes her hand vigorously.* Don't worry about it. You're free to leave any time. You're a very pretty girl. Excep-tional.

NANCY: Thank you, I—

ARTHUR: Don't worry about it. *Sits opposite her, on sand dune.* I'm just going to sit here and you sit there and every-thing'll be beautiful. You want some coffee?

NANCY: Great; yes.

ARTHUR: Oh; I don't have any. How did you know my name? You must be freezing. Hey, I'll give you my coat.

NANCY: Truth is, I am cold, if it isn't—

ARTHUR: Beautiful. Beautiful. *Taking off his coat:* Situation like this, believe me; you know how to handle yourself. May I ask your name?

NANCY: Nancy Scott.

ARTHUR: Beautiful. I like the way you handle yourself. *He has forgotten to give her the coat.*

NANCY: Excuse me . . .

ARTHUR: Right, baby.

NANCY: Your coat, I—

ARTHUR: Oh, my God, of course—*(rolls it up, tosses it to her like a basketball)*

NANCY: Thank you.

ARTHUR: So what're ya doin' around here? I come to see the sunrise, but I fall asleep.

NANCY: Don't worry; great thing about the sun is that it comes back every morning.

ARTHUR: Even fell asleep on this crazy old guy today . . .

NANCY: He's my father.

ARTHUR: Weather like this, how come you don't wear a coat or something?

NANCY: That crazy old guy, he's my—

ARTHUR: I mean, it's February.

NANCY: Well, when I go to buy coats I think I'm very tall. I've got six tall coats and they all look terrible on me.

ARTHUR: Beautiful.

NANCY: So if I was tall I'd be warm. Meanwhile I'm short and cold.

ARTHUR: Beautiful. Beautiful. See what we're doing? We're talking. Opening up. This is terrific. *After a moment:* You got to let it happen. Letting it happen is what it's all about. *Silence; he picks up his banjo case, opens it, takes out banjo.* This is called a Whyte Lady, this banjo. Great sound. Haven't made 'em for thirty, thirty-five years. *Sits next to her on chunk of driftwood, holding the banjo with great affection.* See this here; carved bone pegs . . . pearl inlay on the frets . . .

NANCY: Would you play something for me? *He holds the banjo in playing position; plucks one of the strings, listens to it critically, tightens it. Silence for a moment. He puts it back in the case.*

ARTHUR: Tell ya what, it wouldn't be a good idea.

NANCY: Why not?

ARTHUR: Because I don't play the banjo.

NANCY: What are you doing with it?

ARTHUR: Carrying it. I carry it.

NANCY: Oh.

ARTHUR: I carry things. Idea is you carry something around long enough you become obligated to it, see; to learn what to do with it. Got the instruction book in there too. And my sculpture tools. Used to do sculpture and I'd like to get back to it, so I carry my tools in there and it reminds me. Of my obligation. *He snaps the case shut. He looks off at the horizon for a few moments; sings softly to himself:*

"If you don't get a letter

Then you'll know I'm in jail . . ."

Silence. Well; 'bye now. *Rises; picks up banjo case.* Yessir, that ol' clock really ticks away, doesn't it? *Shaking her hand vigor-*

ously: This was great. Talking to you. Beautiful to meet you. Beautiful experience here. *Walking briskly to the stairs:* Right; but now it's time to start the ol' day goin', huh?

NANCY: Your . . . your coat, I . . .

ARTHUR, *going up the stairs:* Keep the coat. It's your coat. I want you to have it; it's February.

NANCY, *unbuttoning the Mackinaw:* Take your coat. I don't want it . . .

ARTHUR, *at the top of the stairs; he turns to her:* Please. Please keep it . . .

NANCY, *holding the coat out to him:* I really don't want it. Here . . .

ARTHUR, *a casual wave of his hand:* Hey, keep the coat . . . *(suddenly, desperately, clutching the banjo case)* Please . . . Keep it . . . Keep the goddamn coat, will ya? Lady, I gotta leave now. The gaps. The gaps in the conversation. The gaps are coming! Get out while you can! Believe me, you're in for a losing experience. That's it, lady; that's all I do. You've just seen everything I do. That was it. I don't follow up with anything. I'd like to play you a song on my banjo or invite you for a swim but I don't play I just carry and it's too cold. Forgive me, I'm sorry; goodbye—*(he starts to exit left down the boardwalk)*

NANCY, *shouting:* This is a four-thousand-dollar nose! *Throws his coat down on the sand.* You're walkin' out on a four-thousand-dollar nose here, dummy! *He turns, startled by her outburst.* Don't stand there! Go away! Alla you! I don't need *any* of you! This is Dr. Graham's nose! A top nose! This is Mr. Gaston's hair! Mr. Gaston of Lexington Avenue! This is my agent's name and this is Dr. Berman's attitude and this voice I'm talking to you with is from Madame Grenier, the vocal coach! I'm not just a pretty girl, I'm a *crowd* of pretty girl! A convention . . . a parade . . . a . . . *(There are tears in her eyes. She turns away from him, sits down on the beach chair.)* So who needs you; I got company . . . *(she hugs herself against the cold, trembling)* Go away, goodbye; we're goin' over great here . . . Graham, Gaston, Berman, my agent, the madame and me. . . . *Silence. A gust of wind.*

ARTHUR, *gently:* Lady, I . . .

NANCY: You still here? *She remains seated with her back to him.*

ARTHUR: Listen, all those people . . . I want you to know something, they did a terrific job on ya. *Silence.* You really look . . . fine. Just fine. *Silence; he comes down the stairs, picks up his coat, stands behind her.* Here. You're shivering. Please take this. . . . *She does not respond; he drapes the coat very delicately over her shoulders.* When it gets windy you can put the hood up, O.K.? *She reaches behind her head, letting her longish hair fall outside the coat. He assists her carefully with a strand or two.* Very real; the hair. . . . *She continues to look the other way. He touches her shoulder gently:* I'm sorry that I upset you. You mustn't take it personally . . . Believe me, you're a pretty girl. You must be a pretty girl because I can't talk to you. I can't talk to you people . . . There's a special code. Some guys know the code. I don't know the code. . . . *Silence.* Please, give me your number. I'll call you. I'm terrific on the telephone. *No reply. He shrugs sadly, turns to leave.* I know I could have a great life if there was just some way to phone it all in. *Starts to walk slowly away.*

NANCY, *quietly:* The hair, y'know . . . the hair *is* real. *He stops, delighted to hear her voice.*

ARTHUR: I thought so. It had to be.

NANCY: It's just the color that was changed, see.

ARTHUR: Well, it's very suitable.

NANCY, *after a moment:* Thank you.

ARTHUR: I think it's *all* very suitable.

NANCY: Thank you. *After a moment:* It's just the nose, actually, that's not mine.

ARTHUR: Really? It certainly *looks* like—

NANCY: I know it's not mine because yesterday at Bloomingdale's I saw another girl with it. Dr. Graham, he does a certain style of nose and it turns out there's a goddamn *army* of us walking around New York with it. *They both laugh at this for a moment.*

ARTHUR: Coats . . . *(looks up at the sky)* Tall coats, you've got six of them . . .

NANCY: Yes, I—

ARTHUR: The old guy . . . the old guy, you said he was your father . . .

NANCY: I thought you didn't hear that.

ARTHUR: I didn't. I just heard it now. It takes about twenty

minutes for sound to reach me.... *She laughs, enjoying him.*
See what you're doing? You're listening. How do ya do that?
You even look like you're listening. That's the hard part. I gotta
work so hard on that part I can't hear a thing ... there's one
now ...
NANCY: What?
ARTHUR: A gap. And that's just the beginning, that was just a
little one—
NANCY: Hey, Arthur—
ARTHUR: Wait'll the big ones come, they can kill ya—
NANCY: Take it easy, we've got plenty to talk about—

YOU KNOW I CAN'T HEAR YOU
WHEN THE WATER'S RUNNING

by Robert Anderson

———————•———————

SCENE 2

Robert Anderson's comedy is a quartet of one-act plays, each
dealing with the topic of sex. The scene included here is from
"The Footsteps of the Dove."

The setting is the basement of a bedding store. George and
Harriet have come to pick out a new mattress. Harriet has decided she wants twin beds to replace the old double bed they
have used during the twenty-five years of their marriage.
George protests. As the salesman continues to explain his mer-
chandise to the couple, George tries to convince his wife of the
virtues of their old bed. The salesman, who has witnessed similar scenes before, discreetly leaves them alone for a while. In the

ensuing scene George and Harriet reveal the nature of their relationship and the state of their married life.

HARRIET, *turning on George:* You're drunk.

GEORGE: On two martinis at lunch? And you drank most of
the second one.

HARRIET: Yes, to try to prevent something like this. Stop acting like a baby.

GEORGE: I am not acting like a baby.

HARRIET: Well, like a damned clown, then. We had this all
out, over and over again at home. We've discussed it for
months.

GEORGE: I've changed my mind.

HARRIET: It's too late to change your mind. My mind
is made up. My God, humiliating me here in front of that
man.

GEORGE: That man is of no importance to me. My marriage
and my sex life are.

HARRIET: Yes. The whole store heard about your sex life in
graphic detail. You painted me as a bitch who turns you down
all the time, and yourself as a man very unsure of his power.

GEORGE: I did not.

HARRIET: That's the way it sounded. When it wasn't sound-
ing like that, it was like babes in the woods, going to sleep
all wrapped around each other. *She sits on the foot of a single
bed.*

GEORGE: Well, that's the way we do it. You know damned
well you pull my left arm up over your shoulder like a blanket.
It's your damned night-night, and you couldn't sleep without it.
He demonstrates, sitting beside her.

HARRIET: Night-night or no night-night, I haven't slept
soundly in twenty years.

GEORGE: I'm fighting for our marriage, Harriet. You may not
think I'm serious about it, but I am. Nietzsche said the big cri-
ses in our lives do not come with the sound of thunder and
lightning, but softly like the footsteps of doves. That is not exact, but it is close enough.

HARRIET: Oh, honestly!

GEORGE: A man of forty-seven. It's a dangerous age. In a double bed he's got his wife there all the time, just the touch of her, the warmth, is exciting. After twenty-five years the image of the beloved wife is not always sexually stimulating in and of itself. But the touch always is.

HARRIET: The image of the beloved husband is not always so stimulating either.

GEORGE: I understand that. And I say we're taking a big chance. Across the room alone, a man could lie there night after night saying to himself . . . "Do I really feel like it? It's cold out there." And soon he just forgets about it more and more, and then that distance between them is like the Persian Gulf. And he finally decides he doesn't want to get his feet wet sloshing from bed to bed . . . and then they've had it. The family that lies together dies together.

HARRIET, *trying to reason with him, appealing:* George, we've discussed this.

GEORGE: We've also discussed divorce. . . . Three times. But when we came up to it, we couldn't do it. And I can't do this. *He gestures at the twin beds.*

HARRIET: Well, I've got to. My back. The doctor said. . . .

GEORGE: —That damned quack. *Our* doctor didn't say anything about it. But you trekked around to doctor after doctor till one told you . . . some faggot, no doubt . . . to get a single bed.

HARRIET: He's a perfectly good doctor.

GEORGE: He's a quack and a faggot who thinks it's disgusting for you to sleep with me anyway. What's he know about it? What are you going to do when you get up and go to the john?

HARRIET: Oh, for God's sake.

GEORGE: You know damned well you hurry back and snuggle up to me and say, "Oh, warm me up." You pull that old left arm over like a blanket. *He hugs her in demonstration.*

HARRIET: George, that was all lovely. I'm not regretting any of that. Only times change. People change.

GEORGE: People change, and *go* through changes. I know. And I'm trying to be sympathetic about that. I know right now you feel kind of . . . you want to be left alone. But, Harriet, that's temporary. I know.

HARRIET: How do you know and what?

GEORGE, *being very considerate and delicate:* A woman comes back later with fierce desires!

HARRIET, *amused:* Who told you that?

GEORGE: I read it. The *Ladies' Home Journal. (Defensively)* . . . I like to know. I like to be informed . . . what's going on inside your head. It's been very helpful to me on several occasions. "Can This Marriage Be Saved?"

HARRIET: —Now, George, please. Let's stick to facts. First, my back is breaking. Second, my nerves are shattered from sleeplessness. Third, you are a morning person, and I am a night person. I like to read in bed and sleep late. You like to go right to sleep and get up early. For twenty years I have turned out the light for you, and. . . . Oh, this is nonsense. We've been over it all. *She rises and goes to the single beds.*

GEORGE: What about a queen size or a king size?

HARRIET: We've discussed that. It won't fit in the bedroom. A fifty-four or twins along each wall is all that will fit.

GEORGE: Under the windows?

HARRIET: And drafts blowing down our necks?

GEORGE: Then let's sell the house.

HARRIET: Stop being ridiculous.

GEORGE: The house is meant to serve *our* purposes, not the other way around. That damned house. I've been breaking my ass to support it, and now it's going to separate me from my wife . . . I want a divorce!

HARRIET: All right.

GEORGE: You don't care. You don't take me seriously.

HARRIET: You have a right to say "I want a divorce" three times a day. I have a right not to take you seriously. Besides, you keep looking at it from your point of view. . . . Old cuddly bears under a quilt . . . a couple of soup spoons nestled in a drawer . . . old night-night. A very romantic picture. Old everready. . . . Subconsciously I may be rebelling against that. I may want the space so that you'll have to make the effort, wade across the Persian Gulf. Get your feet wet. . . . Not just suddenly decide you might as well since you hardly have to move to get it.

GEORGE: That's damned unfair. I have never taken you for granted. I have scrupulously concerned myself with your moods and preferences and responses . . . I could have been like some husbands who just use their wives ... bang-bang! Thanks for the use of the hall. That's what some husbands do, in case you're interested.

HARRIET: Not in our cultural and educational bracket. I've read the articles too ... so stop congratulating yourself.

GEORGE: You sound as though you'd had a miserable time.

HARRIET: I haven't, and you know it. Now stop acting like a martyr.

GEORGE: A martyr ... a baby ... a clown. ... It's lucky I have a fairly firm image of myself. It will be a miracle now if I can function at all.

HARRIET: Really. ...

GEORGE: Lying in a single bed ... with seven feet between us. How do I feel tonight? She's lying there thinking of me as a baby, a clown, a martyr ... and I've never given her anything more than every other man in my cultural and educational bracket gives his wife. ... Better not risk it.

HARRIET: Please decide what firmness of mattress you want. Because I would like to order and get this over with and get back to our right minds.

GEORGE: What happens six months from now when you return to combat with fierce desires? But I'm over the hill from disuse. Muscles atrophy, you know.

HARRIET: People will hear you.

GEORGE: I want people to hear me. Specifically, you!

HARRIET: I hear you.

GEORGE: You hear me, but you're not listening.

HARRIET, *low:* We'll get the thirty-nine-inch width. If you insist, we'll start the nights wrapped around each other ... and then when you've decided what's playing or *not* playing that night, you can either stay for a while or go back to your own bed.

GEORGE: I get the cold bed!

HARRIET: *I'll* go to the other bed. My God!

GEORGE: How long do I get to make up my mind each night? Do we set an oven timer?

HARRIET: Now, I'm going to look at headboards. You decide on the firmness you want for your mattress. *She moves toward another showroom.*

GEORGE: I warn you, Harriet. We are at the Rubicon.
HARRIET: I thought it was the Persian Gulf.
GEORGE: I can hear the doves!

DAYS OF WINE AND ROSES

by JP Miller

————————•————————

ACT III

Joe Clay is working in the fast-moving and hard-drinking world of Madison Avenue when he meets Kirsten Arnesen. They fall in love and marry. Both have found in each other the perfect drinking companion, and soon their increasing drinking habits become a serious problem for them. Before they can admit to themselves that they are alcoholics, Joe's career collapses, their marriage fails, and they lose the respect of friends and family. In the midst of this deteriorating situation Joe finds the courage and strength to try again—without alcohol and with the help of Alcoholics Anonymous. But Kirsten cannot stop drinking despite Joe's help and encouragement. He realizes the only way he can conquer his alcoholism is by separating from her.

In this final scene of the play Kirsten returns to beg Joe to take her back. Their daughter, Debbie, is asleep in the bedroom.

JOE: Kirs . . . *She smiles wanly, he motions her in. She enters, unable to disguise the slight sag of her shoulders and the hint of shuffle in her walk.*
KIRSTEN, *looking about her furtively:* Debbie asleep?
JOE, *nodding:* It's after eleven.
KIRSTEN: I didn't want her to see me.
JOE: You don't look— *(he stops himself)*
KIRSTEN: So bad? Not as bad as you imagined I would.

Thanks for trying. But I know how I look. This is the way I look when I'm sober. That's enough to make a person drink, wouldn't you say? *Joe answers her little joke with a smile.* Joe—I haven't had a drink in two days.

JOE: Well, that's—that's terrific.

KIRSTEN: It wasn't easy. But—I wanted to talk to you, so I thought I would try to make myself deserve it, at least a little. Sort of a penance, you might say.

JOE: You'd be surprised how much fun you can have sober, once you get the hang of it.

KIRSTEN: And you've got the hang of it.

JOE: I think so. And believe me, it's the greatest. *She turns away, barely able to keep herself in check.*

KIRSTEN: I want to come home.

JOE, *finally:* It's been a long road, a lot of detours. I can forgive you, I can try to help you, but I don't know if I can take you back. I don't know if I can forget enough. I thought I could, but now I don't know.

KIRSTEN: You're talking about them. Yes, there were plenty of them. But they were nothing. I never looked at them. They had no identity. I never gave anything out of myself to them. I thought they would keep me from being so lonely, but I was just as lonely, because love is the only thing that can keep you from being lonely, and I didn't have that.

JOE: I'm listening, Kirs. *Points left:* There's a little kid in there asleep who sure would like to wake up and find you here, so all you have to do is say the right words.

KIRSTEN: I don't know if I have the right words. That's why it took me so long to get here. You see—the world looks dirty to me when I'm not drinking—like the water in the Hudson when you look too close. I don't think I can ever stop drinking, Joe—not completely, like you, I couldn't.

JOE: You could—

KIRSTEN: —if I wanted to, really wanted to. But I don't. I know that now. I want things to look prettier than they are. But I could control it if I had you to help me. I know I could. I know I could be all right if we were back together again and things were like they used to be and I wasn't so nervous. But I need to be loved. I get so lonely from not being loved, I can't stand it.

JOE: I want to love you, Kirs, but I'm afraid of you. I'm an alcoholic. I can't take a drink. But I'm afraid of what we do to each other. If you'd only say you'd try—

KIRSTEN: I know this sounds crazy but—I can't face the idea of never having another drink.

JOE: One day at a time. One day at a time.

KIRSTEN, *overlapping:* I can't. I can't.

JOE: Doesn't it impress you at all that I've been sober for almost a year, that I'm delighted to be this way, that I'm working steady and feeling great, that Debbie and I are moving out of this dump into a decent place? And all because I'm sober.

KIRSTEN: You're strong, Joe. That's why I know you can help me now. If we only had it back like it was—

JOE, *too loud:* Back like it—! *He stops himself, remembering Debbie. Then he continues in a low voice:* Do you remember how it really was, Kirs? It was you and me and booze. A threesome. A threesome! Remember? Oh, it was great while it lasted, don't get me wrong—

KIRSTEN, *pathetically eager:* And we can have it back that way! I know we can! If—

JOE: If I'd drink with you! Right? But I'm not going to drink with you! That's finished!

KIRSTEN: I wouldn't ask you to drink with me. I'd control myself—

JOE: You can't control yourself! You're an alcoholic, same as I am!

KIRSTEN: No!

JOE: You and I were a couple of drunks on a sea of booze in a leaky boat! And it sank! But I've got hold of something to keep me from going under, and I'm not going to let go, not for you, not for anybody. If you want to grab on, grab on, but there's only room for you and me. No threesome. *She turns away abruptly with a kind of desperate anguish, crosses to the "door" and opens it. Then she stops, as though staring out at the world, struggling with herself.*

KIRSTEN, *finally:* I can't get over how dirty everything looks.

JOE: Try it one more day.

KIRSTEN, *turns to face him, hopeless, dead voiced:* Why?

JOE, *motioning left toward Debbie's room:* For her.

KIRSTEN: I'm afraid I'm not that unselfish. You'd better give up on me, Joe.

JOE: Not quite yet.
KIRSTEN, *after a moment:* Thanks. Good night. *She turns quickly and starts through the door.*
JOE: Kirs— *(she stops)* Take care of yourself. *She nods, goes quickly through the "door" and disappears off right. Joe stares after her. For a moment or two it looks as though he is going to call her back. He takes two or three strides toward the door, then stops, holding himself precariously in check. He stands this way for several seconds, rigid, trembling, grimly fighting for the biggest victory of his life. Then, praying:* God—grant me the serenity to accept the things I cannot change. *Lights fade slowly to black.*

DID YOU EVER GO TO P.S. 43?

by Michael Schulman

———•———

This one act play depicts a very unlikely romance emerging from a very inauspicious first encounter in Central Park, New York City. ("P.S." refers to "Public School" in the New York City school system.)

A bench in Central Park, New York City, late afternoon in mid-autumn. She is sitting, reading an abnormal-psychology book, not pleased with what she is discovering. He enters. He is clearly upset. As He walks he gazes toward the horizon, apparently looking for something or someone. He is dressed in a suit and tie, but is somewhat disheveled now. He spots her on the bench. He is very interested—even excited. He seems to recognize her—perhaps, perhaps not. She becomes aware that she is being stared at. She turns away, hoping He will go away. He moves in on her.

HE: Hey, did you ever go to P.S. 43?
SHE, No.
HE: Damn, I thought you might have.
SHE: No.

HE: Are you from Crotona Avenue?

SHE: No. I'm sorry, you must . . .

HE: The Bronx?

SHE: No. Look, I'm trying to read this . . .

HE: Goddamn it! *Cries out:* Did anyone around here go to P.S. 43? *To an off-stage person in the direction of the audience:* Hey, did you go to P.S. 43? Yeah, well fuck you too. *To She as she starts to get up:* No, don't go. You can stay. I'm not crazy. Really, I'm not.

SHE: I have to go.

HE: Look, you can stay. I'm not crazy. I won't hurt you. I'm just upset.

SHE: I really have to . . . *(As she picks up her briefcase all her books and papers fall out.)*

HE: Please, I'm sorry. *He tries to help her pick up her belongings.* Look, I'm upset, that's all. I'm just . . . I'm just looking for my past.

SHE: Oh my, that sounds awfully poetic. Are you a poet?

HE, *missing her sarcasm:* Well, no, I . . .

SHE: God!

HE, *defeated:* Shit! I'm desperate and you throw some sarcastic crap at me. *Slumps onto bench.*

SHE: I throw crap at you? I'm sitting here reading a book and you come around . . . First I just think you're on the make with that line, Did you ever go to P.S. whatever it was . . .

HE: Forty-three.

SHE: But then I see you're just another nut in the park. Well I am up to my esophagus with nuts in the park. *She decides to sit to defend her territory.* Twice a week I come here after work and I have just one hour to calm myself before going to the shrink. All I want to do is read my book and relax so I can make a good appearance. And every goddamn time either some creep tries to pick me up with some stupid line like didn't you go to P.S. something or other . . .

HE: Forty-three . . . but I . . .

SHE: Or else some nut comes over with some kind of bullshit trying to get a rise out of me. On Monday it was a big guy with a suitcase and a Texas accent who asks me if I want to see his large snake. I figured it's just some creep who on his first day in town wants to give a city girl a thrill by pulling his pants down in front of her. But I'm not so lucky. No, this is a super creep who is not into euphemisms. This nut opens his suitcase, pulls out a boa constrictor, and puts it right down in my lap. Dolores is friendly, he says. She only wants to hug, he says. Crazies! Nuts!

HE: Wait a minute, I just ...

SHE: Oh, last Friday it was a baldheaded fag who wanted to show off his new dentures to me. *This* creep kept taking his teeth out of his mouth and snapping them in my face. In his mouth; in my face. Then this prunefaced queen asks me if I think the pretty young boys will like him better if he takes his teeth out of his mouth when he gives them ... Ech! I don't even want to think about it. Crazies! Creeps! They all come to the park, and they all come to my bench.

HE: Miss, I'm not ...

SHE: No! I walked away from that Texas boa constrictor and I walked away from those snapping teeth—I walked away from all of them—but mister, I have had it. Maybe your craziness, objectively speaking, is not as bad as some of those others, but mister, unfortunately for you, today you are the straw and I am the camel. Now you creeps have your problems and I have mine, and mine right now is to stay very, very, very, calm, so if you don't right now, immediately, this very instant—fuck off— right now, immediately, and get your creepiness away from my bench, I am going to scream so loud it will ... *(the intensity of her "fuck off" has lifted him off the bench)*

HE: Look, I'm sorry. I only wanted to ... *(he tries to move in to explain)*

SHE: Don't sit down. Get away from my bench. Get away!

HE: I ...

SHE: Get away. Get away. *Takes breath to scream.*

HE: I'm going ... Please ... I'm sorry. *She takes breath again.* I'm going, I'm going. *He runs off. She is quite pleased with herself. She sits on the bench, opens her briefcase and takes out the book* On Aggression. *She resumes reading, trying to relax. Shortly, she finds something discomforting in the text. He reenters from behind her; carefully, desperately, He sneaks up on her and covers her mouth with his hand.* Don't scream. Please. Don't scream. I'm not going to hurt you. Please. I couldn't just leave with you thinking I was that kind of person, some maniac who comes to the park to frighten people. *She struggles to get loose; tries to hit him with book.* I'm not a nut. I'm not a creep.

I'm sane. There's nobody saner. No boa constrictor. My teeth don't come out. I'm . . . I'm a . . . regular person . . . You know . . . People like me. Animals like me. I'm a member of the Humane Society . . . I . . . I don't know what to say. I read books too. I . . . uh . . . I keep my apartment neat . . . You know, I'm regular. *She starts to laugh.* I have a regular job, a good job. I run a private school. I make a lot of money. *She bites him hard, still laughing.* Ow! *He lets go.* Damn. Oh God, what are you, crazy? You're crazy. What are you laughing at?

SHE, *laughing all the way through:* I'm sorry, but that was so funny . . . I keep my apartment neat? . . . Did I hurt you?

HE: Yes, you did.

SHE, *laughing:* I'm sorry . . . so funny . . . I'm a member of the Humane Society . . .

HE, *takes out wallet; angry:* It's true. I am. Here, look. *Shows her card.* And I do run a school, and I do make a lot of money. *Shows her money. . . .* Would you stop laughing.

SHE, *laughing:* I can't. Once I start, sometimes I just can't . . .

HE: Look, I was just trying to explain to you . . . Big joke, huh? You know, you ought to tell your shrink that you're not a very sensitive person.

SHE, *laughing:* I am, I am. Look, my eyes are tearing. *She finds this very funny. At times she tries to stop laughing, but it bursts out of her.*

HE: You are something. Go on, laugh. I hope you swallow your tongue . . . You know, you're the one who is crazy . . . You've probably given me rabies . . . *He shows her his hand, then suddenly realizes what he has done and is very embarrassed. He backs away, but is too embarrassed to leave.* Oh my God. That was the dumbest thing I have ever done. I can't believe I grabbed you like that. I just can't believe it. I guess I really made a fool of myself.

SHE: Yes, you did . . . No, no, it's okay. How else could you explain yourself. I mean, what would I say if I tried to let a stranger I was choking in the park know that I wasn't crazy. That's really a hard one. The only things that come to my mind are that I study yoga—that's sane, isn't it? And . . . and I read the *Times* . . . and I don't know what else I would say.

HE: Well, don't forget you go to a therapist twice a week.

SHE, *suddenly very upset, as if she is jolted back to reality:* Oh, yeah, that sounds supersane, doesn't it?

HE, *not quite sure why she has become upset. He sits . . . carefully:* Well, I mean, that at least shows that you're working on your problems.

SHE, *tries to pull herself together; takes out her compact and applies powder:* Please, don't remind me. Don't take this personally, but these afternoons in the park are destroying my therapy. In my hour from five to six he only hears about my adventures in the park from four to five. I'm sure Dr. Monska—that's my therapist—thinks I'm insane. I try so hard to show him how calm and normal I am, but something always comes along and messes it up. You know, it's pretty disgraceful when your own therapist thinks you're crazy.

HE: But isn't that why you go to a . . . Hey, I know it's not usually done, but if you want I can go with you today and swear to him it was all my fault.

SHE: Thanks, but no. They don't allow you witnesses for the defense. Never. Whatever happens, they always find you guilty . . . Hey. *She has thought of something delightful.* Hey! Come to think of it, you have already done me an enormous favor.

HE: After the series of miseries I just put you through, I can't imagine what.

SHE: It's wonderful! For eight months Dr. Monska has been trying to get me to show my anger, and now I can finally tell him that I did it; that between four and five o'clock today during my adventures in the park, I did it. I let it all out—thanks to you.

HE, *trying to be ingratiating:* Anytime, anytime, but I'm not sure whether to congratulate you or to start mourning for your enemies. You were pretty vicious.

SHE, *delighted with herself:* Yeah. It really felt good. You were actually scared, weren't you? You really looked scared when you thought I was going to scream.

HE, *pointing to his hand:* My only mistake was that when you opened your mouth like that I didn't notice how sharp your teeth were.

SHE, *ignoring him; self-possessed with her newly discovered strength:* You know, I've never scared anybody before. I think I could have, and I think sometimes I would even begin to scare somebody; but then I'd feel . . . oh, I don't know, I guess guilty . . . like it's not right to show someone you're stronger than they are—emotionally stronger—because it might hurt their feelings, especially a man's. But you got me so pissed, I just didn't give a damn.

HE, *has had enough; starts to walk away:* Yeah, well, I'm happy to have helped you on your climb toward meanness. You keep at it and I'm sure you'll be king of the park soon. Sorry to have bothered you . . .

SHE, *realizing he is hurt, goes after him:* No, don't take it that way. Sometimes I just talk too much. That's another one of my problems.

HE: Well, that's really tough, but one cure a day is all I'm good for. See you around . . .

SHE: Wait. Please. It's just that you happened to come along after all those other guys, and actually it was just what I needed to finally rescue me from my guilt. You did me a big favor . . . I'm serious . . . Really . . . Really. *For the first time each notices that the other is quite attractive.*

HE: Okay.

SHE: Okay . . . How's your hand?

HE: It's okay . . . *A flirtation begins:* Those are some teeth marks. Are you a vampire?

SHE: Oh, wow. Come here. I have some hand cream. I'm really sorry. *She applies cream.* Maybe I should have stuck with my guilt.

HE: No. *Mock poetic:* The pains of the flesh are no match for the pains of the spirit . . . You missed a spot.

SHE: Oh.

HE, *gives her other hand:* Try this hand.

SHE: You're silly.

HE: No, it's having sympathy pains. It's a neurological phenomenon. You know, the sympathetic nervous system.

SHE: Come on.

HE: What did you expect from a crazy nut in the park, huh? *He likes her.*

SHE: Well . . . something different. *She likes him.* I guess since we're holding hands I should know your name. It's only proper.

HE: Jerry.

SHE: Jerry, thank you for ridding me of my guilt. *She shakes his right hand, the one she bit. He grimaces.* Oh, sorry. I feel so good. If I had my box of gold stars . . . Oops, I guess that's a giveaway.

HE: What?

SHE: That I'm a school teacher. Anyway, if I had a gold star, I'd pin it on you.

HE: Some gilt for some guilt? *Very proud of this.*

SHE: Some gilt ... for ... some guilt? Huh? Oh, I get it ... Gilt, guilt. Gold is gilt and you get some gilt for helping me to get rid of my guilt ... Jerry, I know you're going to think I'm insensitive again, but I hope you don't use puns like that when you write your poems.

HE: You are not only insensitive to people, but you are also obviously insensitive to art. I thought that was pretty good.

SHE: Well ... *They look into each other's eyes and stop for a moment.*

HE: Nice eyes ... *A bit embarrassed; recovering:* Actually, I don't write poems. I wasn't kidding before when I said I run a private school. The Hanley School on West Seventy-ninth Street. I'm the director.

SHE: That sounds like it's a long way from P.S. ... forty ... ?

HE: It was forty-three.

SHE: Yes, forty-three.

HE: And it was a long way away and a long way back, if I'm not being too poetic again.

SHE: What were you after before? Did you really think that you remembered me from there?

HE: Yeah ... *Something quickly changes in Jerry. His troubled state from the beginning of the play is becoming visible again.* Well, no, not exactly. I'm not sure. I thought you might have looked familiar. No ... I just thought ... maybe ... I don't know. *Tries to recover his composure:* Forget it. It's over.

SHE: I don't understand. We're friends, right? You choked me; I bit you. So you can tell me anything.

HE: Forget it. It was a mistake. You're one up on me. I bet you have a name, too.

SHE: What's happening? Why are you getting upset?

HE: I'm not getting upset. Don't start turning sensitive on me now. Forget it. *Checking his pockets:* Do you have a pen?

SHE: Come on, Jerry. Something is obviously wrong. You don't seem like the kind of guy that ordinarily screams out in the park like that. Everybody knows that guys with neat apartments who belong to the Humane Society don't do that sort of thing. Come on. I'm serious. Maybe I shouldn't pry, but ...

HE: No. It's nothing. It's ... *He is bothered by something he* *doesn't quite understand.*

SHE: What?

HE: It's really nothing ... it's ... just ... lately ... I've been thinking a lot about when I was a kid ... and sometimes I think I see someone I remember. I think I recognize someone, that's all.

SHE: But can't you ...

HE: Actually, it's more like I've been looking for someone from when I was a kid. Yes, It's more like looking for someone than actually recognizing someone. *He is getting caught up in some kind of inner turmoil.*

SHE: Is it someone ...

HE: Actually ... it's kind of hard to describe, but there was a feeling I had then, a special kind of feeling ... it's hard to describe ... a feeling ... that I seem to be missing now. I don't know why.

SHE: Do you think ...

HE: Actually, everything is really going very well. I took over this school recently, and it's been very successful, and I like what I'm doing. I'm my own boss, and I really like working with kids, and with the teachers and parents. It's very interesting, really, and I'm good at it. The school has been very successful and I feel I'm pretty well liked. The kids seem to like me, and my teachers seem to like me. I mean everything is really okay.

SHE: Well, have you ever ...

HE: Actually, I really haven't been thinking that much about when I was a kid. *Making discoveries as he goes along:* No ... at least not in general ... Actually, I've been thinking a lot ... kind of imagining ... reliving in a way, one particular time. Actually, it was a basketball game when I was in the ninth grade. I used to play a lot of basketball when I was a kid and I was pretty good. Actually, I was very good. Toward the end of the ninth grade we had a basketball all-star game. You see, it was a junior high school and we were the seniors. The best players in the school were divided into two teams and the whole school came to watch: friends, teachers, parents—even the man from the candy store came. It was a big event ... and I could do no wrong. I mean I scored more than anybody else. I got the most rebounds, the most assists. *Remembering a special moment:* I could dribble the ball well ... with my left hand too ... I used to practice for hours with my left hand. Towards the end of the

game I froze the ball for four minutes by myself. I just kept
dribbling and dribbling and dribbling and nobody could get the
ball away from me. And then, with six seconds left I hit a jumpshot from the corner and we won by five points. It's strange
how I remember that jumpshot. I remember it, somehow, in my
muscles. It's as if I can still feel it . . . some kind of muscular
image. I don't know if it makes sense to you—a junior high
school basketball game—but it was a fabulous moment. You
see, everybody was there, everybody saw it, everybody knew. I
played basketball a bit in college, and it was good. But when I
look back . . . my junior high school was in my neighborhood,
you see, and everybody knew. And it felt great. Somehow it's
different now. Now . . . well, now I feel . . . I guess I feel . . . dis-
connected? Anonymous? I don't know how else to put it. You
see, it's not that I don't have friends now. I do. I have good
friends, and I still get my share of cheers. You should hear the
parents tell me what wonderful things I'm doing for their kids;
and I don't even need them to tell me. I know what I do. But
somehow it's not the same. I don't know, maybe it's that they're
not really connected to my life, they're not really important to
me—in a personal way, I mean. And with my friends, I guess
we just try to enjoy ourselves together. Oh, sometimes we get
serious and we help each other out sometimes, but still it's not
like it was then at that game when everybody was there. Everybody who was important to me saw it and shared it with me.
And now I wonder if I'm the only one who remembers. I wonder if that event has simply vanished, except for my own memory of it. Somehow, that's frightening. Maybe that's why lately
I've been thinking I recognize people who went to P.S. 43. I've
stopped a lot of people and asked if they went to P.S. 43, but I
haven't found anyone. For some reason I don't want that game
to have been forgotten. It's as if in some way if only one other
person remembers—if I can talk to one person who saw that
game—some meaning, some connection could be reestablished
. . . a kind of commemoration of something I'm afraid I'll never
really experience again. I need to find someone who remembers
that basketball game. *By now he is fully back in his earlier troubled state, gazing again toward the horizon.*
SHE: That's very sad.
HE, *shocked:* You bastard. You are the most sarcastic son of a
bitch I have ever . . .

SHE: No.

HE: I tell you—share with you—some of my deepest feelings ... and you make fun of me? You better get yourself a smarter therapist, sweetheart. You don't have any trouble with aggression—only you disguise it in bitchy, sarcastic remarks. *He starts to leave.*

SHE, *going after him:* No, I mean it. It's sad. I mean I really think what you're saying is sad. It really made me feel sad. I'm sorry it sounded sarcastic, but Dr. Monska says that that's another one of my problems, showing compassion. He says I can't show anger and I can't show love.

HE: Yeah, well, that doesn't leave much does it? Look it doesn't matter anyway. We just don't ...

SHE: No please, give me a chance. It's my problem ... Please ... Let me work on it. I do feel sad ... I do ... for you. *She starts to cry.* I do.

HE: Hey, don't. Please don't.

SHE: No, let me. *Her crying is very full.*

HE: Come on.

SHE: It feels so good. Dr. Monska will be so proud.

HE: You don't have to ...

SHE, *an idea:* Hey, Jerry, would you do me a favor?

HE: What?

SHE: Would you let me watch you play basketball?

HE: What? You're kidding?

SHE: No. I'd really like to watch you play.

HE: Oh, that's ridiculous. I'd feel foolish.

SHE: Are you still good?

HE: Well, yeah, I'm still pretty good. I mean, I don't play much anymore. Sometimes I take jumpshots in front of the mirror, and I still look almost as good as Bob Cousy. You ever hear of Bob Cousy?

SHE: Sure I did ... sure.

HE: Cousy was the greatest. Cousy, Carl Braun, Max Zaslofsky, they were some players. And they weren't much bigger than me. It's a game for giants now.

SHE: Is there a basketball court around here?

HE: Yeah, there's one just over there.

SHE: Play for me, Jerry. I'll cheer and I'll clap. I always wanted to be a cheerleader. Play for me, please. I'm serious. For me, so I can tell Dr. Monska that I can show enthusiasm.

HE: It's ridiculous.

SHE: Please Jerry.

HE: Oh . . . I don't know . . . Okay.

SHE: Oh, great, great.

HE: When?

SHE: How about tomorrow, same time . . . *(suddenly remembering)* Oh my God, I better go or I'll be late. Do I look okay?

HE: Fine.

SHE: Not too frazzled?

HE: You're just fine. Be a little frazzled. You never know, he might like challenges in his work.

SHE: Yeah, maybe you're right . . . maybe you're right . . . Hey, you're not a fag are you?

HE: No!

SHE: Didn't think so . . . Tomorrow?

HE: Yes.

SHE: Do you have a basketball?

HE: Yes.

SHE: Okay—see you tomorrow.

HE: Hey, what's your name?

SHE: Sheila. *Rushes off. He is delighted, but then . . .*

HE: Holy God . . . I must really be crazy. What did I do? Play for her? I can't do . . . *About to call her back, then hesitates. He pantomines dribbling and a jumpshot. Shouts:* I'll see you tomorrow, Sheila. *Exits.*

THE ONLY GAME IN TOWN

by Frank D. Gilroy

———•———

ACT I, SCENE 5

Joe is a compulsive gambler (and inveterate joker) who plays the piano for a living in a Las Vegas nightclub. His goal is to save up $5,000 in order to move back to New York City. One night he meets Fran, a chorus girl, and goes home with her. Fran has been trying to end the unsatisfying ten-year-old involvement she has had with a married man. Her guarded nature and self-protective style do not make it easy for her to enter into a new relationship.

At the time of the following scene, Joe and Fran have known each other for a few days. A day earlier Joe won $8,000 in a casino, more than enough to set up his new life in New York; and last night, ready to bid a fond farewell to Las Vegas, he took Fran out on the town to celebrate. The scene takes place at 7:00 the next morning. Fran is alone in her apartment, still dressed from the night before. She is watching television, sitting "in an attitude of troubled preoccupation." There is a knock at the door. Joe enters, "a little drunk, a little disheveled, and totally spent." (The Harold C. Carver referred to is someone Joe met at the casino during his big win.)

JOE: Top of the morning. "Won't you come in?" "Don't mind if I do." *He enters; closes the door; regards her.* Okay, say it.
FRAN: What is there to say?
JOE: For openers you could call me a fool, a jackass, a moron, an idiot.
FRAN: Would that make you feel better?
JOE: A little.
FRAN: All right: You're a fool, a moron, a weakling, a baby.
JOE: Stick to the script.
FRAN: I thought you wanted to be punished.
JOE: I think I'm in the wrong apartment.
FRAN: So do I.
JOE: So much for small talk—can you lend me twenty bucks?
FRAN, *shocked:* You lost it *all?*
JOE: Every farthing—every sou.
FRAN: You still had five thousand when I left.
JOE: Want to search me?
FRAN: How *could* you?
JOE: It was easy.
FRAN: *I've had enough jokes!*
JOE: Give me the twenty and I'll never darken your door again.

FRAN, *placing herself between him and the door, mimicking cruelly:* "I used to gamble a little. Haven't touched the stuff in months."

JOE: Do I get the twenty—yes or no?

FRAN: "As soon as I have five thousand I'm going to flee this cesspool."

JOE: I didn't come here for a lecture!

FRAN: Do I detect anger?

JOE: *Get out of my way or . . .*

FRAN: Or what?

JOE, *caving in:* Or you're going to see a grown man cry.

FRAN: I'd prefer that to jokes.

JOE, *close to tears, he turns away:* I had eight thousand dollars. Had it in my hand. Am I crazy—or what? *Slams the fist of one hand against the palm of the other.* God damn me! *God damn me!*

FRAN: I can't tell you how sorry I am.

JOE: Eight grand . . . *Eight thousand dollars.*

FRAN: How about a drink?

JOE: Got any hemlock?

FRAN: I'll see. *She prepares drinks.*

JOE: Did you know that Las Vegas has the highest suicide rate, per capita, in the country?

FRAN: I don't like that kind of talk—even kidding.

JOE: Who's kidding?

FRAN: Now look—

JOE: Relax. I don't have the guts. If I did, I wouldn't be here.

FRAN: Maybe you better stick to jokes. *She hands him his drink.*

JOE: All I needed was *five* thousand—and I had *eight.*

FRAN: Shut up and drink your whiskey.

JOE, *raising his glass:* To Harold C. Carver—may he rot in hell. *He drinks.* All I needed was *five*—and I had *eight.*

FRAN: Why do you need *anything?* Why can't you just leave?

JOE: You have to be in New York six months to get your eight-o-two card. Until you get it, you can only work one nighters.

FRAN: You need five thousand dollars to live six months?

JOE: I'm a big tipper.

FRAN: That's two hundred dollars a week.

JOE: *I'm not in the mood for an economics lesson.*

FRAN: Sorry.

JOE: Speaking of economics—do I get the twenty?

FRAN: No.

JOE: Why not?

FRAN: You'd go to the nearest casino and blow it.

JOE: You've got it all figured out.

FRAN: Well, wouldn't you?

JOE, *drains his drink:* Thanks for the use of the hall. *Starts out.*

FRAN: Hey . . . You're welcome to spend the night.

JOE: Is that an indecent proposal—or pity?

FRAN: Pity.

JOE: In that case—I accept. The fact is I'm not up to the other.

FRAN: How would you like a warm bath?

JOE: I wouldn't.

FRAN: It'll relax you.

JOE: I don't want to relax.

FRAN: I'll scrub your back.

JOE: I don't want my back scrubbed.

FRAN: Get undressed. I'll run the water. *She exits into the bathroom.*

We hear the sound of running water.

JOE: Five grand—and I had eight . . . Five, and I had eight. *He breaks down; cups his head in his hands.*

FRAN, *returning:* The bath will be ready in a—*(she sees him; stops; goes to him; puts her arms about him)* You'll be all right.

JOE: How could I do it? . . . How?

FRAN: Tomorrow it will hurt less. The next day, a little less. The next day, still less . . . You'll see . . . Come now—take your bath.

THE SUBJECT WAS ROSES

by Frank D. Gilroy

———————————•———————————

ACT I, SCENE 3

Timmy Cleary comes back from World War II (to the New York apartment of his parents) an independent and self-assured young man. His arrival is greeted joyfully by his parents, John and Nettie. But soon it becomes clear that his presence only exacerbates the friction and frustration that have come to dominate their interaction. The failure of their marriage quickly infects each parent's attempt to get close to Timmy, and soon he decides to leave home and make his way on his own.

Prior to the following scene, the family went out for a night on the town. John and Timmy came back tipsy and playful and John began reminiscing about his courtship of Nettie—the first dance, the early romance. But Nettie, in no mood for either playfulness or amorous recollections, sends Timmy off to bed. Before putting herself to bed she takes care of the roses that were given to her earlier in the day (she believes by John, but they actually were sent by Timmy). John's amorous mood quickly incites an ugly scene of sexual advances and rejections. (The Ruskin mentioned by Nettie is a business associate of John's.)

NETTIE: Home two days and both nights to bed like that.
JOHN: He's entitled. You should hear some of the things he's been through. They overran one of those concentration camps—
NETTIE: —I don't want to hear about it now.
JOHN, *crosses to her left:* You're right. It's no way to end a happy evening.
NETTIE: I think we have some aspirin in the kitchen. *She moves into the kitchen. He follows; watches her take a bottle of aspirin from counter drawer.*

JOHN, *crossing to kitchen table:* You didn't say anything before about a headache.

NETTIE: I don't have a headache.

JOHN: Then what—

NETTIE: I read that if you put an aspirin in cut flowers they keep longer. *She drops an aspirin in the vase; regards the roses:* I wonder what made you get them?

JOHN: I don't know.

NETTIE: There must have been some reason. *Smells them.*

JOHN: I just thought it would be nice to do.

NETTIE, *she turns to him:* It was.

(They regard each other a moment.)

JOHN: I like your dress.

NETTIE, *crosses to counter with aspirin bottle:* You've seen it before.

JOHN, *crossing to above her:* It looks different. . . . Everything about you looks different.

NETTIE, *turns to him:* What mass are you going to?

JOHN: Ten o'clock.

NETTIE, *picking up the vase of roses and starting toward the living room:* I better set the alarm.

JOHN: Nettie? *She turns to him.* I had a good time tonight.

NETTIE: So did I. *Nettie enters the living room and places the roses on coffee table; arranges them.*

JOHN, *following her into the living room, to left of phone:* Did you really? Or were you putting it on for his sake?

NETTIE: I really did.

JOHN, *crosses to her right:* So did I.

NETTIE, *crosses to chair and picks up Timmy's jacket:* I'll set the alarm for nine-fifteen. *She starts away again.*

JOHN: Now that he's back we'll have lots of good times.

NETTIE, *she stops:* What's wrong between you and I has nothing to do with him.

JOHN, *crosses to her left:* I didn't say it did.

NETTIE: We have to solve our own problems.

JOHN, *crosses to her right:* Of course.

NETTIE: They can't be solved in one night.

JOHN, *takes jacket from her and puts it on chair:* I know.

NETTIE, *she crosses to center:* One nice evening doesn't make everything different.

JOHN, *crosses with her and puts his arm around her waist:* Did I say it did? *His lips brush the nape of her neck.*

NETTIE: I guess you don't understand.

JOHN, *kisses her neck:* I forgot how nice you smelled.

NETTIE: You'll spoil everything.

JOHN, *squeezes her waist:* I want things right between us.

NETTIE: You think this is going to make them right?

JOHN, *his hands moving to her breasts:* We have to start someplace.

NETTIE, *breaking away right:* Start?

JOHN: Bless us and save us.

NETTIE: *That's not my idea of a start.*

JOHN: Nettie, I want you . . . I want you like I never wanted anything in my life.

NETTIE, *covering her ears:* Stop.

JOHN, *crosses to her left:* Please?

NETTIE, *crosses to chair, picks up Timmy's jacket and crosses to left of couch:* You're drunk.

JOHN: *(turns left) Do you think I could ask again if I wasn't?*

NETTIE: I'm not one of your hotel-lobby whores.

JOHN: If you were I wouldn't have to ask.

NETTIE: A couple of drinks, a couple of jokes, and let's jump in bed.

JOHN: Maybe that's my mistake.

NETTIE: How do you suppose Ruskin managed without you today? *Crosses upstage.*

JOHN, *follows to her left:* Maybe you don't want to be asked! *He seizes her.*

NETTIE: Let me alone.

JOHN: *(as they struggle at couch) You've had the drinks! You've had the jokes!*

NETTIE: Stop! *She breaks free of him, regards him for a moment, then picks up the vase of roses and hurls them against the floor.*

AT HOME

by Conrad Bromberg

———————•———————

SCENE 1

This short play takes place in the New York apartment of Bob
and Nancy, a young couple who have been married for five
years. Bob is a struggling actor who has had "exactly four paying jobs in the last six years." Nancy is an assistant editor on a
trade journal. Bob is trying to memorize his part in an Off-Off
Broadway play. Nancy begins to help him. What starts out as
an innocent attempt on her part to clarify a section of the script
for him turns into a family spat about their sex life. From here
they move through a series of confrontations concerning their
true feelings about themselves and each other.

BOB: *practicing lines:* "Oh, really?" *Thinks of other character's
line, then:* "Why do you do that?" *Other's line.* "That's really
something." *Other's line, then he can't remember his response.*
"Uh. . . ." *Mutters other's line.* "That's very brave of you . . .
that's very brave of you . . . beg pardon?" *Consults script.* Is that
right? No! "What?" Of course, "what?" Not the hardest word
in the English language. "What?" *Reads other character's next
line, then reads:* "That's very brave of you." Hmmm. *He thinks,
then calls out to Nancy:* You about done?
NANCY: Be right there.
BOB, *to himself, musing over it:* "That's very brave of you." Je-
sus, avant-garde plays.
NANCY, *entering from kitchen:* What?
BOB: This play doesn't make much sense. *He hands her script.
She sits across from him on sofa.* Doesn't relate to anything. I
have to make up stories to justify every line.
NANCY: You wanted to do it.
BOB: To be doing something.
NANCY: It's good practice.

BOB: For what, "The World Cellar Theater Festival"? Jesus, I've been in more plays in more cellars and more lofts. Lofts and cellars. If I ever get a job in a real theater, I'll probably go down to the boiler room out of sheer habit.

NANCY, *pertly:* Don't worry, you'll get something soon. Where shall we start?

BOB: Page 15, from the top. *He rises.* The two guys are standing there after the booth light goes off, we do the thing about what I like to do, then I say, "What do you like to do?"

NANCY, *reads:* "Promise you won't tell?"

BOB, *looking out toward imaginary booth:* "Promise."

NANCY: "I like to pee in the middle of the bowl."

BOB, *paces a bit as he works:* "Oh, really?"

NANCY: "It sounds like a thousand waterfalls."

BOB: "Why do you do that?"

NANCY: "The danger. Someone might be listening."

BOB: Uh . . . "That's really something." *To her:* Is that right? *She nods.* "That's really something."

NANCY: "That's very brave of you."

BOB, *stops, thinks:* "What?"

NANCY: "Say it. That's very brave of you."

BOB: "That's very brave of you."

NANCY: "Louder."

BOB: "Louder . . . louder . . . do I say it again?" *She nods.* "That's very brave of you."

NANCY: "With gestures."

BOB, *gestures wildly:* "That's very brave of you!" *Flops his arms down.* Shit, I don't understand this at all. What does he want? Why am I doing this for him?

NANCY: Well, he's your boss, isn't he?

BOB: In the studio, yes.

NANCY: And he's insecure.

BOB: Yes, but what a ridiculous thing to applaud a man for peeing in the middle of the bowl.

NANCY: It's that kind of play, dear.

BOB: It's totally unbelievable. So unrelated to life.

NANCY: Oh, I don't know. It does strike a note.

BOB: Nancy, come on. Where did you ever hear two people talking like that?

NANCY: Maybe not like that, but . . .

BOB: Or even close to it.

NANCY: Well . . . *(suddenly remembers, in all innocence)* as a matter of fact I can think of something. You know when you and I make love? And you say to me, "Do you know what I'm doing to you?" Well, of course I know what you're doing to me, but you want me to say it, so I say it.

BOB: That's lovemaking. These two guys aren't making love.

NANCY: But it's the same thing is all I mean.

BOB: Not at all. The situation's different, the relationship is different. *Goes to her, takes script.* See here, when I say, "That's very brave of you"? The stage direction reads "uncomfortably," as if there's something holding me back, as if I don't want to say it. That's not the case with us. You love to say it. *She is silent. He waits for her to affirm what he's said.* Don't you?

NANCY, *a bit uncomfortable:* Well . . .

BOB: You always said you did.

NANCY, *trying to gracefully retract:* I love to please you.

BOB: No, you've said time and again that you love to talk dirty in sex.

NANCY: Well, I do . . . sometimes.

BOB: Sometimes? What about the other times?

NANCY: Well . . . look, Bob, it's not important. I only raised it to make a point about the play.

BOB: It is important. You're saying that for five years of a marriage, you've been doing something you don't like to do.

NANCY: I didn't say that.

BOB: You implied it.

NANCY: I only meant that I get pleasure from pleasing you.

BOB, *pained:* I thought it excited you. *She doesn't respond.* Didn't it? *No response.* It didn't.

NANCY: Not really. *He is crestfallen. She rushes in to retrieve the situation:* It's just that I'll be feeling something and thinking something, and then, when you ask the question, it sort of distracts me. It's like patting your head and rubbing your tummy at the same time. I was never very good at that. *She rises, goes and embraces him, fondly.* Bobby, it's not a big thing, really. Please, let's go on with the cueing. *He's not convinced.* I love making love with you. *She takes the script and returns to the sofa.* Shall we go back?

BOB, *muted thinking:* No let's go on.

NANCY: All right.

BOB, *she looks to him, waits. He flails his arms feebly as his character:* "How brave of you."

NANCY, *correcting him:* "That's very brave of you."

BOB, *repeats:* "That's very brave . . ." *Thinks.* I won't do it anymore.

NANCY: Do what?

BOB: Ask you that question in bed.

NANCY, *shyly:* It's all right if you do.

BOB: No, you should have your own pleasure undistracted by me. *Catches himself:* What am I saying? I'm the one you're making love with. What I mean is, I shouldn't impose on you something you don't like. Never again.

NANCY, *softly:* All right. *A moment of silence.*

BOB, *a bit concerned:* What'll I do instead?

NANCY, *shrugs:* Just make love.

BOB, *nonplussed:* Without talking? Just go at it in silence?

NANCY: What's wrong with that?

BOB: It's lonely.

NANCY: Well, we can say things like "Oh, Bob," "Oh, Nancy."

BOB: You never say, "Oh, Bob."

NANCY: But I will, if you like it.

BOB: I don't want you to say it, because I like it. That's the point of all this.

NANCY, *after a moment:* Why do you feel the need to talk at all?

BOB: I enjoy it. It's . . . ribald. It's festive. Like the guest and the hostess exchanging toasts. "Do you know what I'm doing to you?" "Yes, you're blah-blah-blah!" Cheers! *He looks at her. She is unconvinced.* I don't know why I like it. I guess to make some sort of contact. That's usually why people talk.

NANCY: But I'm there with you.

BOB: Yes, I guess I don't trust it enough. I look at you, and you seem to be into your own world. Not really with me.

NANCY: I'm with you. *Then quickly:* It's not a big problem. Let's do the lines. *She picks up script again.* All right, from the last "That's very brave of you."

BOB, *again the feeble flopping of arms:* "That's very brave of you."

NANCY: "Yes, I feel myself, strong, capable, defiant."

BOB, *by rote:* "Very good."

NANCY: "I assert my individuality."

BOB, *stops, shakes his head:* Gee, I really liked those lines.

NANCY: Which, these last?

BOB: No, "Do you know what I'm doing to you?" etc., etc. . . . Sorry, go ahead.

NANCY: Take it back. You say, "Very good."

BOB: "Very good."

NANCY: "I assert my individuality."

BOB: Uh, "You're quite an individual."

NANCY: "Louder."

BOB, *louder:* "You're quite an individual!"

NANCY: "With gestures!" *Bob stops, studies her, thinks.* What is it?

BOB: Do you think I'm insecure?

NANCY: No. Why?

BOB: Before, you described this character as insecure, because he had to have my character applaud him all the time. Do you think that's what my sex talk reflects?

NANCY: No!

BOB: But you said it. You related it to us.

NANCY: I was talking about the play. Only the play.

BOB: If the analogy fits, we have to wear it.

NANCY, *sighs:* Bob, you are not insecure.

BOB: Why not?

NANCY: Why *not*?

BOB: I have every reason to be.

NANCY: But you're not!

BOB: Wait. Listen to this. Pretend I'm speaking of a stranger. *He paces.* In his six-year career he's has exactly four paying jobs. In one he actually spoke the author's words. For the rest he did a variety of parts. Can you ever forget his performance as "Passerby"? Or his stirring portrayal of "Third Juror"? He is thirty years old (a moment of silence for that). Every other month he gets a check from his younger brother, the real estate whiz! And last but not least his monthly rent check is signed by his wife! In the face of all that why would this man not be insecure?! *She starts to respond, but he continues:* I'll tell you why! Because he runs! Winter and summer, fair and foul weather, he suits up and runs. He runs two miles a day. He regards it as *the* test of his character and strength. And every day he passes the test! That's why he's not insecure! Any man who can run two miles a day is not insecure! In the face of that why are you implying I am insecure?!

NANCY: I'm not! I don't understand why you're suddenly so defensive.

BOB: I'm not! I just want it clear that if there is a sex problem between us, it doesn't stem from my need for applause.

NANCY: I never said it did. I don't think there's any problem.

BOB: Right! Okay, let's go on. *She looks for place in the script, but he starts in again:* In fact, the more I think about it, there's nothing wrong with talking during sex. I mean outbursts, exclamations, things like that. What if, in the heat of it, I burst out "I love you!" What's wrong with that?

NANCY: Nothing!

BOB: Would it distract you?

NANCY: Well, no, of course not . . . not really.

BOB: Not *really*?

NANCY: Not at all.

BOB: Wait a minute. You said not really. Just exactly what are you thinking of when we make love?

NANCY: Nothing!

BOB: But before you said you were!

NANCY, *rises:* I don't like this conversation. It's silly and dangerous. Do you want to run lines or not?

BOB: I want to know your thoughts while in bed with me!

NANCY: I have none!

BOB: Nancy, I can tell when you're evading! I need to know for my peace of mind!

NANCY: It won't give you peace of mind! *It's out of the bag. Both stand there shocked at it in the air between them.*

BOB, *with dreadful quiet:* Tell me.

NANCY, *falls back on sofa:* Do you remember Youssef?

BOB: Your old boyfriend from college?

NANCY: Yes, from the Arab legation. Well, when we made love, which was only a few times, he did a certain thing for me. . . .

BOB: Which I do for you, too!

NANCY: I know! And every time you do it, it starts me thinking of Youssef!

BOB, *turns away:* Oh, shit!

NANCY, *goes to him:* It's terrible, I know. I didn't want to tell you.

BOB: I'm competing with the ghost of a talented Arabian!

NANCY, *with wholehearted honesty:* Oh, Bob, you're every bit as good as he was! Better!

BOB: Then why don't you think of me?

NANCY: I don't know! It's just that every time you start, there's Youssef! I've thought about it constantly! I'm just so guilty about it, I don't know what to do! But I can't stop it!

BOB, *sits, shakes his head:* Terrific. Five years of innocent pleasure gone, wiped out. Replaced by the leering smile of a Syrian economist.

NANCY, *drops to her knees beside him:* I'm sorry.

BOB: Don't be. I pursued it and I got it. *A silence.* Let's forget it. Let's do the lines. Where were we?

NANCY, *consults script:* "I assert my individuality."

BOB: Is that the line?

NANCY: What?

BOB: Is that the line or are you saying it?

NANCY: It's the line. I'll take it back further. "Yes, I feel myself, strong, capable, defiant."

BOB: "Very good." *He thinks.* About the sex thing. It's not a problem. Let's forget it.

THE TIGER

by Murray Schisgal

————————◆————————

Ben is a disgruntled New York City mailman who is outraged and feels victimized by the unfair "system" that forces him to carry mail for a living. In an attempt to assert his power he kidnaps a young suburban housewife while she is in town for her weekly bridge game. This is the beginning of a rather strange and humorous relationship between an initially unwilling woman and her seemingly ferocious abductor.

The scene that follows opens the play. It is a stormy night. Ben enters his basement apartment with Gloria thrown over his shoulder. His raincoat is over her head.

GLORIA, *muffled voice, kicking her legs:* For your own sake . . . Put me down. Put me down . . .

BEN, *carries her across to bed:* Stop it! Stop it! Do you think I'm playing games with you? Is that what you think? Ha! That's a laugh. This is strength you're feeling on your bones, lady, primitive, animal strength. There's no arguing with that. Oh, no. *Gloria is seated on edge of bed, Ben turns on lamp.* Now you stay there. Don't move. Don't budge an inch. I'll be right with you. In a minute . . . In a minute . . . *He runs to door, closes it, pulls curtains over small window above bureau. Gloria rises, moves blindly about the room. Ben grabs her, drags her to the wooden chair.* Come back. Come back here. *He ties her wrists behind the chair with the belt of his raincoat.*

GLORIA, *muffled voice:* What are you doing? Take this off. Please. I can't breathe under here, I can't . . .

BEN: Scream; scream all you want. You have my permission. It's not going to help you, though. Not here, it won't. We're quite alone. Quite, quite alone. No conditions. I insist on that. I don't accept conditions of any kind. That's a point for you to keep in mind. *She is tied to chair, he moves around to face her.* There: that's it. Each of us in his proper place. *Removes raincoat from her.* You like flirting, don't you, lady? Do anything for a good time. I had those propositions before. Don't make any mistake about that. *He takes towel from line, wipes his face.*

GLORIA: But I never flirted with you. I didn't. I swear, that's the truth. This is silly. Please, let me go.

BEN: Go? Let you go? After all that trouble of dragging you through those back alleys? After getting my new pants wet? Oh, no. Not a chance. Not tonight, lady. I've got something else in mind for you.

GLORIA: I don't know what you want; really, I don't. But I won't tell anyone anything. I promise. So far as I'm concerned none of this ever happened. I didn't see you. I kept my eyes closed. Look. They're still closed. I have no idea what you look like. Just let me go. Please, let me go . . . *(she sobs)*

BEN, *sits on steps, removes shoes, wet socks, takes pair of light blue socks from bureau, puts them on, shoes remain off:* Cry. Yes. Cry. Your tears are beautiful. I can watch you all night. It's as natural for you to cry as it is for the tiger to stalk its prey and gorge itself. Cry. Go ahead. Human history is filled with countless relevant examples.

GLORIA: Why did you take me? Why out of everybody did you have to take me?

BEN: Things are what they have to be, that's why they are. You don't get it, do you? I stood in the doorway of that decrepit stationery store for three hours, for more than three hours, who knows for how many. I let six, seven, eight of you go by, and then you came click-clacking along in those high-heeled shoes of yours, and I knew you were the one, it was you. At first I had a . . . a almost uncontrollable impulse to finish you off right there. Finish you off and be done with it. But when I touched you, when my fingers grabbed hold of you, a voice deep inside of me said, "No. Don't. Wait. Take her. Let it be something special . . . and sacred even. A ritual, a ritual of . . ."

GLORIA: You're not that inhuman.

BEN: That human! That human! *Hangs wet socks on line, in despair:* Nobody understands. Not even Schopenhauer or . . . or Nietzsche. They always have that carrot dangling in front of your nose. Be more than you are, be more than human, transcend, go above, beyond, up, up, up . . . *At blackboard.* But no! That isn't it. I say, be less than you are. To be what you are. *Draws a descending line.* Be less! less! less! than you are. *Erases blackboard.*

GLORIA: I can't talk to you. You're . . .

BEN: I'm what?

GLORIA: Nothing. Nothing.

BEN: Insane? Is that what you wanted to say? Insane? *Paces around her chair.* I hope so. Oh, God. I hope so. I am insane, right? You wanted to say it. I didn't tell you. I didn't influence that remark. But you knew; you sensed it. I agree with your judgment. Emphatically. You don't meet people like me every day, people with my ideas, with the courage of my convictions. I am insane, say it!

GLORIA: If you'd listen to me . . .

BEN: Not until I give you permission! Is that clear? Between us, between you and me, there's only one thing that counts. Power, strength, my physical superiority, this fist and this arm. Here, tonight, I say to you I am insane so that I can be human. You see how great it is? You see how everything falls into place? You don't understand anything, do you? Linguistic concepts are too much for your female birdbrain. But that's all right. You have other assets. You're nice to touch, I assume. You're soft. Your blood is warm and alive. *He tries to kiss her. She moves her head away. He presses his nose to her cheek.* Now? Do I end your miserable life now? Quickly and suddenly . . . *(looks about)* All right. All right. *Takes record out of album cover, puts it on phonograph: music, Tchaikovsky's Concerto No. 1.* We'll do it. You sit there. Right there. We'll do it now and we'll do it properly. With all the trimmings. With all . . . *(She turns her head back toward him. He kisses her, daintily, on the cheek, then shuts phonograph.)* That was a little better. Sometimes the tiger has to claw the tigress; then she understands what it's all about.

GLORIA: Let me tell you . . .

BEN: Did I give you permission to speak? Did I?

GLORIA: *May* I have your permission?

BEN: All right. You're learning. You can speak to me now if you wish.

GLORIA: I . . . I'm a married woman. I have been married for the last six years. My husband is an . . . honest hard-working man. We have our own home; it isn't fully paid. We're not what you'd call well-off by any means. We have two small children, two little girls. And you can ask anyone out on the Island where we . . .

BEN: Enough! Enough of that noise! I don't like babbling women. You can cry, but don't babble. Is that clear? Any woman who leaves her kids to go tramping around at night is a whore and she deserves, ipso facto, what she gets.

GLORIA: I wasn't . . .

BEN: What?

GLORIA: Can I please say something?

BEN: All right, now.

GLORIA: I wasn't tramping around all night. I wasn't. Every

Thursday . . . I belong to a bridge club and a few other girls whom I worked with when I was single . . . It all goes to charity!

BEN: Continue. I didn't say stop, did I?

GLORIA: It's only one night a week. I'm in every other night. I get out so little, that when I get the chance . . .

BEN, *stands behind her, strokes her hair, gently:* Your husband takes you out on Saturdays. All husbands take their wives out on Saturdays.

GLORIA: Not for some time now. I swear to you, that's the truth. He's so tired when the weekend comes and . . . It costs so much for a baby-sitter, even if you can get someone . . . reliable. Please, don't.

BEN, *facing her:* I want you to kiss me.

GLORIA: No, no . . .

BEN: I said I want you to kiss me.

GLORIA: I can't, please . . . *She lowers her head.*

BEN: Pick up your head! Pick it up! *She raises her head. Without kissing her:* I'll accept that for now. But you'd better learn and learn quickly. I'm not to be contradicted. Not in word, thought or deed. I'm all your world tonight. Remember that, lady.

GLORIA: I won't ask you to consider what you're doing for myself. It isn't myself I'm concerned with right now. But I do have a husband and a family. All of them will suffer. It's not only me. Why don't you consider them? Why don't you . . .

BEN: I didn't hear a word you said because . . . *(flaring petulantly)* because you didn't have my permission to speak! You can cry whenever you want, however. That much I allow you because you're a woman.

GLORIA: I'm not going to cry. There's no reason to cry. I believe that there's goodness in you. I can see it in your eyes. Isn't there someone whom you love very much?

BEN: Besides myself?

GLORIA: Besides yourself.

BEN: No one.

GLORIA: There must be someone. Your mother . . .

BEN: Don't make me laugh.

GLORIA: A wife? .

BEN: Do you think I'm that dumb?

GLORIA: Then friends. You must have had friends.
BEN: No one. No one. I have no one but myself and that's all
that counts. Me. Myself. The fulfillment of my own body and
my own primitive soul. Sometimes . . . Sometimes I walk along
the street at night and my feet, as I walk, my feet feel like large
soft paws, and the moon, the moon shining overhead, so brightly, so primeval, I want to raise my head and . . . and let loose
from inside of me some wild strange . . . a sound that hasn't
been heard for thousands of years, but it's inside of us, you see,
deep, deep inside of us . . . Tonight I don't have to hold anything in. Tonight I have you. To play with. To destroy. To do
whatever I want with. After that, I don't care. I want you to
kiss me. Now.
GLORIA: You're driving me out of my mind.
BEN: You don't want to? *She does, on his cheek.* Not good
enough!
GLORIA: Leave me alone, leave me alone . . .

LOU GEHRIG DID NOT
DIE OF CANCER

by Jason Miller

———————•———————

Barbara and Victor Spinilli are a suburban couple whose marriage is on the rocks. As she has become more involved in local
community theater, he has spent more time coaching his little-
league baseball team. After five years of marriage they have little in common.

The play opens with Barbara rehearsing for the opening that
night of *Hedda Gabler*, in which she stars. Her rehearsal was interrupted, first, by phone calls for Victor from angry parents
whose children are on the team, and then, by a visit from a parent who claimed her son didn't play often enough. Victor returns from a little-league game, buoyant after punching the

umpire. A frustrated athlete who now works for his family's company, Victor is still trying to win the love of his unyielding father.

In the scene below, Victor has just gotten off the phone after telling an irate father that his son belongs in dancing school and not on the baseball field. Barbara voices her displeasure at Victor's behavior, and during the argument that follows, both of them become aware of how little they respect each other's values.

BARBARA: You are hard to believe, Victor Spinilli. You're just too much.

VICTOR: Am I? Look, Greta, save the acting for the stage, all right?

BARBARA: I will, I certainly will. If you'll save your antics for the boxing ring.

VICTOR: Oh! Who called?

BARBARA: That moron Phil. The man is going to sue us, Victor.

VICTOR: Let him sue. Honey, I really laid one on that loud mouth. Bam! His ears almost fell off.

BARBARA: There are other ways of settling disputes than hitting someone in the mouth with a catcher's mitt.

VICTOR: What catcher's mitt? I hit him with my fist . . . this fist, closed just like this . . . and I hit him like so. *Slowly demonstrates on Barbara's chin.*

BARBARA: Really? Then Phil must have made a mistake because he said you hit him with a catcher's mitt.

VICTOR: Listen, sweetie, I don't need weapons.

BARBARA: Mrs. Martin must be mistaken too. She said you hit him with a catcher's mitt and she was there.

VICTOR: Who's Mrs. Martin?

BARBARA: Her son plays on your team. I believe he's the one who sits on the end of the bench alone.

VICTOR: Oh, Mary Jane . . . Mrs. Martin is Mary Jane's mother?

BARBARA: No, she's Jeffrey's mother. That boy adores you and you won't even give him the time of day. He's deeply hurt by all this juvenile name-calling. Mrs. Martin came here to talk to you about it. She's very upset.

VICTOR: You want to know the truth? I gave the kid a suit, right? A gift. Because he's so bad it's unbelievable, but I felt sorry for this skinny bloodless kid and I put him on the team. And I let him bat once, just once, the first game I let him bat and I thought that kid would pee all over home plate . . . one . . . two . . . three. He came back and sat at the end of the bench and that's where he's staying until the end of the season.

BARBARA: She's going to call you tomorrow; use a little tact when you talk to her, please.

VICTOR: I'll charm the pants right off her.

BARBARA: Figuratively speaking, of course.

VICTOR: Is there any other way?

BARBARA: Put a little juice in you and you're just a wit.

VICTOR: You know, I think I'll try out for one of your plays, I'd probably electrify everyone.

BARBARA: Well, Stephen was thinking of doing *The Hairy Ape.*

VICTOR: Is it a good role? Would I be the hero?

BARBARA: Victor, you wouldn't have to memorize a line. Just walk out there and burp and belch and scratch.

VICTOR: Forget it, I don't think I'd get along with that faggoty friend of yours.

BARBARA: Stephen is not a faggot. He's a gentleman and an excellent director.

VICTOR: He's also an excellent faggot.

BARBARA: Don't tell me I worked with the man for six months and . . .

VICTOR: I saw the guy for six minutes and I'm telling you he's sweet . . . come on, that tight-assed little walk, holding his cigarette like a baton, ascots, lisping . . . baby, he's three feet off the ground. Flies like a little birdie looking for a nest . . .

BARBARA: It's just so you, Victor, to mistake breeding and culture for something crude.

VICTOR: Fine. So he's read a few books. Went to N.Y.U. . . . uses hundred-dollar words. Fine. Live and let live, that's my philosophy. But I wouldn't take a shower with him, that's all I'm saying.

BARBARA: You're just jealous of him.

VICTOR: Jealous of him? Come on. Look . . . stop, look, listen. If he was Adam and you were ever Eve, you'd still be in the Garden of Eden, alone.

BARBARA: Why do you resent people with intelligence and ability and class? People who have exciting minds. People who can think and feel beyond all the rest of your ordinary, drab, beer-belly friends.

VICTOR: Because my beer-belly friends are not phony. They don't have fake smiles, fake laughs, fake words. And they don't wear pants five sizes too small. Does that answer your question?

BARBARA: I know what it is. I know why the people from the theater bother you so.

VICTOR: Oh yeah!

BARBARA: Because they make you feel stupid. They make you feel awkward and nervous and stupid. They make you feel just like that little Martin boy because you almost pee in your pants every time I have them over here.

VICTOR: Are you serious, come on.

BARBARA: It's true. Last week when the group was here and we were talking about books and Stephen asked you if you had ever read Proust and you said sure all the time, he was one of your favorite writers. Everybody just froze with embarrassment. Just absolutely went rigid with embarrassment, because they knew you never even heard of Proust let alone read him. God, it was humiliating.

VICTOR: I went to college. I know who Proust is, Proost, Prusti!

BARBARA: You graduated with a business degree from N.Y.U.! I don't call that going to college. And that even took you six years to get.

VICTOR: Well, that's just too Goddamn bad about you and your intellectual friends. Sitting around talking about Proust, drinking all my liquor, sitting around drinking all my booze and talking about . . . what's his name, the guy that ended up a drunk? You know they made a movie about him, the guy that . . .

BARBARA: F. Scott Fitzgerald had terrifying problems.

VICTOR: Sure he did and one of them was alcohol. And the other guy, the one who shot himself in the mouth with a shotgun . . . Hemingway. There you are sitting around for two hours talking about a drunk and a suicide. Talking like crazy, "Oh, he was marvelous." "What perception, what depth . . ." Depth? Ah fongo, depth! Those two guys couldn't even face life.

One drowns in scotch and the other scatters his brains all over the living room. So, what's all the cheering about?

BARBARA: Please don't use yourself as a model of life-facing, Victor.

VICTOR: I stare it right in the face, baby. I don't sit around talking about how other people face it because I face it every day of my life. I think my thoughts, I don't steal them from books. I don't pick dead men's brains for ideas so I can impress a bunch of people who aren't going to be impressed because they are too busy trying to impress me. You know what I noticed about your little sewing circle the other night? Everybody talked but nobody listened. Everybody sat around doing monologues and nobody gave a good Goddamn what anyone else was saying.

BARBARA: And you just sat back there like Buddha, like a big fat Buddha, silly grin and all, and said nothing.

VICTOR: Right.

BARBARA: Just like you sit back and say nothing every time your father comes to this house. *Pause.*

VICTOR: Let's leave my father out of this, Barbara.

BARBARA: No, let's not. Let's really clear the air. You can face anything, right. Old King Kong Spinilli can face a little thing like the truth. Do you know you are terrified of your father just as you are terrified of my friends? *Victor puts a Caruso record on the phonograph.*

VICTOR: You're going to say that once too often and I'm going to knock you right on your fat bitchy ass.

BARBARA: Do you have your catcher's mitt ready?

VICTOR: Keep it up, mouth! My relationship with my father is my business, not yours.

BARBARA: It's very much my business when he comes in here telling me how to run my house.

VICTOR: He tells you nothing. *Victor, during Barbara's speech, starts to sing in a mock-Caruso manner, very loudly.*

BARBARA: No? How come everytime he arrives here for his semimonthly visit he has the nerve to ask me if I'm pregnant. He doesn't ask anymore, he demands it. "Are you pregnant yet?" He gives me that Neanderthal look and I'm afraid to say no.

VICTOR: He wants a grandchild, so what?

BARBARA: He's got two from your sister and one from your brother. What does he want, an army of grandchildren?

VICTOR: He wants a boy . . . he wants the name continued . . . he's from the old country, all right?

BARBARA: He's from the old country, all right . . .

VICTOR: All right, you've said enough.

BARBARA: I just want to tell him we are living our lives separate from him. He is not going to terrorize me into having a child before I want one.

VICTOR: How can you have a child, Barbara, you've got a little piece of steel up there between your legs, remember?

BARBARA: Tell him then about the coil.

VICTOR: He wouldn't understand. He's old-fashioned about that.

BARBARA: Well, your father and I are going to come to an understanding. What's he going to do, stop his annual donation to us? Cut you out of your share of the company? Fire you?

VICTOR: He'd be very hurt.

BARBARA: He had the nerve to ask me to go to a specialist to see if I could make babies, make babies . . .

VICTOR: We've been married for five years, it's a legitimate question, for Christ's sake.

BARBARA: The man owns us.

VICTOR: I do a good job for him. We're paying our own way.

BARBARA, *quietly:* Victor, that is not true, not really.

VICTOR: Look, they've accepted my new advertising line, "Spinilli gives you the sauciest spaghetti." The old man was delighted with that line. We might even put it to music.

BARBARA: Accepting it and using it are two different things.

VICTOR: He'll use it, I know it.

BARBARA: He accepted "Spinilli, the sauce that made spaghetti famous," but did he use it? No! He used "Spinilli is spaghetti" instead, which was Bob's suggestion. But I tell everybody it was yours.

VICTOR: You don't have to do that.

BARBARA, *sad:* Victor, all you're doing is collecting your check every Friday.

VICTOR: I sold them on the idea of sponsoring the little-league team, didn't I? He bought the uniforms, jackets, everything.

BARBARA: Only because he loves baseball. He didn't even ask you about the team the last time he was here.

VICTOR: It bothers him because we're in last place.

BARBARA: Victor, this is insane, honey. I'd leave here tomorrow with you if you'd go back to the city and start with Harry again. Face the facts, Victor, here with your father's firm you will always be a lackey, the son of the boss.

VICTOR: I face the facts, but I am going to prove to the old man that I can carry the weight of my share of the company.

BARBARA: For God's sake. You've been trying to prove something to your father for the last thirty years. You thought he wanted you to be a baseball player. You tried it, you know what happened. He wanted you to be a doctor, you flunked out. You did everything he wanted you to and nothing you wanted. You keep telling yourself lies, pretending you're important to the company.

VICTOR: Let's not talk about lying to ourselves. Don't tell me about daydreams.

BARBARA: And what does that mean?

VICTOR: It means that this stupid community play acting has gone straight to your head. Dancing lessons on Thursday, speech lessons on Monday. And you're not going to New York with any faggot, to see any agent, about any commercials, understand?

BARBARA: That agent is coming to the show tonight, at Stephen's request, and if he likes my work, I'm going to New York and read for anything that might come up.

VICTOR: He's coming to see the play tonight, huh ... well, forget about New York, baby, wake up, because tonight the dream's over. Bye bye, big city.

BARBARA: You saw a dress rehearsal last week. Dress rehearsals are never very good.

VICTOR: Do you know that it was so rotten, everybody was so terrible that I almost puked? Everybody falling all over everybody else. The guy that plays your old lover or something opens the door and the Goddamn door falls down ... he's just standing there with a doorknob in his hand. The agent will die laughing.

BARBARA: If he doesn't die of laughter, if by some small miracle he wants to get me work, I am going to New York. Do you understand?

VICTOR: Hey, you know where your talent is? Your talent is in your boobs. Everybody goes to see your enormous boobs. I'm not kidding. Your boobs come on stage first, and then you follow. That should be your stage name, Barbara Boobs. Old Bullet Breasts.

BARBARA: Thank you for your confidence in me, Victor. But I'm still going to work in New York.

VICTOR: You better move out of my house then.

BARBARA: Whose house?

VICTOR: Mine, this house is mine. My house!

BARBARA: You know, this play acting started as just a simple diversion, an escape from all the sterility that surrounds me. Just a little exercise of female vanity, but now it's become all I have, it's become a necessity. And you're right, Victor, it's a daydream, but it's mine and nobody gave it to me and so I'm not afraid of anyone taking it away. And as things stand now, it may very well be the most important thing in my life.

VICTOR: I swear to you, if you go to New York, never come back to this house again.

BARBARA: I am through sitting with your father and you every third Thursday like clockwork, sitting in this living room, listening to the Goddamn grieving voice of Caruso for three hours. I am done inflicting that torture upon myself. And now I shall go upstairs and finish dressing for the theater. *She exits. Phone rings. He answers.*

VICTOR: What! . . . Hello, Phil . . . yeah . . . look, Phil, nobody calls me a wop . . . no, with my fist, Phil, the mitt was in the other hand . . . I know it doesn't look good for the league . . . what . . . what do you mean fired? . . . You can't fire me, I'm the sponsor, remember? My old man bought the suits, balls and bats, I own the team . . . you did . . . my old man said what? . . . *(unbelieving)* . . . Are you serious, my old man said that? . . . No, I do not want to coach the eight to ten year olds, Christ, that's like being shipped to the minors . . . no, no hard feelings, I'll see you around. *Hangs up phone. Goes to record player, puts on a Caruso record, a sad mournful one, fixes a drink. Barbara enters. Victor is pretty high by now.*

BARBARA: If you drive me down to the theater now, you'll still have time to come back and get dressed.

VICTOR: I'm not going to the theater.

BARBARA: Where are the keys? *Victor hands them to her.* You know what I think? We've simply outgrown each other. After five years together I have to remind myself.

VICTOR, *quietly:* Hey, I never made love to you without getting the feeling that you were defending yourself against something, and that's not booze talking, either!

BARBARA: I'm going to the party, I'll be very late.

VICTOR: Have a nice time.

PART II

———•———

Scenes for Two Women

IN THE BOOM BOOM ROOM

by David Rabe

---•---

ACT II

The play tells the story of Chrissy, a go-go dancer in the late
sixties. It is the story of her search for love, of her failure to find
anything but abuse and rejection, and, ultimately, of the destruction of her spirit.

Chrissy is a big-hearted, pretty, and very naïve girl who loves
to dance and yearns for the romance depicted in pop and rock
music. Rejection was there right from the beginning of her life
when her mother tried to have her aborted. The abuse started
with her father's drunken sexual assaults when she was a young
child. In the following scene Chrissy confronts her mother, Hel-
en, about the abortion. She has just been talking to her father.

HELEN: How was he? *And she is dumping the Kool-Aid into
the pitcher.*
CHRISSY: Fine.
HELEN, *as the water in the pitcher is turning red:* Don't they
play so many nice songs on the radio nowadays? I peeked in the
window of your apartment, you know, bringing you oranges.
You looked so worried, Chrissy. Are you in the right line of
work, every person must ask herself. Every person must. Is it
your new line of work you're so worried about? I bet you diet
and diet.
CHRISSY: I'm overweight. Don't like it.
HELEN: To look pretty for your father. He always liked a pretty figure. *Handing Chrissy a glass of Kool-Aid, Helen sits down
with a glass of her own to sip.* Except it's a silly business how
you gotta wanna have a nice little figure so a man'll wanna get
you pregnant and ruin your nice little figure. How tall are you?

CHRISSY: Why?

HELEN: Oh, forgive me honey, I don't mean to pry. It's just I been so nervous and short-tempered lately and so worried about your father. There are moments, I tell you, when I see him sittin' off somewhere lookin' at a wall, or out scratchin' in that dirt, I wish he would want to steal again. The way he used to. He loved to steal things. Made big elaborate plans for big jobs he was goin' to pull someday. Start his own gang.

CHRISSY, *advancing on her:* Don't you know he's thinkin' about leavin' you is what he's thinkin' about?

HELEN, *sitting quietly, calmly, a little dreamily:* Chrissy, no, no; he's so tired. Home to stay this time. And that's a fact. We gotta be gettin' ready for our little old age. Savin' our money. Doin' our little jobs. Wanna come inside? I'm gonna make him chocolate pudding.

CHRISSY: But he hates you. I mean, that's what we were talkin' about—how you was a hateful liar. I mean, you never even had any a those abortions I been so worried about.

HELEN: Did he tell you that? He never did like to think about it. Still don't. He's a squeamish man, in a lotta ways. But my God, he had women sittin' down with coat hangers all across this state. Toilets flushin'; stomach's goin' empty. He just don't bear to think about it—always lovin' little children so. Just never understood the connection. Wanna come in the kitchen? *She is walking away.* It's nice inside. Gonna make some chocolate pudding.

CHRISSY: I mean, I am here to tell you how I am never gonna forgive you—not ever, for how you didn't wanna have me.

HELEN: Then how come I did? I loved him. How are you to know I loved him? He would lift a can of beer or I would see him standing deep in thought, I would feel such a hurt of love. But I could never make him do what I wanted—be careful—use a thing. "Man don't wear galoshes to take a shower," he would say. So, "I'm pregnant," I would tell him and he would nod and say, "That's good," and pretty soon I would feel him lookin' at my lumpy body, and in his lookin' at me his leavin' of me was clear. I couldn't bear it. So I would get rid of whatever was inside me. I would get rid of it. Except for you. I wanted you.

CHRISSY: I don't feel good—like my head is shaking; all vibrating. *She is going sideways a step or two, her knees weak; she looks for a place to rest.*

HELEN: I mean, sometimes I forget all 'bout that other stuff. I swear I do, honey.

CHRISSY: I feel like maybe I can hear what you're thinkin' and I been able maybe all my life. How you hate me. You are in the room with me, I hear you. Outside my door, you stand hatin' me—

HELEN: No, no.

CHRISSY: Sendin' rays a hate in at me—I hear your thinkin' how I am hateful, all these rays a hate sent in at me into my head! *And she falls to her knees:* SHUT UP, SHUT UP! You ain't tellin' me anymore. You are done tellin' me. You tried to get rid of me, and you ain't changin' it now. You used to sit on the floor and bounce up and down tryin' to get me out like a hunk a ole blood in that belly and so that's how you always looked at me and me at myself, like I was a little bit dead or that oughta be dead, which is how I regard and look at myself a lot. But I don't oughta be dead. I mean, Christ almighty, sometimes I think about what it musta been to be me inside you bouncin' up and down and I wasn't ready to come out. I would only die if I did. How did I feel? How did I feel? *She has bounced on the floor; she has fallen forward.*

HELEN: It wasn't you, Chrissy; that wasn't you. No, no.

CHRISSY, *begging:* Who, then?

HELEN: I didn't want you dead.

CHRISSY: Who?

HELEN: That thing inside me and all the way it was gonna hurt my life.

CHRISSY: That was me! *And she collapses; Helen runs to console her.*

HELEN: No! No, I was hesitant in my bouncing. I was hesitant. Something tugged at my heart. I know it did. *She is embracing Chrissy, the two of them on the floor.* I coulda bounced harder. I coulda bounced much harder. I coulda jumped off the table. Some tugging at my heart for you held me back or you wouldn't be here. But you are. That's proof of my innermost wishes of hope and love and how they prevailed.

CHRISSY: Noooo. *Pulling away.* I don't oughta be dead.

HELEN: No.

CHRISSY: Tell me.

HELEN: You don't oughta be dead, honey.

CHRISSY: I gotta stop. I'm gonna stop.

HELEN: You wanna stay the night? You look so tired.

CHRISSY: No. I don't wanna be here, even. I don't wanna see you anymore. You go away.

HELEN: All right. *And Chrissy is kneeling, Helen moving backward.*

CHRISSY: You go away.

HELEN: I'm going. *Still backing away:* See you later.

CHRISSY: No. Noooo. *Helen is gone.* Don't wanna see you ever again. Not either one a you. No more. I gotta stop. *And she sits, shaking her head as the lights are fading.* No more.

HELLO FROM BERTHA

by Tennessee Williams

———————•———————

This one-act play takes place in a bedroom of an East St. Louis brothel. Bertha, a prostitute, is very sick and has been lying in bed for two weeks. Goldie, the madam, needs the room for business. She wants Bertha to leave, and tells her to go back home or to a hospital. Many terms are applicable to Bertha: she is *in pain,* she is *delirious,* she is *drunk,* she is *frightened,* she is *belligerent*—but most of all, Bertha is very much *alone.* The following excerpt is from the beginning of the play. Bertha is in bed. Goldie enters.

GOLDIE: Well, Bertha, what are you going to do? *For a moment there is no answer.*

BERTHA, *with faint groan:* I dunno.

GOLDIE: You've got to decide, Bertha.

BERTHA: I can't decide nothing.

GOLDIE: Why can't you?

BERTHA: I'm too tired.

GOLDIE: That's no answer.

BERTHA, *tossing fretfully:* Well, it's the only answer I know. I just want to lay here and think things over.

GOLDIE: You been layin' here thinkin' or somethin' for the past two weeks. *Bertha makes an indistinguishable reply.* You got to come to some decision. The girls need this room.

BERTHA, *with hoarse laugh:* Let 'em have it!

GOLDIE: They can't with you layin' here.

BERTHA, *slapping her hand on bed:* Oh, God!

GOLDIE: Pull yourself together, now, Bertha. *Bertha tosses again and groans.*

BERTHA: What's the matter with me?

GOLDIE: You're sick.

BERTHA: I got a sick headache. Who slipped me that Mickey Finn last night?

GOLDIE: Nobody give you no Mickey Finn. You been layin' here two solid weeks talkin' out of your head. Now, the sensible thing for you to do, Bertha, is to go back home or—

BERTHA: Go back nowhere!—I'm stayin' right here till I get on my feet. *She stubbornly averts her face.*

GOLDIE: The valley's no place for a girl in your condition. Besides we need this room.

BERTHA: Leave me be, Goldie. I wanna get in some rest before I start workin'.

GOLDIE: Bertha, you've got to decide! *The command hangs heavily upon the room's florid atmosphere for several long moments. Bertha slowly turns her head to Goldie.*

BERTHA, *faintly:* What is it I got to decide?

GOLDIE: Where you're going from here? *Bertha looks at her silently for a few seconds.*

BERTHA: Nowhere. Now leave me be, Goldie. I've got to get in my rest.

GOLDIE: If I let you be, you'd just lay here doin' nothin' from now till the crack of doom! *Bertha's reply is indistinguishable.* Lissen here! If you don't make up your mind right away, I'm gonna call the ambulance squad to come get you! So you better decide right this minute.

BERTHA, *her body has stiffened slightly at this threat:* I can't decide nothing. I'm too tired—worn out.

GOLDIE: All right! *She snaps her purse open.* I'll take this nickel and I'll make the call right now. I'll tell 'em we got a sick girl over here who can't talk sense.

BERTHA, *thickly:* Go ahead. I don't care what happens to me now.

GOLDIE, *changing her tactics:* Why don't you write another letter, Bertha, to that man who sells . . . hardware or something in Memphis?

BERTHA, *with sudden alertness:* Charlie? You leave his name off your dirty tongue!

GOLDIE: That's a fine way for you to be talking, me keeping you here just out of kindness and you not bringing in a red, white or blue cent for the last two weeks! Where do you—

BERTHA: Charlie's a real . . . sweet. Charlie's a . . . *(her voice trails into a sobbing mumble)*

GOLDIE: What if he is? All the better reason for you to write him to get you out of this here tight spot you're in, Bertha.

BERTHA, *aroused:* I'll never ask him for another dime! Get that? He's forgotten all about me, my name and everything else. *She runs her hand slowly down her body.* Somebody's cut me up with a knife while I been sleeping.

GOLDIE: Pull yourself together, Bertha. If this man's got money, maybe he'll send you some to help you git back on your feet.

BERTHA: Sure he's got money. He owns a hardware store. I reckon I ought to know, I used to work there! He used to say to me, Girlie, any time you need something just let Charlie know. . . . We had good times together in that back room!

GOLDIE: I bet he ain't forgotten it neither.

BERTHA: He's found out about all the bad things I done since I quit him and . . . come to St. Louie. *She slaps the bed twice with her palm.*

GOLDIE: Naw, he ain't, Bertha. I bet he don't know a thing. *Bertha laughs weakly.*

BERTHA: It's you that's been writing him things. All the dirt you could think of about me! Your filthy tongue's been clacking so fast that—

GOLDIE: Bertha! *Bertha mutters an indistinguishable vulgarity.* I been a good friend to you, Bertha.

BERTHA: Anyhow he's married now.

GOLDIE: Just write him a little note on a postcard and tell him you've had some tough breaks. Remind him of how he said he would help you if you ever needed it, huh?

BERTHA: Leave me alone a while, Goldie. I got an awful feeling inside of me now.

GOLDIE, *advancing a few steps and regarding Bertha more critically:* You want to see a doctor?

BERTHA: No. *There is a pause.*

GOLDIE: A priest? *Bertha's fingers claw the sheet forward.*

BERTHA: No!

GOLDIE: What religion are you, Bertha?

BERTHA: None.

GOLDIE: I thought you said you was a Catholic once.

BERTHA: Maybe I did. What of it?

GOLDIE: If you could remember, maybe we could get some sisters or something to give you a room like they did for Rose Kramer for you to rest in, and get your strength back—huh, Bertha?

BERTHA: I don't want no sisters to give me nothing! Just leave me be in here till I get through resting.

GOLDIE: Bertha, you're . . . bad sick, Bertha!

BERTHA, *after a slight pause:* Bad?

GOLDIE: Yes, Bertha. I don't want to scare you but . . .

BERTHA, *hoarsely:* You mean I'm dying?

GOLDIE, *after a moment's consideration:* I didn't say that. *There is another pause.*

BERTHA: No, but you meant it.

GOLDIE: We got to provide for the future, Bertha. We can't just let things slide.

BERTHA, *attempting to sit up:* If I'm dying I want to write Charlie. I want to—tell him some things.

GOLDIE: If you mean a confession, honey, I think a priest would be—

BERTHA: No, no priest! I want Charlie!

GOLDIE: Father Callahan would—

BERTHA: No! No! I want Charlie!

GOLDIE: Charlie's in Memphis. He's running his hardware business.

BERTHA: Yeah. On Central Avenue. The address is 563.

GOLDIE: I'll write him and tell what condition you're in, huh, Bertha?

BERTHA, *after a reflective pause:* No. . . . Just tell him I said hello. *She turns her face to the wall.*

GOLDIE: I gotta say more than that, Bertha.

BERTHA: That's all I want you to say. Hello from—Bertha.

GOLDIE: That wouldn't make sense, you know that.
BERTHA: Sure it would. Hello from Bertha to Charlie with all her love. Don't that make sense?
GOLDIE: No!
BERTHA: Sure it does.

THE MIRACLE WORKER

by William Gibson

———•———

ACT II

The play is based on the early life of Helen Keller. Helen was blind, deaf, and mute; she was wild and uncontrollable. As a last resort her parents hired Annie Sullivan, trained as a teacher of blind children, *to work a miracle*. The play focuses on Annie's efforts to break through the sensory barriers that have kept Helen isolated and uncivilized. Annie comes to believe that Helen can learn if she is properly disciplined. Helen is used to poking her hands in everyone's food at dinner time. When Annie prevents her from doing this Helen has a tantrum and begins to kick the floor. The family members ask Annie to let Helen do as she pleases so that they might have some peace and continue their conversations. Annie demands that they leave her alone with Helen. Just prior to the following scene the family has exited reluctantly. Annie locks the door behind them. She is resolved: Helen will learn to eat in a civilized manner and show respect for others.

Annie meanwhile has begun by slapping both keys down on a shelf out of Helen's reach; she returns to the table upstage. Helen's kicking has subsided, and when from the floor her hand finds Annie's chair empty she pauses. Annie clears the table of Kate's, James's, and Keller's plates; she gets back to her own across the table just in time to slide it deftly away from Helen's

*pouncing hand. She lifts the hand and moves it to Helen's plate,
and after an instant's exploration, Helen sits again on the floor
and drums her heels. Annie comes around the table and resumes
her chair. When Helen feels her skirt again, she ceases kicking,
waits for whatever is to come, renews some kicking, waits again.
Annie retrieving her plate takes up a forkful of food, stops it halfway to her mouth, gazes at it devoid of appetite, and half-lowers
it; but after a look at Helen she sighs, dips the forkful toward
Helen in a for-your-sake toast, and puts it in her own mouth to
chew, not without an effort.*

*Helen now gets hold of the chair leg, and half-succeeds in pull-
ing the chair out from under her. Annie bangs it down with her
rear, heavily, and sits with all her weight. Helen's next attempt to
topple it is unavailing, so her fingers dive in a pinch at Annie's
flank. Annie in the middle of her mouthful almost loses it with
startle, and she slaps down her fork to round on Helen. The child
comes up with curiosity to feel what Annie is doing, so Annie resumes eating, letting Helen's hand follow the movement of her
fork to her mouth; whereupon Helen at once reaches into Annie's
plate. Annie firmly removes her hand to her own plate. Helen in
reply pinches Annie's thigh, a good mean pinchful that makes
Annie jump. Annie sets the fork down, and sits with her mouth
tight. Helen digs another pinch into her thigh, and this time Annie slaps her hand smartly away; Helen retaliates with a roundhouse fist that catches Annie on the ear, and Annie's hand leaps
at once in a forceful slap across Helen's cheek; Helen is the startled one now. Annie's hand in compunction falters to her own
face, but when Helen hits at her again, Annie deliberately slaps
her again. Helen lifts her fist irresolute for another roundhouse,
Annie lifts her hand resolute for another slap, and they freeze in
this posture, while Helen mulls it over. She thinks better of it,
drops her fist, and giving Annie a wide berth, gropes around to
her mother's chair, to find it empty; she blunders her way along
the table upstage, and encountering the empty chairs and missing
plates, she looks bewildered; she gropes back to her mother's
chair, again touches her cheek and indicates the chair, and waits
for the world to answer.*

*Annie now reaches over to spell into her hand, but Helen yanks
it away; she gropes to the front door, tries the knob, and finds the*

*door locked, with no key. She gropes to the rear door, and finds it
locked, with no key. She commences to bang on it. Annie rises,
crosses, takes her wrists, draws her resisting back to the table,
seats her, and releases her hands upon her plate; as Annie herself
begins to sit, Helen writhes out of her chair, runs to the front
door, and tugs and kicks at it. Annie rises again, crosses, draws
her by one wrist back to the table, seats her, and sits; Helen escapes back to the door, knocking over her mother's chair en
route. Annie rises again in pursuit, and this time lifts Helen bodily from behind and bears her kicking to her chair. She deposits
her, and once more turns to sit. Helen scrambles out, but as she
passes Annie catches her up again from behind and deposits her
in the chair; Helen scrambles out on the other side, for the rear
door, but Annie at her heels catches her up and deposits her
again in the chair. She stands behind it. Helen scrambles out to
her right, and the instant her feet hit the floor Annie lifts and deposits her back; she scrambles out to her left, and is at once lifted
and deposited back. She tries right again and is deposited back,
and tries left again and is deposited back, and now feints Annie
to the right but is off to her left, and is promptly deposited back.
She sits a moment, and then starts straight over the tabletop,
dishware notwithstanding; Annie hauls her in and deposits her
back, with her plate spilling in her lap, and she melts to the floor
and crawls under the table, laborious among its legs and chairs;
but Annie is swift around the table and waiting on the other side
when she surfaces, immediately bearing her aloft; Helen clutches
at James's chair for anchorage, but it comes with her, and halfway back she abandons it to the floor. Annie deposits her in her
chair, and waits. Helen sits tensed motionless. Then she tentative-
ly puts out her left foot and hand, Annie interposes her own
hand, and at the contact Helen jerks hers in. She tries her right
foot, Annie blocks it with her own, and Helen jerks hers in. Finally, leaning back, she slumps down in her chair, in a sullen bid-
ing.*

*Annie backs off a step, and watches; Helen offers no move. An-
nie takes a deep breath. Both of them and the room are in considerable disorder, two chairs down and the table a mess, but
Annie makes no effort to tidy it; she only sits on her own chair,
and lets her energy refill. Then she takes up knife and fork, and
resolutely addresses her food. Helen's hand comes out to explore,*

and seeing it Annie sits without moving; the child's hand goes over her hand and fork, pauses—Annie still does not move—and withdraws. Presently it moves for her own plate, slaps about for it, and stops, thwarted. At this, Annie again rises, recovers Helen's plate from the floor and a handful of scattered food from the deranged tablecloth, drops it on the plate, and pushes the plate into contact with Helen's fist. Neither of them now moves for a pregnant moment—until Helen suddenly takes a grab of food and wolfs it down. Annie permits herself the humor of a minor bow and warming of her hands together; she wanders off a step or two, watching. Helen cleans up the plate.

After a glower of indecision, she holds the empty plate out for more. Annie accepts it, and crossing to the removed plates, spoons food from them onto it; she stands debating the spoon, tapping it a few times on Helen's plate; and when she returns with the plate she brings the spoon, too. She puts the spoon first into Helen's hand, then sets the plate down. Helen, discarding the spoon, reaches with her hand, and Annie stops it by the wrist; she replaces the spoon in it. Helen impatiently discards it again, and again Annie stops her hand, to replace the spoon in it. This time Helen throws the spoon on the floor. Annie after considering it lifts Helen bodily out of the chair, and in a wrestling match on the floor closes her fingers upon the spoon, and returns her with it to the chair. Helen again throws the spoon on the floor. Annie lifts her out of the chair again; but in the struggle over the spoon Helen with Annie on her back sends her sliding over her head; Helen flees back to her chair and scrambles into it. When Annie comes after her she clutches it for dear life; Annie pries one hand loose, then the other, then the first again, then the other again, and then lifts Helen by the waist, chair and all, and shakes the chair loose. Helen wrestles to get free, but Annie pins her to the floor, closes her fingers upon the spoon, and lifts her kicking under one arm; with her other hand she gets the chair in place again, and plunks Helen back on it. When she releases her hand, Helen throws the spoon at her.

Annie now removes the plate of food. Helen grabbing finds it missing, and commences to bang with her fists on the table. Annie collects a fistful of spoons and descends with them and the plate on Helen; she lets her smell the plate, at which Helen ceases banging, and Annie puts the plate down and a spoon in Helen's hand. Helen throws it on the floor. Annie puts another spoon in her hand. Helen throws it on the floor. Annie puts another spoon in her hand. Helen throws it on the floor. When Annie comes to her last spoon she sits next to Helen, and gripping the spoon in Helen's hand compels her to take food in it up to her mouth. Helen sits with lips shut. Annie waits a stolid moment, then lowers Helen's hand. She tries again; Helen's lips remain shut. Annie waits, lowers Helen's hand. She tries again; this time Helen suddenly opens her mouth and accepts the food. Annie lowers the spoon with a sigh of relief, and Helen spews the mouthful out at her face. Annie sits a moment with eyes closed, then takes the pitcher and dashes its water into Helen's face, who gasps, astonished. Annie with Helen's hand takes up another spoonful, and shoves it into her open mouth. Helen swallows involuntarily, and while she is catching her breath Annie forces her palm open, throws four swift letters into it, then another four, and bows toward her with devastating pleasantness.

ANNIE: Good girl.

THE KILLING OF SISTER GEORGE

by Frank Marcus

———•———

ACT II, SCENE 1

As the curtain rises, June enters her flat; she is agitated. She lights a cigar and says to her roommate and lover, Alice (nicknamed Childie): "They are going to murder me." But we are not about to encounter one of those tense British murder mysteries: June is a well-known character in a soap opera—Sister George, a gentle and good-hearted nurse—and she suspects that Sister George is about to be written out of the story. In contrast to her kindly BBC character, June is, in real life, domineering, acerbic, and extremely possessive. She is also wonderfully witty and terribly frightened of losing her job and losing Alice to a man. As it turns out, she does, in fact, lose both (although she loses Alice to another woman).

The following scene takes place at 4 A.M. June has been up all night, drinking and going over her scrapbook of memorabilia on Sister George. Alice has gotten up early to wait on line for tickets to the ballet. At this point in the scene Alice is dressed and about to leave. They have just exchanged some serious words about their relationship: about June's jealousy and Alice's remorse over not having a baby. (The Mr. Katz referred to in the scene is Alice's employer.)

ALICE: There's a performance of *Petrushka* on the nineteenth. I might try for that.
JUNE, *rising; suddenly:* Shh! Shh! *She pauses and listens.* Was that the post?
ALICE: At this time in the morning? It won't be here for hours yet. You really ought to go to bed.

There is a pause.

JUNE, *crossing below the table left center to left of it; seriously:* What am I going to do? They're driving me round the bend.
ALICE: You're driving yourself round the bend. *She crosses to center.* Why don't you go to bed?
JUNE, *sitting left of the table left center; desperately:* Because I can't sleep.
ALICE, *moving above the table left center:* Shall I get you some hot milk?
JUNE: Urghh!
ALICE: You'll catch cold, you know, sitting up like this.
JUNE: I've already got a cold.
ALICE, *moving above June to left of her:* Well, keep your throat covered up, then. *She arranges June's collar.* Put your dressing-gown on properly. It's time we got you a new dressing-gown—this collar is all frayed. I'll put some new braid on it tomorrow. There, better?
JUNE: Thanks.
ALICE, *moving above the table left center and indicating the gin bottle:* Shall I put this away?

JUNE, *picking up the bottle:* No, I just want to hold it for a moment. *She hugs the bottle.*

ALICE, *moving center and looking at the clock:* I ought to be going—it's half past four. *She turns to June. Worried:* Will you be all right? *She moves to right of the table left center and faces June across it.*

JUNE: Childie, they won't do it, will they? They *can't,* after all I've done for them

ALICE: Of *course* they won't, George. You must stop brooding about it. You'll make yourself ill. *She sits right of the table left center.* Why don't you go to bed and try and sleep it off? You can set the alarm to wake you for rehearsal tomorrow.

JUNE: There no rehearsal tomorrow.

ALICE: That's good, then. You can get a nice long rest. *She pauses a moment, then rises and moves right.* Now George, I've got to go.

JUNE, *looking yearningly across at Alice:* No, wait a minute.

ALICE: Oh, George, they'll be waiting for me. *She picks up the knapsack and puts it on.* I'll be at the back of the queue.

JUNE, *rising and moving center:* You can't go like *that,* you know.

ALICE: Like what?

JUNE, *pointing to the knapsack:* You're not going on a hike, you know. Mind you, donkeys are best for loading.

ALICE: There's only a change of clothing in it, to take to the office. And a few provisions. *She backs towards the arch right and puts on her scarf.* Please, may I go now?

JUNE: Did you speak?

ALICE: Yes, I said 'May I go now?'

JUNE, *considering the request:* Not before you have made your obeisances to me in the proper manner.

ALICE, *alarmed:* What do you mean?

June breathes heavily and alcoholically for a few moments.

JUNE: You must kiss the hem of my garment. *With an imperious gesture:* On your knees. Go on! Down, boy, down! *She snaps her fingers and motions Alice downstage.*

Alice removes her knapsack and shrugs.

ALICE: Oh, all right. *She goes on her knees down right of the pouffe.*

JUNE, *moving to left of Alice:* Now repeat after me: 'I hereby solemnly swear—'

ALICE, *mechanically:* 'I hereby solemnly swear—'

JUNE: '—that I will not allow—'

ALICE: '—that I will not allow—'

JUNE: '—anyone whooomsoever—'

ALICE: '—anyone—*(she imitates June)* whoomsoever—'

JUNE: '—including Mr. Katz, gratification of his fleshly instincts with me today or at any other time.'

ALICE, *quickly:* All right, all right, I swear. *She kisses the hem of June's dressing-gown.*

JUNE, *making sweeping gestures over Alice's head:* Mind you remember, or may the curse of Satan fall on your head.

ALICE, *rising and quickly reiterating:* That's one *Giselle*, one *Petrushka*, and no *Lac*—right?

JUNE: *(with enormous effort) Rien de 'Lac de Cygnes'. C'est juste. (She holds on to Alice's scarf. With maudlin affection:) Mon petit chou.*

ALICE: All right, all right, George, let go. Let go.

JUNE, *still with affection:* What's this? *She looks at the scarf.*

ALICE: What?

JUNE: This isn't yours, is it? *She jerks the scarf away from Alice and looks suspiciously at it.* Where did you get it?

ALICE: Oh, come on now, give it back to me.

JUNE, *moving center and looking at the label on the scarf:* Who is J.V.S. Partridge?

ALICE: A young Liberal. Satisfied? *She makes a grab for the scarf.*

JUNE, *jerks the scarf out of Alice's reach:* Far, far from satisfied. How long have you been entangled with this—youth?

ALICE: He's not a youth. He's forty-six.

JUNE: Bit long in the tooth for a young Liberal, isn't he? *Fiercely:* Who is he?

ALICE, *shifting from foot to foot:* The chap from downstairs, daftie. Madame Xenia's lodger. *She crosses behind June to left of her and makes a grab for the scarf.*

JUNE, *jerking the scarf out of Alice's reach:* Ah—I thought there was some monkey business going on there.

ALICE: There is not. I've only ever seen him twice.

JUNE: How did you get his scarf, then?

ALICE, *after a pause; sheepishly:* I pinched it off the hall-stand.

JUNE: D'you expect me to believe that?

ALICE, *shaken, but sincerely:* Look, George, I've never even spoken to him. It's nothing.

JUNE: That's what you said when you went off with that estate agent for a weekend in Birmingham.

ALICE, *moving left:* That was five years ago.

JUNE: It happened once—it can happen again.

ALICE, *looking away:* Nothing happened.

JUNE, *suspiciously:* Oh?

ALICE, *rounding on June; almost screaming:* Nothing!

JUNE: Well, *nothing's* going to happen now because I forbid you to speak to him.

ALICE: You must be raving mad. He's a neighbor, there's no harm in being friendly.

JUNE, *shouting:* I forbid you to speak to him, do you hear?

ALICE: I'll flipping well speak to him if I want to—why shouldn't I?

JUNE, *venomously:* You fancy him, don't you? *She shouts:* Don't you?

ALICE: He seems perfectly agreeable. *June's face is contorted with suspicion.* Yes, I do fancy him—he's a dish. *June steps threateningly toward Alice, who shrinks back against the sideboard.* Don't you touch me—you've no right to . . .

JUNE: I've got every right.

ALICE: I'm not married to you, you know. *There is a long pause, then June hands the scarf to Alice and moves up center. In a low voice:* I'm sorry, George, but you asked for it.

JUNE: You'd better get along, you'll be late. *She moves center.*

Alice crosses to right, picks up the knapsack, but does not put it on.

ALICE: Look after yourself. Don't forget the party tonight.

Alice makes a kissing motion to June, but June has turned away and does not see it.

ANTIGONE

by Jean Anouilh,
adapted by Lewis Galantière

———•———

ACT I

By order of her uncle, Creon, king of Thebes, the body of Polynices, Antigone's brother, must not be given a religious burial.
Anyone attempting to bury the body will be punished by death.
Polynices was killed in battle while attempting to overthrow
Creon's government. According to custom, because he was a
traitor his soul must be punished and must not be allowed to
rest. Antigone, daughter of Oedipus, will not let her brother's
body rot and his soul wander homeless forever. It is against religious law; it is contrary to what she knows is right (although
she admits later in the play that she is not really sure why she
feels that she must take this action). She buries her brother,
knowingly and willingly (and even eagerly) accepting the death
penalty that the law must mete out to her. Creon's attempts to
avoid killing her are fruitless. She will not cooperate at all and,
as a result, she is buried alive in a cave.

The following scene between Antigone and her nurse takes
place at the beginning of the play. It is early morning. Antigone
enters. She has already secretly buried her brother during the
night.

NURSE: Where have you been?
ANTIGONE: Nowhere. It was beautiful. The whole world was
gray when I went out. And now—you wouldn't recognize it.
It's like a postcard: all pink, and green, and yellow. You'll have
to get up earlier, Nurse, if you want to see a world without col-
or.
NURSE: It was still pitch black when I got up. I went to your
room, for I thought you might have flung off your blanket in
the night. You weren't there.
ANTIGONE, *comes down the steps:* The garden was lovely. It

was still asleep. Have you ever thought how lovely a garden is when it is not yet thinking of men?

NURSE: You hadn't slept in your bed. I couldn't find you. I went to the back door. You'd left it open.

ANTIGONE: The fields were wet. They were waiting for something to happen. The whole world was breathless, waiting. I can't tell you what a roaring noise I seemed to make alone on the road. It bothered me that whatever was waiting wasn't waiting for me. I took off my sandals and slipped into a field. *She moves down to the stool and sits.*

NURSE, *kneels at Antigone's feet to chafe them and put on the sandals:* You'll do well to wash your feet before you go back to bed, Miss.

ANTIGONE: I'm not going back to bed.

NURSE: Don't be a fool! You get some sleep! And me, getting up to see if she hasn't flung off her blanket; and I find her bed cold and nobody in it!

ANTIGONE: Do you think that if a person got up every morning like this, it would be just as thrilling every morning to be the first girl out-of-doors?

Nurse puts Antigone's left foot down, lifts her other foot and chafes it.

NURSE: Morning my grandmother! It was night. It still is. And now, my girl, you'll stop trying to squirm out of this and tell me what you were up to. Where've you been?

ANTIGONE: That's true. It was still night. There wasn't a soul out of doors but me, who thought that it was morning. Don't you think it's marvelous—to be the first person who is aware that it is morning?

NURSE: Oh, my little flibbertigibbet! Just can't imagine what I'm talking about, can she? Go on with you! I know that game. Where have you been, wicked girl?

ANTIGONE, *soberly:* No. Not wicked.

NURSE: You went out to meet someone, didn't you? Deny it if you can.

ANTIGONE: Yes. I went out to meet someone.

NURSE: A lover?

ANTIGONE: Yes, Nurse. Yes, the poor dear. I have a lover.

NURSE, *stands up; bursting out:* Ah, that's very nice now, isn't it? Such goings-on! You, the daughter of a king, running out to meet lovers. And we work our fingers to the bone for you, we slave to bring you up like young ladies! *She sits on chair, right of table.* You're all alike, all of you. Even you—who never used to stop to primp in front of a looking glass, or smear your mouth with rouge, or dindle and dandle to make the boys ogle you, and you ogle back. How many times I'd say to myself, "Now that one, now: I wish she was a little more of a coquette—always wearing the same dress, her hair tumbling round her face. One thing's sure," I'd say to myself, "none of the boys will look at her while Ismene's about, all curled and cute and tidy and trim. I'll have this one on my hands for the rest of my life." And now, you see? Just like your sister, after all. Only worse: a hypocrite. Who is the lad? Some little scamp, eh? Somebody you can't bring home and show to your family, and say, "Well, this is him, and I mean to marry him and no other." That's how it is, is it? Answer me!

ANTIGONE, *smiling faintly:* That's how it is. Yes, Nurse.

NURSE: Yes, says she! God save us! I took her when she wasn't that high. I promised her poor mother I'd make a lady of her. And look at her! But don't you go thinking this is the end of this, my young 'un. I'm only your nurse and you can play deaf and dumb with me; I don't count. But your Uncle Creon will hear of this! That, I promise you.

ANTIGONE, *a little weary:* Yes. Creon will hear of this.

NURSE: And we'll hear what he has to say when he finds out that you go wandering alone o' nights. Not to mention Haemon. For the girl's engaged! Going to be married! Going to be married, and she hops out of bed at four in the morning to meet somebody else in a field. Do you know what I ought to do to you? Take you over my knee the way I used to do when you were little.

ANTIGONE: Please, Nurse, I want to be alone.

NURSE: And if you so much as speak of it, she says she wants to be alone!

ANTIGONE: Nanny, you shouldn't scold, dear. This isn't a day when you should be losing your temper .

NURSE: Not scold, indeed! Along with the rest of it, I'm to like it. Didn't I promise your mother? What would she say if she was here? "Old Stupid!" That's what she'd call me. "Old Stupid. Not to know how to keep my little girl pure! Spend your life making them behave, watching over them like a mother hen, running after them with mufflers and sweaters to keep them warm, and eggnogs to make them strong; and then at four o'clock in the morning, you who always complained you never could sleep a wink, snoring in your bed and letting them slip out into the bushes." That's what she'd say, your mother. And I'd stand there, dying of shame if I wasn't dead already. And all I could do would be not to dare look her in the face; and "That's true," I'd say. "That's all true what you say, Your Majesty."

ANTIGONE: Nanny, dear. Dear Nanny. Don't cry. You'll be able to look Mamma in the face when it's your time to see her. And she'll say, "Good morning, Nanny. Thank you for my little Antigone. You did look after her so well." She knows why I went out this morning.

NURSE: Not to meet a lover?

ANTIGONE: No. Not to meet a lover.

NURSE: Well, you've a queer way of teasing me, I must say! Not to know when she's teasing me! *Rises to stand behind Antigone.* I must be getting awfully old, that's what it is. But if you loved me, you'd tell me the truth. You'd tell me why your bed was empty when I went along to tuck you in. Wouldn't you?

ANTIGONE: Please, Nanny, don't cry anymore. *Antigone turns partly toward Nurse, puts an arm up to Nurse's shoulder. With her other hand, Antigone caresses Nurse's face.* There now, my sweet red apple. Do you remember how I used to rub your cheeks to make them shine? My dear, wrinkled red apple! I didn't do anything tonight that was worth sending tears down the little gullies of your dear face. I am pure, and I swear that I have no other lover than Haemon. If you like, I'll swear that I shall never have any other lover than Haemon. Save your tears, Nanny, save them, Nanny dear; you may still need them. When you cry like that, I become a little girl again; and I mustn't be a little girl today.

THE CHILDREN'S HOUR

by Lillian Hellman

———————— • ————————

ACT III

Martha Dobie and Karen Wright run a girls' boarding school. One of their pupils spreads an unfounded rumor that they are lesbians. Although it is later discovered that the gossip was the invention of a malicious youngster, it is too late to spare them tragedy. They are forced to close their school, and Karen's engagement to Joe Cardin ends because he believed the rumor.

The following scene is from the end of the play. Karen reveals the circumstances of her broken engagement. Martha, in despair over the incident, confesses her secret belief that she has, indeed, always loved Karen "that way." Martha's guilt over having possibly caused Karen's unhappiness leads her to eventually take her own life.

The scene begins with Karen onstage. Martha, who has been preparing dinner, comes in with a small tray and dust cloth.

MARTHA, *goes to lamp on downstage left table, lights it:* It gets dark so early now. *Crosses to desk, puts down tray, empties ashtray into it:* Cooking always makes me feel better. I found some purple scylla for the table. Remember! They were the first things we planted here. And I made a small cake. Know what? I found a bottle of wine. We'll have a good dinner. *Crosses to below right end of sofa, picks newspaper up from the floor. No answer. She crosses back to above desk.* Where's Joe?

KAREN: Gone.

MARTHA, *puts newspaper on desk:* A patient? Will he be back in time for dinner?

KAREN: No.

MARTHA, *watching her:* We'll wait dinner for him, then. Karen! What's the matter?

KAREN, *in a dull tone:* He won't be back.

MARTHA, *speaking slowly, carefully:* You mean he won't be back anymore tonight? *Slowly crossing left, above desk.*

KAREN: He won't be back at all.

MARTHA, *quickly, walks to right of Karen:* What happened? *Karen shakes head.* What happened, Karen?

KAREN: He thought we had been lovers.

MARTHA, *tensely:* I don't believe you. I don't believe it. What kind of awful talk is that? I don't believe you. *I don't believe it.*

KAREN: All right, all right.

MARTHA: Didn't you tell him? For God's sake, didn't you tell him it wasn't true?

KAREN: Yes.

MARTHA: He didn't believe you?

KAREN: I guess he believed me.

MARTHA, *moves upstage angrily:* Then what have you done? It's all wrong. It's crazy. I don't understand what you've done. You "guess" that he believed you. *Comes back to right of Karen.* There's no guessing about it. Why didn't you——?

KAREN: I don't want ever to talk about it, Martha.

MARTHA, *sits in chair left of desk:* Oh God, I wanted that for you so much!

KAREN: Don't carry on. I don't feel well.

MARTHA: What's happened to us? What's really happened to us?

KAREN: I don't know. I think I'll make a cup of tea and go to bed now.

MARTHA: Whatever happened, go back to Joe. It's too much for you this way.

KAREN, *irritably:* Stop talking about it. Let's pack and get out of here. Let's take the train in the morning.

MARTHA: The train to where?

KAREN: I don't know. Some place; any place.

MARTHA: A job? Money!

KAREN: In a big place we could get something to do.

MARTHA: They'd know about us. We've been in the headlines. We're very famous.

KAREN: A small town, then.

MARTHA: They'd know more about us, I guess.

KAREN: We'll find a place to go.

MARTHA: I don't think we will. Not really. I feel as if I couldn't move, and what would be the use? It seems to me I'll be sitting the rest of my life, wondering what happened. It's a bad night, tonight, but we might as well get used to it. They'll all be like this.

KAREN, *gets up, goes to stove. Hands in front of it, warming herself:* But it isn't a new sin they tell us we've done. Other people aren't destroyed by it.

MARTHA: They are the people who believe in it, who want it, who've chosen it for themselves. That must be very different. We aren't like that. We don't love each other. We don't love each other. We've been close to each other, of course. I've loved you like a friend, the way thousands of women feel about other women.

KAREN, *turns her back to stove:* I'm cold.

MARTHA: You were a dear friend who was loved, that's all. Certainly there's nothing wrong with that. It's perfectly natural that I should be fond of you. Why, we've known each other since we were seventeen and I always thought——

KAREN, *as if she were tired :* Why are you saying all this?

MARTHA: Because I love you.

KAREN, *sits on downstage left chair.* Yes, of course. I love you, too.

MARTHA: But maybe I love you *that* way. The way they said I loved you. I don't know——Listen to me.

KAREN: What?

MARTHA: *(kneels down next to Karen) I have loved you the way they said.*

KAREN, *idly:* Martha, we're both so tired. Please don't——

MARTHA: There's always been something wrong. Always—as long as I can remember. But I never knew it until all this happened.

KAREN, *for first time looks up, horrified, turns to Martha:* Stop that crazy talk—

MARTHA: You're afraid of hearing it; I'm more afraid than you.

KAREN, *turns away, hands over her ears:* I won't listen to you.

MARTHA: You've got to know it. I can't keep it to myself any longer. I've got to tell you that I'm guilty.

KAREN, *deliberately:* You are guilty of nothing.

MARTHA: I've been telling myself that since the night we heard the child say it. I lie in bed night after night praying that it isn't true. But I know about it now. It's there. I don't know how. I don't know why. But I did love you. I do love you. I resented your marriage; maybe because I wanted you; maybe I wanted you all these years; I couldn't call it by a name but maybe it's been there ever since I first knew you——

KAREN, *tensely, grips arms of chair:* It's not the truth. Not a word of it. We never thought of each other that way.

MARTHA, *bitterly:* No, of course *you* didn't. But who says I didn't? I never felt that way about anybody but you. I've never loved a man— *(Stops. Softly)* I never knew why before. Maybe it's that.

KAREN, *carefully:* You are tired and sick.

MARTHA, *as though talking to herself:* It's funny. It's all mixed up. There's something in you and you don't do anything about it because you don't know it's there. Suddenly a little girl gets bored and tells a lie—and there, that night, you see it for the first time, and you say it yourself, did she see it, did she sense it—?

KAREN, *turns to Martha. Desperately:* What are you saying? You know it could have been any lie. She was looking for anything—

MARTHA: Yes, but why this one? She found the lie with the ounce of truth. I guess they always do. I've ruined your life and I've ruined my own. I swear I didn't know it, I swear I didn't mean it— *(Rises, crosses upstage left. In a wail)* Oh, I feel so Goddamned sick and dirty—I can't stand it anymore.

KAREN: All this isn't true. We don't have to remember it was ever said. Tomorrow we'll pick ourselves up and—

MARTHA: I don't want tomorrow. It's a bad word.

KAREN, *who is crying:* Go and lie down, Martha. And in a few minutes, I'll make some tea and bring it to you. You'll feel better.

MARTHA, *looks around room, slowly, carefully. She is now very quiet. Moves, turns, looks at Karen:* Don't bring me any tea. Thank you. Good night, darling.

CURSE OF THE STARVING CLASS

by Sam Shepard

———————•———————

ACT I

The action of this odd but actually quite naturalistic play takes place in the kitchen of Ella and Weston and their son and daughter, Wesley and Emma. The family owns a run-down farm in the western United States. Ella, who mostly eats, has plans to sell the farm behind her husband's back, and dreams of using the money to go off to Europe. Weston, who mostly drinks, tried to kill her the night before when she locked him out of the house. He smashed in the front door, but left when she started screaming for the police. Emma, dressed in a white and green 4-H Club uniform, is having her first period. She decided (just minutes before the excerpt below begins) to leave home on a horse, intending to ride down the freeway to California. She made this decision when she learned that her mother ate the chicken that she had been saving for today's 4-H Club demonstration, and that her brother urinated on the charts she had prepared for her talk ("How to Cut Up a Frying Chicken").

As the scene begins, Ella has eaten everything in the house and is staring into the empty refrigerator. Emma enters, covered with mud. She is holding a horse's rope halter.

EMMA: That bastard almost killed me.

Ella shuts refrigerator and turns toward Emma.

ELLA: What happened to you?
EMMA: He dragged me clear across the corral.
ELLA: I told you not to play around with that fool horse. He's insane, that horse.
EMMA: How am I ever going to get out of here?
ELLA: You're not going to get out of here. You're too young. Now go and change your clothes.

EMMA: I'm not too young to have babies, right?

ELLA: What do you mean?

EMMA: That's what bleeding is, right? That's what bleeding's for.

ELLA: Don't talk silly, and go change your uniform.

EMMA: This is the only one I've got.

ELLA: Well, change into something else then.

EMMA: I can't stay here forever.

ELLA: Nobody's staying here forever. We're all leaving.

EMMA: We are?

ELLA: Yes. We're going to Europe.

EMMA: Who is?

ELLA: All of us.

EMMA: Pop too?

ELLA: No. Probably not.

EMMA: How come? He'd like it in Europe wouldn't he?

ELLA: I don't know.

EMMA: You mean just you, me, and Wes are going to Europe? That sounds awful.

ELLA: Why? What's so awful about that? It could be a vacation.

EMMA: It'd be the same as it is here.

ELLA: No, it wouldn't! We'd be in Europe. A whole new place.

EMMA: But we'd all be the same people.

ELLA: What's the matter with you? Why do you say things like that?

EMMA: Well, we would be.

ELLA: I do my best to try to make things right. To try to change things. To bring a little adventure into our lives and you go and reduce the whole thing to smithereens.

EMMA: We don't have any money to go to Europe anyway.

ELLA: Go change your clothes!

EMMA: No. *She crosses to table and sits stage right end.*

ELLA: If your father was here you'd go change your clothes.

EMMA: He's not.

ELLA: Why can't you just cooperate?

EMMA: Because it's deadly. It leads to dying.

ELLA: You're not old enough to talk like that.

EMA: I was down there in the mud being dragged along.

ELLA: It's your own fault. I told you not to go down there.

EMMA: Suddenly everything changed. I wasn't the same person anymore. I was just a hunk of meat tied to a big animal. Being pulled.

ELLA: Maybe you'll understand the danger now.

EMMA: I had the whole trip planned out in my head. I was going to head for Baja California.

ELLA: Mexico?

EMMA: I was going to work on fishing boats. Deep-sea fishing. Helping businessmen haul in huge swordfish and barracuda. I was going to work my way along the coast, stopping at all the little towns, speaking Spanish. I was going to learn to be a mechanic and work on four-wheel-drive vehicles that broke down. Transmissions. I could've learned to fix anything. Then I'd learn how to be a short-order cook and write novels on the side. In the kitchen. Kitchen novels. Then I'd get published and disappear into the heart of Mexico. Just like that guy.

ELLA: What guy?

EMMA: That guy who wrote *Treasure of Sierra Madre.*

ELLA: When did you see that?

EMMA: He had initials for a name. And he disappeared. Nobody knew where to send his royalties. He escaped.

ELLA: Snap out of it, Emma. You don't have that kind of a background to do jobs like that. That's not for you, that stuff. You can do beautiful embroidery; why do you want to be a mechanic?

EMMA: I like cars. I like travel. I like the idea of people breaking down and I'm the only one who can help them get on the road again. It would be like being a magician. Just open up the hood and cast your magic spell.

ELLA: What are you dreaming for?

EMMA: I'm not dreaming now. I was dreaming then. Right up to the point when I got the halter on. Then as soon as he took off I stopped. I stopped dreaming and saw myself being dragged through the mud.

ELLA: Go change your clothes.

EMMA: Stop saying that over and over as though by saying it you relieve yourself of responsibility.

ELLA: I can't even follow the way you talk to me anymore.

EMMA: That's good.

ELLA: Why is that good?

EMMA: Because if you could then that would mean that you understood me.

Pause. Ella turns and opens the refrigerator again and stares into it.

EMMA: Hungry?
ELLA: No.
EMMA: Just habit?
ELLA: What?
EMMA: Opening and closing?
ELLA, *closes refrigerator and turns toward Emma:* Christ Emma, what am I going to do with you?
EMMA: Let me go.
ELLA, *after pause:* You're too young. *Ella exits.*

MOONCHILDREN

by Michael Weller

ACT 1, SCENE 3

The play takes place in a student apartment in an American university town. In outline, it is the story of a senior college year in the mid-sixties, and the time of the play runs from fall through graduation. During the course of the play the characters go through antiwar riots, love affairs, an expulsion from school, an attempted self-immolation, and the death of a parent. In this excerpt Ruth and Kathy are airing their frustrations with their boyfriends.

Kathy is sitting at the table, staring blankly ahead. The front door opens. Ruth comes back, her clothes from the previous scene slightly scuffed. Ruth sees that Kathy is upset.

RUTH: Hey, what's wrong? Bob here?
KATHY: No.
RUTH: Want some coffee.
KATHY: Please.

RUTH, *takes off her coat and starts making coffee:* I thought you and Bob were coming. You were on the bus and everything. I got lost when the cops charged. Man, they really got some of those guys.

KATHY: When we got there he said he didn't feel like marching.

RUTH: Why not?

KATHY: Oh, Ruthie, I don't know. I don't know anything any more. You devote two years to a guy and what does he give you? He didn't even tell me about being drafted.

RUTH: He's not drafted. For chrissakes, Kathy, that letter's for the physical, that's all. All he has to do is act queer. They're not gonna take a queer musician.

KATHY: That's what I told him on the bus. He wouldn't even listen to me until I called him Job. He said from now on he's dead, Bob is dead and everybody has to call him Job.

RUTH: Oh, come on, Kathy, he's just putting you on.

KATHY: That's what I mean. *Me.* He's even putting *me* on. Ungrateful bastard. After all the things I've done for him. *Pause.* Shit, I sound just like my mother. It's just you get tired of giving all the time and nothing's coming back. You know what I told him? I said he was the first guy I ever had an orgasm with. I mean, it really made him feel good. Now I gotta live with it.

RUTH: Hey, for real, is he really worried about that letter?

KATHY: He says he's gonna try to pass.

RUTH: What!?

KATHY: He wants to join. That's what he told me. He wants to study engineering in the army and when he gets out he's gonna get some kind of plastic job and marry a nice little plastic wife and live in a plastic house in some plastic suburb and have 2.7 plastic children.

RUTH: Bullshit.

KATHY: Ruthie, I'm telling you, he's serious. You know what he told me? He thinks the whole antiwar movement is a goddamn farce. That's what he said. I mean, Jesus, I really thought we were relating on that one. It's not like I'm asking the guy to go burn himself or anything. It's just, I mean, he knows how I feel about this war and he's just doing it to be shitty. I know what it is. He's, like, reaching out, trying to relate to me on a personal level by rejecting me but, like, I don't know how to break through. Oh, Ruth, it's all too much. He went to a cowboy film.

RUTH: Well, you know, that's how it is.

KATHY: Ruthie!

RUTH: Well, I mean, you know, like maybe he's serious. Mike's got this thing about physics. He really digs it and his advisor says he's a genius, okay, maybe he is, like what do I know about physics? The thing is, he knows he's gonna end up working for his old man in the lumber business. It's all laid out from the start. You have to just sort of fit in.

KATHY: You don't want him to do that, do you? I mean, if the guy is really into physics you have to stand behind him and make it all happen for him.

RUTH: I don't know. You have some kids and everything. I mean, it's not like you can't have a meaningful life if you get married and have kids. Look, I don't want the guy to saw wood for the rest of his life but what can I do about it? Why shouldn't he get into wood? Like, what if he does physics for the rest of his life and he's a genius and ends up head of department at some asshole university. You find out one day he's being financed by the CIA.

KATHY: These guys. They think they don't need you so you go away and they fall to pieces. You should've seen Bob when I first met him.

RUTH: I did.

KATHY: He used to compose all this really shitty music and like when he did something good he didn't even know it. I had to keep telling him yes, it's good, it's really great. A whole year it took him to believe it. He's writing some brilliant stuff now, ever since, you know, I told him he was the first guy.

RUTH: Yeah, and look at him now.

KATHY, *weeping:* I don't know. You think you're really relating like crazy and then, suddenly, it's a whole new scene.

RUTH: Maybe you ought to stop relating so hard.

FATHER'S DAY

by Oliver Hailey

———————•———————

ACT I

Marian, Estelle, and Louise are three divorcées sharing an after-noon in the sun while their former spouses spend Father's Day with the children. During the course of the play they reveal and share their thoughts on marriage and sex, their fears of a future without mates, and their struggle to maintain a sense of security in an insecure world. In the end each has to confront the reality of her shattered marriage and learn to face the future.

The scene below takes place on the terrace of the Manhattan apartment house in which they live. The three women have been chatting about their past married lives and discussing preparations for a Father's Day party later that day which their ex-husbands will attend. Estelle, the youngest and most naïve of the three has just left to get some of her homemade gazpacho. Marian and Louise are sophisticated, articulate women whose acerbic wits are often directed at each other. When left alone they begin to gossip about Estelle. Their conversation quickly turns to their broken marriages and, with humor that belies their painful sense of rejection, they share their concerns about their families. (The "Fred and Sammy" mentioned by Marian are the roommates of Harold, Estelle's ex-husband.)

LOUISE, *a long beat as Louise stares at Marian:* I don't like her gazpacho either.
MARIAN: There is nothing worse than bad gazpacho. *A beat.* Unless it's bad Quiche Lorraine. Have you ever had bad Quiche Lorraine?
LOUISE: I've had bad everything.
MARIAN: I always thought Estelle's gazpacho might have been one of the reasons Harold left her. Whatever else you say about Fred and Sammy, they make *marvelous* gazpacho.
LOUISE: Any theories on why Tom left me? I don't even make gazpacho.

MARIAN: You hated each other, didn't you? I believe you've made that clear enough.

LOUISE: It's the reason I give—yes—but, God, I don't know a good marriage that doesn't have a chunk of hate mixed in. I'd like to say something kind, Marian.

MARIAN, *stunned:* To me?

LOUISE: Yes, I envy you. That's why I'm so bitchy with you. I'm sorry.

MARIAN: Envy?

LOUISE: You know *why* you divorced your husband. You caught him committing adultery and you divorced him. That's such a good, solid, middle-class reason.

MARIAN: I thought you were going to say something kind.

LOUISE: That is kind. I have great respect for middle-class logic. It doesn't make for great essayists, of course—and I'm afraid that's your problem there. But as for Richard, you caught him with another woman and you kicked him out. That's so simple—a woman can live with that.

MARIAN: I am not middle-class! My father was a Communist and probably still is!

LOUISE: It'd been raining a couple of weeks the morning Tom and I decided to split.

MARIAN, *and then muttering to herself:* Middle class!

LOUISE: And I suppose Tom and I got nastier when it rained—close quarters—but it finally cleared. We slept late—and when we woke, he turned to me and said, "Why don't we quit playing this game?" I smiled and said, "Wonderful idea." I thought he meant the game of hating one another. But he said, "Fine. I'll call the lawyer right now." He meant the game of being married to one another.

MARIAN: Oh, poor Louise.

LOUISE: No—dumb Louise. When he asked which of us should make the trip to Tia Juana, I can remember my big thought was how much I loved Mexican food. On the way down on the plane, I kept thinking, "I'll have a good meal and then I'll go to whomever you go to—but when they see my papers—how legally married I am—church *and* state—they'll say, 'Oh, señora, we can't do anything about this one—not even in Mexico!'" Well, those Goddamn Mexicans had me divorced in twenty minutes! All those wonderful churches down there— all that fucking religious art. What God has joined let no man put asunder. Ha! To this day I haven't been able to eat another enchilada. And now she's in there pouring up that Goddamn gazpacho.

MARIAN: That's Spanish—gazpacho.

LOUISE: Yeh? Ever meet a Mexican who didn't tell you he was? *Suddenly a piano is heard playing Chopin in the distance. The selection is Ballade No. 1 in G Minor, Op. 23.* There goes that Chopin nut again. What floor does he live on anyway? That damn thing sounds like it's coming from above *and* below. Ever have sex with a pair of twins, Marian?

MARIAN, *shocked:* No.

LOUISE: Well, neither have I—but that's exactly what that Goddamn piano sound makes me think of—above *and* below.

MARIAN: You have an incredible mind.

LOUISE: Thanks. *And then shouting at the ledge:* Hey, there— I got a cat down here. My cat hates Chopin. How about a little Debussy for my pussy?

MARIAN, *she jumps up, tries to hide against the wall from fear of being spotted by anyone on the other decks.* Really, Louise— he's quite a sensitive young man.

LOUISE: *You* know him?

MARIAN: Ronnie? Not well—but I've spoken with him.

LOUISE: Ronnie who?

MARIAN: Ronnie Michner.

LOUISE, *again at the ledge—shouting:* Ronnie! Ronnie Michner! CUT THAT SHIT OUT! *The music stops abruptly.*

MARIAN: To refer to Chopin in such a manner. Oh, Louise, I must say I've never seen you quite like you are this afternoon.

LOUISE: There's a reason.

MARIAN: Oh?

LOUISE: I hoped it wouldn't show so quickly—but it does, doesn't it?

MARIAN: Well, you're always unpleasant, of course—but no, I'll be fair—you've reached your nadir today.

LOUISE: They want to take Christopher away.

MARIAN: Away? Christopher? Who?

LOUISE: Who do you think? Tom and the Fat One. They want him to come live with them.

MARIAN: You mean permanently?

LOUISE: That's right. I'll get visiting privileges, of course. Mother's Day—things like that.

MARIAN: But Christopher's only seven. A child always stays with his mother.

LOUISE: Marian—you are *so* middle-class.

MARIAN: Medea killed her children rather than let Jason take them. And what kind of class was she?

LOUISE: That kind of behavior shows no class at all.

MARIAN: How could Tom ask such a thing? It was cruel even to ask.

LOUISE: Chris is his son, too. And he wants him. What's cruel?

MARIAN: I'd lie. If it came to that I'd lie. I'd swear Augustus was not Richard's son.

LOUISE, *she suddenly laughs sharply:* That's very funny.

MARIAN: What's funny?

LOUISE: Well ... if you're going at it that literally, I'm not sure Chris is.

MARIAN: Not Tom's son?

LOUISE: Not *sure.*

MARIAN: Are you lying again? You lie a lot, you know.

LOUISE: All right, skip it.

MARIAN: Whose son is he?

LOUISE: I just said I'm not *that* sure. I was an actress, remember? And a very popular one—offstage. When I found I was with child, I decided on Tom. He knew it was going to be a seven-month baby. He assumed *his* seven-month baby. Me, I was never that sure. All those bad jokes about "only the mother knows for sure." Well, here's one mother who really doesn't have the foggiest. There were three very serious contenders.

MARIAN: I'm shocked, Louise.

LOUISE: Oh, you're not.

MARIAN: I know I'm not supposed to be, but I am. I was just saying to Estelle that nothing shocks me today. Well, that's a lie! I'm shocked every day of my life! I don't know how much more my system can take. Every day new outrages. I'm glad the Tribune didn't live to have to print them! And now this. Why did you tell me? I don't want to know things like this, damn it!

LOUISE: All right, I'm sorry.

MARIAN: Who were the other two? Anyone I knew?

LOUISE: No one worth naming. After me they both went gay. The life of an actress is not that easy.

MARIAN: Well, if they became homosexuals, then Tom probably *is* the father—since he's the only one of the three who chose to assume the role of a father.

LOUISE: There's not a court in the country could follow that reasoning. *A beat.* They leave in a month.

MARIAN: Leave? You mean leave New York?

LOUISE: They're moving to Iowa. Sioux City.

MARIAN: Tom's changing jobs?

LOUISE: No—the whole firm's moving. It's another one of those "We've had it with New York" company moves.

MARIAN: They want to take Christopher to Iowa? To Sioux City, Iowa? My God, that place is in the Midwest, isn't it?

LOUISE: You want to know my first thought? It was pretty horrible. I thought—thank God Tom and I aren't still married—*I'd* have to go to Iowa. This way it's only Christopher.

MARIAN: Don't talk like that. You'd never let him go. All the way to Iowa? With a man and woman he's probably not even related to?

LOUISE: I'm letting him decide.

MARIAN: Who? Christopher?

LOUISE: Yes.

MARIAN: A child? A child make a decision like that?

LOUISE: Who better?

MARIAN: *You* better—that's who better. This way all you're doing is testing his love. Don't. Because he'll go with the one who offers him the most. It'll have nothing to do with love. I'll tell you something. *A beat—this is not easy for her.* Augustus has tried to run off four times to live with his father.

LOUISE: I didn't know that.

MARIAN: I couldn't tell it for a long time. Until I came to understand why. And yet it's really quite simple. His father has more than I do. It's greed. They're hopelessly greedy little creatures. And nothing feeds that greed quite like divorce. Christopher is only seven. Augustus is almost twelve. I've heard him actually boasting to friends—what a great racket he's got going—what a great setup it is!

LOUISE: I don't want that to happen to my child.

MARIAN: Who the hell does?

LOUISE: Then I think he should have a crack at a set of parents . . . or, as Christopher puts it . . . "a mother and father who both live in."

MARIAN: I picked a parent, you know.

LOUISE: Your parents were never divorced.
MARIAN: No—but I picked one anyway. I loved my mother, of course—but I picked my father. I listened to him. I modeled myself after him. My poor mother had virtually nothing to do. She died quite young, you know. Some take it better, of course. But I should never have picked a parent. No child should be permitted to.

THE DAYS AND NIGHTS OF
BEEBEE FENSTERMAKER

by William Snyder

———•———

ACT I

Beebee Fenstermaker is a young woman just out of college and living in an American city on her own in her first apartment. Her aspirations are to live a creative and independent life. She tries writing and then painting, but is forced to recognize both the limitations of her talents and that, at best, she is a dilettante. Further deterioration of her self-esteem and hopes are brought about by the realities of having to work at a mundane full-time job, and by unsuccessful relationships with men. One by one her romantic illusions crumble as she is forced to confront her unrealistic expectations about men, her career, and her own abilities.

Nettie Jo is an unambitious, but fun-loving young woman who is Beebee's neighbor and friend. In the following scene Nettie Jo stops by Beebee's apartment on her way out on a date. She tells Beebee that she will soon be getting married and moving away. She expresses concern about Beebee's recent reclusiveness and tries to convince her to get out more often. During the conversation the two women begin to criticize each other's lifestyles and goals. Finally, Beebee confesses to herself that her approach to life is based on self-deception and her fear of failure.

NETTIE JO: Beebee?

BEEBEE: Hey, Nettie Jo. *Nettie Jo stands in front of armchair and takes a modeling pose. Beebee gets a sketchbook and pencil out of coffee-table drawer, sits on sofa, and begins to sketch Nettie Jo.*

NETTIE JO: You antsy about somethin?

BEEBEE, *shakes her head:* Uh-uh.

NETTIE JO: Ever since you dropped your novel and took up art, you seem much more moody to me.

BEEBEE: I haven't dropped my novel. I put it aside to let the ideas solidify.

NETTIE JO: Since you put it aside then. You seem much more moody to me. *Crosses to kitchen, gets Coke out of refrigerator and opens it.*

BEEBEE: I don't think I am.

NETTIE JO: I do. I think you are.

BEEBEE: Hold still, Nettie Jo.

NETTIE JO, *returns to her position in front of armchair:* Don't you want me to be evanescent?

BEEBEE: Not tonight.

NETTIE JO: That's the way I feel tonight.

BEEBEE: You look very pretty.

NETTIE JO: Thank you. *She smiles.*

BEEBEE: Don't smile.

NETTIE JO: How's your new art teacher?

BEEBEE: I stopped goin to him.

NETTIE JO: Stopped goin to this one too? Why?

BEEBEE: He was talkin more than he was teachin.

NETTIE JO: Who will you go to now?

BEEBEE: Nobody for a while. I thought I'd work on my own. Hold still, Nettie Jo. I wish you'd have your hair cut. All I can see is hair.

NETTIE JO: Most people like it long. *Sits in armchair.* Mother could sit on hers. I've got a picture of her doin it. Lookin up into a sterlin silver handmirror. *Poses like her mother.*

BEEBEE: Come on now, Nettie Jo.

NETTIE JO: How many teachers have you been to?

BEEBEE: What difference does it make?

NETTIE JO: Two or three anyway.

BEEBEE: What difference does it make? None of them fit the bill. I don't either, I guess. When I first go to them they all think I'm wonderful. They say how expressive and sensitive and all that. *Nettie Jo pulls at her skirt to even the hem.* Nettie Jo will you hold still? *Nettie Jo resumes posing.* And the first few days I am good. Then I get so bugged I freeze up and I get just horrible. And I stay horrible. And I tell myself I'm not doin it for them. And all right so I'm horrible now, if I was good once I'll be good again. But I'm not. Well, I'll have to work harder, that's all. Keep workin is the important thing. *Closes sketchbook and puts it in coffee-table drawer.*

NETTIE JO, *sits in armchair:* I wish you'd date more.

BEEBEE: I've told you a thousand times those T. D. Hackameyer boys don't interest me.

NETTIE JO: You don't give yourself a chance to meet anybody else. Then when you do you never will date em more than once. I wish I had a nickel for every boy I've had Tommy bring up here that you've turned thumbs down on.

BEEBEE: Nettie Jo, stop talkin like my mother.

NETTIE JO: I think you're workin too hard.

BEEBEE, *rises:* And I think you're just breezin along with the breeze, aren't you, Nettie Jo? Lettin the rest of the world go by.

NETTIE JO: I might as well. I certainly can't change it.

BEEBEE, *circling Nettie Jo:* You go right down the years sittin on your one spot. You sit on your one spot at the office. You sit on your one spot in your folks' split-level ranch house. You have no outside interests other than men. No hobbies, handicrafts or sports. No religious convictions or philosophical leanins. Just sittin. One spot Nettie Jo Repult. The girl who never gets off her behind. *Moves around in upstage right area.*

NETTIE JO: Correct, Beebee. And I'm havin a grand time doin it.

BEEBEE: You live a day at a time with never a passin thought for tomorrow or the day after.

NETTIE JO: Correct, Beebee.

BEEBEE: And what beats me is you're satisfied.

NETTIE JO: I don't have any ambition, Beebee.

BEEBEE: That's the kind sails right to the top like a gas balloon.

NETTIE JO: What do you want me to do?

BEEBEE: I don't know. But there's somethin wrong about bein so satisfied with everything the way it is and goin along with the crowd. You have to gain special recognition in some way. In *some* way, Nettie Jo. If you don't you end up nothin—a nonentity. Another face in the crowd. And that's like bein dead. Do you want to wind up dead without one person to remember your name?

NETTIE JO, *rises, crosses to bureau and gets nailfile:* If I'm dead, why should I care if people remember my name? *Crosses back to armchair, sits and files nails.* And I've got enough to keep in mind without worryin whether I'm leavin behind some mark that I won't even be able to look at. Anyway, what's wrong with bein another face in the crowd?

BEEBEE: It's death in life, that's what. It's walkin through the world without touchin a thing. It's blendin in instead of stickin out. And God knows folks try to push you into the wallpaper from the minute you're born. Startin with your family. She gets this from so and so. That from somebody else. Eyes, ears, character, bad habits, good habits. Just when you think you finally got somethin on your own, as sure as Christmas somebody comes along and says, "Isn't that exactly like Uncle Whatchamacallit." There you are locked tighter than a Chinese puzzle without knowin where one person ends and the other ones begin. *Sits on coffee table.* Then your mother starts sayin why aren't you more like people your own age? Why don't you join a sorority, a club, go to dances?

NETTIE JO: Did you ever do any of those things, Beebee?

BEEBEE: No.

NETTIE JO: Why?

BEEBEE: I didn't want to. *Pauses, then reflectively:* The funny thing is, if I had gone along with the rest, I would have been last in line.

NETTIE JO: Why?

BEEBEE: They weren't interested in me and I wasn't interested in them. It was like they had something extra. A gift I didn't have. And it made me feel cut off.

NETTIE JO: What gift was that?

BEEBEE, *absorbed in her words:* The gift of ease. Of comradeship. Of . . . belongin to somethin.

NETTIE JO: Beebee, I don't know if you realize it or not but you just contradicted yourself.

BEEBEE: How? I didn't.

NETTIE JO: You just finished sayin the last thing you wanted to be was part of a group.

BEEBEE: And I meant it. But a person can still be momentarily seduced by the *idea* of somethin they think is *wrong*.

NETTIE JO: Beebee, do you want to be like me?

BEEBEE: Like you! *Rises, crosses downstage left then circles around Nettie Jo.* Like you, Nettie Jo. Nettie Jo, like you! Why Nettie Jo, you're the last person to step on grass I'd want to be like. Why I'd take a flyin leap off anything high enough if I thought I was anything approachin bein like you.

NETTIE JO: If that's so, it makes me wonder sometimes why I'm your only friend.

BEEBEE, *holds upstage right above coffee table:* You're not.

NETTIE JO: Who else do you see?

BEEBEE: I live in the same apartment building with you. I couldn't get away from you if I tried.

NETTIE JO: You haven't tried very hard. In fact it's been just the opposite. You're always askin me up here every hour of the day or night on any pretext other than just to visit. I don't know why you can't admit sometimes you'd just like to visit.

BEEBEE, *crosses downstage right between coffee table and bed:* Well I'm admittin now that I'm gonna avoid you from now on like the bubonic plague!

NETTIE JO: O.K., Beebee, but I'll tell you this. For my money and for all your talkin—you're not much further along than me.

BEEBEE: I'm not huh? I'm not huh?

NETTIE JO: No.

BEEBEE: All that proves is that you're blind in one eye and can't see good out of the other.

NETTIE JO: And you can see out of both of yours I suppose.

BEEBEE: At least I use mine for somethin besides Maybelline!

NETTIE JO: Maybe so, but two years ago you said . . .

BEEBEE, *stunned:* Two years ago?

NETTIE JO: Yes, Beebee, two years ago. I met you two years ago.

BEEBEE: What month is this?

NETTIE JO: June.

BEEBEE: I thought it was the tag end of May.

NETTIE JO: No, it's the second of June. You were doin all that talk about love and a career bein God's answer to hundred-proof bourbon. And I thought it was a fine idea. Still do for that matter. But what have you done?

BEEBEE: What do you mean what have I done?

NETTIE JO: What have you got to show for your two years besides a stab at a novel and a few weeks of art school. What have you settled on?

BEEBEE: I've settled on paintin.

NETTIE JO: With writin on the side and music in the background. Well, I'm sorry, Beebee, but I don't see where all your "doin" gives you any right to criticize my "sittin"—cause from where I'm sittin, your doin don't look like much. *Beebee sits on coffee table. Pause.* Oh, Beebee, I didn't mean to say all that.

BEEBEE: Never mind, Nettie Jo.

NETTIE JO: When you jumped on me with all fours you just got my back up.

BEEBEE: I don't blame you.

NETTIE JO, *rises and crosses to Beebee:* Beebee, I'm worried about you.

BEEBEE: Well don't be.

NETTIE JO, *kneels beside Beebee:* The thing of it is I'll be leavin pretty soon.

BEEBEE: Leavin?

NETTIE JO: See. Tommy's asked me to marry him. And I'm goin to.

BEEBEE: Married. *Moved:* Oh. Oh, Nettie Jo. How wonderful. *She hugs Nettie Jo.* When did it happen?

NETTIE JO: Last night. I was really bowled over. I've known for a long time he's been the one I wanted, but I didn't think I was the one he wanted.

BEEBEE: How wonderful. He's a very nice boy.

NETTIE JO: I think so.

BEEBEE: Where will you live?

NETTIE JO, *crosses to armchair:* He's had a real good job offered to him in L.A. so we'll be movin out there.

BEEBEE: Soon, you say.

NETTIE JO: In about a month. It'll take me that long to quit my job and give up this place and get ready.

BEEBEE: Well. Oh, Nettie Jo. It's wonderful.

NETTIE JO, *crosses to Beebee:* I wish you were comin to California with us.

BEEBEE, *crosses to bureau:* Nettie Jo stop.

NETTIE JO, *follows Beebee:* I do. We could all take an apartment together.

BEEBEE: Now wouldn't that be fun.

NETTIE JO: It would. I know Tommy wouldn't mind.

BEEBEE: You ought to try asking him.

NETTIE JO: I already have. And he thought it was a wonderful idea.

BEEBEE: Nettie Jo.

NETTIE JO: The thing of it is I think a change of scene might give you a fresh viewpoint.

BEEBEE: Well, thanks, Nettie Jo but . . .

NETTIE JO: My thought is a fresh scene and fresh faces might help you get settled on somethin. And I'd certainly feel better about you. Will you think about it?

BEEBEE, *distracted:* What?

NETTIE JO: I say will you think about it.

BEEBEE: Yes, I'll think about it.

NETTIE JO: Well. I'll see you later. I'll come up when I get home if it's not too late.

BEEBEE: Goodbye, Nettie Jo. *Nettie Jo exits. Beebee crosses upstage center. With emotion:* Two years! That's three hundred and sixty-odd days times two! And how many hours and how many minutes and how many seconds? God, what have I been doing all this time? *The sound of the ticking begins under and increases in volume as the speech progresses.* You must have put me in a trance. I'm so dogged by time all I been doing is lettin it go by. I been here two years! People ask me what are my interests, and I say I'm a writer/pianist or a pianist/writer or a pianist/painter or a writin piano-playin painter. When all I am is a nine-to-five worker at T. D. Hackameyer's with an unfinished novel, a grubby sketchbook, and an apartment that's drivin me stark starin crazy. I *need* somebody! Somebody for *me!* If I had somebody I'd know what to do and how to do it. Well, what do you want, Miss Beebee? *Fiercely:* I want a man in the image of God! Isn't that what you're supposed to be producin? Then do it goddamit! If I'm my own worst enemy make me not my own worst enemy. I've got strings attached and they're tying me in knots! *The ticking has become almost louder than her voice. It stops abruptly.*

THE BAD SEED

by Maxwell Anderson

———•———

ACT I, SCENE 4

Rhoda is as sweet, well behaved, and innocent-seeming as a young girl can be. Yet, as this play of intrigue and suspense unfolds, her mother, Christine, learns that Rhoda is a malevolent murderer, totally devoid of conscience. Christine also learns that she herself is an adopted child, and that her *own* mother was "the most amazing woman in all the annals of homicide." Rhoda has apparently inherited her grandmother's traits (thus the *bad seed*). Prior to the following scene Christine hears on the radio that one of Rhoda's classmates, a little boy, Claude Daigle, who had just won a penmanship medal that Rhoda wanted, was found drowned on a school picnic. (The medal was not found.) Rhoda's casual reaction toward the incident surprises her mother, but the event is soon forgotten. A few days later, Miss Fern, the school headmistress, arrives at the house seeking some information about the drowning. After Rhoda leaves the room the questions begin.

MISS FERN, *she waits till Rhoda exits:* It did occur to me that—that Rhoda might have told you a detail or two which she hadn't remembered when she talked with me. You see, she was the last to see the little Daigle boy alive—
CHRISTINE: Are you sure of that?
MISS FERN: Yes.
CHRISTINE: I hadn't realized— (*Christine rises, crosses, and sits left end of sofa.*)
MISS FERN: About an hour after we arrived at the estate one of our older pupils came on Rhoda and the Daigle boy at the far end of the grounds. The boy was upset and crying, and Rhoda was standing in front of him, blocking his path. The older girl was among the trees, and neither child saw her. She was just about to intervene when Rhoda shoved the boy and snatched at

his medal, but he broke away and ran down the beach in the direction of the old wharf where he was later found. Rhoda followed him, not running, just walking along, taking her time, the older girl said.

CHRISTINE: Has it occurred to you that the older girl might not have been telling the truth?

MISS FERN: That isn't at all likely. She was one of the monitors we'd appointed to keep an eye on the younger children. She's fifteen and has been with us since kindergarten days. No, Mrs. Penmark, she was telling precisely what she saw. We know her well.

CHRISTINE: And this was the last time Claude was seen?

MISS FERN: Yes. A little later—it might have been about noon—one of the guards saw Rhoda coming off the wharf. He shouted a warning, but by then she was on the beach again and he decided to forget the matter. The guard didn't identify the girl by name, but she was wearing a red dress, he said, *(Christine looks toward front door)* and Rhoda was the only girl who wore a dress that day. *Christine rises slowly, looking toward door.* At one o'clock the lunch bell rang and Claude was missing when the roll was called. You know the rest, I think.

CHRISTINE, *turns, crosses below coffee table to dining table looking out window:* Yes. But this is very serious—if Rhoda was on the wharf—

MISS FERN: Not serious, really, when you've seen as much of how children behave as I have. Children conceal things from adults. *Christine crosses slowly downstage center.* Suppose Rhoda did follow the Daigle child onto the wharf—so many things could have happened quite innocently. He may have concealed himself in the old boat house, and then, when discovered, may have backed away from Rhoda and fallen in the water.

CHRISTINE: Yes, that could have happened.

MISS FERN: Now, Claude, although he looked frail, was an excellent swimmer—and, of course, Rhoda knew that. Once he was in the water she would have expected him to swim ashore. How could she know that the treacherous pilings were at the exact spot where he fell?

CHRISTINE: No, she couldn't possibly . . .

MISS FERN: Perhaps the thought in Rhoda's mind when he fell in the water was that he'd ruin his new suit and she'd get a scolding for causing it. When he didn't swim ashore at once she may have thought, with the logic of childhood, that he'd hidden under the wharf to frighten her—or to escape her. Later on, when it was too late to do anything, she was afraid to admit what had happened.

CHRISTINE: Then you think Rhoda knows something she isn't admitting?

MISS FERN: Yes. I think that, like many a frightened soldier, she deserted under fire. *Christine starts to reply.* This is not a serious charge. Few of us are courageous when tested.

CHRISTINE: She has lied, though.

MISS FERN: Is there any adult who hasn't lied? Smooth the lines from your brow, my dear. You're so much prettier when smiling.

CHRISTINE: I shall question Rhoda.

MISS FERN: I wish you would, though I doubt that you'll learn more than you know.

CHRISTINE, *crosses, sits on a stool:* Miss Fern, there's something I want to ask you. There was a floral tribute at Claude's funeral sent by the children of the Fern School. I suppose the children shared in the expense—but I haven't been asked to pay any part of it.

MISS FERN: The tribute wasn't nearly so expensive as the papers seemed to think. The money has been collected, and the flowers paid for.

CHRISTINE: Perhaps you telephoned me, and I was out.

MISS FERN: No, my dear. We thought perhaps you'd want to send flowers individually.

CHRISTINE: But why should we have sent flowers individually? Rhoda wasn't friendly with the boy, and my husband and I had never met the Daigles.

MISS FERN, *flustered:* I don't know, my dear. I really—— There are three of us, you know, and in the hurry of making decisions—*(she pauses)*

CHRISTINE: You make excuses for Rhoda—and then you admit that you didn't ask me to help pay for the flowers—and the reasons you give for not asking are obviously specious. *Rises and stands below stool.* Does this mean in your mind, and the minds of your sisters, there is some connection between the Daigle boy's death and Rhoda's presence on the wharf?

MISS FERN: I refuse to believe there is any connection.

CHRISTINE: And yet you have acted as if there were.

MISS FERN: Yes, perhaps we have.

CHRISTINE: This is a terrible tragedy for Mrs. Daigle, as you say. She has lost her only child. But if there were any shadow over Rhoda—from what has happened—I shall have to live under it—and my husband, too. As for Rhoda—she would not be happy in your school next year. *Turns upstage toward window.*

MISS FERN: No, she would not. *Christine stops and turns toward Miss Fern.* And since she would not, it would be as well to make up our minds now that she will not be there.

CHRISTINE, *crosses downstage center:* Then there is a shadow over her—and you have already decided not to invite her back?

MISS FERN: Yes. *Rises and faces Christine:* We have made that decision.

CHRISTINE: But you can't tell me why?

MISS FERN, *crosses to Christine:* I think her behavior in the matter of the medal would be sufficient explanation. She has no sense of fair play. She's a poor loser. She doesn't play the game.

CHRISTINE: But you're not saying that Rhoda had anything to do with the Daigle boy's death.

MISS FERN: Of course not! Such a possibility never entered our minds! *At this moment the doorbell chimes.*

CHRISTINE: I'd better answer.

MISS FERN: Of course, my dear.

NO EXIT

by Jean-Paul Sartre,
translated by Stuart Gilbert

———•———

Sartre's one-act play takes place in Hell. Three people—two women and one man—are locked together in one bricked-up room, hideously decorated in Second Empire style, where the electric lights can never be turned off. Each character has a story that reveals the circumstances of his or her death on earth, and all three deny that they deserve to be punished for their deeds. Sartre's Hell is not the fire and brimstone of the Bible but the psychological cruelty that people can inflict on each other.

Toward the beginning of the play Inez, a lesbian, tries to be-friend Estelle, a lovely but exceedingly vain young woman who has eyes only for Garcin, the male of the group. Estelle is very concerned with her appearance and falls into despair when she discovers there are no mirrors in Hell. Inez seizes this opportu-nity to coerce Estelle into a relationship. Garcin, the man, is present throughout this excerpt, but he does not speak.

Estelle has been plying her powder puff and lipstick. She looks round for a mirror, fumbles in her bag, then turns towards Gar-cin.

ESTELLE: Excuse me, have you a glass? *Garcin does not an-swer.* Any sort of glass, a pocket mirror will do. *Garcin remains silent.* Even if you won't speak to me, you might lend me a glass.

His head still buried in his hands, Garcin ignores her.

INEZ, *eagerly:* Don't worry. I've a glass in my bag. *She opens her bag. Angrily:* It's gone! They must have taken it from me at the entrance.
ESTELLE: How tiresome!

A short silence. Estelle shuts her eyes and sways, as if about to faint. Inez runs forward and holds her up.

INEZ: What's the matter?
ESTELLE, *opens her eyes and smiles:* I feel so queer. *She pats herself.* Don't you ever get taken that way? When I can't see myself I begin to wonder if I really and truly exist. I pat myself just to make sure, but it doesn't help much.
INEZ: You're lucky. I'm always conscious of myself—in my mind. Painfully conscious.
ESTELLE: Ah yes, in your mind. But everything that goes on in one's head is so vague, isn't it? It makes one want to sleep. *She is silent for a while.* I've six big mirrors in my bedroom. There they are. I can see them. But they don't see me. They're reflecting the carpet, the settee, the window—but how empty it is, a glass in which I'm absent! When I talked to people I always made sure there was one nearby in which I could see myself. I watched myself talking. And somehow it kept me alert, seeing

myself as the others saw me. . . . Oh dear! My lipstick! I'm sure I've put it on all crooked. No, I can't do without a looking glass for ever and ever, I simply can't.

INEZ: Suppose I try to be your glass? Come and pay me a visit, dear. Here's a place for you on my sofa.

ESTELLE: But— *(points to Garcin)*

INEZ: Oh, he doesn't count.

ESTELLE: But we're going to—to hurt each other. You said it yourself.

INEZ: Do I look as if I wanted to hurt you?

ESTELLE: One never can tell.

INEZ: Much more likely *you'll* hurt *me*. Still, what does it matter? If I've got to suffer, it may as well be at your hands, your pretty hands. Sit down. Come closer. Closer. Look into my eyes. What do you see?

ESTELLE: Oh, I'm there! But so tiny I can't see myself properly.

INEZ: But *I* can. Every inch of you. Now ask me questions. I'll be as candid as any looking glass.

Estelle seems rather embarrassed and turns to Garcin, as if appealing to him for help.

ESTELLE: Please, Mr. Garcin. Sure our chatter isn't boring you?

Garcin makes no reply.

INEZ: Don't worry about him. As I said, he doesn't count. We're by ourselves. . . . Ask away.

ESTELLE: Are my lips all right?

INEZ: Show! No, they're a bit smudgy.

ESTELLE: I thought as much. Luckily *(throws a quick glance at Garcin)* no one's seen me. I'll try again.

INEZ: That's better. No. Follow the line of your lips. Wait! I'll guide your hand. There. That's quite good.

ESTELLE: As good as when I came in?

INEZ: Far better. Crueler. Your mouth looks quite diabolical that way.

ESTELLE: Good gracious! And you say you like it! How maddening, not being able to see for myself! You're quite sure, Miss Serrano, that it's all right now?

INEZ: Won't you call me Inez?

ESTELLE: Are you sure it looks all right?

INEZ: You're lovely, Estelle.

ESTELLE: But how can I rely upon your taste? Is it the same as *my* taste? Oh, how sickening it all is, enough to drive one crazy!

INEZ: I *have* your taste, my dear, because I like you so much. Look at me. No, straight. Now smile. I'm not so ugly, either. Am I not nicer than your glass?

ESTELLE: Oh, I don't know. You scare me rather. My reflection in the glass never did that; of course, I knew it so well. Like something I had tamed. . . . I'm going to smile, and my smile will sink down into your pupils, and heaven knows what it will become.

INEZ: And why shouldn't you "tame" *me*? *(The women gaze at each other, Estelle with a sort of fearful fascination.)* Listen! I want you to call me Inez. We must be great friends.

ESTELLE: I don't make friends with women very easily.

INEZ: Not with postal clerks, you mean? Hullo, what's that— that nasty red spot at the bottom of your cheek? A pimple?

ESTELLE: A pimple? Oh, how simply foul! Where?

INEZ: There. . . . You know the way they catch larks—with a mirror? I'm your lark mirror, my dear, and you can't escape me. . . . There isn't any pimple, not a trace of one. So what about it? Suppose the mirror started telling lies? Or suppose I covered my eyes—as he is doing—and refused to look at you, all that loveliness of yours would be wasted on the desert air. No, don't be afraid, I can't help looking at you, I shan't turn my eyes away. And I'll be nice to you, ever so nice. Only you must be nice to me, too.

A short silence.

ESTELLE: Are you really—attracted by me?

INEZ: Very much indeed.

Another short silence.

ESTELLE, *indicating Garcin by a slight movement of her head:* But I wish he'd notice me, too.

INEZ: Of course! Because he's a Man! *To Garcin:* You've won. *Garcin says nothing.* But look at her, damn it! *Still no reply from Garcin.* Don't pretend. You haven't missed a word of what we've said.

LADIES AT THE ALAMO

by Paul Zindel

———————•———————

ACT II

Dede Cooper is the founder and artistic director of the Alamo, a multi-million-dollar regional theater complex in Texas City, Texas. Through her fierce will, hard work, and shrewd manipulation, Dede has parlayed this once small theatrical operation into a major cultural center. Now her power is being threatened. Joanne Remington, chairman of the board and important financial contributor, is critical of Dede's style, her artistic vision, and her inability to produce full-capacity audiences. She plans to replace Dede with Shirley Fuller, an ex-Hollywood star whom she will be able to manipulate and control. During the course of the play Joanne and Dede trade accusations and threats.

The scene below, set in the posh conference room of the theater, is between Dede and Joanne, and takes place just after Dede has exposed Shirley Fuller's history of alcoholism, sexual indiscretions, and mental instability. The "goober" referred to is a dried bull's penis, described as a "cane-like object." It was given to Dede as a gift. (For scene study purposes the single interchange between Dede and Bella may be ignored.)

DEDE, *shutting off the intercom and crossing center:* Well, I guess you owe me an apology, Joanne.

JOANNE, *crossing to Dede:* I owe you no such thing. Just because I made a mistake about Shirley Fuller doesn't mean I've made a mistake about you.

DEDE: And what is that supposed to mean?

JOANNE: It means I'm still going to bring someone down here to ride herd on you, that's what it means. *Crossing to the downstage right bar.* And that much I am still going to tell the Board of Trustees tonight. I don't think we misunderstand each other on that point.

DEDE, *crossing to the desk:* I don't think the problem is in the area of misunderstanding. I think it's more like misestimation.

JOANNE: Ha! You're the last one to correct my English.

DEDE, *picking up the goober:* Yes, but I am the first one to know you don't get very far in Texas by misestimation. Oh, I come from the dirt, all right—I'm just like a Prairie Dog—you know, you can't catch them. I'm here, I'm there—I'm over yonder—you can never tell where I'm going to be next. But I'm always out there somewhere. You know how those Prairie Dogs are. Just when you think you've got them, and you've run them down a hole—they pop up somewhere else. You just can't catch them.

JOANNE: If I were you, I wouldn't misestimate me. If you think that because I was raised with money and properly educated, that I'm weak, you're mistaken. *Crossing behind the desk.* I'll take over the Alamo myself tonight if necessary.

DEDE, *moving upstage, around the desk and behind Joanne:* Joanne, you're not a member of the family of clowns—as much as you would like to be. You have to be a poor clown to be in the theater. *Dede touches Joanne with the goober as she passes behind her, and then continues moving downstage right.*

JOANNE: Get that away from me, or I'll wrap it around your neck!

BELLA: Oh, Dede, did you hear that? She threatened you with physical violence!

DEDE, *crossing left:* Shut up, Bella.

JOANNE: What did you think? Just because you were born a poor hick you cornered the market on grit? You have no idea how strong a gal had to be to survive the onslaught of Biblical passages which defined a woman in my parents' house: "And the head of the woman is man" that's Corinthians; and Timothy, "Every woman should be ashamed of the thought that she is a woman." *With a yell, Dede holds the goober in front of her like a weapon and charges at Joanne. Joanne merely lifts a hand and stops her with her icy tone:* Stop that, you animal!

DEDE: That is what you find repulsive about me, isn't it? I bleat like some kind of animal. *Crossing to left center.* Is that why, in all these years, you have never once invited me to your house, you son-of-a-bitch!

JOANNE, *crossing to right center:* You'd be out of place at any party I gave. You're raised like a mongrel, you can't just put on a lime-green dress and expect the mud doesn't show anymore.

DEDE, *crossing to downstage right of Joanne:* You belong to some other race, don't you? You and your herd are a genetically pure pack of cows. All the right brands. *Dede turns and again smacks Joanne with the goober.*

JOANNE: I told you to keep that away from me!

DEDE, *moving right:* Well, my mama told me, "You keep a cattle prod around, Dede, sometimes one of them high-bred cows doesn't want to go into the corral. You've got to give her a good whack!" *Dede whirls about in order to hit Joanne again, but Joanne catches it in her hand and pulls it away from Dede.*

JOANNE: Don't you dare touch me with that filthy thing again, or I'll smack you across the face with it. *Joanne realizes that she is now holding the goober in her hand and is repulsed by the contact. She throws it away upstage.* You disgusting mutt!

DEDE: Joanne, we are ladies here at the Alamo! Ladies!

JOANNE: You are not a lady! You are a rodent—that's what a prairie dog is! Something I was taught to despise ever since I was a child. You are a destructive mammal burrowing under the earth, tearing apart and chewing at the roots of anything that's trying to grow! You are devouring this theater with no sense of where you're going or the importance of what it is you're destroying! *Crossing to the desk to pick up her bag.* I and the Board of Trustees will begin legal action tomorrow and we'll have you out of here in a week. *Dede grabs the hammer from the desk, and crashes it down on the desk. She then holds it above her head and crosses to block Joanne's exit.*

DEDE, *screaming:* Is that what you goddamn think! Huh?

JOANNE: You're as sick as the others.

DEDE, *exploding, wielding the hammer high over Joanne's head, and forcing Joanne back downstage left till she ends up sitting on the edge of the platform:* BULLSHIT! If I was a man you'd just say I'm belligerent. But just because I'm a lady, I'm sick, huh? Now, I want you to stay here, and you're going to stay a while or this hammer is going to come right down and crack open your skull. You just don't blink an eye, or I will tear off your scalp with the hook on this thing, you understand me? You will at best go running down the hall with this protruding right out of your temple! I am not devouring this theater, lady! Everything this theater has, I gave it! And I have given it as an

amateur. Yes! Out of love. And I am proud to be an amateur,
and I am ashamed that I had tried to forget it for so long. You
know, you made the mistake of reminding me how immune I
am to your kind of bigoted aristocracy. And if I want to I can
invent a story about you being a dyke. I'll make up that you are
a dyke, you've been living with a dyke and Bella and I say we
have seen you be a dyke—and if that don't work, we can make
you black! And I point out to you that the members of the
Board that I have not charmed, Bella has amused. Now I'm
telling you what you're going to do. You came in here tonight
and you made a fuss. And the kind of fuss you made in here tonight is the kind of thing that I can kill you for. You are not in
this room with the Persian Lamb Set, honey. You are in here
with the Monkey Fur Set. I did not drip my blood around this
town for almost twenty years to have you fussing me out. Now
the only thing I want to know is am I going to have to kill you?
Lifting the hammer again and moving in on Joanne: Did you
hear me, you female son-of-a-bitch? Do I have to kill you?
JOANNE, *screaming and covering her head:* No!
DEDE: No? *Crossing to the desk:* Well, I didn't think I'd have
to. *Crossing to center.* Tonight you will resign as President of
the Board. In fact, you *have* resigned and your resignation is accepted! Tomorrow I will appoint another Miss Moneybags and
if she does not have a foundation I'll help her invent one. There
are fifty people in this town just dying to be what you are—a
parasite! A leech that sucks on the backs of talented people.
And there's twenty different kinds of talent—and one of them is
the talent to survive! Now you just go on sitting around in your
basic black and your goddamn pearls! You never did an honest
day's work in your life. All you ever did was ring your bell and
some servant came running to wipe your ass. Well, honey, I
don't come running when you ring your bell. I may be a national joke, you son-of-a-bitch, but I am a local success! And I don't
care where you see me, if it's in a theater lobby or a restaurant
or in the street, you get up and get out of my way. Now go on,
get! Get! Get! *She chases Joanne out the door with the hammer.
Dede stops at the door. She is exhausted. She turns and throws
the hammer across the floor, then crosses down right to the bar.*

THE GIRL ON THE
VIA FLAMINIA

by Alfred Hayes

———•———

ACT I

Rome in the winter of 1944. The American army has occupied
Italy. The action takes place in the apartment of the Pulcini
family. There is little work to be had in Italy. To survive, the
family has turned their apartment into a meeting place for lonely soldiers and young Italian women, a place where companionship and sexuality are exchanged for chocolates, warm food,
and a safe roof.

Lisa, young, pretty—but homeless, jobless, and hungry—
agrees to become the companion of Robert, a lonely American
soldier. The bitterness and self-hatred generated by their "arrangement" brings into sharp relief the degradation that befalls
both conqueror and conquered in the aftermath of war.

In the following scene, early in the play, Lisa is convinced by
Nina (who already has her own "arrangement" with a soldier)
that she should go ahead with the planned meeting with Robert—that it is not as unpleasant to have sex with a strange man
as it is to starve to death.

NINA, *sits left at dining table:* I'm exhausted. Such a day. Such
excitement.
LISA: When will he come?
NINA: Who?
LISA: Your Roberto.
NINA: Mine? Yours, dear.
LISA: When will he come?
NINA, *rises. Opening purse to get at nail equipment in cosmetic
bag:* I telephoned. Dio! To telephone an American! First one
answers: who do I want? I say il sergente Roberto. Roberto?
What Roberto? They never heard of a— *(above table)* Roberto
in their company. Oh, he says—Bob! Si, Bob! Well, he says, this

one on the telephone, how about me, babbee, instead of Bob? Finally he goes. Va bene. Comes another one to the telephone. Again who do I want. Again the Roberto; again the Bob. Then he says: 'allo. 'allo, who's speaking? I say Nina. *Nina! (Lisa shushes Nina up, stands center)* This one shouts, on the telephone. *Loudly:* How's the old tomato, Nina? Che pomodoro? Who has a tomato? But that is how one telephones an American.

LISA: And when you spoke to him?

NINA: Who?

LISA: Roberto.

NINA: He was happy you had agreed. Why not? Look how pretty his girl will be.

LISA: Pretty?

NINA: But you are pretty.

LISA, *crosses back to dining table:* Yes, and this is pretty, too. To wait, like this, in a strange house for a man I've never seen.

NINA: Why do you have to see him? If he's nice, he's nice, sight unseen. Listen to me, cara. For three weeks he's bother me to introduce him to a nice girl. *Lisa turns.* Have you eaten today?

LISA, *crosses. Sits by Nina, right:* It's not important.

NINA: Have you paid your rent? So. At least with Roberto you'll eat, and you'll have somewhere to live. *During the following Lisa has to fight back the tears.* I've told Adele you are married to him. I've explained to Roberto how it will be—that you are not a street girl, and that the arrangement will be a permanent one. He's anxious too. The Army's a cold place.

LISA: But I can't.

NINA: You can't what?

LISA: Make love to a stranger. *Banging on the table, she causes Nina to accidentally smear the nail polish she is applying.*

NINA: One learns.

LISA: Oh, Nina— *(To above table)*

NINA: What do you want me to say? *Repairing fingernail job with a tissue:* One learns. One learns everything. Wars are all the same. *Rises.* The men become thieves, and the women— *(crosses to left of table)* And it's the same everywhere. *Throws tissue on floor.*

LISA, *turns:* Not in America.

NINA: In America, too, if they had gone through what we've

gone through. *Lisa sits left of dining table. Nina crosses to Lisa. Gently touching her hair:* No, cara, one doesn't live as one likes to, but as one must. *Crosses up right center.* Go through the city! On the Corso, on the Via Veneto, on all the bridges—it's the same. Everywhere the soldiers and the women. Why? *To right of dining table.* Because there is nothing else, cara mia, except to drink and to make love and to survive. Our men? Poof! They guts are gone. Let them whimper and shout—the cigarettes they smoke, and the coffee they drink, we buy them.

LISA, *loudly; rises:* I'm not one of the women who stand on the bridges.

NINA: Did I say you were? We are all unlucky in the same way. We were born, and born women, and in Europe during the wars. *Sits above dining table. Closing her cosmetic bag:* Besides, who will it harm? Adele will have her rent—and if you won't be happier, at least you won't be hungrier—

LISA: But what will I say to him?

NINA: Madonna!

LISA: I've never gone with a soldier.

NINA: Ask him how's his old tomato! *Lisa turns away left. Nina throws down purse:* Dio, you've talked to a man before.

LISA, *back to Nina:* Not the Americans.

NINA: They speak exactly the same language.

LISA, *bitterly:* The liberators!

NINA, *rises:* We lost the war.

LISA, *moves in to the table:* Only the war?

NINA: Oh you make me sick! *Crosses up center.*

LISA, *crosses up to Nina. Holding chair back of table:* Yes, he'll feed me because he's won the war, and that's part of the arrangement, and then after he's fed me we'll go to bed, because that's part of the arrangements, too. *Cross down left.* But why should I be better or different than the women standing on the bridges? How stupid to think one is different or better. *Crosses to couch, sits dejectedly.* I'll have my American. Everybody has one now.

NINA, *follows Lisa to couch. Impatiently:* No, you'll jump in the Tiber.

LISA: Why not?

NINA: They'll fish out another fool!

LISA: There will be one less in the world.

NINA, *turns away:* I ought to let you!

LISA: It's not important either way.

NINA, *turns back:* Except I went through all the trouble of getting you a nice one!

LISA: You take him. You like Americans.

NINA, *crosses down left, sits on couch below Lisa:* Like them? Some I could spit on. You should see their officers as I've seen them—what animals! Screaming in the hotel corridors, and such jokes! To them it's a wonderful joke to hang toilet paper from a chandelier—

LISA: Che brutta guerra.

NINA: Si. But what shall I do—cry my eyes out? Or jump in the Tiber? There's enough corpses on the bottom now—and it's better to eat and *(leans back)* to go to Firenze when one can—

LISA: Or wait for some Roberto.

NINA: Or wait for some Roberto.

LISA: But—

Lights build before Adele's entrance.

NINA: But what?

LISA: He may not like me.

NINA, *looks at her and smiles slightly:* Would you like to bet?

THE GINGHAM DOG

by Lanford Wilson

———•———

ACT I

Lanford Wilson's play is a portrait of a dissolving interracial marriage on its final day. Gloria, a black woman, and Vincent, her white husband, are dividing up the belongings of their East Village apartment. The air is full of recriminations and painful accusations as Vincent packs his things. Vincent's sister, Barbara, has come by to help her brother move. She is a young, naïve southerner who has been in New York only a short time. Vincent has just exited to get more packing boxes, leaving Barbara and Gloria alone. Gloria is upset and tries to ignore Barbara's attempts at conversation. As the scene progresses, the underlying hostilities the two women feel toward each other are revealed.

GLORIA: Barbara, Barbara, Barbara, before you get all snug and cuddly there—I've got a lot to do and I don't want to be rude, but I just don't feel like a chat. To be perfectly frank I've never liked you and I can't pretend to—
BARBARA: Oh, I don't blame you, actually. I've known you didn't like me really. But I've always liked you. A lot. I didn't want to chat or anything. I just—
GLORIA: I just don't care to talk about my private life with you.
BARBARA: I'm not interested in your and Vincent's sex life—
GLORIA: —Oh, my god—
BARBARA: —Anyway, I'm sure that it was probably just as normal as anyone. I just wanted you to know that I'm sorry you and Vincent are divorcing like this. *Gloria looks up sharply.* I still feel that if you had talked about it, you wouldn't have to be, is all.
GLORIA: Vince and I have spent the whole day *avoiding* talking about it and I think that's best. The thought of a girl-to-girl chat nauseates me.

BARBARA, *exiting to the bathroom, quite cool:* I know why you don't like me—and I don't think it's fair, really.

GLORIA, *to herself in the second she is gone:* Phoney white tramp.

BARBARA, *reentering, a few articles in her hand:* You feel that I'm Southern. Because I speak the way I do; you feel I'm just a typical Southerner.

GLORIA: Barbara, I don't think of you as typically anything— exactly.

BARBARA: Yes you do, you think I sound like a hillbilly and you're right: I can tell I don't talk as well as you, that I don't sound like people in New York. Are these his?

GLORIA: Yes. Barbara, in you a hillbilly accent is charming. In my brother, or one of my sisters, it would be a sure sign of stupidity. You can be vapid and dumb and wide-eyed as all hell but if Cynthia or Nora looked wide-eyed it would be comical. They have to practically *squint!* It's a joke.

BARBARA: Well, they joke about hillbillies, too. I don't think it's so damn charming. And you're wrong about people laughing at the way Negroes talk. I haven't heard a good colored-people joke in two years— And on TV the only people who can put on a dumb accent anymore are Negroes.

GLORIA: Yes. Well, we've earned the privilege.

BARBARA: Is Cynthia and Nora the names of your sisters? I didn't know you had more than one sister, Gloria.

GLORIA: I have four sisters and two brothers living.

BARBARA: I didn't know that. How old are they?

GLORIA: I don't know. I haven't seen them in a long time; Cynthia's fourteen; Nora's eight or nine.

BARBARA: Why did you say "living?"

GLORIA: One brother died at birth and a sister died in infancy.

BARBARA: Oh. I didn't know that.

GLORIA: Well, you asked—

BARBARA: I didn't—

GLORIA: —It's an occupational hazard of being a poor Harlem Black. You shouldn't trouble yourself with it—

BARBARA: —Well, not just Black—

GLORIA: —It's something the "outside" shouldn't and doesn't trouble itself with. What did you say?

BARBARA: I said, not just Black. Not just the poor Harlem

Black. Back home—our home, near Louisville—they aren't city slum or black, they're just poor. But they have baby after baby dying like flies. They have—every shack along the road has a screaming, dirty, skinny mess of kids on the porch, and a grave plot alongside the house with four or five markers. It's no different.

GLORIA: It's a great deal different, when it's your own sister dead on the bed in front of you, my dear.

BARBARA: You don't think about other people, Gloria, you never once do; and you're very smart, actually, about other things—

GLORIA: —When every apartment is wall-to-wall screaming and filth, every pore of the rotting building you live in is death, you don't consider other people's misery, Barbara. I *lived* in misery.

BARBARA: Well, so did millions of other people. *Worse.* Not me, although it wasn't much better. It's not so crowded in Harlem as it is in Indonesia. In Indonesia people, millions of people, are living on just one bowl of—

GLORIA: —Fuck Indonesia! *Beat.* Fuck the Indonesians. What the hell are the Indonesians to me?

BARBARA: Well, I'm not saying you didn't. We sound like a contest of who knows the worst conditions. I didn't want to start something like that. I just came here to help Vincent.

GLORIA: Well, everything is between Vince and me; I didn't intend to go into my dingy family heritage for you.

BARBARA: I didn't know you had a brother and sister that died.

GLORIA: Well, now that you do, I'm sure you won't let it trouble you any.

BARBARA: Of course it will. Maybe I can think that that helps to explain how you feel about—

GLORIA: It doesn't explain anything about me!

BARBARA: It's you're so—I honestly don't know! You tell me all that like you were *proud* of your sister dying and *proud* of—

GLORIA: *I AM! PROUD! I am proud!*

PATIO/PORCH

by Jack Heifner

———————•———————

Set on the porch of an old Victorian house somewhere in Texas, *Porch* depicts the relationship between Dot and Lucille. Dot is a cranky, irritable old woman who dominates her spinster daughter. Throughout this one-act play their dialogue reveals the frustration and mutual torment they inflict on each other.

This scene takes place at the end of the play. Dot is complaining about the noisy fan Lucille uses in her room. The argument quickly turns into accusations and threats as mother and daughter attack each other with their arsenals of long-standing grievances.

DOT: That thing sure is loud.

LUCILLE: Yes.

DOT: I can hear it running at night. I can hear it running in your room.

LUCILLE: So?

DOT: You have this buzz fan for coolness, don't you?

LUCILLE: Sure.

DOT: I don't suppose you use it to drown out noise?

LUCILLE: What?

DOT, *yelling:* What do you do in your room?

LUCILLE: Nothing.

DOT: Good.

LUCILLE: Why good?

DOT: I'm glad to know nothing's going on that I shouldn't hear. I don't want you sneaking around on me. You don't do sneaky things do you, Lucy?

LUCILLE: No ... well, no. Well, sometimes Helen comes over. It's not sneaky, she just comes in.

DOT: When? Helen? Helen who?

LUCILLE: Helen ... from down the block. I went to school with her and sometimes she drops by when she gets off work at the movie.

DOT: At night?

LUCILLE: She works at night.

DOT: She comes over often? Comes in when I'm asleep?

LUCILLE: What difference does it make? It's my room. I can ask over whoever I like.

DOT: Can you? Can you? Well I know what you like! I suppose you have men in?

LUCILLE: What?

DOT: Men! Men! For God's sake, get rid of this buzz fan! Turn it off! Get rid of it!

LUCILLE: Why?

DOT: I want to know what's going on! I won't have a Watergate under my own roof! Turn that evil fan off! Off! *Lucille turns the fan off.*

LUCILLE: Okay, it's off.

DOT: What have you done to me?

LUCILLE: Nothing. I had a friend over.

DOT: Keep that Helen out! And don't bring men in here. I don't want strangers in my house.

LUCILLE: It's mine, too.

DOT: Daddy left it to me.

LUCILLE: He was my daddy!

DOT: He was my husband! *A pause.* I earned this house. I deserve it. It's mine. Children aren't supposed to own their own homes.

LUCILLE: I'm not a child. I wish I had my own house.

DOT: How would you get your own home? Huh? How'd you pay for it? What money you have belongs to me. I won't give you the money.

LUCILLE: You won't even give me enough to take a bus ride.

DOT: I've given you money. I gave you nine ninety-five and look what you bought.

LUCILLE: I get your point!

DOT: Do you? Do you, Lucille? Your own home? Are you crazy? How in the world would you get one?

LUCILLE, *this is an outcry of white anger and force ... she makes perfect sense:* I could walk across the street and marry old man Ferguson. I could do that. After all, that's what you did. Marry an old man, sit on his porch, have a kid, got your own home. What you did didn't take any brains or money. I could walk across the street, do what you did, sit on Freddy's porch and stare at you. I could do that! Unless it's God's will that I should stay here for forty-five more years letting you make me miserable.

DOT: You wouldn't marry that old man!

LUCILLE: Sit on your porch and watch.

DOT: You don't even know old man Ferguson that well.

LUCILLE: I do. I talk to him at night, when you're asleep. Other times I wander down the block and see Tommy Vickery's daddy. Another nice widower. Ferguson's old, Vickery's young . . . both are lonely. So am I.

DOT: Well, you have yourself quite a nightlife. I'll bet you even hang out with the beatniks at the *Dairy Queen?*

LUCILLE: Oh, Mama, I have the time of my life when it's past your bedtime.

DOT: What makes you think any man would want to marry you?

LUCILLE: Out of pity. Out of loneliness. I don't know.

DOT: No, you don't know. You see, the whole world's lonely, Lucille. That's the state of things. That's no reason to wander up and down the block talking to the menfolk. Shame on you! That's no reason to marry one.

LUCILLE: But you did! Marry one!

DOT: That don't make it right. It was the one mistake I ever made, but I recovered . . . got over it.

LUCILLE: And got a house.

DOT: Oh, for Pete's sake, Lucy . . . hold your horses! I'm an old woman. I'll be dead soon.

LUCILLE: How soon?

DOT: What?

LUCILLE: How soon? If you make it short, I might stay around to see the end.

DOT: That's silly, you make it sound like you want me dead?

LUCILLE: Right now I wish I knew an elephant.

DOT: You've certainly got a smart mouth. I didn't raise you to be a tart!

LUCILLE: No, well, what did you raise me for?

DOT: Because . . . because you were born, you came along, you were there.

LUCILLE: Well, that's why the chicken crosses the road, Mama. Because it's there. Like Freddy Ferguson's.

DOT: Well . . . well . . . I don't know what to say.

LUCILLE: Finally.

DOT: Well ... this is a fine how do you do. Well, I think it's time for you to go in. You've had too much exposure, Miss.

LUCILLE: I don't want to go in, thank you.

DOT: Well, I won't sit here and talk to a crazy. You ought to get inside, get on some clothes and get ahold of yourself.

LUCILLE: Freddy's bound to be back soon with my magazines.

DOT: You wouldn't do that, would you? Leave poor old me and marry that poor old man?

LUCILLE: I'm the one who's poor.

DOT: I'll be gone soon. Just wait. Then you can have this house, run all over creation at night in your silly swimsuit, get yourself involved with a hot rodder ... if you want. I won't know. Right now I need you.

LUCILLE: For years you've said, "Lucy, don't go, I need you." So I didn't go and all you've needed me for has added up to nothing. I need to go. I got a lot to do.

DOT: After the Lord takes me, you'll be on your own.

LUCILLE: Finally.

DOT: And I'll bet you find out there's nothing to do, Lucy. Nothing is what there is to do. There's no need to go looking for anything you can't have right here. This is the best of nothing. Oh, I know you have dreams. Wild ideas put there by your newspapers and magazines about what's going on in the world. But this is the best place to be, Lucy ... out here on this porch. When I go to my eternal rest, you can rest right here. Swing on the swing. Rock in the rocker. Watch the world go by. The view is so much better here than it is from old man Ferguson's. But don't go outside ... in the world, Baby. You're a little person and you might get lost. *Dot reaches out and touches Lucille ... as a mother would touch a child.*

LUCILLE: I'm just going to read, Mama. Read the news of people who got robbed, arrested or shot. People who got out and did something.

DOT: Good for you.

LUCILLE: Good for me?

DOT: After all, you wouldn't want to wander off. I might start to die and you wouldn't be here. I'm ready to go. Been just waiting for ages. I can't wait to get to heaven. Every night, before I go to sleep, I pray, "Dear God, take me." I've seen the world for seventy some odd years. Seen my neighbors come and go. Watched Tommy Vickery swipe my roses and old man Ferguson trot off to the post office. See Lucille grow from a little girl into a grown woman. I've had an eyeful. Seen it all. Everything there is to see from this porch. Yes, Lord, I'm ready to come to heaven and see what the angels are up to! *A short pause.* Well ... I've had it with the porch. I'm going inside, Lucille, and wait. *Dot puts down her fan and rolls her wheelchair inside the house. We hear Dot yell from inside:* Don't run off! *Lucille picks up Dot's fan and begins to fan herself.*

LUCILLE: *to herself:* Sit and rock. Sit and rot. *A short pause.* God, it's hot. *A short pause.* God, I got to be going. *Lucille puts down the fan, goes to the steps of the porch and begins to step off. She does not leave. The sound of ice cream truck is heard again playing "Pop Goes The Weasel."*

DOT, *yelling from inside the house:* Lucy? Is that the ice cream man again? Lucille? *A short pause.* Yoo hoo? Lucille? Come put me in the bed! *Lucille stares out at the world beyond the steps ... torn between leaving and the calls from Dot. A short pause.* Lucy? I need you. Are you there? *A short pause. She sings.* "When I'm calling you ... ooh ... ooh ... ooh ... ooh ... ooh." *She yells:* Yoo-hoo? *Lucille turns and exits into the house.*

AND MISS REARDON DRINKS
A LITTLE

by Paul Zindel

———————•———————

ACT I

The play focuses on the lives of three sisters. Anna is a science teacher in a junior high school. Catherine is an assistant principal in the same school. Ceil, formerly a teacher, has become an administrator in the Board of Education. The setting is Anna and Catherine's apartment. They are unmarried, clearly embarked on their respective spinsterhoods. Anna has been teetering on the edge of a nervous breakdown since the death of her mother some months earlier. Catherine has taken to drink. (She has also taken to hiding raw chopped meat in the candy box since Anna has become a vegetarian.) Four days before this scene takes place, Anna had some sort of sexual relations with a male student. His parents learned of this event and lodged an angry complaint with the school. Ceil, trying to contain the scandal that could damage her own career, convinces Catherine to send Anna to a mental institution. During the course of the evening old resentments are revealed (Ceil enticed and then married the one beau that Catherine ever had) and fresh wounds are inflicted. The scene begins with Ceil's entrance.

CATHERINE: Well, well, well. I never thought you'd show up. Of course, that's not quite true.

CEIL: I had asked to come.

CATHERINE: Oh, sure, but it wouldn't be the first time your busy, busy schedule would cancel out a lovely family dinner. What do they have you supervising down there at the Board of Ed? The Christmas Party? It's October, so I guess they're ... starting to ... make the tree decorations.

CEIL: I had intended to call before this.

CATHERINE: Oh yes, I'm sure. Super-intended. Do you realize you haven't been here to see us since we put Mother in her grave? A couple of lousy phone calls in seven months, you little bitch.

CEIL, *after a suitable pause:* Where's Anna?

CATHERINE: She's "sedated." Do you want a Manhattan?

CEIL: Yes, please. She hasn't been teaching since last Thursday?

CATHERINE: Oh, cut the crap, Ceil.

CEIL: Look, I wouldn't be here now if Hamilton didn't call and ...

CATHERINE: Sister—that tone of voice of yours butchers me, dear.

CEIL: He suggested ...

CATHERINE: Sibling, sweets—your penultimate shortcoming has become the fact that you've taken so many graduate education courses you've ended up with euphemism of the brain. Nobody does anything at that Board without checking with you first, the overdressed Sheena of the Blackboard Jungle.

CEIL: Jesus Christ, you forget!

CATHERINE: Forget! Nobody forgets! Every teacher in that demented little school looks at me and silently burps in my face every day of the week. Where would you be if it wasn't for that powerhouse of a sister of yours? Know what the faculty has nicknamed you this year? Well, it's "Superman." You have finally transcended womanhood entirely.

CEIL: Catherine, what's the matter with Anna?

CATHERINE: Matter? Who says there's anything the *matter?* Just because she started crying now and then—like right in front of her classes? I don't know where you got the idea something was the matter. Well, maybe she just wanted a little change of routine like Mrs. Miniken, at Oakwood High. Remember Mrs. Miniken? Mrs. Miniken, who leaped from the school roof, and splattered herself all over the handball courts. Now, that was a change of routine. Mrs. Miniken—splat—all because of some marital difficulties, wasn't it? And she taught Family Living.

CEIL: She hasn't been the same since Mama died, has she?

CATHERINE: Now look, Ceil. We might as well be honest about this whole thing. The only thing you're disquieted about is how much nuisance Anna is going to cause you. How much trouble. How much mortification. How much money. I mean, let's face it. That's what's got you out of your condominium, isn't it?

CEIL: Actually, Catherine, the only unkind remarks I've heard lately have been about you.

CATHERINE: Oh, is that so? Well, I'm not interested. In fact, you may not even have to worry much longer about my nepotistically endowed assistant principalship because I'm thinking of quitting and becoming a waitress. I could do with a little honest work for a change.

CEIL: They say you've started to drink a little.

CATHERINE, *involved in making a huge batch of Manhattans:* What a preposterous and cruel disestimation. Who would hoot such a thing about me? Could it be one of your old friends from around here? One of our mutual friends before your nuptials? Was it Mr. Pollack in Apartment 2A who beats his wife because she's having sex with the Fuller Brush man? Or was it Mrs. Pedowicz in 4C who beats her husband because he's having sex with the Fuller Brush man?

CEIL: It doesn't matter who said it.

CATHERINE: What do you mean, it doesn't matter? They've got *one hell* of a nerve.

CEIL: Actually, it was someone from your own school.

CATHERINE: Someone from that bibliophilic looney bin? Who? Mrs. Drisser, that pygmyess with the face like Toto, the kissless bride? Or Lipschitz who wears the same suit for six months and putts around with gorgonzola of the breath? That whole pack of academically defunct eternally matriculated and fuckingly overpaid nuts and what are they saying? Miss Reardon drinks a little. Jesus Christ! *She pours some Manhattans.*

CEIL: Look, if you've already had too much, I'll come back in the morning.

CATHERINE: No! *Beat.* Well, maybe it was Mama's death that got her. And maybe it wasn't. I thought she got over that nicely, considering . . . don't you, Ceil? *She takes the candy box and nibbles at its contents intermittently.*

CEIL: Was she all right on the trip?

CATHERINE: Oh, she did fine, just fine, till we got to Rome, that is; then she picked up on this flea-bitten ugly cat. There she was . . . running around the whole city picking up cats: black ones, green ones, yellow ones, three legged ones, one eyed ones, picking up any mangy sad thing she could get her hands on . . . while I was trying to get picked up by some of those two legged smooth Italian Tom cats.—Oh, I'm sorry, Ceil. I must sound crude to a happily married woman like yourself. Happily nuptialed to a big handsome man like Edward. How's Edward? Does he ask about me? *Beat.* Oh, we mustn't go into that— must not we? Anyway, the night before we were going to leave for Naples for the tourist barge back, I finally found the Trevi Fountain and I was tossing my eighty-third coin when Anna found this huge white cat, a tortured-looking thing, with a face like Goya's "St. Sebastian" . . .

CEIL: El Greco's . . .

CATHERINE: *Somebody's* St. Sebastian—and she picked it up, saying right into that hairy, festooned face, "nice little pussy, pussykin, nice little pussy, pussy" and the dear little thing responded by burying its front fangs into Anna's wrist. Right down to the bone. *She takes a huge mouthful of chopped meat.*

CEIL: What the hell are you eating? Chop meat? *Raw* chop meat?

CATHERINE: It's *chopped* meat, not chop meat. Fanny Farmer Chopped Meat.

CEIL: Are you crazy? What on earth for?

CATHERINE: Hold your water—your rushing the story. So anyway, we laughed the cat bite off and go to Naples for this Christoforo Trawler to get back here in time for school which was to begin on September something or other.

CEIL: School started September 16th.

CATHERINE: Yes, Ceil, you're utterly correct. Utterly precise as usual. September 16th. And the afternoon before we docked around September 3rd ... try to pardon me for this temporal equivocation—docked in New York, Anna took an afternoon nap and had a nightmare—an afternoon-mare, if you will—and that evening she fainted in the dining room. To tell the truth, I was ready to pass out myself from the table-mates we got stuck with. I knew I should have tipped the Maitre d' on the gangplank—this whole table of stag matrons who were so desperate they were sprinting after the busboys like piranha in evening gowns.

CEIL: Why did Anna faint?

CATHERINE: Well, Anna came to the conclusion she had rabies. But the ship's doctor told her not to worry because if her symptoms were those of rabies she'd be dead in three days—which was sort of a fun prognosis. But three days later we were back here and she was still having nightmares about some pregnant guppy or something, and we ran from doctor to doctor, each of whom told her not to take the anti-rabies injections because they were dangerous and anyway the odds were a million to one that she had it. But she insisted on the shots so for fourteen days she went to this senile quack down at the Board of Health and he stuck fourteen needles in her stomach, right *here* ... pow, pow, pow!

CEIL: My God, how painful.

CATHERINE: On the contrary, Anna delighted in them. She looked like Somebody's St. Sebastian *smiling*.

CEIL: Then she was all right?

CATHERINE: No, she got worse. So I took her to a private senile quack and he put her on tranquilizers so she could get back to school, back to the beloved classroom, and he said everything she was bellyaching about was in her head. Anyway, I thought Anna was all right then or I wouldn't have let her go back to work. So she began once more to face the cheerful loving children. But they began to stalk her.

CEIL: What do you mean *stalk* her?

CATHERINE: In class. First they did the spit-ball routine—wang! Then the airplanes—zooooom! And the cow sounds . . . moooo! Moooo! And the big thing last week, they were pinning flowers on her skirt without her knowing it and Scotch-taping little notes on her back like: *One of my tits is rubber* and *Please mount me.* Do you have any idea how embarrassing it can be to be the assistant principal of a high school and have your own sister arrive at the faculty conferences wearing a *One of my tits is rubber* sign on her back? It got so I had to check her clothes every period.

CEIL: Why do you think they began to do . . . dirty things to her?

CATHERINE: Well, Jesus Christ, you've got us teaching condoms in kindergarten, positions in the third grade, abortion in the sixth—perverts, nymphos, satyrs, and succubi in the eighth— If you ask me it's a wonder our kids aren't balling in the aisles.

CEIL: Did Anna do anything to encourage the things they did?

CATHERINE: I think she wore lipstick.

CEIL: Catherine—the boy . . .

CATHERINE: Oh, the boy! I was wondering how long it was going to take you to get to that. The cherub.

CEIL: She sent for him.

CATHERINE: The succulent seraphim who was present when Anna broke down—the McCloud boy . . .

CEIL: He's saying . . .

CATHERINE: You want to know about that little shit, I'll tell you. The nicest biographical detail on his grammar school record was that in the third grade he was caught pissing on a doll. During his first year in junior high he's taken dope, sold porno, and drew pictures of rhinoceri fornicating on the cover of his world geography text book. Granted he quieted down this term. He only punched a truant officer in the gut and just winks a lot as he walks around with his fly open. One of the semi-literate teachers in the English department dubbed him the Intermedable Tumescence. *She takes a big mouthful of meat.*

CEIL: Would you stop eating that?

CATHERINE: No. If I don't get some protein into me before Anna un-sedates herself, I'm going to collapse.

CEIL: What the hell does Anna have to do with your eating that disgusting raw meat?

CATHERINE: Well, it's like this—ever since she broke down we're not allowed to eat flesh. You see, she's caressed vegetarianism. She made me throw out every piece of meat we had in the house. Even the bouillon cubes.

CEIL: You're joking.

CATHERINE: Yeah, I'm joking, but you'd better like zucchini because that's what you're getting for supper. Saturday we had sauteed zucchini, Sunday we had boiled zucchini, Monday night for variety we called it squash. I can't even cook a cod fish cake—"You've got no right to kill anything," she says. Monday night she rescued a cockroach out of the toilet bowl. It isn't bad enough we're paying over two hundred bucks a month for a co-op with cockroaches, I have to have a sister who acts as a lifeguard for them.

CEIL: She's afraid of death . . . maybe the way Mama died . . .

CATHERINE: Oh, for Christ's sake, she's always been like that and you know it. Remember when Mama took us to St. Mary's Bazaar and we put her on that little ferris wheel. There was only enough money for one, and Mama said she could go alone . . . remember?

CEIL: Yes.

CATHERINE: Jesus, I'll never forget her face when that motor started and she went up and up and up.

PART III

—•—

Scenes for Two Men

AMERICAN BUFFALO

by David Mamet

———————•———————

ACT II

Don's Resale Shop—a junkshop. It is Friday, a robbery is being planned. This is the setting and basic situation. The robbery never takes place. But what emerges—through the planning, the waiting, the arguing, the complaining, and the outbursts of physical violence that comprise the actions of this play—is the story of three friends: of their fear of being deceived or left out; of their need to be respected and liked; of their efforts to balance loyalty and self-interest. The writing style captures the essential rhythms and sparseness of a modern urban dialect; yet it goes beyond mere replica to create a tone that is unique and poetic.

The excerpt that follows comes in the second act. It is night, approaching the hour of the robbery.

TEACH: What time is it?
DON: It's midnight.

Pause.

TEACH: I'm going out there now. I'll need the address. *Teach takes out revolver and begins to load it.*
DON: What's that?
TEACH: What?
DON: That.
TEACH: This "gun"?
DON: Yes.
TEACH: What does it look like?
DON: A gun.
TEACH: It *is* a gun.
DON, *rises and crosses to center:* I don't like it.

TEACH: Don't look at it.

DON: I'm serious.

TEACH: So am I.

DON: We don't need a gun, Teach.

TEACH: I pray that we don't, Don.

DON: We don't, tell me why we need a gun.

TEACH: It's not a question do we *need* it . . . *Need* . . . Only that it makes me comfortable, okay? It helps me to relax. So, God forbid, something inevitable occurs and the choice is (and I'm *saying* "God forbid") it's either him or us.

DON: Who?

TEACH: The guy. I'm saying God forbid the *guy* (or somebody) comes in, he's got a knife . . . a cleaver from one of those magnetic *boards* . . .?

DON: Yeah?

TEACH: . . . with the two *strips* . . . ?

DON: Yeah?

TEACH: And *whack,* and somebody is bleeding to death. This is all. Merely as a deterrent. *Pause.* All the preparation in the world does not mean *shit,* the path of some crazed lunatic sees you as an invasion of his personal domain. Guys go nuts, Don, *you* know this. Public *officials* . . . *Ax* murderers . . . all I'm saying, look out for your own.

DON: I don't like the gun.

TEACH: It's a personal thing, Don. A personal thing of mine. A silly personal thing. I just like to have it along. Is this so unreasonable?

DON: I don't want it.

TEACH: I'm not going without it.

DON: Why do you want it?

TEACH: Protection of me and my partner. Protection, deterrence. (We're only going around the fucking *corner* for chrissake . . .)

DON: I don't want it with.

TEACH: I can't step down on this, Don. I got to have it with. The light of things as they are.

DON: Why?

TEACH: Because of the way *things* are. *He looks out window:* Hold on a second.

DON: Fletcher?

TEACH: Cops.

DON: What are they doing?
TEACH: Cruising.

Pause.

DON: They turn the corner?
TEACH: Hold on. *Pause.* Yes. They have the right idea. Armed to the hilt. Sticks, mace, knives . . . who knows what the fuck they got. They have the right idea. Social customs break down, next thing everybody's lying in the gutter.

A VIEW FROM THE BRIDGE

by Arthur Miller

———————•———————

ACT I

Eddie Carbone is the central character in this modern tragedy, set in the Brooklyn waterfront district. Eddie is a longshoreman, respected by his coworkers, his friends, and his family for his integrity and generosity. He has brought up his dead sister-in-law's child, Catherine, who has turned into a beautiful, vivacious young woman. He shares his apartment with his wife's cousins, two young men who are illegal aliens from Italy, and who have come to New York to earn money for their families back home. And that's where the trouble begins. Catherine, and one of the young men, Rudolpho, fall in love, and for Eddie it ignites a caldron of jealous rage and suspicion that overwhelms all reason. He cannot give Catherine up, but camouflages his feelings (even to himself) in accusations that Rudolpho is "not right," a homosexual, and that he is just marrying Catherine to acquire U.S. citizenship. Eddie searches in vain for a way to end their relationship and finally—violating what amounts to a sacred code of the community—reports the cousins to the immigration authorities. The play ends with Eddie's humiliation and death.

In the scene that follows, Eddie seeks the help of an attorney, Mr. Alfieri.

ALFIERI: It was at this time that he first came to me. I had represented his father in an accident case some years before, and I was acquainted with the family in a casual way. I remember him now as he walked through my doorway— *(enter Eddie down right ramp)* His eyes were like tunnels; my first thought was that he had committed a crime. *Eddie sits beside the desk, cap in hand, looking out.* But soon I saw it was only a passion that had moved into his body, like a stranger. *Alfieri pauses, looks down at his desk, then to Eddie as though he were continuing a conversation with him.* I don't quite understand what I can do for you. Is there a question of law somewhere?

EDDIE: That's what I want to ask you.

ALFIERI: Because there's nothing illegal about a girl falling in love with an immigrant.

EDDIE: Yeah, but what about it if the only reason for it is to get his papers?

ALFIERI: First of all you don't know that.

EDDIE: I see it in his eyes; he's laughin' at her and he's laughin' at me.

ALFIERI: Eddie, I'm a lawyer. I can only deal in what's provable. You understand that, don't you? Can you prove that?

EDDIE: I know what's in his mind, Mr. Alfieri!

ALFIERI: Eddie, even if you could prove that—

EDDIE: Listen . . . will you listen to me a minute? My father always said you was a smart man. I want you to listen to me.

ALFIERI: I'm only a lawyer, Eddie.

EDDIE: Will you listen a minute? I'm talkin' about the law. Lemme just bring out what I mean. A man, which he comes into the country illegal, don't it stand to reason he's gonna take every penny and put it in the sock? Because they don't know from one day to another, right?

ALFIERI: All right.

EDDIE: He's spendin'. Records he buys now. Shoes. Jackets. Y'understand me? This guy ain't worried. This guy is *here.* So it must be that he's got it all laid out in his mind already—he's stayin'. Right?

ALFIERI: Well? What about it?

EDDIE: All right. *He glances at Alfieri, then down to the floor.* I'm talking to you confidential, ain't I?

ALFIERI: Certainly.

EDDIE: I mean it don't go no place but here. Because I don't like to say this about anybody. Even my wife I didn't exactly say this.

ALFIERI: What is it?

EDDIE, *takes a breath and glances briefly over each shoulder:* The guy ain't right, Mr. Alfieri.

ALFIERI: What do you mean?

EDDIE: I mean he ain't right.

ALFIERI: I don't get you.

EDDIE, *shifts to another position in the chair:* Dja ever get a look at him?

ALFIERI: Not that I know of, no.

EDDIE: He's a blond guy. Like . . . platinum. You know what I mean?

ALFIERI: No.

EDDIE: I mean if you close the paper fast—you could blow him over.

ALFIERI: Well that doesn't mean—

EDDIE: Wait a minute, I'm tellin' you sump'm. He sings, see. Which is—I mean it's all right, but sometimes he hits a note, see. I turn around. I mean—high. You know what I mean?

ALFIERI: Well, that's a tenor.

EDDIE: I know a tenor, Mr. Alfieri. This ain't no tenor. I mean if you came in the house and you didn't know who was singin', you wouldn't be lookin' for him you be lookin' for her.

ALFIERI: Yes, but that's not—

EDDIE: I'm tellin' you sump'm, wait a minute. Please, Mr. Alfieri. I'm tryin' to bring out my thoughts here. Couple of nights ago my niece brings out a dress which it's too small for her, because she shot up like a light this last year. He takes the dress, lays it on the table, he cuts it up; one-two-three, he makes a new dress. I mean he looked so sweet there, like an angel— you could kiss him he was so sweet.

ALFIERI: Now look, Eddie—

EDDIE: Mr. Alfieri, they're laughin' at him on the piers. I'm ashamed. Paper Doll they call him. Blondie now. His brother thinks it's because he's got a sense of humor, see—which he's got—but that ain't what they're laughin'. Which they're not goin' to come out with it because they know he's my relative, which they have to see me if they make a crack, y'know? But I know what they're laughin' at, and when I think of that guy layin' his hands on her I could—I mean it's eatin' me out, Mr. Alfieri, because I struggled for that girl. And now he comes in my house and—

ALFIERI: Eddie, look—I have my own children. I understand you. But the law is very specific. The law does not . . .

EDDIE, *with a fuller flow of indignation:* You mean to tell me that there's no law that a guy which he ain't right can go to work and marry a girl and—?

ALFIERI: You have no recourse in the law, Eddie.

EDDIE: Yeah, but if he ain't right, Mr. Alfieri, you mean to tell me—

ALFIERI: There is nothing you can do, Eddie, believe me.

EDDIE: Nothin'.

ALFIERI: Nothing at all. There's only one legal question here.

EDDIE: What?

ALFIERI: The manner in which they entered the country. But I don't think you want to do anything about that, do you?

EDDIE: You mean—?

ALFIERI: Well, they entered illegally.

EDDIE: Oh, Jesus, no, I wouldn't do nothin' about that, I mean—

ALFIERI: All right, then, let me talk now, eh?

EDDIE: Mr. Alfieri, I can't believe what you tell me. I mean there must be some kinda law which—

ALFIERI: Eddie, I want you to listen to me. *Pause.* You know, sometimes God mixes up the people. We all love somebody, the wife, the kids—every man's got somebody that he loves, heh? But sometimes . . . there's too much. You know? There's too much, and it goes where it mustn't. A man works hard, he brings up a child, sometimes it's a niece, sometimes even a daughter, and he never realizes it, but through the years—there is too much love for the daughter, there is too much love for the niece. Do you understand what I'm saying to you?

EDDIE, *sardonically:* What do you mean, I shouldn't look out for her good?

ALFIERI: Yes, but these things have to end, Eddie, that's all. The child has to grow up and go away, and the man has to learn to forget. Because after all, Eddie—what other way can it end? *Pause.* Let her go. That's my advice. You did your job, now it's her life; wish her luck, and let her go. *Pause.* Will you do that? Because there's no law, Eddie; make up your mind to it; the law is not interested in this.

EDDIE: You mean to tell me, even if he's a punk? If he's—

ALFIERI: There's nothing you can do. *Eddie stands.*

EDDIE: Well, all right, thanks. Thanks very much.

ALFIERI: What are you going to do?

EDDIE, *with a helpless but ironic gesture:* What can I do? I'm a patsy, what can a patsy do? I worked like a dog twenty years so a punk could have her, so that's what I done. I mean, in the worst times, in the worst, when there wasn't a ship comin' in the harbor, I didn't stand around lookin' for relief—I hustled. When there was empty piers in Brooklyn I went to Hoboken, Staten Island, the West Side, Jersey, all over—because I made a promise. I took out of my own mouth to give to her. I took out of my wife's mouth. I walked hungry plenty days in this city! *It begins to break through.* And now I gotta sit in my house and look at a son-of-a-bitch punk like that—which he came out of nowhere! I give him my house to sleep! I take the blankets off my bed for him, and he takes and puts his dirty filthy hands on her like a goddam thief!

ALFIERI, *rising:* But, Eddie, she's a woman now.

EDDIE: He's stealing from me!

ALFIERI: She wants to get married, Eddie. She can't marry you, can she?

EDDIE, *furiously:* What're you talkin' about, marry me! I don't know what the hell you're talkin' about!

ALFIERI, *after a pause:* I gave you my advice, Eddie. That's it.

EDDIE, *gathers himself. A pause:* Well, thanks. Thanks very much. It just—it's breakin' my heart, y'know. I—

ALFIERI: I understand. Put it out of your mind. Can you do that?

EDDIE: I'm— *(he feels the threat of sobs, and with a helpless wave)* I'll see you around. *He goes out up the right ramp.*

ALFIERI, *sits on desk:* There are times when you want to spread an alarm, but nothing has happened. I knew, I knew then and there—I could have finished the whole story that afternoon. It wasn't as though there was a mystery to unravel. I could see every step coming, step after step, like a dark figure walking down a hall toward a certain door. I knew where he was heading for, I knew where he was going to end. And I sat here many afternoons asking myself why, being an intelligent man, I was so powerless to stop it. I even went to a certain old lady in the neighborhood, a very wise old woman, and I told her, and she only nodded, and said, "Pray for him . . ." And so I—waited here.

EQUUS

by Peter Shaffer

———————•———————

ACT I, SCENES 19, 20, 21

The setting is a psychiatric hospital in England. But the real locales explored in this play are the minds of Martin Dysart, a disillusioned psychiatrist, and Alan Strang, his seventeen-year-old patient. Alan has committed a baffling and cruel crime: late one night he entered the stable in which he worked and blinded six horses with a metal spike. Dysart, feeling useless and weary of a life with neither passions nor goals (suffering from what he calls "professional menopause"), is assigned to be Alan's psychiatrist. Dysart pursues the normal course of treatment with this most unusual boy, but soon finds himself envying Alan the intensity of his feelings and his ability to yield completely to the dictates of his passions. The therapy is designed to make Alan normal, able to take his place in a civilized society. Yet Dysart believes that this normality can be achieved only by cutting away from Alan something vital and precious.

The play has a number of theatrical conventions: the central square serves as office, stable, field, etc.; Dysart, at times, speaks his thoughts directly to the audience; the horses are played by actors in suggestive costume pieces. (For scene-study purposes, the actor playing Alan may wish to create the horses through his imagination.)

In the following scene Alan enters for his regular therapy session. The action continues through the scene changes.

Alan rises and enters the square. He is subdued.

DYSART: Good afternoon.

ALAN: Afternoon.

DYSART: I'm sorry about our row yesterday.

ALAN: It was stupid.

DYSART: It was.

ALAN: What I said, I mean.

DYSART: How are you sleeping? *Alan shrugs.* You're not feeling well, are you?

ALAN: All right.

DYSART: Would you like to play a game? It could make you feel better.

ALAN: What kind?

DYSART: It's called *Blink*. You have to fix your eyes on something: say, that little stain over there on the wall—and I tap this pen on the desk. The first time I tap it, you close your eyes. The next time you open them. And so on. Close, open, close, open, till I say Stop.

ALAN: How can that make you feel better?

DYSART: It relaxes you. You'll feel as though you're talking to me in your sleep.

ALAN: It's stupid.

DYSART: You don't have to do it, if you don't want to.

ALAN: I didn't say I didn't want to.

DYSART: Well?

ALAN: I don't mind.

DYSART: Good. Sit down and start watching that stain. Put your hands by your sides, and open the fingers wide. *He opens the left bench and Alan sits on the end of it.* The thing is to feel comfortable, and relax absolutely ... Are you looking at the stain?

ALAN: Yes.

DYSART: Right. Now try and keep your mind as blank as possible.

ALAN: That's not difficult.

DYSART: Ssh. Stop talking ... On the first tap, close. On the second, open. Are you ready? *Alan nods. Dysart taps his pen on the wooden rail. Alan shuts his eyes. Dysart taps again. Alan opens them. The taps are evenly spaced. After four of them the sound cuts out, and is replaced by a faint, metallic sound, on tape. Dysart talks through this, to the audience—the light dims around him—while the boy sits staring at the wall, opening and shutting his eyes.* The Normal is the good smile in a child's eyes:—alright. It is also the dead stare in a million adults. It both sustains and kills—like a god. It is the Ordinary made beautiful: it is also the Average made lethal. The Normal is the indispensable, murderous God of Health, and I am his priest. My tools are very delicate. My compassion is honest. I have honestly assisted children in this room. I have talked away terrors and relieved many agonies. But also—beyond question—I have cut from them parts of individuality repugnant to this god, in both his aspects. Parts sacred to rarer and more wonderful gods. And at what length ... Sacrifices to Zeus took at the most, surely, sixty seconds each. Sacrifices to the Normal can take as long as sixty months. *The natural sound of the pencil resumes. Light changes back. To Alan.* Now your eyes are feeling heavy. You want to sleep, don't you? You want a long, deep sleep. Have it. Your head is heavy. Very heavy. Your shoulders are heavy. Sleep. *The pencil stops. Alan's eyes remain shut and his head has sunk on his chest.* Can you hear me?

ALAN: Mmm.

DYSART: You can speak normally. Say Yes, if you can.

ALAN: Yes.

DYSART: Good boy. Now raise your head, and open your eyes. *He does so.* Now, Alan, you're going to answer questions I'm going to ask you. Do you understand?

ALAN: Yes.

DYSART: And when you wake up, you are going to remember everything you tell me. All right?

ALAN: Yes.

DYSART: Good. Now I want you to think back in time. You are on that beach you told me about. The tide has gone out, and you're making sandcastles. Above you, staring down at you, is that great horse's head, and the cream dropping from it. Can you see that?

ALAN: Yes.

DYSART: You ask him a question. "Does the chain hurt?"

ALAN: Yes.

DYSART: Do you ask him aloud?

ALAN: No.

DYSART: And what does the horse say back?

ALAN: "Yes."

DYSART: Then what do you say?

ALAN: "I'll take it out for you."

DYSART: And he says?

ALAN: "It never comes out. They have me in chains."

DYSART: Like Jesus?

ALAN: Yes!

DYSART: Only his name isn't Jesus, is it?

ALAN: No.

DYSART: What is it?

ALAN: No one knows but him and me.

DYSART: You can tell me, Alan. Name him.

ALAN: Equus.

DYSART: Thank you. Does he live in all horses or just some?

ALAN: All.

DYSART: Good boy. Now: you leave the beach. You're in your bedroom at home. You're twelve years old. You're in front of the picture. You're looking at Equus from the foot of your bed. Would you like to kneel down?

ALAN: Yes.

DYSART, *encouragingly:* Go on, then. *Alan kneels.* Now tell me. Why is Equus in chains?

ALAN: For the sins of the world.

DYSART: What does he say to you?

ALAN: "I see you." "I will save you."

DYSART: How?

ALAN: "Bear you away. Two shall be one."

DYSART: Horse and rider shall be one beast?

ALAN: One person!

DYSART: Go on.

ALAN: "And my chinkle-chankle shall be in thy hand."

DYSART: Chinkle-chankle? That's his mouth chain?

ALAN: Yes.

DYSART: Good. You can get up ... Come on. *Alan rises.* Now: think of the stable. What is the stable? His temple? His Holy of Holies?

ALAN: Yes.

DYSART: Where you wash him? Where you tend him, and brush him with many brushes?

ALAN: Yes.

DYSART: And there he spoke to you, didn't he? He looked at you with his gentle eyes, and spake unto you?

ALAN: Yes.

DYSART: What did he say? "Ride me?" "Mount me, and ride me forth at night?"

ALAN: Yes.

DYSART: And you obeyed? *Pause.*

ALAN: Yes! *Pause.*

DYSART: How did you learn? By watching others?

ALAN: Yes.

DYSART: It must have been difficult. You bounced about?

ALAN: Yes.

DYSART: But he showed you, didn't he? Equus showed you the way.

ALAN: No!

DYSART: He didn't?

ALAN: He showed me nothing! He's a mean bugger! Ride—or fall! That's Straw Law.

DYSART: Straw Law?

ALAN: He was born in the straw, and this is his law.

DYSART: But you managed? You mastered him?

ALAN: Had to!

DYSART: And then you rode in secret?

ALAN: Yes.

DYSART: How often?

ALAN: Every three weeks. More, people would notice.

DYSART: On a particular horse?

ALAN: No.

DYSART: How did you get into the stable?

ALAN: Stole a key. Had it copied at Bryson's.

DRYSART: Clever boy. *Alan smiles.* Then you'd slip out of the house?

ALAN: Midnight! On the stroke!

DYSART: How far's the stable?

ALAN: Two miles. *Pause.*

DYSART: Let's do it! Let's go riding! . . . Now! *He stands up, and pushes in his bench.* You are there now, in front of the stable door. *Alan turns upstage.* That key's in your hand. Go and open it.

Alan moves upstage, and mimes opening the door. Soft light on the circle. Humming from the Chorus: the Equus noise. The horse actors enter, raise high their masks, and put them on all together. They stand round the circle—Nugget in the mouth of the tunnel.

DYSART: Quietly as possible. Dalton may still be awake. Sssh ... Quietly ... Good. Now go in. *Alan steps secretly out of the square through the central opening onto the circle, now glowing with a warm light. He looks about him. The horses stamp uneasily: their masks turn toward him.* You are on the inside now. All the horses are staring at you. Can you see them?

ALAN, *excited:* Yes!

DYSART: Which one are you going to take?

ALAN: Nugget. *Alan reaches up and mimes leading Nugget carefully round the circle downstage with a rope, past all the horses on the right.*

DYSART: What color is Nugget?

ALAN: Chestnut. *The horse picks his way with care. Alan halts him at the corner of the square.*

DYSART: What do you do, first thing?

ALAN: Put on his sandals.

DYSART: Sandals? *He kneels, downstage center.*

ALAN: Sandals of majesty! Made of sack. *He picks up the invisible sandals, and kisses them devoutly.* Tie them round his hooves. *He taps Nugget's right leg: the horse raises it and the boy mimes tying the sack round it.*

DYSART: All four hooves?

ALAN: Yes.

DYSART: Then?

ALAN: Chinkle-chankle. *He mimes picking up the bridle and bit.* He doesn't like it so late, but he takes it for my sake. He bends for me. He stretches forth his neck to it. *Nugget bends his head down. Alan first ritually puts the bit into his own mouth, then crosses, and transfers it into Nugget's. He reaches up and buckles on the bridle. Then he leads him by the invisible reins, across the front of the stage and up round the left side of the circle. Nugget follows obediently.* Buckle and lead out.

DYSART: No saddle?

ALAN: Never.

DYSART: Go on.

ALAN: Walk down the path behind. He's quiet. Always is, this bit. Meek and milk legs. At least till the field. Then there's trouble. *The horse jerks back. The mask tosses.*

DYSART: What kind?

ALAN: Won't go in.

DYSART: Why not?

ALAN: It's his place of Ha Ha.

DYSART: What?

ALAN: Ha ha.

DYSART: Make him go into it.

ALAN, *whispering fiercely:* Come on! ... Come on! ... *He drags the horse into the square as Dysart steps out of it.*

Nugget comes to a halt staring diagonally down what is now the field. The Equus noise dies away. The boy looks about him.

DYSART, *from the circle:* Is it a big field?

ALAN: Huge!

DYSART: What's it like?

ALAN: Full of mist. Nettles on your feet. *(He mimes taking off his shoes—and the sting)* Ah!

DYSART, *going back to his bench:* You take your shoes off?

ALAN: Everything.

DYSART: All your clothes?

ALAN: Yes. *He mimes undressing completely in front of the horse. When he is finished, and obviously quite naked, he throws out his arms and shows himself fully to his god, bowing his head before Nugget.*

DYSART: Where do you leave them?

ALAN: Tree hole near the gate. No one could find them. *He walks upstage and crouches by the bench, stuffing the invisible clothes beneath it. Dysart sits again on the left bench, downstage beyond the circle.*

DYSART: How does it feel now?

ALAN, *holds himself:* Burns.

DYSART: Burns?

ALAN: The mist!

DYSART: Go on. Now what?

ALAN: The Manbit. *He reaches again under the bench and draws out an invisible stick.*

DYSART: Manbit?

ALAN: The stick for my mouth.

DYSART: Your mouth?

ALAN: To bite on.

DYSART: Why? What for?

ALAN: So's it won't happen too quick.

DYSART: Is it always the same stick?

ALAN: Course. Sacred stick. Keep it in the hole. The Ark of the Manbit.

DYSART: And now what? . . . What do you do now? *Pause. He rises and approaches Nugget.*

ALAN: Touch him!

DYSART: Where?

ALAN, *in wonder:* All over. Everywhere. Belly. Ribs. His ribs are of ivory. Of great value! . . . His flank is cool. His nostrils open for me. His eyes shine. They can see in the dark . . . *Eyes! (Suddenly he runs in distress to the farthest corner of the square.)*

DYSART: *Go on!* Then? *Pause.*

ALAN: Give sugar.

DYSART: A lump of sugar? *Alan returns to Nugget.*

ALAN: His Last Supper.

DYSART: Last before what?

ALAN: Ha ha. *He kneels before the horse, palms upward and joined together.*

DYSART: Do you say anything when you give it to him?

ALAN, *offering it:* Take my sins. Eat them for my sake . . . He always does. *Nugget bows the mask into Alan's palm, then takes a step back to eat.* And then he's ready.

DYSART: You can get up on him now?

ALAN: Yes!

DYSART: Do it, then. Mount him. *Alan, lying before Nugget, stretches out on the square. He grasps the top of the thin metal pole embedded in the wood. He whispers his god's name ceremonially.*

ALAN: Equus! . . . Equus! . . . Equus! *He pulls the pole upright. The actor playing Nugget leans forward and grasps it. All the other horses lean forward also, all round the circle, so that each places a hand on the rail. Alan rises and walks right back to the* *upstage corner, left.* Take me! *(He runs and jumps high on to Nugget's back. Crying out:) Ah!*

DYSART: What is it?

ALAN: Hurts!

DYSART: Hurts?

ALAN: Knives in his skin! Little knives—all inside my legs. *Nugget mimes restiveness.* Stay, Equus. No one said Go! . . . That's it. He's good. Equus the Godslave, faithful and true. Into my hands he commends himself—naked in his chinkle-chankle. *He punches Nugget.* Stop it! . . . He wants to go so badly.

DYSART: Go, then. Leave me behind. Ride away now, Alan. Now! . . . Now you are alone.

ALAN, *he stiffens his body and raises his hand ritually:* Equus— son of Fleckwus—son of Neckwus—Walk. *A hum from the Chorus. Very slowly the horses standing on the circle begin to turn the square by gently pushing the wooden rail. Alan and his mount start to revolve. The effect, immediately, is of a statue being slowly turned round on a plinth. During the ride, however, the speed increases, and the light decreases until it is only a fierce spotlight on horse and rider, with the overspill glinting on the other masks leaning in toward them.* Here we go. The King rides out on Equus, mightiest of horses. Only I can ride him. He lets me turn him this way and that. His neck comes out of my body. It lifts in the dark. Equus, my Godslave! . . . Now the King commands you. Tonight, we ride against them all.

DYSART: Who's all?

ALAN: My foes and His.

DYSART: Who are your foes?

ALAN: The Hosts of Hoover. The Hosts of Philco. The House of Remington and all its tribe!

DYSART: Who are His foes?

ALAN: The Hosts of Bowler. The Hosts of Jodhpur. All those who show him off for their vanity. Tie rosettes on his head for their vanity! Come on, Equus. Let's get them! . . . *Trot! (The speed of the turning square increases.)* Stead-y! Stead-y! Stead-y! Stead-y! Cowboys are watching! Take off their Stetsons. They know who we are. They're admiring us! Bowing low unto us! Come on now—show them! *Canter!* . . . CANTER! *He whips Nugget.*

And Equus the Mighty rose against All!
His enemies scatter, his enemies fall!

TURN!
Trample them, trample them,
Trample them, trample them,
TURN!
TURN!!
TURN!!!
(The Equus noise increases in volume. Shouting.)
WEE! . . . WAA! . . . WONDERFUL! . . .
I'm stiff! Stiff in the wind!
My mane, stiff in the wind!
My flanks! *My* hooves!
Mane on my legs, on my flanks, like whips!
Raw!
Raw!
I'm raw! Raw!
Feel me on you! *On* you! *On* you! *On* you!
I want to be *in* you!
I want to BE you forever and ever!—
Equus, I love you!
Now!—
Bear me away!
Make us One Person!
(He rides Equus frantically.) One Person! One Person! One Person! One Person! (He rises up on the horse's back, and calls like trumpet.) Ha-HA! . . . Ha-HA! . . . Ha-HA! (The trumpet turns to great cries.) HA-HA! HA-HA! HA-HA! HA-HA! HA! . . . HA! . . . HAAAAA! (He twists like a flame. Silence. The turning square comes to a stop in the same position it occupied at the opening of the Act. Slowly the boy drops off the horse's back to the ground. He lowers his head and kisses Nugget's hoof. Finally he flings back his head and cries up to him.) AMEN! (Nugget snorts, once.)

THE BASIC TRAINING
OF PAVLO HUMMEL

by David Rabe

———————•———————

ACT II, SCENE 1

Pavlo Hummel is as much a misfit as a character can be, awkward and dumb, an object of ridicule and abuse. Lonely and desperate for acceptance and friendship, he joins the army (it is during the Vietnam War), but gains neither companionship nor self-confidence. Ultimately, he kills himself with a hand grenade.

In this scene he is on leave before being shipped overseas. He goes home and vainly tries to get his brother, Mickey, to acknowledge that he has changed and is worthy of respect.

PAVLO: Hey, Mickey, it's me. I'm home! *Mickey, in T-shirt, slacks, shoes, combs hair.* It's me. I'm home, I'm home, I'm home.

MICKEY: Whata you say, huh? Hey, hey, what happened? You took so long. You took a wrong turn, huh? Missed your stop and now you come home all dressed up like a conductor. What happened? You were down in that subway so long they put you to work? Huh? Man, you look good though; you look good. Where were you again?

PAVLO: Georgia.

MICKEY: Hot as a bitch, right?

PAVLO: No. Cold.

MICKEY: In Georgia?

PAVLO: Yeh, it was real cold; we used to hide out in the furnace room every damn chance we ever got.

MICKEY: Hey, you want a drink? Damn, that don't make much sense, does it?

PAVLO: What?

MICKEY: They send you to Georgia for the winter and it's like a witch's tit. Can you imagine that? A witch's tit?

Eeeeeegggggg. Put ice on your tongue. That ever happens to
me, man, I'd turn in my tool. Ain't you gonna ask about the ole
lady? How's she doin' and all that, 'cause she's doin' fine.
Pickin' and plantin' daisies. Doin' fine. *And Pavlo laughs softly,
shaking his head, taking the drink Mickey has made him.*
Whatsa matter? You don't believe yo-yos can be happy? Psy-
chotics have fun, man. You oughta know that.

PAVLO: I just bet she's climbin' some kinda wall. Some kinda
wall and she's pregnant again, she thinks, or you are or me or
somebody.

MICKEY: Noo, man, noo, it's everybody else now. Only non-
family.

PAVLO, *laughing, loudly:* THAT'S ME AND YOU! NON-
FAMILY MOTHERFUCKERS!

MICKEY: All the dogs and women of the world!

PAVLO: Yeh, yeh, all the guys in the barracks used to think I
was a little weird so I'd—

MICKEY: —you are a little weird—*(slight pause)*

PAVLO: Yeh, yeh, I'd tell 'em, "You think I'm weird, you
oughta see my brother, Mickey. He don't give a big rat's ass for
nothin' or nobody."

MICKEY: And did you tell 'em about his brains, too? And his
wit and charm. The way his dick hangs to his knees—about his
eighteen thou a year? Did you tell 'em all that sweet shit?

PAVLO: They said they hoped you died of all you got.

MICKEY, *has been dressing throughout: shirt, tie, jacket:* How
come the troops were thinkin' you weird? You doin' that weird
stuff again. You say "Georgia" and "the army." For all I know
you been downtown in the movies for the last three months and
you bought that goddamn uniform at some junk shop.

PAVLO: I am in the army.

MICKEY: How do I know?

PAVLO: I'm tellin' you.

MICKEY: But you're a fuckin' liar; you're a fuckin' myth mak-
er.

PAVLO: I gotta go to Vietnam, Mickey.

MICKEY: Vietnam don't even exist.

PAVLO: I gotta go to it.

MICKEY: Arizona, man; that's where you're goin'. Wyoming.

PAVLO: Look at me! I'm different! I'm different than I was!
This is with fury and there is a pause. I'm not the same anymore.

I was an asshole. I'm not an asshole anymore. I'm not an asshole anymore! *Slight pause.* I came here to forgive you. I don't need you anymore.

MICKEY: You're a goddamn cartoon, you know that.

PAVLO, *rapidly, a rush of words:* I'm happier now than I ever was, I got people who respect me. Lots of 'em. There was this guy Kress in my outfit. We didn't hit it off . . . and he called me out . . . he was gonna kill me, he said. Everybody tried to stop me because this guy had hurt a lot of people already and he had this uncle who'd taught him all about fightin' and this uncle had been executed in San Quentin for killing people. We went out back of the barracks. It went on and on, hitting and kicking. It went on and on; all around the barracks. The crowd right with us. And then . . . all of a sudden . . . this look came into his eye . . . and he just stopped . . and reached down to me and hugged me. He just hugged and hugged me. And that look was in all their eyes. All the soldiers. I don't need you anymore, Mickey. I got real brothers now.

MICKEY: You know . . . if my father hadn't died, you wouldn't even exist.

PAVLO: No big thing! We got the same mother; that's shit enough. I'm gonna shower and shave, O.K.? Then we can go out drinkin'.

MICKEY: All those one-night stands. You ever think of that? Ghostly pricks. I used to hear 'em humpin' the ole whore. I probably had my ear against the wall the night they got you goin'.

PAVLO, *after a slight silence:* You seen Joanna lately?

MICKEY: Joanna?

PAVLO: Joanna. My ole girl. I thought maybe she probably killed herself and it was in the papers. You know, on account of my absence. But she probably did it in secret.

MICKEY: No doubt.

PAVLO: No doubt.

MICKEY: Ain't she the one who got married? I think the ole lady tole me Joanna got married and she was gonna write you a big letter all about it. Sure she was. Anyway, since we're speaking of old girls and pregnant people, I've got to go to this little party tonight. Got a good new sweet young thing and she thinks I'm better than her daddy. I've had a run a chicks lately you wouldn't believe, Pavlo. They give away ass like Red Cross

girls dealin' out donuts. I don't understand how I get half a
what I get. Oh yeah, old lady comes and goes around here.
She's the same old witch.
PAVLO: I'm gonna go see Joanna. I'll call her up. Use the
magic fuckin' phone to call her up.
MICKEY: I'll give you a call later on.
PAVLO: I'll be out, man. I'll be out on the street.
MICKEY: You make yourself at home. *Exiting.*

PLAY IT AGAIN, SAM

by Woody Allen

———————•———————

ACT III

Allan Felix is a small, homely young man who has never had
much success with women. He dreams about acquiring Bogart's
suave techniques, but, despite private direction from his fantasy
hero, Allan always manages to muff it. However, Allan's best
friend's wife, Linda, finds his ineptness charming and they pro-
ceed to spend the night together. Now the trouble begins. Filled
with remorse and guilt for deceiving his best friend, Allan contemplates the most terrifying (and humorous) possibilities. In
the following scene Allan daydreams about what would happen
if Dick found out about his night with Linda. His fantasies are
interrupted when Dick actually arrives.

ALLAN: Gee, I can't believe it. This bright, beautiful woman is
in love with me. Of course she's in love with me. Why shouldn't
she be? I'm bright, amusing . . . sensitive face . . . fantastic body.
Dick'll understand. Hell, we're two civilized guys. In the course
of our social encounters a little romance has developed. It's a
very natural thing to happen amongst sophisticated people.
DICK, *appearing in dream light:* You sent for me?
ALLAN: Yes.

DICK: Good.

ALLAN: Drink?

DICK: Quite.

ALLAN: Scotch?

DICK: Fine.

ALLAN: Neat?

DICK: Please.

ALLAN: Soda?

DICK: A dash.

ALLAN: Linda and I are in love.

DICK: It's just as well. I've come from my doctor. He gives me two months to live.

ALLAN: Good, then you don't mind?

DICK: Not a bit.

ALLAN: Cheers.

DICK: Cheers. *He vanishes.*

ALLAN, *rises:* Sure . . . things are going to be okay. Hell, Dick and I have been through tougher situations than this. Dick and I have been through a lot together. He's my best friend. This is terrible. This is going to hurt him . . . I know it.

DICK, *enters in dream light:* Thanks a lot.

ALLAN: Dick . . .

DICK, *crosses left of the sofa:* How could you? My wife and my best friend. I trusted you both. I feel I've been made such a fool of. I love her. I love you. Why didn't I see it coming? Me—who had the foresight to buy Polaroid at eight and a half! *He disappears.*

ALLAN: This is awful . . . he'll do something rash. Dick's an emotional guy. He'll kill himself. Kill himself? Did you ever think what he might do to you? Didn't you ever hear of the unwritten law? You take a guy's wife . . . you humiliate him. You've seen enough Italian movies. Dick's got a temper!

DICK: *(enters in undershirt and scarf) Bastado! Pezzo di curnutu. Tu mai tradutto me!*

ALLAN: *(backing up the steps onto the platform) Ma non e vero.*

DICK: *Tu mi pigli per stupido!*

ALLAN: *Non e culpa mia.*

DICK: *(leaps over the railing) Bugiardo! Proco! Carogna! Imbesile! (He draws a dagger.)*

ALLAN: No . . . no . . .

DICK: *Solo chisto me tuo sadisfari mio onore. (He stabs Allan.)*

ALLAN: Oh boy, that hurt! *Dick exits. Allan stands at the railing.* This is ridiculous! What am I going to do? I love her. She loves me. We could have a wonderful life together. Why does Dick have to be in the picture? Hell, take it easy. Why do you have to make everything into a Warner Brothers production? She'll come back, we'll have breakfast together. Shape up. She'll be back in a minute. You'll spend the day together . . .

The doorbell rings. Alan opens the door to find Dick with his suitcase and coat.

DICK, *leaves his coat and case at the railing:* I had to come home, Allan. I have to speak to you. Allan, I think Linda's having an affair. I just called home. She's not there. These past few weeks she's seemed distracted, distant, little things only a husband would notice. You've seen her a lot these past couple of weeks . . . she's changed. The other night she talked about an affair in her sleep.
ALLAN: Did she mention any names?
DICK: Only yours. When I woke her and questioned her she said it was just a nightmare. *He crosses up the steps and onto the platform.* I try to think of who it might be. It has to be someone I don't know . . . some guy she met through work . . . an agent, a photographer, some ad executive, or actor.
ALLAN: Why are you so upset . . . I thought she was just your corporate image?
DICK: I love her. If she leaves me I'll kill myself.
ALLAN: Since when are you so emotional?
DICK: I've never been in love with anyone before. If I find out who the guy is I'll kill him, I swear. I've neglected her and now she's involved with some stud! *Allan sits in the swivel hassock; Dick sits on the edge of the coffee table.* If I haven't already lost her to someone, I'm going to make up for everything to her. I'm going to change. I'm going to do everything I can to make her life with me exciting and fun because without her it wouldn't be worth living. I was up all last night in a Cleveland hotel room. I figured, all right, I'm losing her . . . too bad . . . I'll survive. Then I panicked and phoned her. She was out. When I called her here last night she said she was going home. Where'd she stay?
ALLAN, *rising:* Calm yourself.
DICK, *rises, crosses, then moves back to Allan:* I've got to find

her. I've got to stop her and beg her forgiveness before it's too late. I want her to get on that plane with me and fly back to Cleveland. I want her with me all the time. I want to pamper her. I want to hear her laugh and speak . . . I'm sorry for carrying on like this, Allan, but you're the only friend in the world who would understand.

ALLAN: I . . . I understand.

DICK: Look, if she calls, tell her I'll see her home. Tell her I've got to speak to her, will you?

ALLAN: Sure . . . sure.

DICK: Thanks . . . thanks a lot. *He gets his coat and suitcase and exits.*

ALLAN, *sits on the coffee table:* I'm going to faint. How could I tell him? The guy's desperately in love with her. I never realized how much. He never realized how much. I couldn't do that to a stranger, much less a friend. But what if it's too late? What if Linda's really hooked on me now? You know, once a woman's been made love to by somebody who can really do it great! I was fantastic last night! I never once had to sit up and consult the manual. Love is very different for a woman. It's a complicated phenomenon. I don't know what to expect. I've never broken off with a woman before.

CAT ON A HOT TIN ROOF

by Tennessee Williams

———————•———————

ACT II

It is Big Daddy's sixty-fifth birthday and the whole family is gathered at the plantation house to celebrate. But Big Daddy—unbeknownst to himself—is dying of stomach cancer; and, since he has never written a will, his son Gooper, and his daughters-in-law Mae and Margaret, are maneuvering for control over his considerable estate. Big Daddy has just returned from the hospital where he was lied to when he was told that he has only a minor ailment. He has come home rejuvenated and determined to lead a full and pleasurable life without lies or pretense. He is also determined to find out why his fair-haired son, Brick, a former star football player, has turned into a failure and a drunk.

Prior to the following scene Big Daddy cleared everyone out of the bedroom/sitting room that Brick and his wife Margaret (Maggie) are occupying during their visit. He reveals to Brick his own recommitment to life (Brick knows the truth about the cancer) and wants to know why Brick has become so bitter and unmotivated. He also wants to know why Brick went jumping hurdles on the athletic field at 3 A.M. the night before (Brick broke his ankle during this drunken jaunt and wears a cast throughout the play); and, finally, he wants to know why Brick quit his job as a sports announcer, why his marriage is failing, and why he has become an alcoholic. Brick refuses to talk, but Big Daddy strikes a bargain with him: he will give Brick the drink he so desperately wants if Brick will answer his questions.

In this section of their scene, Gooper has just tried to get Big Daddy to return to the birthday celebration, but was thrown out of the room. Just before the interruption Brick said he was disgusted with mendacity, with "lyin' and liars." Big Daddy resumes his interrogation at this point.

BIG DADDY, *crosses to bar to pour Brick's drink:* Who's been lyin' to you? Has Margaret been lyin' to you, has your wife been lyin' to you about somethin', Brick?
BRICK: Not her. That wouldn't matter.
BIG DADDY: Then who's been lyin' to you, an' what about?
BRICK: No one single person an' no one lie.
BIG DADDY: Then what, what then? Then who, about what?
BRICK, *rubs head:* The whole, the whole—thing.
BIG DADDY, *crosses to Brick with drink:* Why are you rubbin' your head? You got a headache?
BRICK: No, I'm tryin' to—
BIG DADDY, *hands Brick the drink:* Concentrate, but you can't because your brain's all soaked with liquor, is that the trouble? Wet brain! What do you know about this mendacity thing? Hell, I could write a book on it! *Crosses downstage center, faces front.* I could write a book on it an' still not cover the subject! Well, I could, I could write a goddam book on it an' still

not cover th' subject anywhere near enough! Think of all th' lies I got to put up with! Pretenses! Ain't that mendacity? Havin' to pretend stuff you don't think or feel or have any idea of? Havin' for instance to act like I care for Big Mama! I haven't been able to stand the sight, sound or smell of that woman for forty years! Church! It bores the bejesus out of me, but I go! I go an' sit there an' listen to that dam' fool preacher! Clubs! Elks! Masons! Rotary! *(turns to Brick)* You I *do* like for some reason, did always have some kind of real feelin' for—affection—respect— *(bows on each word)* Yes, always, I don't know why, but it is! *(crosses to Brick)* *I've* lived with mendacity! Why can't *you* live with it? Hell, you *got* to live with it, there's nothin' *else* to *live* with except mendacity, is there?

BRICK: Yes, sir, yes, sir, there is somethin' else that you can live with.

BIG DADDY: What?

BRICK, *raising glass:* This!

BIG DADDY: That's not livin', that's dodgin' away from life.

BRICK, *drinks:* I want to dodge away from it.

BIG DADDY: Then why don't you kill yourself, man?

BRICK: I like to drink.

BIG DADDY: God! I can't talk to you. *Crosses upstage center.*

BRICK: I'm sorry, Big Daddy.

BIG DADDY, *turns to Brick from center:* Not as sorry as I am. I'll tell you somethin'. A little while back when I thought my number was up, before I found out it was just this—spastic— colon, I thought about you. Should I or should I not, if the jig was up, give you this place when I go? I hate Gooper an' those five screamin' monkeys like parrots in a jungle an' that bitch Mae! Why should I turn over 28,000 acres of the richest land this side of the Valley Nile to not my kind? But why in hell on the other hand, Brick, should I subsidize a dam' fool on the bottle? Liked or not liked, well, maybe even—loved! Why should I do that? Subsidize worthless behavior? Rot? Corruption? *Crosses downstage center, face front:* An' this I will tell you frankly. I didn't make up my mind at all on that question an' still to this day I ain't made out no will! Well, now I don't *have* to! The pressure is gone. *Crosses to Brick.* I can just wait an' see if you pull yourself together or if you don't.

BRICK: That's right, Big Daddy.

BIG DADDY: You sound like you thought I was kiddin'.

BRICK, *rises:* No, sir, I know you're not kiddin'.

BIG DADDY: But you don't care—?

BRICK, *crosses above couch to right gallery doors:* No, sir, I don't care—

BIG DADDY: WAIT! WAIT, BRICK. *Crosses to above wicker seat, facing Brick:* Don't let's leave it like this, like them other talks we've had, we've always—talked around things, we've— just talked around things like some rotten reason, I don't know what, it's always like somethin' was left not spoken, somethin' avoided because neither of us was honest enough with the other—

BRICK: I never lied to you, Big Daddy.

BIG DADDY: Did I ever to *you?*

BRICK: No, sir.

BIG DADDY, *his arm on Brick's arm:* Then there is at least two people that never lied to each other.

BRICK: Yes, sir, but we've never *talked* to each other.

BIG DADDY: We can *now.*

BRICK: Big Daddy, there don't seem to be anything much to say.

BIG DADDY: You say that you drink to kill your disgust with lyin'.

BRICK: You said to give you a reason.

BIG DADDY: Is liquor the only thing that'll kill this disgust?

BRICK: Now. Yes.

BIG DADDY: But not once, huh?

BRICK: Not when I was still young an' believin'. A drinkin' man's someone who wants to forget he isn't still young an' believin'.

BIG DADDY: Believin' what?

BRICK, *starts back for downstage gallery door:* Believin'—

BIG DADDY, *following, above wicker seat, to left of Brick at door, downstage:* Believin' *what?*

BRICK: Believin' . . .

BIG DADDY: I don't know what th' hell you mean by believin', an' I don't think you know what you mean by believin', but if you still got sports in your blood, go back to sports announcin' an'—

BRICK: Sit in a glass box watchin' games I can't play. Describin' what I can't do while players do it? Sweatin' out their disgust an' confusion in contests I'm not fit for? Drinkin' a Coke, half bourbon, so I can stand it? That's no dam' good any more—time just outran me, Big Daddy—got there first.

BIG DADDY, *turns to Brick:* I think you're passing the buck.

BRICK: You know many drinkin' men?

BIG DADDY: I have known a fair number of that species.

BRICK: Could any of them tell you why he drank?

BIG DADDY: Yep, you're passin' the buck, you're passin' the buck to things like time an' disgust with "mendacity," an'—crap! If you got to use that kind of language about a thing, it's ninety-proof bull, and I'm not buying any.

BRICK: I had to give you a reason to get a drink!

BIG DADDY: What did you say?

BRICK: I said: I had to give you a reason to get a drink.

BIG DADDY: You started drinkin' when your friend Skipper died.

BRICK: What are you suggesting?

BIG DADDY: I'm suggestin' nothin'. *Brick starts for the bar, crossing below Big Daddy.* But Gooper an' Mae suggested that there was something not right, exactly, in your—

BRICK: "Not right"?

BIG DADDY: Not, well, exactly *normal* in your—friendship with—

BRICK, *turning back to Big Daddy:* They suggested that, too? I thought that was Maggie's suggestion. Who else's suggestion is it, is it *yours?* How many others thought that Skipper and I were—

BIG DADDY: Now, hold on, hold on a minute, son. —I knocked around in my time.

BRICK: What's that got to do with it?

Rev. Tolker enters from right on gallery and eases into the room through doors, right, to behind wicker seat.

BIG DADDY, *crosses down center stage, front:* I said "Hold on!"—I bummed, I bummed this country till—

BRICK, *following:* Whose suggestion, who else's suggestion was it?

BIG DADDY: Slept in hobo jungles an' railroad Y's an' flophouses in all cities before I—

BRICK: Oh, *you* think so, too, you call me your son and a queer.

BUTLEY

by Simon Gray

———————•———————

ACT II

The setting is the shared office of Ben Butley and Joey Keyston, English teachers at London University. With his irascible manner and acerbic wit, Butley has managed to alienate all those who have cared about him. His wife, Anne, from whom he is separated, is divorcing him, and Joey, his former student and present roommate and lover, is leaving him for another man, Reg. Joey has just informed Butley that he is not available for dinner, that he is dining with Reg, and that Butley is not invited. The "Tom" mentioned in the scene (also referred to by Butley as "the most boring man in London") is a mutual friend of Butley and Reg who is about to marry Anne and have his new novel published by Reg's publishing company. The scene begins with Butley marking exams, alone in his office, a while after having learned of his wife's intention to remarry and just after having argued with Joey about the evening's plans. There is a knock on the door.

BEN: Come. *The door opens. Reg enters. Ben goes on working at his essay.* Minute please. *Then looks up.*

REG: Is Joey here?

BEN: Good God, it's Reg, isn't it? Of course it is. *He gets up, goes over, holds out his hand. As they shake hands:* I'm terribly sorry, do come in.

REG: Your porter said he was here.

BEN: And so he will be. He just went off to have a brief word with a colleague in distress. How are you?

REG: Very well, thanks. And you?

BEN, *gestures toward his desk:* As you see. *Laughs.*

REG: Yes. *He glances at the desk, appalled.* Look, you're obviously very busy. If you just tell Joey I'm at the porter's desk—

BEN: Don't be silly. You sit yourself down over there— *(he offers him a chair)* — and I'll just finish this off, I won't be a minute. *Reg hesitates, glances at Joey's desk and bookshelves and lights a cigarette. Ben pretends to go on marking, makes a few exclamations under his breath. Not looking up:* What brings you down here, anyway?

REG: I just thought I'd look in.

BEN, *writes furiously:* Have to make my script illegible so that they don't find out about my spelling. There. *He pushes the essay away.* To check up, eh?

REG: Check up?

BEN: Joey's always saying that if you got your hands on our little room, which is an everywhere, or rather on me, eh? as I'm responsible for the mess we're in— *(laughs)* But you should see our flat. Even Joey's room is like a pigsty—naturally, I'm the pig that made it that way. You really must come around and help us out. He says you've done wonders with your little kitchen.

REG: I'm in publishing.

BEN, *puzzled:* Yes?

REG: Not in interior decorating. *He sits on the hard chair by Joey's desk.*

BEN: Oh God, yes. *Laughs.* I'm sorry about that. No, I don't get your job wrong any more. It would be inexcusable. I'm always making Joey tell me about it, in fact.

REG: I know. He's always telling me about having to tell you about it.

BEN: He says you're a marvelous cook.

REG: I'm glad he eats well.

BEN: And keeps his figure, lucky sod. *Little pause. Gets up and sits on hard chair opposite Reg.* You know, Reg, I'm very glad to have the chance to speak to you privately—I behaved abominably the last time we met. I do hope—well, you've forgiven me for your shoes. I never apologized properly.

REG: It's all right. These things happen.

BEN: But your shoes survived, did they?

REG: They were suede.

BEN: Oh dear. Suede.

Pause.

REG: Look, you must want to get on. I'll go back to the porter— *(He gets up.)*

BEN: No, you mustn't do that. *He gets up.*

REG: I don't mind. In point of fact we were doing a little business together. He's an Arsenal supporter.

BEN: Good God. Is he really? In point of fact?

There is a pause.

REG: So I can let you get on with—

BEN: Have a drink? *He goes to his desk, opens the drawer.*

REG: I don't think I ought to.

BEN, *coming back with the Scotch and two soiled glasses:* You are lucky. Then you'll really enjoy it. *He pushes one of the glasses into Reg's hand. Reg peers down into the glass, winces at its condition. Ben dashes Scotch into it, then into his own.* I understand you've met my friend Tom. Tom Weatherley, by the way.

REG: I know Tom, yes.

BEN: You know all my domestic news, too, I gather. I only heard it myself today.

REG: Yes, I heard something about it. I'm sorry.

BEN: Do you detest warm Scotch? I don't know how you drink it in your part of the world?

REG: This is fine.

BEN: Good. Cheers.

REG: Cheers.

BEN: Thanks. *He drinks. Reg goes to Joey's bookshelves.* Its nice to have some company. These last few hours I've felt quite like Antony at his close—the air is full of the gods' departing musics. So do forgive any tendency to babble, eh?

REG: No, that's all right. I understand.

BEN: Cheers. *He sits on the hard chair by his desk.* Actually what this whole business has brought home to me is how dependent I am on my past.

REG, *turning to him:* But it was—excuse me—but it was quite a short marriage, wasn't it?

BEN: No, I was talking about Joey.

REG: Oh.

BEN: It's as if my marriage were an intermission, if you see. Now I'm catching up with my past again, which is where I suppose my future is also.

REG: Really?

BEN: Sorry. I'm being literary. But I always think of *you* as a born romantic. From Joey's descriptions of *your* past. A touch of the butterfly, eh?

REG: Really? And what does Joey say to make you think that?

BEN: Oh, I don't know—the way you've pulled up your roots in the North, what I imagine to be your emotional pattern, your love of the bizarre.

REG, *pause:* And how does that express itself?

BEN: Joey's always recounting your experiences—for example with the Gurkhas. You were with them, weren't you?

REG: I was stationed with them, yes. About ten years ago, during my National Service.

BEN: Exactly. And I scarcely knew what a Gurkha was—I still tend to think he's something you get with a cocktail.

REG: Do you?

BEN: They must be tough little towsers.

REG: They are. *He sits at Joey's desk.* You didn't do your National Service, I take it.

BEN: Oh Christ! Sorry, I mean no.

REG: How come?

BEN: I got took queer. *There is a pause. Reg puts his glass down.* Oh! You're ready for another one.

REG: No, I—in point of fact, I'd rather not.

BEN: This is an altogether different suburb. *He refills Reg's glass.*

REG: Sorry? What suburb?

BEN: Oh, it's a little joke of Joey's. Almost impossible to explain out of context. *He pours himself a drink and leans on the front of his desk.* But how is the world of fiction?

REG: Can't complain.

BEN: Cheers. What have you got coming out at the moment?

REG: At the moment I'm doing two cookery books, an authoritative guide to bird watching in Lincolnshire, the only intelligent account of the farce of El Alamein—by an N.C.O. needless to say—and a New Testament Commentary.

BEN: That's your *fiction* list?

REG: No, that's our list for next month.

BEN: No novels at all then?

REG: Well, just one of those historical romances where the hero shoves his sword into assorted villains and his cock into assorted ladies. It won't get the reviews but it'll make us money.

BEN: If he did it the other way around you might get both.

REG, *laughs briefly:* But the point is, you see, by putting that one through we can afford to do something worthwhile later. For instance, I've just made a decision about a novel on National Service life.

BEN: Oh, one of those. I thought that vogue was eight years dead.

REG: No, not one of those. This is something special, in my opinion. Of course it mightn't interest you as you didn't do National Service, but personally I found it moving, witty, gracefully organized—genuinely poetic.

BEN: The National Service? Good God! Those qualities are hard enough to come by in art. It's never occurred to me to look for them in life, especially as run by the armed forces. Cheers.

REG: Nevertheless I expect you *will* be curious in this case. Theoretically I can't tell you our author's name as the board doesn't meet until tomorrow, but if I just mention that he's a comprehensive school teacher— *(he raises his glass slowly)* Cheers.

BEN, *after a pause:* Well, well. *He sits in the armchair.* The most boring man in London strikes again.

REG: I'm sorry.

BEN: Why?

REG: It must be painful for you.

BEN: Why?

REG: Because of his relationship with you. It was wrong of me to have mentioned it.

BEN: On the contrary. It was the correct move. Has Joey read it?

REG: Not yet. It was offered to me in strict secrecy—at least until I'd made up my mind. But I can tell him about it now. I think he'll like it.

BEN: That's because you don't know him very well, perhaps. He may be something of a dilettante in personal relationships, but he holds fast to standards on important matters. We once drew up a list of the five most tedious literary subjects in the world. National Service came fifth, just behind the Latin poems of Milton.

REG: Really? And what occupied the other three places?

BEN: The English poems of Milton.

REG: When I was at Hull I chose Milton for my special subject.

BEN: That sounds an excellent arrangement. The thing is to confine him to the North. Down here we can dally with Suckling and Lovelace.

REG: And Beatrix Potter? Joey says you've got great admiration for the middle-class nursery poets.

BEN: With reservations. I find some of the novellae a trifle heavy going. *A pause.* I call Joey Appley Dappley, did you know?

REG: Do you?

BEN: And he calls me Old Mr. Prickle-pin. After

Old Mr. Prickle-pin, with never a coat to
Put his pins in.

Sometimes I call him Diggory Diggory Delvet, when he's burrowing away at his book.

There is a pause.

REG: What did you mean by being took queer?

BEN, *coyly:* Oh, you know, I'm sure. *Laughing.* You do look shocked, Reg.

REG: That's surprising, because I'm not surprised even.

BEN: You don't think there's anything shameful in it, then?

REG: In what?

BEN: Dodging the draft.

REG: There are thousands of blokes from working-class homes who couldn't. They didn't know the tricks. Besides, they'd rather have done ten years in uniform than get out of it that way.

BEN: Then you think there's something shameful in being taken queer?

REG: I'm talking about people pretending to be what they're not.

BEN: Not what?

REG: Not what they are.

BEN: But if people do get taken queer, it's nature we must blame or their bodies, mustn't we? Medicine's still got a long way to go, Reg.

REG: Why do you use that word?

BEN: What word?

REG: "Queer."

BEN: Does it offend you?

REG: It's beginning to.

BEN: Sorry. It's an old nursery habit. One of our chars used to say it. Whenever I came down with anything it would be, "Our Ben's took queer again, poor little mite." *There is a silence.* Although I can see it's a trifle inappropriate for a touch of T.B.—

REG: T.B.?

BEN: They found it just in time. At my board medical, in fact. Why *do* you object to the phrase though?

REG: No, no, it doesn't matter. A misunderstanding. I'm sorry.

BEN: Oh, I *see. Queer!*—of course. Good God, you didn't think I'd sink quite so low, did you? *Laughs.*

REG: I'm sorry.

BEN: Its all right. *There is a pause.* Cheers. *He raises his glass.*

REG: Cheers.

Another pause.

BEN: Homosexual.

Another pause.

REG: What?

BEN: Homosexual. I was just wondering—should one say that instead of "queer"—in your sense of the word. Homosexual.

REG: It doesn't really matter at all. I don't really care—

BEN: Do you feel the same about "fairies" as you do about "queers?"

REG: Yes, in point of fact. Since you ask.

BEN: Right, I've got that. *He gets up and moves toward Reg.* Of course they've almost vanished anyway, the old-style queens and queers, the poofs, the fairies. The very words seem to conjure up a magical world of naughty thrills, forbidden fruits— sorry—you know, I always used to enjoy them enjoying themselves. Their varied performances contributed to my life's varieties. But now the law, in making them safe, has made them drab. Just like the heterosexual rest of us. Poor sods. *Little pause.* Don't you think?

REG, *stands up and puts his glass on the desk:* Oh, there's enough affectation and bitchiness in heterosexuals to be getting on with. *He glances at his watch.* Don't you think?

BEN: Oh don't worry. He'll be here in a minute. *Pause.* How are things between you two, by the way?

REG: What things?

BEN: No complications?

REG: What kind of complications would there be?

BEN: In that our routine doesn't interfere with your—plural meaning—routine.

REG: Plural meaning? Meaning what?

BEN: Yours and his. Your routines together.

REG: Ah. Well, it has done, frankly, yes. Now you ask. But I don't think it will from now on.

BEN, *sits on the hard chair opposite Reg:* Then you're beginning to get the hang of it? Good. Because sometimes I've suspected that our friendship—going back so far and including so much— so much of his history and so much of my history which has really become *our* history—singular meaning this time—must make it difficult for any new people we pick up on the side.

REG: Like your wife, do you mean?

BEN: Well done. Yes, like poor old Anne. She must have felt her share amounted to a minor infidelity, really. I speak metaphorically, of course, but then I suppose marriage is the best metaphor for all our intense relationships. Except those we have with our husbands and wives. *Laughs.* Naturally.

REG: So you think of yourself as married to Joey, do you?

BEN: Metaphorically. *A pause. The telephone rings. Ben picks it up.* Butley, English. Oh, hello, James—no, I'm afraid I still can't talk properly. I'm in the middle of a tutorial. *He winks at Reg.* O.K. Yes. Goodbye.

REG: What metaphor would you use when you learned that Joey was going to move in with someone else? Would that be divorce, metaphorically?

BEN, *after a long pause:* What?

REG, *laughs:* Sorry. I shouldn't do that. But I was thinking that it must be odd getting news of two divorces in the same day.

BEN, *pause:* Joey hasn't said anything.

REG: No. I'm giving the news. You might say that when he comes to me our Joey will be moving out of figures of speech into matters of fact. Ours will be too much like a marriage to be a metaphor.

BEN, *little pause:* I thought you didn't admit to being—what? different?

REG: There are moments when frankness is necessary. No, our

Joey's just been waiting for the right queen, fruit, fairy, poof, or
homosexual to come along. He's come.
BEN, *after a pause:* Well, isn't he lucky.
REG: Time will tell. I hope so. But I'm tired of waiting to make
a proper start with him. I'm tired of waiting for him to tell you.
You know our Joey—a bit gutless. No, the truth of the matter is
I've been trying to get Joey to bring you around to dinner one
evening and tell you straight, so we could get it over with. I
knew he'd never find the nerve to do it on his lonesome. But
he's kept dodging about, pretending you were busy, one excuse
after another. It's worked out quite well though, hasn't it?

A MAN FOR ALL SEASONS

by Robert Bolt

———————•———————

ACT II

When Henry VIII failed to obtain a church divorce from Catherine of Aragon, he rebelled against the Catholic church and
the Pope. He issued an Act of Supremacy making himself spiritual as well as temporal leader of England, and he required all
his subjects to sign the document. His Lord Chancellor, Sir
Thomas More, would not sign. More knew he was placing himself in jeopardy by upholding the authority of the Pope, but he
was a profoundly devout Catholic with a strong conscience, and
was morally incapable of lying about his convictions. Pressure
from Henry and his henchman, Thomas Cromwell, increased.
Various plots and threats were used to force More to comply,
but to no avail. Charges of treason were then brought against
him and he was executed.

The scene below takes place in Cromwell's study. More has
been summoned for questioning. Cromwell tries to frighten him
with false evidence implicating him in treasonous acts. More re-
plies with solid evidence absolving himself on each count. Their
conversation is being transcribed by Master Rich.

MORE: If I might hear the charges?

CROMWELL: Charges?

MORE: I understand there are certain charges.

CROMWELL: Some ambiguities of behavior I should like to clarify—hardly "charges."

MORE: Make a note of that will you, Master Rich? There are no charges.

CROMWELL, *laughing and shaking head:* Sir Thomas, Sir Thomas ... You know it amazes me that you, who were once so effective *in* the world and are now so *much* retired from it, should be opposing yourself to the whole movement of the times? *He ends on a note of interrogation.*

MORE, *nods:* It amazes me too.

CROMWELL, *picks up and drops a paper; sadly:* The King is not pleased with you.

MORE: I am grieved.

CROMWELL: Yet do you know that even now, if you could bring yourself to agree with the Universities, the Bishops, and the Parliament of this realm, there is no honor which the King would be likely to deny you?

MORE, *stonily:* I am well acquainted with His Grace's generosity.

CROMWELL, *coldly:* Very well. *Consults the paper.* You have heard of the so-called Holy Maid of Kent—who was executed for prophesying against the King?

MORE: Yes, I knew the poor woman.

CROMWELL, *quickly:* You sympathize with her?

MORE: She was ignorant and misguided; she was a bit mad, I think. And she has paid for her folly. Naturally I sympathize with her.

CROMWELL, *grunts:* You admit meeting her. You met her—and yet you did not warn His Majesty of her treason. How was that?

MORE: She spoke no treason. Our conversation was not political.

CROMWELL: My dear More, the woman was notorious! Do you expect me to believe that?

MORE: Happily there are witnesses.

CROMWELL: You wrote a letter to her?

MORE: Yes, I wrote advising her to abstain from meddling with the affairs of Princes and the State. I have a copy of this letter—also witnessed.

CROMWELL: You have been cautious.

MORE: I like to keep my affairs regular.

CROMWELL: Sir Thomas, there is a more serious charge—

MORE: Charge?

CROMWELL: For want of a better word. In the May of 1526 the King published a book. *He permits himself a little smile.* A theological work. It was called *A Defence of the Seven Sacraments.*

MORE: Yes. *Bitterly:* For which he was named "Defender of the Faith," by His Holiness the Pope.

CROMWELL: By the Bishop of Rome. Or do you insist on "Pope"?

MORE: No, "Bishop of Rome" if you like. It doesn't alter his authority.

CROMWELL: Thank you, you come to the point very readily; what *is* that authority? As regards the Church in Europe; *(approaching)* for example, the Church in England. What exactly *is* the Bishop of Rome's authority?

MORE: You will find it very ably set out and defended, Master Secretary, in the King's book.

CROMWELL: The book published under the King's name would be more accurate. You wrote that book.

MORE: I wrote no part of it.

CROMWELL: I do not mean you actually held the pen.

MORE: I merely answered to the best of my ability certain questions on canon law which His Majesty put to me. As I was bound to do.

CROMWELL: Do you deny that you *instigated* it?

MORE: It was from first to last the King's own project. This is trivial, Master Cromwell.

CROMWELL: I should not think so if I were in your place.

MORE: Only two people know the truth of the matter. Myself and the King. And, whatever he may have said to you, he will not give evidence to support this accusation.

CROMWELL: Why not?

MORE: Because evidence is given on oath, and he will not perjure himself. If you don't know that, you don't yet know him.

Cromwell looks at him viciously.

CROMWELL, *goes apart; formally:* Sir Thomas More, is there anything you wish to say to me concerning the King's marriage with Queen Anne?

MORE, *very still:* I understood I was not to be asked that again.

CROMWELL: Evidently you understood wrongly. These charges—

MORE, *with a sudden, contemptuous sweep of his arm:* They are terrors for children, Master Secretary—an empty cupboard! To frighten children in the dark, not me.

CROMWELL, *it is some time now since anybody treated him like this, and it costs him some effort to control his anger, but he does and even manages a little smile as one who sportingly admits defeat:* True . . . true. Sir Thomas, very apt. *Then coldly:* To frighten a man, there must be something *in* the cupboard, must there not?

MORE, *made wary again by the tone:* Yes, and there is nothing in it.

CROMWELL: For the moment there is this: *(Picks up a paper and reads:)* "I charge you with great ingratitude. I remind you of many benefits graciously given and ill received. I tell you that no King of England ever had nor could have so villainous a servant nor so traitorous a subject as yourself." *During this, More's face goes ashen and his hand creeps up to his throat in an unconscious gesture of fear and protection. Cromwell puts down the paper and says:* The words are not mine, Sir Thomas, but the King's. Believe that.

MORE: I do. *He lowers his hands, looks up again, and with just a spark of his old impudence:* I recognize the style. So I am brought here at last.

CROMWELL: Brought? You brought yourself to where you stand now.

MORE: Yes—Still, in another sense—I was brought.

CROMWELL: Oh, yes. You may go home now. *After a fractional hesitation, More goes, his face fearful and his step thoughtful, and he pauses uncertainly as Cromwell calls after him:* For the present. *More carries on, and exits:* I don't like him so well as I did. There's a man who raises the gale and won't come out of the harbor.

ONE FLEW OVER THE CUCKOO'S NEST
(from the novel by Ken Kesey)

by Dale Wasserman

———•———

ACT II

McMurphy contrives to serve a short prison sentence in what he believes will be the pleasanter setting of a mental institution. In short order, his roguish but honest nature and his enthusiasm for life generate feelings of optimism and confidence in the inmates. But McMurphy breaks the rules of the institution and he encourages the inmates, for the sake of their sanity, to do the same. His adversary, Headnurse Ratched, warns him about his misbehavior; then, in a desperate attempt to regain control of the ward, she submits him to electro-shock therapy. When this fails to surpress his spirit, she finally has him lobotomized. Believing he would rather be dead than live as a vegetable, one of the inmates, Chief Bromden, smothers McMurphy with a pillow.

Prior to the following excerpt, McMurphy became aware that his release from the institution was totally dependent on Nurse Ratched and that, unlike a prison sentence, there is no specified release date for mental patients. At that point, to the disappointment of the inmates—who have come to regard him as a Moses leading them out of slavery—McMurphy decides to abide fully by the institution's rules.

The following scene between McMurphy and Chief Bromden takes place some hours later. It is night. The dayroom is empty and lit only by moonlight. Chief Bromden enters. He is an American Indian, a giant of a man, who is presumed to be deaf and dumb. The "panel" referred to in the dialogue houses all the electrical circuits that feed into the control board (controlling and monitoring sound, light, TV, etc.) in the Nurses' Station.

Chief Bromden enters from the dormitory. He looks about in a puzzled way as though someone had called to him. He is drawn to the windows, magnetized by moonlight. Raises his head looking up at the sky . . . and in the hush is heard the high laughing gabble of wild geese passing overhead. He raises his arms wide, as though to embrace the whole lost world beyond the windows, then folds them about his body. He is standing like that, head thrown back, eyes closed, when McMurphy enters.

MCMURPHY, *whispering:* Chief, you all right? *No acknowledgment.* Saw you get up and figgered maybe you come out here to scrape off some a that thousand-year gum. *Offering a stick of gum; apologetically:* They took away my canteen privileges so this is all I got.

CHIEF BROMDEN, *taking it—then he speaks in a hoarse voice:* Thank you.

MCMURPHY: That's okay. *Starts off, comes to a startled halt:* Hey—! *Coming back:* Try it again—you're a little rusty.

CHIEF BROMDEN, *clears his throat; more clearly:* Thank you. *McMurphy starts to laugh, trying to keep the sound down. Chief Bromden goes toward the dormitory, his feelings hurt.*

MCMURPHY, *stopping him:* 'Scuse me, Chief. What I was laughin' at, I just caught wise to what you been doin' all these years—bidin' your time till you could tell 'em off!

CHIEF BROMDEN: No . . . no, I'd be afraid.

MCMURPHY: How's that?

CHIEF BROMDEN: I'm not big enough.

MCMURPHY: Hoo boy, you *are* crazy, aren't you. I been on a few reservations in my life, but you are the *biggest* damn Injun I have ever seen!

CHIEF BROMDEN: My papa was bigger.

MCMURPHY: Yeah?

CHIEF BROMDEN: He was a full chief and his name was Tee Ah Millatoona. That means The Pine That Stands Tallest on the Mountain. But my mother got twice his size.

MCMURPHY: You must of had a real moose of an old lady!

CHIEF BROMDEN: Oh, she wasn't big *that* way. She wasn't Indian, neither. She was a town woman. Her name was Bromden.

MCMURPHY: Yeah, I think I see what you're gettin' at . . .

when a town woman marries an Indian that's marryin' beneath her, ain't it? And your papa had to take her name?

CHIEF BROMDEN: She said she wouldn't be married to no man with a name like Tee Ah Millatoona. But it wasn't only her that made him little. Everybody worked on him. The way they're workin' on you.

MCMURPHY: They who?

CHIEF BROMDEN: The Combine. It wanted us to go live some place else. It wanted to take away our waterfall. In town they beat up Papa in the alleys and cut off his hair. Oh, the Combine's big . . . big. He fought it a long time till my mother made him too little to fight any more. Then he signed the papers.

MCMURPHY: What papers, Chief?

CHIEF BROMDEN: The ones that gave everything to the government. The village. The falls . . .

MCMURPHY: I remember . . . but I heard the tribe got paid some huge amount.

CHIEF BROMDEN: That's what the government guys said, here's a whole big pot of money. And Papa said, what can you pay for the way a man lives? What can you pay for his right to be an Indian? They didn't understand. Neither did the tribe. They stood in front of our door, holdin' those checks, askin' what should we do now? And Papa couldn't tell them 'cause he was too little . . . and too drunk.

MCMURPHY: What happened to him?

CHIEF BROMDEN: He kept drinkin' till he died. They found him in a alley and threw dirt in his eyes. *Fiercely:* The Combine whipped him. It beats *everybody.*

MCMURPHY: Now, wait a minute—

CHIEF BROMDEN: Yes, yes, it does! Oh, they don't bust you outright. They work on you, ways you can't even see. They get hold of you and they *install* things!

MCMURPHY: Take 'er easy, buddy.

CHIEF BROMDEN: And if you *fight* they lock you up some place and make you stop and—!

MCMURPHY, *closing the Chief's mouth with his hand:* Woops, cool it. *Takes him in his arms, gently, soothingly.*

CHIEF BROMDEN, *in a moment, ashamed:* I been talkin' crazy.

MCMURPHY: Well . . . yeah.

CHIEF BROMDEN: It don't make sense.

MCMURPHY: I didn't say it didn't make sense.

CHIEF BROMDEN: Sh-h! *Raises his head, moves toward the windows, listening:* Hear 'em? *McMurphy comes to him, listens. From the sky the wild, gabbling cry again.*

MCMURPHY: Canada honkers flyin' south. Gonna be an early winter, Chief. Look, there they go. Right across the moon!

CHIEF BROMDEN, *gazing skyward, chanting softly:* Wire, brier, limber lock . . .

MCMURPHY: Huh?

CHIEF BROMDEN: It's a old children's rhyme. My grandmomma taught it to me . . .

MCMURPHY: Oh, lord, yes, I remember! You play it with your fingers. Hold out your hand, Chief. *Ticking off fingers, chanting:* Wire, brier, limber lock—

CHIEF BROMDEN: Three geese in a flock.

MCMURPHY: One flew east—

CHIEF BROMDEN: One flew west—

MCMURPHY: An' one flew over the cuckoo's nest!

CHIEF BROMDEN: O-U-T spells out—

MCMURPHY: Goose swoops down and plucks *you* out! *They embrace, laugh happily; then the Chief sobers.*

CHIEF BROMDEN: McMurphy?

MCMURPHY: Yeah?

CHIEF BROMDEN: You gonna crawfish? *McMurphy doesn't answer.* I mean, you gonna back down?

MCMURPHY, *turning away:* Aw . . . what's the difference?

CHIEF BROMDEN: Are you?

MCMURPHY, *his eyes light on the panel. Brightly:* Hey, remember when I tried to lift that thing? I bet *you* could do it.

CHIEF BROMDEN, *shrinking back:* I'm too little.

MCMURPHY: Whyn't you give it a try?

CHIEF BROMDEN: I'm not *big* enough!

MCMURPHY: How do ya know? That'd be one sure way to find out. *Giving up, cheerfully:* Well, when you're ready, lemme make book on it. Hoo boy, would *that* be a killin'!

CHIEF BROMDEN: McMurphy. *McMurphy pauses.* Make me big again.

MCMURPHY: Why, hell, Chief . . . looks to me like you growed half a foot already!

CHIEF BROMDEN, *shaking his head:* How can I be big if you ain't? How can anybody? *He exits into the dorm. McMurphy is motionless a moment, then follows.*

SHORT EYES

by Miguel Piñero

———————•———————

ACT II

The setting is the dayroom in the House of Detention. The characters are the inmates (mostly Puerto Rican and black) and guards of one section. The play depicts racial encounters, personal encounters, and the self-encounters of men facing their own yearnings, frustrations, rages, and fears. The tenuous stability of the section is disrupted with the arrival of Clark Davis. Clark is white and middle-class. He was arrested for raping a young girl, a crime that, even among these violent and hardened men, is looked on with particular revulsion. He is badly abused and threatened by both inmates and guards. Juan, a Puerto Rican inmate, is the one person who shows him any compassion, and Clark confides to Juan his own self-hatred and all the details of his sordid sexual proclivities.

In the following scene Clark has just returned from the line-up. He believes that he has a chance of being released and asks Juan not to divulge anything from their personal conversation. Juan is faced with the dilemma of breaking the confidence of this pathetic man or allowing him to go back outside "to scar up some more little girls' minds."

JUAN: What you want to see me about, Clark?
CLARK: Look, what I told you earlier . . . er . . . that between me and you . . . like, I don't know why I even said that, just . . . just that . . . man, like everything was just coming down on me . . . My wife . . . she was at the hospital . . . She . . . she didn't

even look at me ... once, not once ... Please ... don't let it out ... please ... I'll really go for help this time ... I promise.

JUAN: What happened at the P.I. stand?

CLARK: Nothing ... nothing ... happened ...

JUAN: Did she identify you? Did she?

CLARK: I don't know. I didn't see anybody. They put me next to a bunch of the other men about my size, weight ... You—the whole lineup routine. I didn't see anybody or anything but the people there and this voice that kept asking me to turn around to say, "Hello, little girl." That's all.

JUAN: Nothing else?

CLARK: No.

JUAN: You mean they didn't make you sign some papers?

CLARK: No.

JUAN: Was there a lawyer for you there? Somebody from the courts?

CLARK: Juan, I really don't know ... I didn't see anybody ... and they didn't let me speak to anyone at all ... They hustled me in and hustled me right out ...

JUAN: That means you have a chance to beat this case ... Did they tell you what they are holding you for?

CLARK: No ... no one told me anything.

JUAN: If they are rushing it—the P.I.—that could mean they only are waiting on the limitation to run out.

CLARK: What does that all mean?

JUAN: What it means is that you will get a chance to scar up some more little girls' minds.

CLARK: Don't say that, Juan. Please don't think like that. Believe me, if I thought I couldn't seek help after this ordeal, I would have never—I mean, I couldn't do that again.

JUAN: How many times you've said that in the street and wind up molesting some kid in the park.

CLARK: Believe me, Juan ... please believe me. I wouldn't any more.

JUAN: Why should I?

CLARK: Cause I told you the truth before. I told you what I haven't told God.

JUAN: That's because God isn't in the House of Detention.

CLARK: Please, Juan, why are you being this way? What have I done to you?

JUAN: What have you done to me? What you've done to me?

It's what you've done, period. It's the stand that you are forcing me to take.

CLARK: You hate me.

JUAN: I don't hate you. I hate what you've done. What you are capable of doing. What you might do again.

CLARK: You sound like a judge.

JUAN: In this time and place I am your judge.

CLARK: No ... no. You are not ... And I'm sick and tired of people judging me.

JUAN: Man, I don't give a fuck what you're sick and tired about. What you told about yourself was done because of the pressure. People say and do weird things under pressure.

CLARK: I'm not used to this.

JUAN: I don't care what you're used to. I got to make some kind of thing about you.

CLARK: No, you don't have to do anything. Just let me live.

JUAN: Let you live?

CLARK: I can't make this ... this kind of life. I'll die.

JUAN: Motherfucker, don't cry on me.

CLARK: Cry ... why shouldn't I cry ... why shouldn't I feel sorry for myself ... I have a right to ... I have some rights ... and when these guys get back from the sick call ... I'm gonna tell them what the captain said to me, that if anybody bothers me to tell him ...

JUAN: Then you will die.

CLARK: I don't care one way or the other. Juan, when I came here I already had been abused by the police ... threatened by a mob the newspaper created ... Then the judge, for my benefit and the benefit of society, had me committed to observation. Placed in an isolated section of some nut ward ... viewed by interns and visitors like some abstract object, treated like a goddamn animal monster by a bunch of inhuman, incompetent, third-rate, unqualified, unfit psychopaths calling themselves doctors.

JUAN: I know the scene.

CLARK: No, you don't know ... electros—sedatives—hypnosis—therapy ... humiliated by some crank nurses who strapped me to my bed and played with my penis to see if it would get hard for "big girls like us."

JUAN: Did it?

CLARK: Yeah ... yes, it did.

JUAN: My father used to say he would fuck 'em from eight to eighty, blind, cripple, and/or crazy.
CLARK: Juan, you are the only human being I've met.
JUAN: Don't try to leap me up ... cause I don't know how much of a human being I would be if I let you make the sidewalk. But there's no way I could stop you short of taking you off the count.

LUV

by Murray Schisgal

——————•——————

ACT I

Harry Berlin is miserable. He is a beaten man, disillusioned with life, despairing over its senselessness. Harry is so miserable that he has decided to end it all this very night by jumping off a bridge. Along comes Milt Manville, Harry's old school chum of fifteen years ago. Milt is successful, wealthy, well tailored, confident—but also miserable. He is madly in love, but not with his wife. So he has arranged to meet his wife on the bridge intending to kill her. While waiting for her, Milt notices Harry's coat on a trash basket; then he spots Harry by the railing and recognizes him. Out of this chance meeting Milt hatches a scheme to pair Harry with his wife; thus, in one bold stroke releasing both men from their unhappiness.

The following is the opening scene of the play. Harry writes a brief note, puts it on the railing, and climbs up.

MILT, *with a sense of recognition, moving up to him:* Is it ... *Harry turns, stares down at him.* No. Harry Berlin! I thought so! I just caught a glimpse of you and I said to myself, "I bet that's Harry Berlin. I just bet that's Harry Berlin." And sure enough, it's old Harry Berlin himself. *Taking Harry's hand, shaking it:* How have you been doing, Harry? What's been happening?

Harry squats and slowly comes down from railing. It must be . . . why, at least fifteen years since I saw you last. We had that party after graduation, I said, "Keep in touch," you said, "I'll call you in a few days," and that's the last I heard of you. Fifteen years.

HARRY, *feigning recognition:* Is it fifteen years?

MILT: Fifteen years.

HARRY: Hard to believe.

MILT: Fifteen years next month as a matter of fact.

HARRY: Time sure flies.

MILT: It sure does.

HARRY: Fifteen years next month.

MILT: Fifteen years.

HARRY, *slight pause:* Who are you?

MILT: Milt! Milt Manville! Your old classmate at Polyarts U.

HARRY, *grabbing his hand:* That's right! Milt! Milt Manville! *They embrace, laugh joyfully. Harry puts on jacket, then crumples note, throws it over railing as Milt speaks.*

MILT: Say, Harry, I've been doing wonderful for myself; terrific. Got into the brokerage business during the day: stocks, bonds, securities, you know. The money's just pouring in; doing fabulous. Got into second-hand bric-a-brac and personal accessories at night: on my own, great racket, easy buck. And, say, I got myself married. Oh, yeah, I went and did it, finally did it. Ellen. A wonderful, wonderful girl. Do anything for her. A home in the suburbs, no kidding, thirty-five thousand, and that's not counting the trees, big tremendous trees; you should see them. Hey. Look at this watch. Solid gold. Twenty-two carats. *Opening his jacket to reveal garish yellow lining:* Notice the label? *Unbuttons shirt.* Silk underwear. Imported. Isn't that something? *Lifts arm.* Hey, smell this, go ahead, smell it. *Harry is reluctant to come too close, Milt presses his head to his armpit, laughing:* Not bad, huh? *Solemnly:* Well, how's it been going, Harry? Let's hear.

HARRY, *mournfully:* Awful, Milt; awful. It couldn't be worse. I'm at the end of the line. Everything's falling apart.

MILT, *perplexed:* I don't get it.

HARRY: The world, Milt. People. Life. Death. The old questions. I'm choked with them.

MILT, *still perplexed:* Oh.

HARRY, *arm around him, leads him forward right:* I must have been out of school for only a couple of weeks when . . . it happened. Out of the blue. Disillusionment. Despair. Debilitation. The works. It hit me all at once.

MILT: Oh. Ohhhh. *Harry sits on curbstone. Milt puts down white handkerchief, sits beside him.*

HARRY: I remember . . . I was sitting in the park. It was Sunday, a hot lazy Sunday. The sun was burning on the back of my neck. An open book was on my lap and I was kind of daydreaming, thinking of the future, my plans, my prospects . . . Then . . . Suddenly . . . Suddenly I looked up and I saw, standing there in front of me . . . How can I put it in words? It was a dog, Milt. A fox-terrier. I'd swear it was a fox-terrier. But who knows, I . . .

MILT, *interrupting:* Let's just say it was a dog, Harry.

HARRY: It was a dog. Right.

MILT: A dog. Go ahead.

HARRY: And . . . And he was there, right in front of me, standing on his hind legs and . . . He looked almost like a little old man with a little white beard and a little wrinkled face. The thing is . . . Milt, he was laughing. He was laughing as loudly and as clearly as I'm talking to you now. I sat there. I couldn't move. I couldn't believe what was happening. And then, he came up to me, now he was walking on all fours and . . . When he got up to me . . . When he got up to me, he raised his leg and . . .

MILT: No.

HARRY, *nodding, with twisted expression:* All over my gabardine pants. And they were wet, through and through. I could swear to that! Then he turned right around and walked off. The whole thing was . . . It was all so unreal, all so damn senseless. My mind . . . I thought . . . *(emotionally)* Why me? Out of everyone in that park, out of hundreds, thousands of people, why me? *Milt looks about bewilderedly.* What did it mean? How do you explain it? *In control of himself:* That started it; right there was the beginning. From that minute on, it changed, everything changed for me. It was as if I was dragged to the edge of the cliff and forced to look down. How can I make you understand. What words do I use. I was nauseous, Milt. Sick to my soul. I became aware . . aware of the whole rotten senseless stinking deal. Nothing mattered to me after that. Nothing.

MILT: Your plans to go to medical school?

HARRY: I couldn't.

MILT: The book you were writing.

HARRY, *throwing up his hands:* No use.

MILT: Your Greek studies?

HARRY: I couldn't. I couldn't go on. *Rises, moves to sandbox, paces around it, Milt also rises.* No roots. No *modus vivendi.* I had to find some answers first. A reason. I traveled, went everywhere, looked everyplace. I studied with a Brahmin in Calcutta, with a Buddhist in Nagoya, with a Rabbi in Los Angeles. Nothing. I could find nothing. I didn't know where to turn, what to do with myself. I began drinking, gambling, living in whorehouses, smoking marijuana, taking guitar lessons . . . Nothing. Still nothing. Tonight . . . Milt, tonight I was going to end it all, make one last stupid gesture of disgust and . . . that would be it!

MILT, *glances at railing:* You don't mean . . .

HARRY: That's right.

MILT, *going to him:* How terrible. How terrible, Harry. I'm ashamed of you at this minute. I'm ashamed to have been your classmate at Polyarts U.

HARRY: Ask me what I believe in, Milt.

MILT: What do you believe in, Harry?

HARRY: I believe in nothing, Milt.

MILT: Nothing? That's terrible. How can someone go on living without believing in anything?

HARRY: That's the problem I'm faced with. And there's no answer to it, none, except down there! *He points to railing, moving to bench.*

MILT, *turns Harry toward him:* Now let's not lose our heads. Let's control ourselves. Keep calm. Keep calm. Now listen to me. I can understand. I can understand everything you said, but, Harry . . . Don't you think it's more than unusual, just a little more than unusual, that I happened to be passing at the very minute, the precise exact minute, that you were contemplating this . . . this horrible thing?

HARRY, *pointing upward:* You don't mean . . . ?

MILT, *throwing both hands up defensively:* I'm not saying it! I didn't say it! *Wagging finger:* But just remember, science doesn't have all the answers!

HARRY: Talking about it only makes it worse, Milt. You don't know what agony I've been through. It's gotten so bad that sometimes, sometimes, in the middle of the day or night, without a warning of any kind, my whole body becomes paralyzed, I can't move a muscle and . . . *(In mid-speech his body stiffens like a board and he topples forward. Milt catches him at the last moment, shouts and shakes him frantically.)*

MILT: Harry! What is it? Harry, for God's sake . . . *(He runs around in a complete circle, holding Harry whose stiff body revolves like the hand of a clock.)* Help! Help! Help, here! Help! Help! *To Harry:* Look at me! Speak to me, Harry!

HARRY, *calmly:* That's the way it happens.

MILT, *sitting on sandbox:* You scared the life out of me. That's terrible. Why don't you see a doctor, a specialist, someone . . .

HARRY: I don't have to see anyone. I know what it is, Milt. The will to live drops out of me, plops right out of me. Why move? I say to myself. Why do anything? But that's not all of it. Sometimes, sometimes, I can't see, I lose the power of sight completely and I grope about . . . *(Throws up his hands, feigns blindness and moves dangerously close to the edge of the stage.)* Milt . . . Milt . . . Where are you? Are you still here, Milt?

MILT, *jumps up, grabs him in the nick of time:* Right here, Harry. I'm right here.

HARRY, *clawing behind him at Milt's face:* Help me, Milt. Help me get to the bench.

MILT, *pushing him forward:* Of course. This way, Harry. That's it. Watch your step. Here, here it is. *They're seated on bench.*

HARRY, *calmly:* Thank you, Milt.

MILT: Is there . . . anything else I can do?

HARRY: No. I'm all right now. That's the way it happens.

MILT: I would never have believed it.

HARRY: Why see? I say to myself. Why be a witness to it? *Grabbing Milt's lapels:* Why, Milt? Why?

MILT: I don't know, Harry. I don't know. *Pulling himself free, straightens tie, etc.*

HARRY: So I go blind and I don't see. The whole thing becomes completely automatic. I have no control over it.

MILT: But there must be something you can do.

HARRY, *cupping hand to ear, feigns deafness, loudly:* What did you say, Milt?

MILT: I said, "There must be something you can do to correct . . . "

HARRY: I can't hear you, Milt. Speak slowly and I'll try to read your lips.

MILT, *speaking slowly, loudly, drawing out words:* I said, "There must be something you can do to ..."

HARRY, *abruptly, calmly:* I hear you now, Milt. That's another one of my ... my fits. Sound becomes so damn painful to me ... Why listen? I say to myself. Why listen?

MILT: Incredible. I wouldn't have believed it was possible.

HARRY: Well, it is. Look at me. I'm a living example of it. Now you can ... *(He feigns muteness, his mouth opening wide and closing without uttering a sound, gesturing.)*

MILT, *becoming increasingly distraught:* Harry? Are you speaking to me, Harry? Harry, I can't hear you. Can you speak? ... *Harry removes pad and pencil from jacket pocket, jots something on pad.* Oh, God, not that, too. *Glances at Harry's note.* I understand, Harry. I ... Give me that. *Takes pencil and pad from Harry, he starts writing:* "Dear Harry. What we have to keep in mind, no matter what ..." *Harry pulls pencil out of Milt's hand. Milt pulls it away from Harry. Angrily:* The least you can do is let me finish! *Starts writing again.*

HARRY: I can hear you, Milt.

MILT: You can?

HARRY: I can't speak when that happens, but I hear all right. Why speak? I say to myself. Words have no meaning; not anymore. They're like pebbles bouncing in an empty tin can.

MILT, *pockets pad, pencil:* I don't know what to say, Harry.

HARRY: What can you say? It's no good, Milt; no good. For cryin'-out-loud, let me get it over with!

A THOUSAND CLOWNS

by Herb Gardner

———•———

ACT III

Murray Burns will not conform. He will not take a steady job,
he will not keep his apartment neat, he will not provide his pre-
cocious nephew, Nick (left in his care years earlier by his sister),
with a home environment that meets the standards of the Child
Welfare Board. He enjoys his life, and enjoys poking fun at the
hypocrisy and stodginess of others. When the Welfare Board
threatens to take Nick away, Murray sets out to put on a "reli-
ability" show for them. He will straighten up his apartment and
get a job. He walked out of a career as a successful TV comedy
writer, but now he asks his brother, Arnold, an agent, to find
him another job. When actually confronted with the reality of
reentering the false and competitive life he left behind, he walks
out of his brother's office. In the excerpt that follows, Arnold
comes to Murray's apartment. Murray, resigned that Nick will
have to go, is "unstraightening" his straightened-up apartment
as Arnold enters. An old recording of a marching band playing
"Stars and Stripes Forever" is playing on the phonograph. (Arnold's mention of a "tangerine" in his opening line refers to the
fact that on past visits he has always brought fruit with him.)

ARNOLD, *after a moment:* I didn't even bring a tangerine with
me. That's very courageous if you think about it for a minute.
*Looks over at Murray, who is not facing him; points at record
player:* You wanna turn that music off, please? *No reply from
Murray.* Murray, the music; I'm trying to— (*No reply from
Murray, so Arnold puts attache case and hat on table, goes
quickly to record player, turns music off; Murray turns to look at
Arnold.*) O.K., I'm a little slow. It takes me an hour to get insulted. Now I'm insulted. You walked out of my office. That
wasn't a nice thing to do to me, Murray. *Murray does not reply.*
You came into my office like George God; everybody's sup-

posed to come up and audition for Human Being in front of you. *Comes over closer to him, takes his arm.* Aw, Murray, today, one day, leave the dragons alone, will ya? And look at the dragons you pick on; Sloan, Leo, me; silly old arthritic dragons, step on a toe and we'll start to cry. Murray, I called Leo back, I apologized, told him my phone broke down; I got him to come over here tonight. He's anxious to see you, everything's O.K.

MURRAY: Hey, you just never give up, do you Arnie?

ARNOLD: Listen to me, Murray, do I ever tell you what to do—?

MURRAY: Yes, all the time.

ARNOLD: If you love this kid then you gotta take any kinda stupid job to keep him.

MURRAY: Now you're an expert on love.

ARNOLD: Not an expert, but I sure as hell value my amateur standing. Murray, about him leaving, have you told him yet?

MURRAY, *softly, realizing Arnold's genuine concern:* Arnie, don't worry, I know how to handle it. I've got a coupla days to tell him. And don't underrate Nick, Arnie; he's gonna understand this a lot better than you think he is.

ARNOLD: Murray, I finally figured out your problem. There's only one thing that really bothers you— *(with a sweep of his hand)* Other people. *With a mock-secretive tone:* If it wasn't for them other people, everything would be great, huh, Murray? I mean, you think everything's fine, and then you go out into the street—and there they all *are* again, right? The other people; taking up space, bumping into you, asking for things, making lines to wait on, taking cabs away from ya—The Enemy. Well, watch out, Murray, they're *every*where—

MURRAY: Go ahead, Arnie, give me advice, at thirty thousand a year you can afford it.

ARNOLD: Oh, I get it, if I'm so smart why ain't I poor? You better get a damn good act of your own before you start giving mine the razzberry. What's this game you play gonna be like ten years from now, without youth? Murray, Murray, I can't *watch* this, you gotta *shape-up—*

MURRAY, *turning quickly to face Arnold, in a surprised tone:* Shape-*up? (looks directly at Arnold, speaks slowly)* Arnie, what the hell happened to you? You got so old. I don't know you any more. When you quit "Harry the Fur King" on Thirty-eighth Street, remember?

ARNOLD: That's twenty years ago, Murray.

MURRAY: You told me you were going to be in twenty businesses in twenty years if you had to, till you found out what you wanted. Things were always going to change. Harry said you were not behaving maturely enough for a salesman; your clothes didn't match or something— *(laughs in affectionate memory of the event)* So the next day, you dressed perfectly, homburg, gray suit, cuff links, carrying a briefcase and a rolled umbrella—and you came into Harry's office on roller skates. You weren't going to take crap from *any*body. So that's the business you finally picked—taking crap from *every*body.

ARNOLD: I don't do practical jokes any more, if that's what you mean.

MURRAY, *grabs both of Arnold's arms tensely:* Practical, that's right; a way to stay alive. If most things aren't funny, Arn, then they're only exactly what they are; then it's one long dental appointment interrupted occasionally by something exciting, like waiting or falling asleep. What's the point if I leave everything exactly the way I find it? Then I'm just adding to the noise, then I'm just taking up some more room on the subway.

ARNOLD: Murray, the Welfare Board has these specifications; all you have to do is meet a couple of specifications—

Murray releases his grip on Arnold's arms, Murray's hands drop to his sides.

MURRAY: Oh, Arnie, you don't understand anymore. You got that wide stare that people stick in their eyes so nobody'll know their head's asleep. You got to be a shuffler, a moaner. You want me to come sit and eat fruit with you and watch the clock run out. You start to drag and stumble with the rotten weight of all the people who should have been told off, all the things you should have said, all the specifications that aren't yours. The only thing you got left to reject is your food in a restaurant if they do it wrong and you can send it back and make a big fuss with the waiter. *Murray turns away from Arnold, goes to window seat, sits down.* Arnold, five months ago I forgot what *day* it was. I'm on the subway on my way to work and I didn't know what day it was and it scared the hell out of me. *Quietly:* I was sitting in the express looking out the window same as every morning watching the local stops go by in the dark with an empty head and my arms folded not feeling great and not feeling rotten, just not feeling, and for a minute I couldn't remember, I didn't know, unless I really concentrated, whether it was a Tuesday or a Thursday—or a—for a minute it could have been *any* day, Arnie—sitting in the train going through any day—in the dark through any year—Arnie, it scared the hell out of me. *Stands up.* You got to know what day it is. You got to know what's the name of the game and what the rules are with nobody else telling you. You have to own your days and name them, each of them, every one of them, or else the years go right by and none of them belong to you. *Turns to look at Arnold.* And that ain't just for weekends, Kiddo. *Looks at Arnold a moment longer, then speaks in a pleasant tone:* Here it is, the day after Irving R. Feldman's birthday, for God's sake— *(takes hat, puts it on)* And I never even congratulated him. *Starts to walk briskly toward the front door.*

ARNOLD, *he shouts in a voice stronger than we have ever heard from him:* Murray!

Murray stops, turns, is startled to hear this loud a voice from Arnold. Arnold looks fiercely at Murray for a moment, then Arnold too looks surprised, starts to laugh.

MURRAY: What's so funny?

ARNOLD: Wow, I scared myself. You hear that voice? Look at that, I got you to stop. I got your complete full attention, the floor is mine now. *Chuckles, awkwardly:* And I can't think of a Goddamned thing to say. *Shrugging his shoulders, picks up his hat from table.* I have long been aware, Murray—I have long been aware that you don't respect me much—I suppose there are a lot of brothers who don't get along. But in reference—to us, considering the factors— *(smiles, embarrassed)* Sounds like a contract, doesn't it? *Picks up his briefcase, comes over to Murray.* Unfortunately for you, Murray, you want to be a hero. Maybe if a fellah falls into a lake, you can jump in and save him; there's still that kind of stuff. But who gets opportunities like that in midtown Manhattan, with all that traffic. *Puts on his hat.* I am willing to deal with the available world and I do not choose to shake it up but to live with it. There's the people who spill things, and the people who get spilled on; I do not choose to notice the stains, Murray. I have a wife and I have children and business, like they say, is business. I am not an exceptional man, so it is possible for me to stay with things the way they are. I'm lucky. I'm gifted. I have a talent for surrender. I'm at peace. But you are cursed; and I like you so it makes me sad, you don't have the gift; and I see the torture of it. All I can do is worry for you. But I will not worry for myself, you cannot convince me that I am one of the Bad Guys. I get up, I go, I lie a little, I peddle a little, I watch the rules, I talk the talk. We fellahs have those offices high up there so we can catch the wind and go with it, however it blows. But, and I will not apologize for it, I take pride; I am the best possible Arnold Burns. *Pause.* Well—give my regards to Irving R. Feldman, will ya? *Starts to leave.*

MURRAY, *going toward him:* Arnold—

ARNOLD: Please, Murray— *(puts his hand up)* Allow me once to leave a room before you do. *Arnold snaps on record player as he walks past it to the front door; exits.*

BECKET
(or THE HONOUR OF GOD)

by Jean Anouilh,
translated by Lucienne Hill

———————•———————

ACT IV

The play tells the story of Henry II, King of England, and Thomas Becket, archbishop of Canterbury, of the conflicting allegiances that destroy their friendship and that ultimately lead to Becket's assassination by the king.

Henry is a Norman (the people that conquered the native British Saxons). He is crude and untutored with simple goals and passions. He loves Becket, his friend and advisor, and he is determined to win his struggle with the Church for wealth and power. Becket, a Saxon, is wiser, subtler, and more complex. He is devoted to his king who has enriched and protected him (he was Henry's faithful companion in drinking, fighting, and whoring); yet through the years of their friendship his allegiance was always tempered by the knowledge that his own conquered people were suffering under Henry's rule.

When his enemy, the old archbishop, dies Henry comes up with a most clever plan. He will appoint his friend Becket to the post, thus bringing the Church and the Saxons fully under his control. But Becket takes his church responsibilities far more seriously than anticipated; most seriously, indeed. For the first time in his life his direction is clear. On the Church's behalf he opposes Henry on a number of crucial issues, and his intelligence and incorruptibility thwart Henry's every strategy.

Feeling betrayed, Henry plots against Becket's life. Becket leaves England seeking the protection of the French king; but soon—realizing the unreliability of that protection and the need to fight his battles on England's soil—he decides to return home. In the scene that follows, Henry and Becket are alone on an open plain in France, battered by wintry winds. They have agreed to meet to try to reconcile their differences—but neither can budge from his position.

KING, *suddenly:* If we've nothing more to say to each other, we might as well go and get warm!

BECKET: We have everything to say to each other, my prince. The opportunity may not occur again.

KING: Make haste, then. Or there'll be two frozen statues on this plain making their peace in a frozen eternity! I am your King, Becket! And so long as we are on this earth you owe me the first move! I'm prepared to forget a lot of things but not the fact that I am King. You yourself taught me that.

BECKET, *gravely:* Never forget it, my prince. Even against God. You have a different task to do. You have to steer the ship.

KING: And you—what do you have to do?

BECKET: Resist you with all my might, when you steer against the wind.

KING: Do you expect the wind to be behind me, Becket? No such luck! That's the fairy-tale navigation! God on the King's side? That's never happened yet! Yes, once in a century, at the time of the Crusades, when all Christendom shouts "It's God's will!" And even then! You know as well as I do what private greeds a Crusade covers up, in nine cases out of ten. The rest of the time, it's a head-on wind. And there must be somebody to keep the watch!

BECKET: And somebody else to cope with the absurd wind—and with God. The tasks have been shared out, once and for all. The pity of it is that it should have been between us two, my prince—who were friends.

KING, *crossly:* The King of France—I still don't know what he hopes to gain by it—preached at me for three whole days for me to make my peace with you. What good would it do you to provoke me beyond endurance?

BECKET: None.

KING: You know that I am the King, and that I must act like a King! What do you expect of me? Are you hoping I'll weaken?

BECKET: No. That would prostrate me.

KING: Do you hope to conquer me by force then?

BECKET: You are the strong one.

KING: To win me round?

BECKET: No. Not that either. It is not for me to win you round. I have only to say no to you.

KING: But you must be logical, Becket!

BECKET: No. That isn't necessary, my Liege. We must only do—absurdly—what we have been given to do—right to the end.

KING: Yet I know you well enough, God knows. Ten years we spent together, little Saxon! At the hunt, at the whorehouse, at war; carousing all night long the two of us; in the same girl's bed, sometimes . . . and at work in the Council Chamber too. Absurdly. That word isn't like you.

BECKET: Perhaps. I am no longer like myself.

KING, *derisively:* Have you been touched by grace?

BECKET, *gravely:* Not by the one you think. I am not worthy of it.

KING: Did you feel the Saxon in you coming out, despite Papa's good collaborator's sentiments?

BECKET: No. Not that either.

KING: What then?

BECKET: I felt for the first time that I was being entrusted with something, that's all—there in that empty cathedral, somewhere in France, that day when you ordered me to take up this burden. I was a man without honor. And suddenly I found it—one I never imagined would ever become mine—the honor of

God. A frail, incomprehensible honor, vulnerable as a boy-King fleeing from danger.

KING, *roughly:* Suppose we talked a little more precisely, Becket, with words I understand? Otherwise we'll be here all night. I'm cold. And the others are waiting for us on the fringes of this plain.

BECKET: I am being precise.

KING: I'm an idiot then! Talk to me like an idiot! That's an order. Will you lift the excommunication which you pronounced on William of Aynsford and others of my liegemen?

BECKET: No, Sire, because that is the only weapon I have to defend this child, who was given, naked, into my care.

KING: Will you agree to the twelve proposals which my Bishops have accepted in your absence at Northampton, and notably to forego the much-abused protection of Saxon clerics who get themselves tonsured to escape land bondage?

BECKET: No, Sire. My role is to defend my sheep. And they are my sheep. *A pause.* Nor will I concede that the Bishops should forego the right to appoint priests in their own dioceses, nor that churchmen should be subject to any but the Church's jurisdiction. These are my duties as a pastor—which it is not for me to relinquish. But I shall agree to the nine other articles in a spirit of peace, and because I know that you must remain King—in all save the honor of God.

KING, *after a pause, coldly:* Very well. I will help you defend your God, since that is your new vocation, in memory of the companion you once were to me—in all save the honor of the Realm. You may come back to England, Thomas.

BECKET: Thank you, my prince. I meant to go back in any case and give myself up to your power, for on this earth, you are my King. And in all that concerns this earth, I owe you obedience.

KING, *after a pause, ill at ease:* Well, let's go back now. We've finished. I'm cold.

BECKET, *dully:* I feel cold too, now. *Another pause. They look at each other. The wind howls.*

KING, *suddenly:* You never loved me, did you, Becket?

BECKET: In so far as I was capable of love, yes, my prince, I did.

KING: Did you start to love God? *He cries out:* You mule! Can't you ever answer a simple question?

BECKET, *quietly:* I started to love the honor of God.

KING, *somberly:* Come back to England. I give you my royal peace. May you find yours. And may you not discover you were wrong about yourself. This is the last time I shall come begging to you. *He cries out:* I should never have seen you again! It hurts too much. *His whole body is suddenly shaken by a sob.*

BECKET, *goes nearer to him; moved:* My prince—

KING, *yelling:* No! No pity! It's dirty. Stand away from me! Go back to England! It's too cold out here! *Becket turns his horse and moves nearer to the King.*

BECKET, *gravely:* Farewell, my prince. Will you give me the kiss of peace?

KING: No! I can't bear to come near you! I can't bear to look at you! Later! Later! When it doesn't hurt any more!

BECKET: I shall set sail tomorrow. Farewell, my prince. I know I shall never see you again.

KING, *his face twisted with hatred:* How dare you say that to me after I gave you my royal word? Do you take me for a traitor?

Becket looks at him gravely for a second longer, with a sort of pity in his eyes. Then he slowly turns his horse and rides away. The wind howls.

KING: Thomas!

STREAMERS

by David Rabe

———————•———————

ACT II

The setting of the play is a stateside army training barracks during the early years of the Vietnam War. But this play is not about the violent clashing of nations. Its bloody and deadly violence erupts from simple misunderstandings between individual men, from frustrations and mistrust and misguided pride. Billy,

Roger, and Richie are three young soldiers sharing a bunk room. Billy is a clean-cut country boy, afraid of being shipped to a war zone. Roger is a black man who has found a home in the army. Richie is urbane and witty—and a homosexual. He is totally out of place in this military environment. Their interactions are amiable and their arguments restrained.

Enter Carlyle—a street-hardened black draftee with intense passions, hatreds, and fears. Ultimately Carlyle, who is not drawn as an unsympathetic character, launches a siege of violence that leaves Billy and an army sergeant dead.

Just before the following excerpt, Carlyle has come into the room and found Richie alone, reading in bed. There is some conversation about a previous evening when Carlyle came in drunk and filled with self-pity, muttering on about his fears as he fell asleep on the floor. Richie gets up, closes the door to the room, offers Carlyle a cigarette, and crosses back to the bed.

CARLYLE: You know what I bet. I been lookin' at you real close. It just a way I got about me. And I bet if I was to hang my boy out in front of you, my big boy, man, you'd start wantin' to touch him. Be beggin' and talkin' sweet to ole Carlyle. Am I right or wrong? *He leans over Richie.* What do you say?
RICHIE: Pardon?
CARLYLE: You heard me. Ohhh, I am so restless, I don't even understand it. My big black boy is what I was talkin' about. My thing, man; my rope, Jim. HEY RICHIE! *And he lunges, then moves his fingers through Richie's hair.* How long you been a punk? Can you hear me? Am I clear? Do I talk funny? *He is leaning close.* Can you smell the gin on my mouth?
RICHIE: I mean, if you really came looking for Roger, he and Billy are gone to the gymnasium. They were—
CARLYLE: No. *He slides down on the bed, his arm placed over Richie's legs.* I got no athletic abilities. I got none. No moves. I don't know. HEY RICHIE! *Leaning close again:* I just got this question I asked, I got no answer.
RICHIE: I don't know . . . what . . . you mean.
CARLYLE: I heard me. I understand me. "How long you been a punk?" is the question I asked—have you got a reply?
RICHIE, *confused, irritated, but fascinated:* Not to that question.

CARLYLE: Who do if you don't? I don't. How'm I gonna? *Suddenly there is whistling in the hall, as if someone might enter, footsteps approaching, and Richie leaps to his feet and scurries away toward the door, tucking his shirt in as he goes.* Man, don't you wanna talk to me? Don't you wanna talk to ole Carlyle?

RICHIE: Not at the moment.

CARLYLE, *he is rising, starting after Richie who stands nervously near Roger's bed:* I want to talk to you, man; why don't you want to talk to me? We can be friends. Talkin' back and forth, sharin' thoughts and bein' happy.

RICHIE: I don't think that's what you want.

CARLYLE, *he is very near to Richie:* What do I want?

RICHIE: I mean, to talk to me. *As if repulsed, he crosses away.*

CARLYLE: What am I doin'? I am talkin'. DON'T YOU TELL ME I AIN'T TALKIN' WHEN I AM TALKIN'! 'COURSE I AM. Bendin' over backwards. Do you know they still got me in that goddamn P Company. That goddamn transient company. It like they think I ain't got no notion what a home is. No nose for no home—like I ain't never had no home. I had a home. IT LIKE THEY THINK THERE AIN'T NO PLACE FOR ME IN THIS MOTHER ARMY BUT K.P. ALL SUDSY AND WRINKLED AND SWEATIN'. EVERY DAY SINCE I GOT TO THIS SHIT HOUSE, MISTER! HOW MANY TIMES YOU BEEN ON K.P.? WHEN'S THE LAST TIME YOU PULLED K.P.? *He has roared down to where Richie had moved, the rage possessing him.*

RICHIE: I'm E.D.

CARLYLE: You E.D.? You E.D.? You Edie, are you? I didn't ask you what you friends call you, I asked you when's the last time you had K.P.?

RICHIE, *edging toward his bed. He will go there, get and light a cigarette:* E.D. is exempt from duty.

CARLYLE, *moving after Richie:* You ain't got no duties? What shit you talkin' about? Everybody in this fuckin' army got duties? That what the fuckin' army all about. You ain't got no duties, who got 'em?

RICHIE: Because of my job, Carlyle. I have a very special job. And my friends don't call me Edie. *Big smile:* They call me Irene.

CARLYLE: That mean what you sayin' is you kiss ass for somebody, don't it? Good for you. Good for you. *Seemingly re-*

laxed and gentle, he settles down on Richie's bed. He seems play-
ful and charming. You know the other night I was sleepin'
there. You know.

RICHIE: Yes.

CARLYLE, *gleefully, enormously pleased:* You remember that?
How come you remember that? You sweet.

RICHIE: We don't have people sleeping on our floor that often,
Carlyle.

CARLYLE: But the way you crawl over in the night, gimme a
big kiss on my joint. That nice.

RICHIE, *he is shocked. He blinks:* What?

CARLYLE: Or did I dream that?

RICHIE, *laughing in spite of himself:* My god, you're outra-
geous!

CARLYLE: Maybe you dreamed it.

RICHIE: What . . . ? No. I don't know.

CARLYLE: Maybe you did it, then, you didn't dream it.

RICHIE: How come you talk so much?

CARLYLE: I don't talk, man, who's gonna talk? YOU? *He is
laughing and amused, but there is an anger near the surface
now, an ugliness.* That bore me to death. I don't like nobody's
voice but my own. I am so pretty. Don't like nobody else face.
And then viciously, he spits out at Richie: You goddamn face
ugly fuckin' queer punk! *And Richie jumps in confusion.*

RICHIE: What's the matter with you?

CARLYLE: You goddamn ugly punk face. YOU UGLY!

RICHIE: Nice mouth.

CARLYLE: That's right. That's right. And you got a weird
mouth. Like to suck joints. *Richie storms to his locker, throwing
the book inside. He pivots, grabbing a towel, marching toward
the door.* Hey, you gonna jus' walk out on me? Where you
goin'? You c'mon back. Hear?

RICHIE: That's my bed, for chrissake. *He lunges into the hall.*

DOES A TIGER WEAR A NECKTIE?

by Don Petersen

———•———

ACT II, SCENE 1

Winters is an English teacher in a rehabilitation center for juvenile narcotic addicts. He is an idealist in a concrete holding pen of violence and fear. Against hopelessness and selfishness he pits Shakespeare and Dickens, and his own honesty and concern. Bickham is an inmate on this island prison. He is a walking volcano of anger—always on the verge of eruption. He is also starving for some loving human contact; he had, in fact, spent years searching for the father that left him as a child. To Bickham, Winters represents both the good and evil of authority: the person who cares and the person who controls and must be overthrown.

It is a wintry evening in December. Winters is alone in the classroom working at the blackboard on a lighting plot for the upcoming Christmas production. Bickham, unnoticed, comes in behind Winters and grabs him. Toward the end of the scene Bickham reveals that he has written a composition that he wishes Winters to read.

BICKHAM: Gimme your wallet, lame, or I'll break your back! *Taken completely off guard, Winters struggles enough to get a glance at his unseen adversary.*
WINTERS: What the!! Bickham!
BICKHAM, *releasing him:* Man, you gotta be on guard. Supposin' that was a real air-raid and not a drill.
WINTERS: Bickham. What the hell you doing up here?
BICKHAM, *takes a seat at the class table:* Saw your light . . . came up the fire escape. Didn't climb nobody's hair, neither.
WINTERS: What do you mean?
BICKHAM: The highwayman. That's *me.* He climbs this bitch's hair and rescues her from the tower. Don't you know the poem?

WINTERS: Yeah. Her name was Rapunzel, wasn't it?

BICKHAM: Yeah, that's it.

WINTERS, *pause:* Hey aren't you supposed to be in the hospital? It's almost eight o'clock.

BICKHAM: Breakin' the rules. Ever try it?

WINTERS: Yeah, when I can get away with it. *Sits at his desk.* I missed you in class today.

BICKHAM, *disgustedly:* Aw, man, I was busy.

WINTERS: Doing what?

BICKHAM: Tryin' to run down my shrink. Kike bastard's hiding. I think he's scared of me.

WINTERS: Whodya have?

BICKHAM: Werner . . . the creepin' sheenie.

WINTERS: Oh, Dr. Werner. Conrad has him, too. Is he doing you any good?

BICKHAM, *with disgust:* Man, it's like screwin' a dead whore. He don't even pretend no more. *Winters rises and doodles at the blackboard.*

WINTERS: Aw, you never know about psychiatrists. Some of them have got a lot under the cap.

BICKHAM: What he's got under his cap, I flushed down the toilet a thousand years ago. *Moves closer to blackboard and gestures to same.* Whatsa matter? Ain't ya got nothin' goin' for ya at home?

WINTERS, *taken slightly off guard, he gestures to the board:* Oh, this? I'm just trying to figure out the lights for the Christmas show.

BICKHAM: Ain't ya afraid your bitch will work overtime, too?

WINTERS, *amused but with some loss of aplomb:* I trust my bitch.

BICKHAM, *flippantly:* Sucker. *He walks calmly around the room.* You know, Winters, I think your old lady got her baskets switched. You're really Mr. Jesus in disguise.

WINTERS, *wryly:* Well, there was some talk in my home town for a while. Never did get it straightened out. *He makes some notation on the board.* You're exceptionally breezy tonight. What are you using? Or is that a personal question?

BICKHAM: Who, me? *(With no coyness, he takes a small tin from his jacket.)* Mace. Ya wanna try some?

WINTERS, *turns to him:* I didn't expect a straight answer. *Takes the tin and examines it.* Mace, huh?

BICKHAM, *pointing to it:* Two teaspoons in a glass of water . . . you can make it with Frankenstein.

WINTERS: Sounds like fun. *Looks closely at it.* Hey, you can buy this at the A & P.

BICKHAM: You better believe it.

WINTERS: It really works?

BICKHAM: It's a boss kick, man. *Grins widely.* Look at me. Can't ya tell?

WINTERS: How come you don't use it all the time? It's cheap.

BICKHAM: Six months on that, ya puke up your liver.

WINTERS: Wheredya get it out here?

BICKHAM, *coyly:* A little old fagarolla flew over and dropped it in my lap.

WINTERS: A *what?*

BICKHAM: A queer, man. I got me a fag social worker over at the hospital. Shock ya, Petey-babe?

WINTERS: Everybody's selling something.

BICKHAM, *laughs with admiration:* Oh, great, cool Father. *Holds out hand for junkie handshake:* Gimme a pound.

WINTERS, *slaps Bickham's open palm with the back of his own hand. Pause:* What do *you sell* in return?

BICKHAM, *coolly:* Nothin'. Come discharge time, my little old social worker will be waitin' on the other side with his magic wand and his Japanese kimono.

WINTERS: And what'll you do?

BICKHAM, *suddenly ruthless:* I'll kick his spade-ass from here to the Congo.

WINTERS: A Negro? That narrows the field.

BICKHAM: How bout it, Pops? You want your junkie to marry a Negro?

WINTERS: Social worker? Professional man? You have my permission. *Then directly . . . seriously:* But don't jack him up, huh, Bickham?

BICKHAM: Why not?

WINTERS: He gave you a box of mace, didn't he? Besides, it's not nice.

BICKHAM: And who's *nice?* Is *he* nice, givin' mace to an addict, lickin' his faggot lips till I get discharged?

WINTERS, *sincerely:* What *he is* has nothing to do with *you,* Bickham. Right or wrong is just like death, buddy. You gotta work it out for yourself.

BICKHAM, *laughs disdainfully:* Sheeit! Where'd ya get that? . . . from a bubble-gum wrapper?

WINTERS, *slightly annoyed:* No, as a matter of fact, it took me a long time to figure that one out.

BICKHAM, *moves away:* Yeah? Me, too. What's right for Bickham . . . is *right*. What's wrong . . . ain't.

WINTERS: Till you meet somebody who thinks the same way. And he cracks your skull.

BICKHAM: If he can do it, let him try.

WINTERS: I think you're better equipped for this world than I am, Bickham.

BICKHAM: That's a fancy way of sayin' I'm a turd and you ain't.

WINTERS: No it isn't.

BICKHAM: You don't like me . . . it's as simple as that. Do ya, Daddy?

WINTERS: I haven't decided yet. And I'm not your daddy. Did *he* like you?

BICKHAM, *rises:* You wanna punch in the snotbox?

WINTERS: Not particularly.

BICKHAM: Don't try to psych me. If I want somebody to clean my skull, I'll go to a cab driver before I rap to a broken-down, chalk-pushin' schoolteacher like you!

WINTERS: Your point is well taken. I'm sorry.

BICKHAM: I mean, you may *think* your butt spits nickels, but you're wrong, man. You're gettin' down wrong.

WINTERS: I said I was sorry.

BICKHAM, *rises and starts to exit:* Squash it. I'm gonna get in the wind anyway.

WINTERS, *shoves the tin of mace down the table:* Don't forget your mace.

BICKHAM, *picks up mace and looks at it:* You got a glass?

WINTERS: Sure. Why?

BICKHAM: I wanna take a little.

WINTERS: Not here you're not.

BICKHAM, *laughs sarcastically:* Punkin' out on me, huh?

WINTERS: Yep. But not for the reasons you think. I got a wife and kid out there. I'm not gonna lose my job because you want a little mace.

BICKHAM: You'd lose it anyway, maybe, if a hack walked in and caught me high.

WINTERS: No I wouldn't. I'd just say you broke in on me, you were high . . . you threatened me. They'd believe me, not you. We lames stick together, didn't you know that?

BICKHAM: Yes . . . "Mr. Winters" that I know. First lesson I ever learned. But you blew your cool. If you could stuff it off now, you could stuff it off after I've had another glass. Right?

WINTERS, *pause. He considers it for a moment:* The glass is in the drawer.

BICKHAM: Thank you, *Mr. Winters. (takes glass from closet, goes to sink and draws water)* A little water. *Holds up glass and turns off water.* Not too much. And a little mace.

WINTERS: You really like that stuff, huh?

BICKHAM: Nope. But it's a high. *Holds up glass.* Rips the shit out of your liver, I'll tell ya that. *Holds glass toward Winters.* Want some?

WINTERS: No, thanks.

BICKHAM, *a toast:* Here's to you, Mr. Winters. Reo habilitator. *Drinks half of it and shudders.*

WINTERS: I'm not too sure of that.

BICKHAM, *downing more of it:* And here's to Daddy.

WINTERS: I'll drink to that.

BICKHAM: You will? *Holds out the glass of mace:* Here.

WINTERS: I meant it figuratively.

BICKHAM: Your heart's pumpin' Kool Aid. Little mace ain't gonna make you no junkie.

WINTERS, *takes glass and drinks a gulp:* Right. *Shudders.* Jesus. Tastes awful.

BICKHAM: Hey, ya know . . . you're all right. You gotta lot of heart.

WINTERS: You're wrong, Bickham. I'm afraid of everything.

BICKHAM: Don't disappoint me. You weren't afraid of me when I flipped in here the other day.

WINTERS: How do you know I wasn't?

BICKHAM: You didn't act like it, Daddy.

WINTERS: There's that "daddy" again.

BICKHAM: What's wrong with that? You're a daddy, ain't ya?

WINTERS, *nods:* A little girl.

BICKHAM: Got a picture?

WINTERS, *gives him his wallet:* Yeah. That was at the zoo.

BICKHAM: She's cute.

WINTERS: I think so.

BICKHAM: What would you do if a junkie put a knife to her throat and asked for your dough?

WINTERS: I'd give it to you. Then I'd hunt you down and kill you if I could.

BICKHAM: Wait a minute. I didn't say *I'd* do that. I know a spick named Valdes over on the east side. That's his speciality. He usually gets what he wants.

WINTERS: Some day he'll get what he *really* wants. What you *all* want.

BICKHAM: What's that?

WINTERS: Death.

BICKHAM: Dig yourself. That's not what I want.

WINTERS: What do *you* want?

BICKHAM, *abruptly:* If you met me on the street, would you have a beer with me?

WINTERS: Sure, why not?

BICKHAM, *shakes his head as if to clear it:* Where'd we go?

WINTERS: To a bar. Hey, is anything the matter?

BICKHAM: This stuff. It screws my head up.

WINTERS, *takes glass and tin of mace:* Do you mind if I get rid of this before we both get in trouble?

BICKHAM: Where would we go? For our beer.

WINTERS: Any place you'd like.

BICKHAM: You ain't kiddin' me?

WINTERS: No.

BICKHAM: What would we talk about?

WINTERS: How 'bout fishing?

BICKHAM: I ain't never been fishing.

WINTERS, *concerned about Bickham:* Hey, you sure you're feeling all right?

BICKHAM, *nods:* What else? Dames?

WINTERS: Sooner or later. Sure.

BICKHAM, *abruptly:* What kind of honeymoon did you have, Pete?

WINTERS, *taken by surprise:* Huh?

BICKHAM: Your honeymoon. Ya have fun?

WINTERS, *chuckles quietly:* Maybe we ought to take that up some other time.

BICKHAM: Why?

WINTERS, *withdraws just slightly:* Well, it's getting late. You should be in the hospital, and I should catch the next boat.

BICKHAM: Ya wanna know somethin', Pete?

WINTERS: Sure. What?

BICKHAM: Straight stuff. You're the nicest guy on this island.

WINTERS, *genuinely moved:* Well, thank you, Bickham. I really appreciate that . . . coming from you.

BICKHAM: There's only one thing wrong with you.

WINTERS: What's that?

BICKHAM: You're like a rich man . . . a very rich man.

WINTERS: Oh? In what way?

BICKHAM: I don't mean uh . . . *really.* I mean uh . . .

WINTERS: Figuratively.

BICKHAM: Yeah, that's right. Figuratively. And what it is, see, it's like this. You walk around with your pockets full of gold, see, and we're a bunch of apes. Every now and then you throw us a piece. It's great . . . and we love it . . . we need the gold *all* the time. Only catch is, lots of times you throw it only when *you* want to throw it. You hip to that, Pete?

WINTERS, *with a touch of sadness:* Maybe I'm not as rich as you think I am.

BICKHAM, *slight pause:* Yeah. Maybe you ain't.

A HATFUL OF RAIN

by Michael V. Gazzo

———————•———————

ACT II, SCENE 2

This is the story of the Pope family and the destruction of that family by drugs. Johnny Pope is a drug addict. He was a hero in the Korean War, a prisoner of war who would not reveal secrets. In an army hospital he was given addictive drugs to ease the pain of the wounds inflicted on him while a prisoner. Now he is living in a New York City apartment with his pregnant wife, Celia, his brother, Polo, and an expensive daily heroin habit. He has become increasingly inattentive to his wife (who only learns of his addiction toward the end of the play), and has used up the life savings of his brother. The family gets an unexpected visit from Johnny and Polo's father. He has quit his job, invested all his money in a business, needs a few thousand dollars more for an outright purchase, and has come to collect on Polo's promise to loan him money. When he learns that Polo has no money to give him, he ignites old family feuds, accuses Polo of being ungrateful and irresponsible, and seeks an ally in his favorite son, Johnny.

Just prior to the following scene, Johnny has come home during the morning after being out all night looking for drugs. He has been given a deadline to pay off his debts and asks Polo for more money. Polo has none to give. The father enters and initiates a bitter exchange with Polo. Johnny, resolved to confess his addiction and to exonerate the brother who has protected him, asks Polo to leave him alone with their father.

FATHER: A good rain cleans the streets . . . huh?
JOHNNY: You're up early, Pop.
FATHER: I didn't get much sleep. I was wondering about something, Johnny. Is today your day off? I mean, how can you take in the ball game if you're working?
JOHNNY: I'm not working.
FATHER: You say you and your wife are getting along . . . ?
JOHNNY: Yeh . . .
FATHER: Last night, when I went back to the hotel, I kept thinking about what your wife said, about believing. About what do I believe in. She's right, I got you kids to believe in. Like I come up here—you got a wife, a little home, a kid on the way, you're making a home for your brother. You did a good job of bringing yourself up . . . but what the hell's your brother doing? Holing up in some dame's apartment? Twenty-five hundred is a—
JOHNNY: I don't know. . . .
FATHER: You talk in awful short phrases, Johnny. . . .
JOHNNY: I'm not used to talking to you, Pop.
FATHER: That's right, we don't talk very much, do we?
JOHNNY: No. . . .
FATHER: I like the letters you write me, Johnny. . . . Life plays funny tricks on people. Hello and Good-bye . . . and nothing in between, but I like the letters you write me.

JOHNNY: I'm glad you do, Pop.

FATHER: You take this believing thing—after your mother died, I used to read to you and your brother ... Hi Diddle Diddle, the Cat and the Fiddle, Easter Bunny, Santa Claus and all that crap. You'd believe everything. I'd tell Polo Santa Claus was coming, and he'd look at me like I was out of my mind. You understand what I mean ... ?

JOHNNY: I'm trying to, Pop....

FATHER: Well, some people can talk, they have all the words. There are some things I feel that I don't have the words for. Maybe you're a little bit like me because you don't seem to be able to talk to me....

JOHNNY: I always wanted to talk to you, Pop, but it's like you never wanted to talk to me, like you were afraid ...

FATHER: What I want to say is that I care what happens to you....

JOHNNY: Thanks....

FATHER: And I love you—that's the thing, see?

JOHNNY: You what?

FATHER: You heard me the first time. Don't make me say it again.

JOHNNY: I feel the same way, Pop—

FATHER: How's that?

JOHNNY: You know what I mean—Polo, you and me, we're all kinda—Pop, willya do something for me. I never asked you for anything. When the kid comes back, tell him it's all water under the bridge.... Oh....

FATHER: What's the matter?

JOHNNY: Headache ...

FATHER: You wouldn't know anything about what happened to that money. Or would you? He doesn't pay a hundred dollars a week board here, does he?

JOHNNY: I'm asking you for something now. When Polo comes—

FATHER: That's the difference between you and Polo, you never asked me for anything.

JOHNNY: He never asked you for anything either, Pop.

FATHER: Yeh, but the way he looked at me sometimes—Maybe I never gave you much either.

JOHNNY: You gave me a coat once!

FATHER: A coat?

JOHNNY: Yeh, you came to the home, and you took me out to a department store—and you let me pick out a coat. And then you took me to a restaurant and made the guy give me some wine. . . .

FATHER: Your brother doesn't gamble, does he?

JOHNNY: No. . . .

FATHER: I always kinda thought that you and your brother and I had a special thing. I thought we were just kinda three men. . . . Your brother did a lot of shouting last night.

JOHNNY: Pop, you did a little shouting yourself last night.

FATHER: I lived with my father until I was twenty-two years old, and I never raised my voice above a whisper . . .

JOHNNY: He lived with his father for nine years. What did you expect, Little Lord Fauntleroy?

FATHER: I expect the same thing I get from you. You don't go around crying like a kid in a crib. I like the letters you write me—'cause they're a man's letter. Dammit, you had a tough life but you made the best of it. Ever since he left home . . .

JOHNNY: He didn't leave home. He was sent away. Every time he gets a letter from you, he goes into his room and reads it. He's got a box of them in there. . . .

FATHER: Yeh . . . ?

JOHNNY: Yeh.

FATHER: Well, how would I know that!

JOHNNY: He's missed you for a long time, Pop. You shipped him out to uncles and aunts . . .

FATHER: And what was I doing? Gambling, drinking, laying on my can in Bermuda. I don't know anything about him. . . .

JOHNNY: Well, when he comes in, you ask him about that time in the orphan home when he wet the bed and they made him stand on a staircase all day long with the wet sheet over his head . . .

FATHER: I shipped him—What was I supposed to do, buy a house, work nights, wash clothes during the day? Uncles and aunts, thank God he had them . . .

JOHNNY: All right, Pop . . .

FATHER: A man has only two hands.

JOHNNY: All right, Pop . . .

FATHER: And don't go around all-righting me. When I came yesterday, I had a funny feeling. Right now I got it again. You're not glad to see me, are you?

JOHNNY: Pop, I don't want to talk about it.

FATHER: You're not glad to see me, are you?

JOHNNY: Nobody's blaming you for anything. . . .

FATHER: You both always had a roof over your heads.

JOHNNY: Yeh, but when we woke up we didn't know what roof we were under.

FATHER: Waking up in a hotel room is no fun . . .

JOHNNY: Nobody's blaming you. When you stand in the snow your feet get cold—if you fall in the water and you can't swim, you drown. We call you Pop, and you call us Son, but it never was . . .

FATHER: You're a pretty cold-hearted cookie, Johnny.

JOHNNY: I don't save your letters . . . and I never saved my money to try to help you out. Don't come around knocking Polo to me . . . because he's my brother.

FATHER: And I'm not your father?

JOHNNY: Don't put words in my mouth . . .

FATHER: What the hell's the matter with you—all the things you say? What are you—the lawyer in the case . . . !

JOHNNY: I know you, Pop—either you clam up, or you start to push. . . .

FATHER: As I listen to you, it sounds like I don't even know you. . . .

JOHNNY: Don't start to steam!

FATHER: I don't even know you!

JOHNNY: All right, you don't even know me.

FATHER: I don't even know you!

JOHNNY: How the hell could you know me? The last time I saw you I was in the hospital. You came to see me for three days. Before that . . . I saw you for two days, when I graduated school. How the hell could you know me? When you came to the hospital . . . you said, Jesus, it must have been rough, kid, but it's all over . . . that's all you had to say . . . we shook hands, like two big men.

FATHER: If you felt that was wrong, why didn't you tell me?

JOHNNY: Tell you what? All I remember is laying there and smiling, thinking the old man's come to take me home.

FATHER: I live in a hotel, Johnny!

JOHNNY: Three big days, Six lousy visiting hours, and you run out. I was so glad to see you. . . .

FATHER: Your wife was there to take you home.

JOHNNY: I knew my wife for one year. I've known you for twenty-seven. Twenty-seven years. Your son! My boy Johnny. I didn't even know who she was.

THE BOYS IN THE BAND

by Mart Crowley

———•———

ACT II

Michael is throwing a birthday party for Harold and has invited some close friends over to celebrate. Unexpectedly, Michael's old, "straight" roommate at college, Alan, calls him. Alan is very upset and desperately needs to talk with Michael. When Alan arrives at the party he finds that Michael is leading an openly homosexual life and that the guests include an assortment of friends ranging from a flamboyant "queen" to a male hustler who is Harold's birthday gift.

Michael suspects that Alan is really a homosexual. To confirm this he devises a telephone game where everyone calls the person they remember loving the most. When Alan makes his call, Michael is surprised to find that it is not a man, but his own wife that Alan has called.

In the following scene, Michael accuses Alan of being a "closet queen" and taunts him into making the telephone call. (The line by Harold may be ignored for scene-study purposes.)

ALAN: Michael, if you are insinuating that I am homosexual, I can only say that you are mistaken.
MICHAEL: Am I? *A beat.* What about Justin Stuart?
ALAN: ... What about ... Justin Stuart?
MICHAEL: You were in love with him, that's what about him. *A beat.* And *that* is who you are going to call.
ALAN: Justin and I were very good friends. That is all. Unfortunately, we had a parting of the ways and that was the end of

the friendship. We have not spoken for years. I most certainly will not call him now.

MICHAEL: According to Justin, the friendship was quite passionate.

ALAN: What do you mean?

MICHAEL: I mean that you slept with him in college. Several times.

ALAN: That is not true!

MICHAEL: Several times. One time, it's youth. Twice, a phase maybe. Several times, *you like it!*

ALAN: IT'S NOT TRUE!

MICHAEL: Yes, it is. Because Justin Stuart *is* homosexual. He comes to New York on occasion. He calls me. I've taken him to parties. Larry "had" him once. *I* have slept with Justin Stuart. And he has told me all about *you.*

ALAN: Then he told you a lie. *A beat.*

MICHAEL: You were obsessed with Justin. That's all you talked about, morning, noon, and night. You started doing it about Hank upstairs tonight. What an attractive fellow he is and all that transparent crap.

ALAN: He *is* an attractive fellow. What's wrong with saying so?

MICHAEL: Would you like to join him and Larry right now?

ALAN: I said he was attractive. That's all.

MICHAEL: How many times do you have to say it? How many times did you have to say it about Justin: what a good tennis player he was; what a good dancer he was; what a good body he had; what good taste he had; how bright he was—how *amusing* he was—how the girls were all mad for him—what close friends you were.

ALAN: We ... we ... were ... very close ... very good ... friends. *That's all!*

MICHAEL: It was *obvious*—and when you did it around Fran it was downright embarrassing. Even she must have had her doubts about you.

ALAN: *Justin ... lied.* If he told you that, he lied. It is a lie. A vicious lie. He'd say anything about me now to get even. He could never get over the fact that *I* dropped *him.* But I had to. I had to because ... he told me ... he told me about himself ... he told me that he wanted to be my lover. And I ... I ... told him ... he made me sick ... I told him I pitied him. *A beat.*

MICHAEL: You ended the friendship, Alan, because you couldn't face the truth about yourself. You could go along, sleeping with Justin, as long as he lied to himself and you lied to yourself and you both dated girls and labeled yourselves men and called yourselves just fond friends. But Justin finally had to be honest about the truth, and you couldn't take it. You couldn't take it and so you destroyed the friendship and your friend along with it. *Michael goes to the desk and gets address book.*

ALAN: No!

MICHAEL: Justin could never understand what he'd done wrong to make you cut him off. He blamed himself.

ALAN: No!

MICHAEL: He did until he eventually found out who he was and what he was.

ALAN: No!

MICHAEL: But to this day he still remembers the treatment— the scars he got from you. *Puts address book in front of Alan on coffee table.*

ALAN: No!

MICHAEL: Pick up this phone and call Justin. Call him and apologize and tell him what you should have told him twelve years ago. *Picks up the phone, shoves it at Alan.*

ALAN: NO! HE LIED! NOT A WORD IS TRUE!

MICHAEL: CALL HIM! *Alan won't take the phone.* All right then, *I'll dial!*

HAROLD: You're so helpful.

Michael starts to dial.

ALAN: Give it to me. *Michael hands Alan the receiver. Alan takes it, hangs up for a moment, lifts it again, starts to dial. Everyone watches silently. Alan finishes dialing. Puts the receiver to his ear.* . . . Hello?

MICHAEL: One point.

ALAN: . . . It's . . . it's Alan.

MICHAEL: Two points.

ALAN: . . . Yes, yes, it's *me.*

MICHAEL: Is it Justin?

ALAN: . . . You sound surprised.

MICHAEL: I should hope to think so—after twelve years! Two more points.

ALAN: I ... I'm in New York. Yes. I ... won't explain now ... I ... I just called to tell you ...

MICHAEL: THAT I LOVE YOU, GODDAMNIT! I LOVE YOU!

ALAN: I love you.

MICHAEL: You get the goddamn bonus. TEN POINTS TOTAL! JACKPOT!

ALAN: I love you and I beg you to forgive me.

MICHAEL: Give me that! *Snatches the phone from Alan.* Justin! Did you hear what the son of a bitch said! *A beat. Michael is speechless for a moment.* ... Fran? *A beat.* Well, of course I expected it to be you! ... *A beat.* How are you? Me, too. Yes, yes ... he told me everything. Oh, don't thank *me*. Please ... Please ... *A beat.* I'll ... I'll put him back on. *A beat.* My love to the kids ...

ALAN: ... Darling? I'll take the first plane I can get. Yes. I'm sorry too. I love you very much. *Hangs up, stands, crosses to the door, stops. Turns around, surveys the group.* Thank you, Michael.

THE SIGN IN SIDNEY
BRUSTEIN'S WINDOW

by Lorraine Hansberry

———————•———————

ACT II, SCENE 3

The play focuses on the struggles of Sidney Brustein, an idealistic intellectual who runs a Greenwich Village newspaper, and his wife, Iris, an unsuccessful actress. Sidney clings to hope—hope for mankind, hope in a reform candidate, hope for the success of a friend's interracial marriage, hope for the renewal of his own foundering marriage. The events of the play confirm for Iris the futility of hope, affirm for her that the cheaters always win, that those with the basest aspirations always come out on top. She sees her husband duped, she sees her sister discard her painful life through suicide, she sees her own dreams crumble under the weight of constant failure. Finally, at the end of the play, she is able to draw strength from Sidney. She comes to understand that the significant stakes are one's honor and integrity and not some elusive and transitory public recognition.

The scene that follows is between Sidney and Alton. They are in Sidney's apartment. The underdog "reform" candidate backed by Sidney's newspaper has just won the election. Sidney is elated, a bit tipsy, and has been rhapsodizing about the perfectability of mankind. Alton is a black man who "is, to the eye of the audience, white." He has worked side by side with Sidney, but is showing no sign of joy. He has learned that his fiancée, Iris's sister Gloria, has been a prostitute. Sidney has been singing "We Did It" (from *My Fair Lady*). He breaks off upon noticing Alton's joylessness.

SIDNEY: What the hell is the matter with you?

ALTON, *his eyes trained on Sidney:* Is it true, Sid?

SIDNEY, *knowing at once:* Is what true—?

ALTON, *rising:* We've hung out together a long time; don't crap around. Is it true? Is it true she's a hooker? And you were going to let me marry her? *Sidney says nothing; he sits on couch, exhaling a great troubled sigh.* Why didn't you tell me?

SIDNEY, *staring at the floor:* It wasn't my place to do so. It was for Gloria to tell you. People change. She'll change. She needs someone. Just don't make me sick today, Alton. Just don't act like a fraternity boy meeting his own girl under the lamppost. *Rises and crosses quickly to the bar for a drink.*

ALTON: How would you act? *To Sidney's back:* When you go into the mines, Sid, you get coal in your skin; if you're a fisherman, you reek of fish! ... She doesn't *know* how to love any more, it's all a performance. It has to be.

SIDNEY, *avoiding a direct reply:* If you could understand it, there is a great compliment to you in how I treated this, Alt. The compliment that I thought you would be man enough to absorb, and help Gloria like you wanted to help the rest of the world once.

ALTON, *crosses to bar and whirls Sidney around to face him.*

Quietly: Talk to me man to man today, Sidney: Would you marry her?

SIDNEY: Alton, for Christ's sake! You were a revolutionary! Doesn't that stand for anything any more? It is one thing to take bread to the Bowery and another to eat it with them!

ALTON: *Would you marry her?*

SIDNEY: If I loved her ... I don't know how to say it to you except that if I loved her ...

ALTON, *screaming:* Don't you know some of the things these girls have to do? *He subsides, crosses downstage right and slumps forward in rocker.*

SIDNEY: All right, I know. You are afire with all the images; every faceless man in the universe has become—

ALTON, *looking off:* Someone who has coupled with my love ... used her like ... an ... inanimate object ... a thing, an instrument ... a commodity ...

SIDNEY, *approaching Alton; with supreme compassion for all:* In an effort to assuage something of his own pathetic needs, Alton ...

ALTON: A commodity! *Looking up at Sidney:* Don't you understand, Sidney? *Rubbing his head.* Man, like I am spawned from commodities ... and their purchasers. Don't you *know* this? I am running from being a commodity. How do you think I got the color I am, Sidney? Haven't you ever thought about it? *Rises in great agitation and crosses downstage left center, away from Sidney.* I got this color from my grandmother being used as a commodity, man. The buying and the selling in this country began with *me.* Jesus, help me.

SIDNEY: All right. *Sidney follows him, but Alton brushes him off. Sidney half-sits on bar stool.*

ALTON, *smiling bitterly to himself:* You don't understand ... My father, you know, he was a railroad porter ... who wiped up spit and semen, carried drinks and white man's secrets for thirty years ... When the bell rang in the night he put on that white coat and his smile and went shuffling through the corridors with his tray and his whisk broom ... his paper bags and his smile to wherever the white men were ringing ... for thirty years. And my mother ... she was a domestic. She always had, Mama did ... bits of this and bits of that from the pantry of "Miss Lady," you know ... some given, some stolen ... And she would always bring this booty home and sit it all out on the kitchen table ... So's we could all look at it ... And my father ... all the time he would stand there and look at it and walk away. And then one night— *(he is reliving the scene)* he had some kind of fit, and he just reached out and knocked all that stuff, the jelly, and the piece of ham; the broken lamp and the sweater for me and the two little vases ... He just knocked it all on the floor and stood there screaming with the tears running down his face ... "I ain't going to have the white man's leavings in my house, no mo'! I ain't going to have his *throw-away* ... no mo'! ... " *He stops, regains control and sits on couch. To Sidney now:* And Mama, she just stood there with her lips pursed together and when he went to bed she just picked it all up, whatever hadn't been ruined or smashed, and washed it off and brushed it off and put it in the closet ... and we *ate* it and *used* it ... because we had to *survive,* and she didn't have room for my father's pride ... I don't want white man's leavings, Sidney. I couldn't *marry* her. *Getting up, and taking out an envelope:* I wrote her a note.

SIDNEY: Aren't you even going to see her? *Alton drops his head.* And if she was a black woman? *It hangs. He stands.* That's racism, Alt.

ALTON: I know it— *(touching his head)* here! *He turns away.*

SIDNEY, *sadly, looking at him:* But—"A star has risen over Africa—"

ALTON, *looking back at him:* Yes.

SIDNEY: Over Harlem ... over the South Side ...

ALTON: Yes.

SIDNEY: The new Zionism is raging.... *Alton hands him the note, crosses quickly to door.* Aren't you even going to see her?

ALTON, *halts, then continues out, Sidney following. In anguish:* No. I don't ever want to see her.

SIDNEY: You are afraid that you would forgive her! *Alton runs off.*

INHERIT THE WIND

by Jerome Lawrence and Robert E. Lee

———————•———————

ACT II, SCENE 2

Inherit the Wind is based on the famous Scopes "Monkey" trial of 1925 in which a schoolteacher, John T. Scopes, was brought to trial for violating a Tennessee statute prohibiting the teaching that man descended from other forms of life. The case was such a cauldron of controversy that it attracted the two foremost lawyers in the nation, William Jennings Bryan (three-time Democratic nominee for the presidency) and Clarence Darrow (a famous civil-liberties lawyer), to the positions of prosecuting and defense attorneys, respectively. The play focuses on the clash between these two men, each advocating different points of view on the right to teach evolution.

In the play, Matthew Harrison Brady (as Bryan is called) is a fundamentalist in his interpretation of the Bible and a staunch believer in the religious tenets of evangelism. Henry Drummond (as Darrow is called) is an atheist who pleads the scientific as well as the legal aspects of the case. Both are expert orators who can sway a courtroom with their arguments and charisma.

The following scene takes place in the crowded courtroom. The judge has denied Drummond the right to call as witnesses experts from the scientific community to support Darwin's theories. In a brillant but risky maneuver, Drummond requests that he at least be allowed to admit into court a witness who is an expert on the Bible. The judge agrees and Drummond calls Brady himself to the witness stand. What follows is a tense, suspenseful, and sometimes humorous interchange upon which the outcome of the case hangs.

BRADY, *with dignity:* Your Honor, I am willing to sit here and endure Mr. Drummond's sneering and his disrespect. For he is pleading the case of the prosecution by his contempt for all that is holy.

DRUMMOND: I object, I object, I object.

BRADY: On what grounds? Is it possible that something *is* holy to the celebrated agnostic?

DRUMMOND: *Yes! (His voice drops, intensely:)* The individual human mind. In a child's power to master the multiplication table there is more sanctity than in all your shouted "Amens!" "Holy, Holies!" and "Hosannahs!" An idea is a greater monument than a cathedral. And the advance of man's knowledge is more of a miracle than any sticks turned to snakes, or the parting of waters! But are we now to halt the march of progress because Mr. Brady frightens us with a fable? *Turning to the jury, reasonably:* Gentlemen, progress has never been a bargain. You've got to pay for it. Sometimes I think there's a man behind a counter who says, "All right, you can have a telephone; but you'll have to give up privacy, the charm of distance. Madam, you may vote; but at a price; you lose the right to retreat behind a powder-puff or a petticoat. Mister, you may conquer the air; but the birds will lose their wonder, and the clouds will smell of gasoline!" *Thoughtfully, seeming to look beyond the courtroom:* Darwin moved us forward to a hilltop, where we could look back and see the way from which we came. But for this view, this insight, this knowledge, we must abandon our faith in the pleasant poetry of Genesis.

BRADY: We must *not* abandon faith! Faith is the important thing!

DRUMMOND: Then why did God plague us with the power to think? Mr. Brady, why do you deny the *one* faculty which lifts man above all other creatures on the earth: the power of his brain to reason. What other merit have we? The elephant is larger, the horse is stronger and swifter, the butterfly more beautiful, the mosquito more prolific, even the simple sponge is more durable! *Wheeling on Brady:* Or does a *sponge* think?

BRADY: I don't know. I'm a man, not a sponge.

There are a few snickers at this; the crowd seems to be slipping away from Brady and aligning itself more and more with Drummond.

DRUMMOND: Do you think a sponge thinks?

BRADY: If the Lord wishes a sponge to think, it thinks.

DRUMMOND: Does a man have the same privileges that a sponge does?

BRADY: Of course.

DRUMMOND: *roaring, for the first time: stretching his arm toward Cates:* This man wishes to be accorded the same privilege as a sponge! *He wishes to think!*

There is some applause. The sound of it strikes Brady exactly as if he had been slapped in the face.

BRADY: But your client is wrong! He is deluded! He has lost his way!

DRUMMOND: It's sad that we aren't all gifted with your positive knowledge of Right and Wrong, Mr. Brady. *Drummond strides to one of the uncalled witnesses seated behind him, and takes from him a rock, about the size of a tennis ball. Drummond weighs the rock in his hand as he saunters back toward Brady.* How old do you think this rock is?

BRADY, *intoning:* I am more interested in the Rock of Ages, than I am in the Age of Rocks.

A couple of die-hard "Amens." Drummond ignores this glib gag.

DRUMMOND: Dr. Page of Oberlin College tells me that this rock is at least ten million years old.

BRADY, *sarcastically:* Well, well, Colonel Drummond! You managed to sneak in some of that scientific testimony after all.

Drummond opens up the rock, which splits into two halves. He shows it to Brady.

DRUMMOND: Look, Mr. Brady. These are the fossil remains of a prehistoric marine creature, which was found in this very county—and which lived here millions of years ago, when these very mountain ranges were submerged in water.

BRADY: I know. The Bible gives a fine account of the flood. But your professor is a little mixed up on his dates. That rock is not more than six thousand years old.

DRUMMOND: How do you know?

BRADY: A fine Biblical scholar, Bishop Ussher, has determined for us the exact date and hour of the Creation. It occurred in the Year 4,004 B.C.

DRUMMOND: That's Bishop Ussher's opinion.

BRADY: It is not an opinion. It is literal fact, which the good Bishop arrived at through careful computation of the ages of the prophets as set down in the Old Testament. In fact, he determined that the Lord began the Creation on the 23rd of October in the Year 4,004 B.C. at—uh, at 9 A.M!

DRUMMOND: That Eastern Standard Time? *Laughter.* Or Rocky Mountain Time? *More laughter.* It wasn't daylight-saving time, was it? Because the Lord didn't make the sun until the fourth day!

BRADY, *fidgeting:* That is correct.

DRUMMOND, *sharply:* The first day. Was it a twenty-four-hour day?

BRADY: The Bible says it was a day.

DRUMMOND: There wasn't any sun. How do you know how long it was?

BRADY, *determined:* The Bible says it was a day.

DRUMMOND: A normal day, a literal day, a twenty-four-hour day?

Pause. Brady is unsure.

BRADY: I do not know.

DRUMMOND: What do you think?

BRADY, *floundering:* I do not think about things that . . . I do not think about!

DRUMMOND: Do you ever think about things that you *do* think about? *There is some laughter. But it is dampened by the knowledge and awareness throughout the courtroom, that the trap is about to be sprung.* Isn't it possible that first day was twenty-*five* hours long? There was no way to measure it, no way to tell! *Could* it have been twenty-five hours?

Pause. The entire courtroom seems to lean forward.

BRADY, *hesitates—then:* It is . . . *possible* . . .

Drummond's got him. And he knows it! This is the turning point. From here on, the tempo mounts. Drummond is now fully in the driver's seat. He pounds his questions faster and faster.

DRUMMOND: Oh. You interpret that the first day recorded in the Book of Genesis could be of indeterminate length.

BRADY, *wriggling:* I mean to state that the day referred to is not necessarily a twenty-four-hour day.

DRUMMOND: It could have been thirty hours! Or a month! Or a year! Or a hundred years! *(He brandishes the rock underneath Brady's nose:) Or ten million years!*

THE WAGER

by Mark Medoff

———•———

ACT I

In the first scene a wager is made—a most peculiar wager: "We are *both* betting that you can seduce Honor Stevens! However, if within forty-eight hours after you've first been to bed with her, her husband makes an attempt on your life or kills you, you lose. If he makes an attempt on your life or kills you *after* forty-eight hours, you win." From that bizzare scheme, the four protagonists embark on a sequence of events that alternates between intrigue, foolishness, and just plain fun.

The wager is proposed by Leeds, a very intellectual graduate student who is eminently unsuccessful with women, to his not very intellectual, superjock roommate, Ward. Leeds's proposition is actually his reply to Ward's boastful challenge that he could seduce Honor Stevens within ten days. Ward's seduction of Honor succeeds within the hour (she is very bored with her husband and her life as an elementary education graduate student); Leeds promptly conveys the news to Ron, Honor's husband, and calmly suggests that Ron kill Ward for revenge. But all of Leeds's plans eventually backfire: Ron learns of the wager and comes stalking Leeds, machine gun in hand; and the final twist—Honor winds up seducing Leeds.

The scene that follows is the opening one between Ward and Leeds. They are in their apartment. Leeds is working at his desk. Ward is dribbling his basketball and shooting baskets at a hoop hung on the wall.

WARD, *dribbling the basketball near Leeds to get his attention:* You wanna make a bet, Leeds?

LEEDS, *without interest and without looking up:* No.

WARD: How do you know?

LEEDS: I don't believe in betting.

WARD: This is an excellent bet. Don't you even wanna hear what it is? *Ward dribbles once, makes a casual head fake, and lays the ball up and in.*

LEEDS, *without interest:* What is it?

WARD, *crossing back to Leeds:* I'm willing to bet you a hundred dollars that I can fuck Honor Stevens inside . . . what?—a month, three weeks? Name it. Make it tough, I need the work. *Leeds is unresponsive.* Okay—make it two hundred that I can get her inside ten days. *Leeds displays no interest.* Three hundred and inside a week. *Nothing from Leeds.* Okay, my final offer, Leeds. Listening? Four hundred dollars and I get her inside five days. That's it. Take it or leave it.

LEEDS, *without looking up:* How about the divorcée downstairs?

WARD: That pig! Look, Leeds, it's got to be Honor Stevens. I've balled everybody in the building but her that I want to. Her number's come up and that's all there is to it.

LEEDS: Why don't you expand your operations to the building next door?

WARD: They've got a kidney-shaped pool. I don't like kidney-shaped pools. I mean, what *is* this sudden interest in Honor Stevens, Leeds? I don't get it.

LEEDS, *trying to end the conversation:* If you get Honor Stevens, her husband *could* find out. If her husband *did* find out, they *might* get a divorce. If they *got* a divorce, I *probably* wouldn't have a ride to class at 7:30 every morning.

WARD: Why not?

LEEDS: Because *he* probably wouldn't take me anymore. *Ward makes a less casual drive on the basket.*

WARD: Maybe she'd get the car.

LEEDS: She has ten o'clock classes.

WARD, *sitting at the counter:* Look, Leeds, whudduya say we forego your eternal self-interests a minute and talk about the practical aspects of this thing.

LEEDS, *fixing on Ward:* How can a mechanical penis taking a master's degree in physical education hope to talk about the practical aspects of anything?

WARD: By feeling like it.

LEEDS: I see.

WARD, *rising and shooting a casual basket:* You know what your trouble is, Leeds?

LEEDS: Yes, I know what my trouble is.

WARD: You don't care about anything or anybody but yourself.

LEEDS: I see.

WARD: Yeah, you *do* see.

LEEDS: That's what I said.

WARD: I know.

LEEDS: But what you really mean is that I don't see.

WARD: That's right.

LEEDS: Which makes you wrong. Because I do see. But not what you think I think you think I see.

WARD: *(crossing to Leeds)* Look—are you gonna offer some resistance and bet or not? *Leeds seems totally uninterested. Ward swoops in on Leeds's ear:* She can't stand you, Leeds. Think about that. Think about the way she's always tearin you to shreds. Think about what I'll do to her for you.

LEEDS: Why would I want to bet against you then?

WARD: Because I need the incentive, goddamn it! I'm tired of balling all these chicks without any incentive! *Leeds ignores him, rises and starts toward bedroom. Ward backs off, turns suddenly and stops Leeds.* How 'bout a buck I get her by midnight?

LEEDS: Why not be done with it, Ward, and simply admit you want any justification you can come up with for wreaking havoc, creating misery, and indulging your psychopathic sexual appetite? *Leeds disappears into bedroom.*

WARD, *casually shooting baskets:* Justification! Of what? *For* what? Justify nothing to no one, Leeds. Just do!

LEEDS, *entering from bedroom engrossed in a book:* You know, you're in the wrong game. You shouldn't be a phys. ed. teacher—uh-uh; you should have made a career of the army with the contingency they keep you a buck private forever.

WARD: Look who's belittling the army. The guy who wouldn't serve.

LEEDS: It's not that I wouldn't serve. It's that they wouldn't take me.

WARD: Oh yeah? Then what if they had taken you?

LEEDS, *focusing on Ward:* I wouldn't have served. But that's not the point of this discussion, is it?

WARD: What *is* the point of this discussion, Leeds?

LEEDS: That there is none.

WARD: It's *my* discussion, I oughta know what the point is.

LEEDS, *crossing to desk and putting book down:* Yes, but you don't. And to prove it, I am going to bet you not one, two, three, or four, but *five* hundred dollars that there is no point to your plot to seduce Honor Stevens. You have five seconds. *Leeds unbares his watch. Ward confidently bounces his basketball.*

WARD: The point to it, Leeds—the point to it is that I *want to do it.*

LEEDS: How do you know you want to do it? You have two seconds left.

WARD, *sitting in director's chair:* I feel it!

LEEDS, *crossing to Ward:* Wrong, and your time's up—sorry. We don't feel reasons, Ward.

WARD: No?

LEEDS: We think reasons.

WARD: Gee.

LEEDS: And in coming to conclusions—even "I want"—there has to be some mental justification process. If you cannot justify, simply mentally, how you know you want, you cannot know, to begin with, *that* you want and therefore cannot want. *Holding out a flat palm to Ward:* You owe me five hundred dollars. Pay up. *Ward slaps the basketball into Leeds's palm and moves away into kitchen.*

WARD: That's very interesting, Leeds.

LEEDS, *crossing to toy box and getting out a pump valve:* I'm glad.

WARD, *with his head in refrigerator:* You are certainly an interesting person. *Leeds inserts valve into basketball, crosses to spool table, and sits on basketball. Ward crosses toward bedroom, sees what Leeds is doing, and crosses down to him.* That's my basketball, Leeds. *Leeds stares at him. The air escapes.*

LEEDS, *finally removing the valve:* That *was* your basketball. It is now your deflated piece of rubber. *Leeds dumps the basketball on the floor. It is dead.*

WARD, *picking up ball:* Well you're takin it down to the gas station, goddamn it, and gettin it blown back up.

LEEDS: Fine. And now that we've exchanged these little pleasantries, Ward, let's get down to it. I will bet you double or nothing on the five hundred you owe me that—

WARD: The five hundred I owe you . . .

LEEDS: Yes, Ward, the five hundred you owe me. And you either bet, pay up, or I'm going to murder you. *Leeds stands and casually crosses his arms, one hand going unseen beneath his shirt to the shoulder holster.* So, what'll it be? Will you bet, will you pay up, or will you be murdered?

WARD, *jocularly defiant:* Murdered. *Leeds draws the revolver from beneath his shirt, checks the cylinder to be sure the bullet is in the right chamber, and aims at Ward's face. Ward snorts and turns and strolls toward his toy box. Leeds alters his aim and fires at one of Ward's pictures, hitting one squarely between the eyes. Ward runs into the bedroom, slamming the door:* Leeds!

LEEDS: Hmm?

WARD: *Are you crazy? Wait! Are you waiting?*

LEEDS: Yes. Will you bet, pay up, or shall we see if a second shot can penetrate this cheap but fire-resistant beaverboard?

WARD: Pay up! Lemme get my checkbook.

LEEDS: Cash.

WARD: *Cash?* It's eight o'clock at night. Where am I gonna get five hundred cash?

LEEDS: Nowhere. So we'll bet.

WARD: You don't believe in betting.

LEEDS: I don't believe in absolutes either.

WARD, *opening the bedroom door a crack and peeking out:* Can I come out?

LEEDS: What do I care?

WARD: Uh, Leeds, how 'bout puttin the gun away?

LEEDS: It's empty.

WARD: Whudduya mean it's empty?

LEEDS: I only had one bullet.

WARD: Whudduya mean ya only had one bullet?

LEEDS: How many bullets does it take to kill someone?

WARD, *coming out of the bedroom. Compulsively defiant:* Evidently more than one. *Leeds suddenly points the gun at Ward's face again. Ward throws himself in terror against the wall. Leeds pulls the trigger. The gun clicks, empty.*

LEEDS: If I had wanted to kill you, Ward, you'd be dead; just as, if I ever *do* want to kill you, you *will* be dead.

WARD: I see, Leeds.

LEEDS, *indicating the hole in Ward's picture:* I certainly hope so. *Crossing to his desk.*

WARD: *(spotting the damage) Goddamn it, Leeds, I don't have the negative to that one. (his competitiveness coming to the fore, crossing to Leeds)* Okay. Okay, what's the bet—even though I *don't* owe you five hundred dollars?

LEEDS, *placing gun and holster in its hiding place on bookshelf:* The wager is double or nothing on the five hundred. The structure of the competition is this: We are *both* betting that you can seduce Honor Stevens. However, if within forty-eight hours after you've first been to bed with her, her husband makes an attempt on your life or kills you, you lose. If he makes an attempt on your life or kills you *after* forty-eight hours, you win. Are you game?

HOGAN'S GOAT

by William Alfred

———————•———————

Act IV

Matthew Stanton was one of thousands of poor Irish immigrants who came to Brooklyn, New York, before the turn of the century. He had known the deep hunger and shame of poverty and made a vow to himself: "I'll fight my way to power if it kills me." The play begins in 1890, as Stanton is about to fulfill his consuming ambition. He is running for mayor of Brooklyn on a reform ticket, and has clear evidence of corruption against the incumbent—an old-line politician named Quinn. But Stanton, too, has secrets to hide: he did not marry his wife in a church service and was married before to a woman he never divorced—offenses that would certainly be considered more se-

rious to the Irish Catholic constituency than Quinn's twenty-
thousand-dollar theft. During the play Quinn learns the truth
about Stanton's past and goes to Stanton's wife with the certifi-
cate from the past marriage. Later, when she tries to leave Stanton, he, desperate to salvage the election, tries to stop her by
pushing her down a flight of stairs. His intention was to sprain
or break her leg, but she dies from the injuries. In the tragic last
scene Stanton confronts the awful pain that his ambition inflicted on those who loved him.

The scene that follows is between Quinn and James "Palsy"
Murphy, political boss of the City of Brooklyn. Stanton has
called a meeting in which he intends to make public his evidence against Quinn unless Quinn immediately resigns his office. Murphy has called Quinn to a private room in Fogerty's
Saloon to tell him that the party, in order to save face, must side
with Stanton.

QUINN:
Does Matthew Stanton think he can oust me
By hole-in-corner meetings in school halls,
With craw thumpers and Sunday-pass-the-plates,
Black Jack the plug and the ga-ga Parish Priest
Both nodding yes to everything he says
Like slobbering dummies?—What is it that he said?

MURPHY:
Do you want to hear?

QUINN:
Would I ask, James, if I didn't?

MURPHY:
Listen then. I have . . . full notes on it.
I took down everything that Stanton said.

QUINN:
Read it. Read it. Do you want applause?

MURPHY:
No, Ned: attention. Here: "My dear old friends,
When Father Coyne asked me to speak to you,
He said it was about Ag Hogan's bills,

A gathering to help raise funds to pay them.
I never thought the purpose of this meeting
Would be political"—

QUINN:
"I never thought
The purpose of this meeting"—Father Coyne!
I roofed his sieve of a church and glazed it too;
And put a tight new furnace in its cellar.
There's not a priest you can trust!

MURPHY:
Will you listen, Ned!

QUINN:
I'm listening. Go on.

MURPHY:
"The Party of Reform"—

QUINN:
"The Party of Reform"! Ah, yes, reform!
A Lutheran lawyer with a flytrap mouth
And a four-bit practice of litigious Swedes
In a closet rank as rats down by the river!
A lecherous broker with a swivel eye
You wouldn't trust with Grandma in a hack!
A tear-drawers arm in arm with a gaping bollocks!

MURPHY:
Will you quit your interrupting!

QUINN:
Read on. Read on.

MURPHY:
"The Party of Reform has in its hands
Sworn affidavits on the city books"—

QUINN:
Got by collusion and by audits forged
As the certificates above their parents' beds!—

MURPHY:
"The Party of Reform has in its hands
Sworn affidavits on the city books,

Drawn up from careful audit, and declaring
A hidden deficit of fifteen thousand"—

QUINN:
Of fifteen thousand! The unfortunates!
They couldn't even get that business right.
It's twenty thousand, Palsy, if it's a cent! *Glum pause*
I'm in the treasury for twenty thousand. *Pause*

MURPHY:
"You say they will expose us to the public,
Unless we guarantee that Edward Quinn
Resigns as candidate in the next election"—

QUINN:
See, that's Matt's game. He's out to get my job;
But he's not the guts to grab it like a man.
Will you listen to the cagey way he puts it:
"*You* say *they* will expose *us* to the public!"
As sneaky as a rat in a hotel kitchen.
Don't you see the cunning of it, James? The craft?
It's not my job he wants, but to save the Party!
And all I did for him. I made him, James.
I picked him up when he first came to me,
Twelve years ago, when he was twenty-five
And lost his job for beating up that grocer.
He'd no knees in his pants; his coat was slick
With grease as a butcher's thumb. He was skin and bones.
I was sitting here in Fogarty's back room.
With poor Ag Hogan codding me, when he
Burst in the door, and asked me for my help.
"I'll do anything that's honest, Mr. Quinn,"
Is what he says. He had that crooked grin—
It reminded me of Patrick that's long dead,
Patrick, my poor brother—

MURPHY:
Go on, now, Ned!
Leave out the soft-soap. He'd a crooked grin
You knew would serve you well among the women—

QUINN:
I should have said, "Go now, and scare the crows,

Raggedy-arse Keho; that's all you're good for!"
But, no, there was that grin; and Ag said, "Take him."
She loved him, the poor slob, from the day she saw him,
Fat good it did her. "You can put him on
With Judge Muldooney," says she; "take him, Ned,
God will bless us for it. . . ." *Pause*
Aggie's dead, James. Dead.

MURPHY:
Yes, Ned. She is.

QUINN:
Did Stanton get to see her? *Pause*
Did he?

MURPHY:
Yes. Hogan.

QUINN:
She wouldn't let me in. *Pause*

MURPHY:
I'm sorry, Ned.

QUINN:
And Stanton's high-toned wife?
What did she say when she found out about them?

MURPHY:
She didn't, Ned. She knows that Ag helped Matt,
But nothing else.

QUINN:
Ah, nothing else? I see.
Where was I, Palsy?

MURPHY:
"All I done for him,"
Fifth book, tenth chapter—

QUINN:
Go to hell, James Murphy.
You think it's funny, do you? I'll give you fun.
If it's jail for me, you know, it's jail for you.
No hundred-dollar suits and fancy feeds
With tarts in Rector's drinking cold champagne

From glasses bright as ice with hollow stems,
But tea from yellowed cups and Mulligan
Foul as the odds and ends they make it from.

MURPHY:
Sure, they'll send us puddings.

QUINN:
Are you mad, or what?
I tell you, I'm in danger. I'm in danger.
Don't shake your head. They're spoiling for the kill.
It's in their blood.

MURPHY:
Whose blood?

QUINN:
Whose blood but our own.
They turn upon the strong, and pull them down,
And not from virtue, James, but vicious pride.
They want to hold their heads up in this city,
Among the members of the Epworth League,
The Church of Ethical Culture and the Elks,
That's why they're taking sides with Ole Olson,
Or whatever the hell his name is, and that whore
From Wall Street in the clean pince-nez. For thirty years
I've kept their heads above the water, James,
By fair means or by foul. Now they've reached the shore
They'd rather not remember how they got there.
They want to disown me. They're a faithless lot,
And Matthew Stanton is the worst of all—
Read on, why don't you? What's the matter with you?
  Pause

MURPHY:
"I would not stand in this school hall before you
If Edward Quinn had not, in his full power,
Made of me what I am. I cannot think,
Since you have shared his generosity
As long as I, that you are asking me
To help you pull him down"—

QUINN:
Good Jesus, James!

MURPHY:
"The way to cope with the Party of Reform's
To raise the funds to make Quinn's deficit up.
I pledge three thousand dollars, and I ask
Each and every one of you who can
To give as much as possible. Ned Quinn
Must not live out his final days in jail
Because he was too kindly to be wise"—

QUINN:
I want no handouts from the likes of him.
Will he pity me?

MURPHY:
What's that?

QUINN:
You heard me, James.
Will he pity me? Does he think I need his pity!
I made him, and I can unmake him too,
And make another in his place. I'm old,
I'm far too old to live on charity
From a greenhorn that I picked up in a barroom
To run my sweetheart's errands. Don't you see, James?
He took Ag from me first; that's how he started.
He ran her roadhouse for her. "He was handsome!
He'd skin like milk, and eyes like stars in winter!"
And he was young and shrewd! She taught him manners:
What clothes to wear, what cutlery to begin with,
What twaddle he must speak when introduced
To the state bigwigs down from Albany.
He told her that he loved her. She ditched me.
I'm twenty years her senior. Then that day,
That famous Labor Day three years ago.
We'd a drink or two, you know, for old times' sake,
And we passed out, and that bitch Josie Finn
Found out about us, and brought Matt in on us,
Our arms around each other like two children.
And he spat on poor Ag's carpet, called her a whore,
Me a degenerate. Three years ago.
The very year he married this Kathleen,

The Lord knows who, James, from the Christ knows
  where,
In some cosy hocus-pocus there in London,
To show Ag he could do without her. He never spoke
To Ag at all until he found her done for,
Dying lung by lung. He'd never speak to me at all
If I were not in trouble
Don't you see the triumph of it, Palsy Murphy!
He takes his vengeance in a show of mercy.
He weeps as he destroys! He's a crocodile—

MURPHY:
Ned, I . . .

QUINN:
Ned what?

MURPHY:
I hope you won't be hurt.
We on the Party board agree with Matt.
We feel the time has come for some new blood—

QUINN:
"We on the Party board agree with Matt"!
Now it comes out at last! It all comes out!
You and your pack of lies, your trumped-up story,
Pretending to be reading what he said
When you can't read a thing that hasn't pictures.
Did you think me such a boob I wouldn't know
What you and Walsh were up to here last night?
It made the rounds of the Ward by half past nine! *Pause*
Bismarck the diplomat! You goddamned fool,
Pouring that vat of soft-soap over me!
"Because he was too kindly to be wise"!
They'll soon be making you the editor
Of *The Messenger of the Sacred Heart.*

MURPHY:
Now, Ned—

QUINN:
"Now, Ned." "Now, Ned." Shut up, or I'll drink your blood.
The only thing rang true in what you said
Was Stanton's offer to be noble to me. *Pause*

MURPHY:
  I wanted to break it easy. Matt made no offer.
  The Party it is will cover you on the books.
  But on one condition, Ned: you must resign.

QUINN:
  I must resign. We'll see who backs out first.
  I didn't stay the mayor of this city
  For thirty years by taking orders, James.
  You tell the Party board I'll rot in prison
  Before I'll let Matt Stanton take my place.
  You tell the Party board I'll meet the debits
  The Party of Reform found in the books.
  You tell the Party board they'd best not cross me.
  Don't look as if you think this all is blather.
  There's not a one of you I can't get at,
  You least of all. Remember that, James Murphy.
  How long, do you think, that knowing what I know
  About your money, James, and how you got it,
  The Jesuit Fathers at St. Francis Xavier's,
  With all their bon-ton notions of clean hands,
  Would let your boys play soldier in their yard?
  Don't glare like that at me. You tell the board
  What I have said. I meant it, every word.

MURPHY:
  The Party will disown you!

QUINN:
  Let them try!
  I'll grease the palm of every squarehead deadbeat
  From Greenwood Cemetery to the Narrows
  Who'll stagger to the polls for three months' rent,
  I'll buy the blackface vote off all the fences
  Down Fulton Street from Hudson Avenue.
  I'll vote from every plot in Holy Cross
  With an Irish headstone on it. I'll win this fight—

MURPHY:
  I'll telegraph to Albany. I warn you!

QUINN:
  Damn Albany! Get out of here. Get out!
    Exit Murphy stage left.

KNOCK KNOCK

by Jules Feiffer

———•———

ACT I

Abe and Cohn have been living together for over twenty years, and for over twenty years they have been bickering. Abe was a stockbroker, Cohn a musician. Now they are retired, spending all their time together, and the bickering goes on incessantly. Abe says to Cohn: "You're rigid. I'm flexible." Cohn calls Abe "mindless." To Abe anything is possible: frogs turning into princes, genies rising out of lamps. So Cohn, the disbeliever, fed up with Abe's irrationality, rubs a lamp to demonstrate that there are no genies and then wishes for "somebody with a brain I could talk to!" In an instant the wish is granted and Abe is replaced in his chair by a bearded "wise man." Thus the tone is set for the strange meanderings of this fanciful and fantastic play that soon brings Joan of Arc onstage as a housemaid, that has strange voices calling out riddles from nowhere, and that has the walls of the house disappear in a flash before the characters' (and the audience's) eyes.

The following excerpt is the opening scene of the play.

At rise: Cohn, overweight and fifty, is at the stove, reading from a cookbook and mixing ingredients into a pot. He is humming a Mozart aria. He hums, cooks, tastes. Across the room, Abe, underweight and fifty, lies in his chair staring into space. He lights a cigar and meditates.

ABE: It's getting better.
COHN, *tastes*: Who says?
ABE: I say.
COHN, *mixes*: With what evidence?
ABE: My eyes are my evidence.
COHN, *turns to Abe and raises two fingers*: How many fingers?
ABE: Five.
COHN: Some eyes. *Goes back to his cooking.*

ABE: All right, two.

COHN, *slams down the pot and turns to Abe:* So if you can see two, why do you say five?

ABE: I prefer five.

COHN: That's not a reason.

ABE: Why does there always have to be a reason?

COHN: Abe, I've known you for twenty-five years and for you there's never a reason.

ABE: And you? You're better off?

COHN: I don't invent.

ABE: I beg your pardon. Neither do I.

COHN: What kind of fool am I living with? You just made up five.

ABE: I didn't make it up.

COHN: Not a minute ago.

ABE: No.

COHN: I was holding up two *(holds up two fingers)* and you said I was holding up five! *Holds up five fingers.*

ABE: You *are* holding up five.

Cohn quickly puts down his hand.

COHN: What's the use?

ABE: Cohn, I'll tell you something—you're rigid. I'm flexible.

COHN: Mindless.

ABE: You only believe in what's in front of your nose. That's not mindless?

COHN: I don't make things up.

ABE, *points to curtained doorway:* What's that?

COHN: Don't bother me. *Abe continues to point.* It's my bedroom! *Goes back to his cooking.* Pest!

ABE: I don't see any bedroom.

COHN: You know it's my bedroom!

ABE: I beg your pardon. All I see is a curtain. *Cohn goes and pulls back the curtain.* Ah hah! A bedroom! *Abe rises, crosses to the doorway, and pulls the curtain back into place.* A curtain. *Pulls the curtain back and forth.* A bedroom. A curtain. A bedroom. A curtain. A bedroom. Is it still a bedroom when you don't see it?

COHN: It's always a bedroom!

ABE: So for you it's always a bedroom and for me it's always five fingers. *Cohn slams the plate down on the table, pours stew* *into it, and begins to eat. Abe joins him at the table, studies the blank sheet in his typewriter, punches one key, and nods seriously at the results.* I'm right, so I don't get any stew?

COHN: You want stew? Here! *Hands him pot.*

ABE, *looks into pot:* It's empty.

COHN, *points to empty pot:* What's that?

ABE: A pot.

COHN: You saw me cook stew in it? *Abe nods.* You saw me pour stew out of it? *Abe nods.* So eat your stew. *Abe, unhappily, watches Cohn eat. Cohn wipes his mouth and points to the empty space in front of Abe:* Eat! That's steak. That's potatoes. That's salad. That's beer. Hearty appetite!

ABE: That's vicious.

COHN, *smiles, self-satisfied:* Abe, you can pull the wool over your eyes but you can't pull it over mine. I know you every step of the way. I know you inside and out.

ABE: I'm hungry.

COHN: So make something.

ABE: You know I don't cook. I burn everything.

COHN: Don't.

ABE: My mind wanders. *Cohn gets up, crosses to stock shelf, takes down a box of spaghetti, sets a plate in front of Abe, and pours the uncooked spaghetti into the plate.* It's not cooked.

COHN: I say it's cooked. Two fingers. Five fingers. Eat your spaghetti. *Abe looks disconsolately at the plate, picks the spaghetti sticks up in his hand, and begins to eat them. Cohn watches for a moment, then relents. He takes the plate away from Abe and pours the spaghetti into a pot of water on the stove.* When will you learn?

ABE: To be like you? I beg your pardon, is that such a blessing?

COHN: Don't get personal.

ABE: I don't like being made a fool of.

COHN: You asked for it.

ABE: I know I'm right. *Cohn groans.* You can win the argument but it doesn't mean you're right. Inside I know who's right.

COHN: You think so?

ABE: I know so. With my ex-wife, I also lost all arguments. But you told me I was right.

COHN: With her you *were* right.

ABE: So if I lost with her and was right, you have to admit that when I lose with you I also could be right. It's consistent.

COHN: Abe, I'm going to tell you a little story. A parable. After I finish, you tell me what it means to you. O.K.?

ABE: Before I eat?

COHN: Here. *Cuts him a slice of cheese. Abe wolfs it down.* Once there was this beautiful, innocent, young maid, golden locks, of eighteen, who lived in a dark forest in the country with her very proud, strict parents, and it was her habit to sit by a pond day in and day out, and moon and mope about the moment when love would first enter her life. One day this lovely young thing is daydreaming by the pond when a frog hops out of the water and into her lap. The beautiful maid recoils. "Don't be frightened," croaks the ugly little frog, "I am not what I appear to be. I am in truth a handsome young prince cast under a spell by a wicked witch and this spell can only be broken when some fair maid takes me into her bed and spends the night by my side." So the girl calms down and decides why not? So she brought the frog home and she took it to bed with her and the next morning she woke up—and lying next to her was this tall, handsome, naked young prince. And that's the way she explained it to her parents when they walked in on the two of them. What's the moral of the story?

ABE: The moral is, you're a very cynical man.

COHN: You want dinner? Then discuss it intelligently.

ABE, *leaves the table and returns to his own chair:* The moral is, you take a classic fable with charm and beauty, that deals with dreams and imagination, and you change it into men's-room humor. That's the moral. What you reveal of yourself. *Leaves his chair, crosses to the typewriter, punches a key, and sits back down again.*

COHN: You would believe the girl's story?

ABE: I beg your pardon, I wouldn't be her prosecutor. I leave that to you.

COHN: Supposing you're the girl's father?

ABE: I would face the problem with compassion.

COHN: First admitting it's a problem!

ABE: A man in bed with my daughter? At first—until the situation's cleared up, I have to admit it's a problem.

COHN: Then she tells you the story of the frog.

ABE: Which clears up everything.

COHN: You believe about the frog?

ABE: What's important is, she believes about the frog. We didn't bring her up to lie.

COHN: You'd rather have her crazy than lie.

ABE: Why is that crazy?

COHN: Or hallucinating.

ABE: Because her mind can conjure with change—with ugliness turning into beauty—you call that hallucinating? And what *you* see—only beauty turning into ugliness—you call that reality? I beg your pardon, Cohn, you're living in a stacked deck. You give me a choice, I prefer frogs into princes over princes into frogs.

COHN: Even if it's not so.

ABE: How do we know? All I'm saying is, we don't know.

COHN: Do we know that you're Abe and I'm Cohn?

ABE: In this life.

COHN: In this life. But in another life, maybe I was Abe and you were Cohn?

ABE: It's possible. Anything's possible.

COHN: —or that I was Mozart and you were Thomas Jefferson?

ABE: It's unlikely. But it's possible.

COHN: —or that I was Moses and you were Christ?

ABE: It's possible.

COHN: Abe, I'm going to give you a chance to listen to what you just said: It's possible you were Christ.

ABE: I didn't say probable. I said possible.

COHN: And it's possible that if I rub this lamp a genie will come out?

ABE: All I'm saying is, we don't know, do we?

Cohn rubs the lamp.

COHN: Now we know.

ABE: I beg your pardon, we know about one lamp. We don't know about all lamps. Also, we don't know that a genie *didn't* come out. We don't know that there isn't a genie in this room this very moment. And that he isn't saying, "Master, I am the genie of the lamp and I have three wishes to grant you and anything you wish will come true." Maybe he's there and maybe we've been taught how not to see genies in our time. Or hear

them. Or take advantage when they offer us three wishes. That's all I'm saying. That it could be us, not him.
COHN: Who?
ABE: The genie.
COHN: Abe, if I had three wishes, you know what would be my first wish? That instead of you to talk to, to drive me crazy for another twenty years, I had somebody with a brain I could talk to! That's what I wish!

COUNT DRACULA

by Ted Tiller

—————•—————

Act II

This relatively recent version of the classic tale of Count Dracula is set in Dr. Seward's Asylum for the Insane in the north of London during the first half of the twentieth century. Mina Murray, Dr. Seward's ward, has been ailing of late. Concern for her health and bafflement over her strange symptoms (bite marks on her neck) have lead the Doctor and Mina's fiancé to call in Professor Van Helsing, a specialist in rare diseases. Other household worries include Dr. Seward's demented sister, Sybil, and Renfield, a schizophrenic inmate who is in cahoots with the "bloodthirsty" count.

In the following scene Dracula commands Renfield to help him carry out his plot to get Mina completely under his control. In the previous moment, Dracula hypnotized Sybil and sent her to her room to await instructions.

DRACULA, *turns sharply to Renfield who crumples to his knees:* Now, you! I have work for you.
RENFIELD: Master, I thought you had renounced me. I ran through the valley, beat on your door, but you would not let me in.

DRACULA: With two men at your heels? The risk was too great. Would you have them learn too much?

RENFIELD: No, Master. Never!

DRACULA: Listen and obey me. *Pulls him to his feet.* You will go upstairs and conceal yourself until Mina is unprotected. Then you will burst into her room, threaten to kill her—

RENFIELD: Oh, Master, no! I beg you—

DRACULA: Be silent and *hear me!* . . . You will frighten her so thoroughly that she will ask her guardian, her lover, and that damnable Dutchman to let her sleep here. The fools will let her. Their tiny minds will not conceive that here she will be more—*accessible* to me.

RENFIELD: Hide myself? Up there? I've never been upstairs. *Scuttles to his stool and sits bunched up, quivering.*

DRACULA: Think of it as an adventure. Consider! You shall also commit your first theft.

RENFIELD: Theft?

DRACULA, *amused at Renfield's fright:* Exactly. You have read your *Oliver Twist?*

RENFIELD: I—I think so, when I was little—

DRACULA: Momentarily, I am your Fagin. Once you have terrified Mina, it is my will that Van Helsing and Dr. Seward shall come to seize you. In the struggle, you will steal their crucifixes.

RENFIELD, *puzzled:* They have crucifixes?

DRACULA: They will, shortly. Tonight each will receive one from Van Helsing—that devotee of Vampire lore. He knows I cannot touch nor look upon a crucifix. He knows too much to live long . . . The sanctimonious cowards will wear their godly artifacts here— *(indicating his breast pocket)* over their hearts. In the melee, as they remove you from Mina's room, you will relieve both Doctor and Professor of their holy burdens.

RENFIELD: And Mr. Harker's crucifix?

DRACULA: Later. I have my own plans for the heroic Mr. Harker. When the three simpletons reach for their crucifixes to stay me— *(begins to laugh)* Without them, they will be helpless!

RENFIELD: Oh, Master, I cannot! To attack Miss Mina, who has always been kind to me—Please, I beg you—!

DRACULA, *approaching him:* Think of it in terms of reward. You shall have fat flies to eat, plump spiders, small succulent chipmunks and, ultimately—if you do well—your first taste of human blood!

RENFIELD, *ecstatic, rocks on stool:* Blood! "The blood is the life!" It says so in the Bible.

DRACULA, *casually:* I've yet to read it. *He moves away.*

RENFIELD, *rises, follows him:* But Hennessey is up there. He will see me.

DRACULA: Hennessey is a simple man, simple to control. He will not hinder you. I shall hypnotize him.

RENFIELD, *amazed:* From *here*, Master?

DRACULA: From *anywhere!* You do not know my powers. Never doubt me. Never question. You are to obey. Nothing more. *Music begins: The Dracula Leitmotif.* Should you not obey, the punishment is death! *Music surges.*

THE CREATION OF THE WORLD AND OTHER BUSINESS

by Arthur Miller

———•———

ACT I

The well-known story of Adam and Eve in the Garden of Eden is retold in this humorous parable by Arthur Miller. The play opens as God tells Adam he is going to create a woman to keep Adam company and to procreate. At first Adam is uneasy, but he soon learns to enjoy his companion. Unfortunately, their relationship remains platonic and procreation does not appear imminent. God is worried. While he is musing on the decidedly nonsexual activities between Adam and Eve, Lucifer appears with a solution to the problem: the apple tree.

GOD: All right, go ahead, say it.

LUCIFER: Nothing for me to say, Lord. *He points below:* You see it as well as I.

GOD, *looking down, shaking his head:* What did I do wrong?
LUCIFER: Why look at it that way? They're beautiful, they help each other, they praise You every few minutes—
GOD: Lucifer, they don't multiply.
LUCIFER: Maybe give them a few more years . . .
GOD: But there's no sign of anything. Look at them—the middle of a perfect, moonlit night, and they're playing handball.
LUCIFER: Well, You wanted them innocent.
GOD: Every once in a while, though, he does seem to get aroused.
LUCIFER: Aroused, yes, but what's the good if he doesn't get it in the right place? And when he does, she walks off to pick a flower or something.
GOD: I can't figure that out. *Pause. They stare down.*
LUCIFER: Of course, You could always— *(he breaks off)*
GOD: What?
LUCIFER: Look, I don't want to mix in, and then You'll say I'm criticizing everything—
GOD: I don't know why I stand for your superciliousness.
LUCIFER: At least I don't bore You like the rest of these spirits.
GOD: Sometimes I'd just as soon you did. What have you got in mind?
LUCIFER: Now, remember, You asked me.
GOD: What have you got in mind!
LUCIFER: You see? You're mad already.
GOD, *roaring furiously:* I am not mad!
LUCIFER: All right, all right. You could take her back and restring her insides. Reroute everything, so wherever he goes in it connects to the egg.
GOD: No-no-no, I don't want to fool with that. She's perfect now; I'm not tearing her apart again. Out of the question.
LUCIFER: Well, then. You've only got one other choice. You've got to thin out the innocence down there. *God turns to him suspiciously.* See? You're giving me that look again; whatever I say, You turn it into some kind of a plot. Like when You made that fish with the fur on. Throw him in the ocean, and all the angels run around screaming hosannahs. *I* come and tell You the thing's drowned, and you're insulted.
GOD: Yes. But I—I've stopped making fish with fur any more.

LUCIFER: But before I can penetrate with a fact I've got to go through hell.

GOD, *He suddenly points down:* He's putting his arm around her. *Lucifer looks down:* Lucifer! *They both stretch over the edge to see better.* Lucifer!! *Suddenly, His expression changes to incredulity, then anger, and He throws up his hands in futile protest.* Where in the world does he get those stupid ideas!

LUCIFER, *still looking down:* Now he's going to sleep.

GOD: Oh, dear, dear, dear, dear. *He sits disconsolately.*

LUCIFER: Lord, the problem down there is that You've made it all so perfect. Everything they look at is not only good, it's equally good. The sun is good, rats are good, fleas are good, the moon, lions, athlete's foot—every single thing is just as good as every other thing. Because, naturally, You created everything, so everything's as attractive as everything else.

GOD: What's so terrible about perfection? Except that you can't stand it?

LUCIFER: Well, simply—if You want him to go into her, into the right place, and stay there long enough, You'll have to make that part better.

GOD: I am not remaking that woman.

LUCIFER: It's not neccessary. All I'm saying is that sex has to be made not just good, but—well, terrific. Right now he'd just as soon pick his nose. In other words, You've got to rivet his attention on that one place.

GOD: How would I do that?

LUCIFER: Well, let's look at it. What is the one thing that makes him stop whatever he's doing and pay strict attention?

GOD: What?

LUCIFER: You, Lord. Soon as you appear, he, so to speak, comes erect. Give sex that same sort of holiness in his mind, the same hope that is never discouraged and never really fulfilled, the same fear of being unacceptable. Make him feel toward sex as he feels toward You, and You're in—*unbeschreiblich!* Between such high promise and deadly terror, he won't be able to think of anything else. *Pause.*

GOD: How?

LUCIFER: Well . . . *(He hesitates a long moment, until God slowly turns to him with a suspicious look.)* All right, look—there's no way around it, I simply have to talk about those apples.

GOD, *stamps His foot and stands, strides up and down, trying to control his temper:* Lucifer!

LUCIFER: I refuse to believe that man's only way to demonstrate his love for God is to refuse to eat some fruit! That kind of game is simply unworthy of my father!

GOD, *angered:* Really now!

LUCIFER: Forgive me, sir, but I am useless to you if I don't speak my mind. May I tell you why *I* think You planted that tree in the garden? *God is silent, but consenting, even if unwillingly.* Objectively speaking, it *is* senseless. You wanted Adam's praise for everything You made, absolutely innocent of any doubt about Your goodness. Why, then, plant a fruit which can only make him wise, sophisticated, and analytical? May I continue? *God half-willingly nods.* He certainly will begin to question everything if he eats an apple, but why is that necessarily bad? *God looks surprised, angering.* He'll not only marvel that the flower blooms, he will ask why and discover chlorophyll— and bless You for chlorophyll. He'll not only praise you that food makes him strong, he will discover his bile duct and praise You for his pancreas. He may lose his innocence, but the more he learns of Your secrets, the more reasons he will have to praise You. And that is why, quite without consciously knowing it, You planted that tree there. It was your fantastic inner urge to magnify Your glory to the last degree. In six words, Lord, You wanted full credit for everything.

GOD: He must never eat those apples.

LUCIFER: Then why have You tempted him? What is the point?

GOD: I wanted him to wake each morning, look at that tree, and say, "For God's sake I won't eat these apples." Not even one.

LUCIFER: Fine. But with that same absence of curiosity he is not investigating Eve.

GOD: But the other animals manage.

LUCIFER: Their females go into heat, and the balloon goes up. But Eve is ready almost any time, and that means no time. It's part of that whole dreadful uniformity down there.

GOD: They are my children; I don't want them to know evil.

LUCIFER: Why call it evil? One apple, and he'll know the difference between good and better. And once he knows that, he'll be all over her. *He looks down.* Look, he's kissing a tree.

You see? The damned fool has no means of discriminating.

GOD, *looking down:* Well, he should kiss trees too.

LUCIFER: Fine. If that's the way You feel, You've got Adam and Eve, and it'll be a thousand years before you're a grandfather. *He stands.* Think it over. I'd be glad to go down and— *(God gives him a look.)* I'm only trying to help!

GOD: Lucifer, I'm way ahead of you.

LUCIFER: Lord, that's inevitable.

GOD: Stay away from that tree.

LUCIFER, *with a certain evasiveness:* Whatever You say, sir. May I go now?

GOD, *after a pause:* Don't have the illusion that I am in conflict about this; I mean, don't decide to go down there and do me a favor, or something. I know perfectly well why I put that tree there.

LUCIFER, *surprised:* Really!

GOD: Yes, really. I am in perfect control over my unconscious, friend. It was not to tempt Adam; it's I who was tempted. I finished him and I saw he was beautiful, and for a moment I loved him beyond anything I had ever made—and I thought, maybe I should let him see through the rose petal to its chemistry, the formation of amino acids to the secrets of life. His simple praise for surfaces made me impatient to show him the physics of my art, which would raise him to a god.

LUCIFER: Why'd You change your mind?

GOD: Because I thought of what became of you. The one angel who really understands biology and physics, the one I loved before all the rest and took such care to teach—and you can't take a breath without thinking how to overthrow me and take over the universe!

LUCIFER: Lord, I only wanted them to know more, the more to praise You!

GOD: The more they know, the less they will need me, Lucifer; you know that as well as I! And that's all you're after, to grind away their respect for me. "Give them an apple!" If it weren't for the Law of the Conservation of Energy I would destroy you! Don't go near that tree or those dear people—not in any form, you hear? They are innocent, and innocent they will remain till I turn out the lights forever! *God goes out. Lucifer is alone.*

LUCIFER: Now what is He *really* saying? He put it there to tempt *Himself!* Therefore he's not of one mind about innocence;

and how could He be when innocence blinds Adam to half the wonders He has made? I will help the Lord. Yes, that's the only way to put it; I'm His helper. I open up the marvels He dares not show, and thereby magnify His glory. In short, I disobey what He says and carry out what He means, and if that's evil, it's only to do good. Strange—I never felt so close to my creator as I do right now! Once Adam eats, he'll multiply, and Lucifer completes the lovely world of God! Oh, praise the Lord who gave me all this insight! My fight with Him is over! Now evil be my good, and Eve and Adam multiply in blessed sin! Make way, dumb stars, the world of man begins!

FAMILY BUSINESS

by Dick Goldberg

———————•———————

Act II

Early winter, 1974, the home of Isaiah Stein in Beverly, Massachusetts. Isaiah Stein, in his mid seventies, his heart failing, calls his sons together to discuss his will. Phil argues against his father's latest plan for disbursing the considerable family estate. Phil, a psychologist, is badly in debt and prefers an arrangement that will provide him with a large sum of ready cash. The argument boils over to the point where Isaiah threatens to cut Phil out of any inheritance. A few minutes later, in his room, Isaiah suffers a severe heart attack. The brothers rush in. Phil is asked to call the doctor. Alone in the main room, he calls, but says nothing of the emergency in the bedroom. Isaiah dies.

The following scene takes place a week later at the end of the traditional Jewish mourning period, the shiva. Phil has set about convincing Jerry, the youngest son, to loan him a large portion of his trust money—but Bobby (as well as Phil) is a trustee and must approve the loan. Norman, who has assumed a maternal role in the family, and who is not very shrewd about business, agrees to argue Phil's cause with Bobby, the brother who has been running the family business and finances with great success.

The scene opens with Norman straightening out the main room. Bobby returns, carrying a sign that reads "For Sale, Schwartz' Realty, 649-8723." Bobby had an appointment with Mr. Schwartz about selling the house. Norman, who does not want the house sold, called and told the realtor that Bobby wasn't coming. When Bobby got there the office was already closed. The two brothers discuss the loan, the house, and Norman brings up Alice, a woman from Bobby's past who became sick and died. Then Norman reveals his feelings over the fact that his mother—who died in an automobile accident while he was driving—loved him more than she loved his father.

BOBBY, *in hall:* Fucking bastard! Leaves me this goddamn sign with a little note. *Reads the note at step:* "Sorry you couldn't make it this evening; why don't you go ahead and stick this in the ground." I'll stick it up his ass, that's what I'll do! First we get eaten out of house and home, then when I should be down at the store, I *schlepp* out in this weather to see Chip Schwartz, the phantom realtor. First thing tomorrow morning, that cock-sucker gets a piece of my mind. *Crosses to closet.*

NORMAN: Why don't you forget about him? It doesn't look like he's very reliable.

BOBBY, *hangs up coat:* Reliable? He's a *gonif*! And I just want him to know that I know it!

NORMAN: Maybe you'll feel different about it in the morning.

BOBBY, *crosses right to sofa:* Will you tell me one thing, Norman? Will you tell me one goddamn thing? How come no matter what the fuck happens, you think people are going to feel different about it in the morning. Somebody shoves some shit in your mouth and you tell yourself, maybe it'll taste different in the morning. Well, I got news, mister, I don't like the taste of shit at no time—breakfast, lunch, or dinner! *Crosses to hall, removes snowshoes.*

NORMAN, *folds up cloth:* Can I get you something, Bobby? Can I do something for you?

BOBBY: Yeah! Get brother Phil to move his fucking car out of the driveway—and then put mine in the garage. I don't feel like scraping off a foot of snow tomorrow morning.

NORMAN: Okay.

BOBBY, *crosses to bar, mixes drink:* You have any idea how long he's going to be here?

NORMAN, *crosses to table, puts tablecloth away:* Not long. He's talking to Jerry. Jerry wants him to handle some of his trust money.

BOBBY, *looking up stairs:* Handle? I'll bet Phil is planning to "handle" it all right—right over to something owned and operated by Dr. Philip M. Stein.

NORMAN: He's your brother.

BOBBY: Yeah. Which means that some of Dad's come went to the same place twice.

NORMAN: Shut up! I won't listen to you talk that way.

BOBBY: And I won't listen to you babble! The money stays where it belongs—in a trust fund in the Bay Bank, formerly the Beverly Trust Company, of Beverly, Massachusetts! *Crosses to sofa right.*

NORMAN: You don't even know what they're talking about.

BOBBY: I know Phil.

NORMAN: You don't want Phil to get his way, do you? That's all it ever is, and that's all it ever comes down to.

BOBBY: Okay. That's all it ever comes down to. I hate my brother.

NORMAN: Be serious, Bobby.

BOBBY: Serious? Okay. I don't like my brother. I don't like him in a big way. And I really don't like the way he goes through money—money that I worked my ass off for. If Pop had wanted Jerry to invest the money, that's what Pop would have written into his will. If you want to go against what Pop wanted, go right ahead. But you won't get very far. Unless you plan on forging my John Hancock. *Crosses to chair.*

NORMAN: What would you do?

BOBBY: Norman, be serious. You haven't done a dishonest thing in your whole fucking life. And I don't think you're going to start now.

NORMAN: You don't think I can do anything, do you?

BOBBY: What the hell are you talking about? We're talking about handing over money to Phil—Phil! Who hasn't paid back a family loan since he borrowed my white *yarmulka* for his *bar mitzvah.*

NORMAN: That's not true, Bobby.

BOBBY: Go look at the books for the stores; look at the balance sheet for the last five years—look under the heading "Bad Business Debts," will ya? I'm going to save everybody a lot of trouble and let the money lay where it lies.

NORMAN: You've got to have my signature to sell the house, don't you?

BOBBY: Yeah.

NORMAN: I don't sign for the house if you don't agree with what Phil and Jerry decide.

BOBBY, *suppressing a laugh:* Are you serious?

NORMAN, *short pause:* Yes.

BOBBY: You're saying if I agree to whatever the hell it is, you'll sell the house.

NORMAN: You know I don't want to sell the house, Bobby— that I think you'd be better off here.

BOBBY: If we sell or if we don't Norman, I'm getting out.

NORMAN: So go. I hope you'll be very happy coming to visit Jerry and me.

BOBBY, *crosses to sofa:* Jerry is leaving too, Norman. I think you've been cooped up in this house too long.

NORMAN: Shut up, Bobby. I am perfectly all right. I'm the one who doesn't want to run out, who wants to stay where he belongs.

BOBBY: I'll tell you where you belong all right—I'll tell you where—

NORMAN, *crosses to Bobby:* Not another word! *He pushes Bobby into sofa, crosses to upstage left.*

BOBBY, *after a moment:* Norman, are you all right?

NORMAN: Yes. I just don't like people saying I'm—I'm different. First, Dad, and now you.

BOBBY: I didn't mean anything by it.

NORMAN, *crosses to table:* I know you didn't. Bobby, don't go.

BOBBY, *gently:* Norman, we don't need this house. It's too big. It was too big when Pop was alive.

NORMAN: I need it.

BOBBY: You'll be happy someplace else—I'm sure you will.

NORMAN: No, I won't. You don't understand. It wouldn't have to be for very long. Just a few years until . . .

BOBBY: Until what, Norman?

NORMAN: I don't know. Jerry got married, you got married.

You could find someone again—someone like Alice. You could raise a family—here!

BOBBY: That's never going to happen, Norman.

NORMAN: Yes, it is.

BOBBY: She's dead. That's all there is to it. Alice got sick and died.

NORMAN: If you had gone ahead and gotten married . . .

BOBBY: Okay, Norman.

NORMAN: People die . . . but you can find other people, people to take their place.

BOBBY: Okay.

NORMAN, *crosses to shiva stool—sits:* Mama loved me more than she loved Pop . . . did you know that, Bobby? She loved me more than she loved Pop. Every day, for as long as I can remember, she would leave him at the store to come home and be with me. She was here before I got home from school almost always. We would watch TV upstairs . . . we'd sit together on the couch with only the desk lamp on in the room . . . and I'd make patterns with the cookies she had given me. From three o'clock to five o'clock. Every day. A little after five, she'd wake Jerry from his nap, and you and Phil'd get home from practice. And then I'd be the one to come down here and wait for Pop. I'd be the one. I'd stand by the window and say to myself, "The sixth car to come by going up the street will be Pop's." Different days I'd guess different numbers. I was right a lot, too. But I didn't tell him when I guessed it. Because Pop would laugh. He'd always laugh. At me . . . and at Mama. *Pause.* I did not kill her. I was home, and Pop wanted someone to take her to the store to pick up some things for dinner. *He* wanted something special for dinner. *Pause.* SHE loved me. She loved me more than she did Pop. *Long pause. Bobby is moved but unable to reach out to him.* I'll find something for us in the kitchen, okay? Some cake or something.

BOBBY: Sure.

THE PRIVATE EAR

by Peter Shaffer

———————•———————

The setting is Tchaik's London apartment. (Tchaik is the nickname given to him by his friend, Ted, because he likes classical music, particularly Tchaikovsky.) Tchaik met a girl at a concert. Usually shy and awkward, he managed to invite her to his flat for dinner. Afraid he would not know what to talk about, he also invited his suave and smooth-talking friend, Ted. Ted has agreed to cook dinner. During the time between the concert and the dinner, Tchaik has built up his image of the girl into a goddess—pure, intelligent, cultured. A rude awakening awaits him. The excerpt below is the opening scene of the play.

The curtain rises on Tchaik's flat. Music is playing: Mozart on the gramophone. The door bursts open; Tchaik rushes in, in bathrobe and slippers, towelling his head. Throughout the scene he displays agitation and indecision in his preparations. There is an iron plugged into the electric light. He throws the towel on the bed, takes trousers from wardrobe, places them on the table and begins to press them. No result. He tests the iron, realizes it is not hot, looks up at the hanging lamp which is off, puts the iron down on the trousers, runs to left of kitchen door and turns on the wall switch. He crosses to the armchair and picks up a paper bag in which there is a deodorant stick, throws bag in wastebasket upstage center and crosses to the dresser, dropping his robe around his waist. He opens the stick and applies it to his armpit—he sniffs it. Satisfied, he applies it to the other. He puts the top on the stick, looks around and sees the iron on his pants. Alarmed, he runs to the table, picks the iron up and gingerly feels it. It is still not warm. He sits in chair above table and looks at it. A transistor is heard through the Mozart and Ted enters from left carrying a shopping bag and a small transistor radio which is playing loudly. He pauses inside the door and looks at Tchaik. He crosses to the red armchair, drops his bag in it, then crosses to the gramophone and takes the arm off it and switches off the gramophone.

TED, *as he rushes to the gramophone:* Christ! D'you know what time it is?

TCHAIK, *seated behind table:* What?

TED, *switching off transistor:* Seven-twenty-two. What the hell have you been up to while I've been doing your shopping? Dreaming, I suppose, as usual.

TCHAIK: I haven't.

TED: You're marvelous! The most important night of your life, and you can't even get yourself dressed. All you can do is listen to bloody music. *He gets a small vase from dresser.*

TCHAIK: I wasn't listening. It was just on.

TED, *crossing to right of table:* I bet. And what are you doing now?

TCHAIK: Pressing my trousers. But it won't get hot.

TED: If she's on time you've got eight minutes. *Crosses to armchair and takes flowers from bag.* I bought you some flowers. *Throws transistor on bed.*

TCHAIK, *trying to press pants:* They're nice. Did I give you enough money?

TED, *takes vase and flowers into kitchen and fills vase with water:* Oh, they're on me. They'll provide that chic touch you're just a tiny bit in need of. *Off:* Did you have a bath?

TCHAIK: Yes.

TED: Did you use that stick I gave you? *He reenters from kitchen.*

TCHAIK: Yes.

TED: It's a hot evening. There's no point in taking any chances. *Puts vase on table.* Did you take that chlorophyll tablet? *Sniffing his breath.*

TCHAIK: Oh, for heaven's sake!

TED: Did you?

TCHAIK: Yes.

TED: I'll do that. *Takes iron and presses pants.* You get your shirt on. *Tchaik gets his shirt, which is hanging in the upstage window, puts it on and crosses to dresser.* What are you wearing over that?

TCHAIK: I thought my blazer.

TED: It's a bit schooly, but she'll probably like that. Makes you look boyish. You'll bring out the protective in her. What tie?

TCHAIK, *taking blue and white striped tie from dresser:* I thought this one.

TED: Oh yes, gorgeous. What is it? The Sheffield Young Men's Prayer Club?

TCHAIK, *holding it out:* Don't be daft. What's wrong with it?

TED, *takes tie:* You really don't know, do you? Look: that sort of striped tie, well, it marks you, see? "I'm a twelve-pound-a-week office worker," it says. "Every day I say, Come on five-thirty, and every week I say, Come on Friday night. That's me and I'm contented with my lot." That's what that tie says to me.

TCHAIK, *he has his shirt on—retrieves tie:* Well, you've got very good hearing, that's what I say.

TED: Where's that green shantung one I gave you last Christmas?

TCHAIK: I lost it.

TED: Typical.

TCHAIK, *putting on tie:* It isn't. I never lose anything.

TED: I think your subconscious would make you lose anything that was chic.

TCHAIK: That's idiotic. And so's that word.

TED: What? Chic?

TCHAIK: Yes. What's it supposed to mean?

TED: It's French for with it.

TCHAIK: "With it"?

TED: Yes, with it. Which is what you're not, and high time you were. You can't stay in the Provinces all your life, you know. I can't do a thing with this material. You'd better put them on. *Throws pants to Tchaik.* Six minutes. *Tchaik crosses upstage to right of bed and puts on trousers. Ted stands on chair and unplugs iron.* You're not going to let me down tonight, are you?

TCHAIK: What do you mean?

TED, *crossing to the kitchen, wrapping the cord around the iron as he goes:* You know what you're going to do this evening? I mean, you know what I'm expecting you to do, don't you? *Pauses in the door, turns off wall switch, puts iron in kitchen. Tchaik puts robe on bed. Ted appears in kitchen door.* Eh?

TCHAIK, *sits foot of bed:* Look, Ted, it's not that way at all.

TED: No?

TCHAIK: No, not at all.

TED, *takes shopping bag into kitchen:* Well then, I'm wasting my time here, aren't I? With all due respect, mate, there are rival attractions to playing chef to you, you know. Do you know where I could be tonight? This very night? *Takes out his wallet and selects a photo.*

TCHAIK: Where?

TED: With her! Look. *Shows Tchaik photo.*

TCHAIK: Goodness.

TED: How about them for a pair of bubbles? And that hair— you can't keep your hands off it. It's what they call raven.

TCHAIK: Raven?

TED: Raven black. It's got tints of blue in it. *He crosses center.*

TCHAIK: Where did you meet this one? *Puts on socks.*

TED, *left of table:* In the Whisky A Go-Go, last night, twisting herself giddy with some little nit. I sort of detached her. She only wanted a date for tonight, didn't she? But I said, "Sorry, doll, no can do. I'm engaged for one night only, at great expense, as chef to my mate Tchaik, who is entertaining a bird of his own. *Très special occasion."* (*The second sock has a large hole in it, through which Tchaik's toes appear.*) Come on! *Ted has seen this and motions Tchaik to the dresser for a fresh pair. Tchaik crosses to dresser, gets another pair from the top drawer, and returns to the bed. Ted folds the blanket from the table and throws it in the wardrobe.* So be grateful. Greater love hath no man, than to pass up a bird like this for his mate. *Ted picks up photo from bed and leans it against vase on table.* Look at the way she holds herself. That's what they used to call carriage. You don't see too much of that nowadays. Most of the girls I meet think they've got it, ignorant little nits. That is the genuine article, that is. Carriage. Miss Carriage.

TCHAIK, *who now has socks and one shoe on—going into the kitchen:* What's her name?

TED: You won't believe me if I tell you. Lavinia.

TCHAIK: Lavinia?

TED, *sits armchair:* Honest. How's that for a sniff of class? The rest of it isn't so good. Botty. Lavinia Botty.

TCHAIK, *reentering with tray on which are three knives, forks, spoons, napkins, place mats, tumblers, and a pitcher of water and a salt cellar:* She's beautiful.

TED: Do you think so?

TCHAIK, *puts tray on chair above table:* Yes.

TED: She's going to go off fairly quickish. In three years she'll be all lumpy, like old porridge.

TCHAIK, *crosses to dresser, gets tablecloth:* I don't know how you do it. I don't, honest.

TED, *raising the upstage leaf of table:* Just don't promise them anything, that's all. Make no promises, they can't hang anything on you, can they? *As Tchaik lays the cloth, Ted picks up vase and photo, then replaces them on the cloth.*

TCHAIK: I wouldn't know.

TED: Well you're going to, after tonight.

TCHAIK, *protesting:* Ted!

TED: Here. I heard a good one the other day. The National Gallery just paid ten thousand pounds for a picture of a woman with five breasts. D'you know what it's called?

TCHAIK: What?

TED: "Sanctity."

TCHAIK, *not understanding:* Sanctity.

TED: Un, deux, trois, quatre, cinq . . . *Tchaik crosses to kitchen door, puzzled. Turns to give a grin of comprehension and exits with tray.* What do you call this, laying a table?

TCHAIK, *reenters and picks up the other shoe:* What's wrong with it?

TED: We're all left-handed, are we?

TCHAIK: Oh, lord. *He hurries to re-lay the table. In his haste he upsets the vase.*

TED: Well, get a cloth. *Tchaik scurries onto the balcony to get it.* You've wet my Lavinia. We'll have to dry you out, love. *He crosses and puts her in the mirror. Tchaik crosses down and begins to mop the table.* You've got the pit-a-pats. Now look, Tchaik: If you get in a state, the evening will be a fiasco. So sit there and calm down.

TCHAIK, *sits in the armchair and puts on his other shoe:* I am calm.

TED, *crosses into kitchen:* After all, this is just a girl, isn't it? Even if you say she looks like a Greek goddess, she's still only flesh and blood.

TCHAIK, *looking at his watch:* What time do you make it?

TED, *takes wine from shopping bag and puts it in the icebox:* Seven thirty just gone.

TCHAIK: Do you think she's not coming?

TED, *reenters and stands at foot of bed:* Of course she's coming. It's a free dinner, isn't it? I hope you've put clean sheets on this bed.

TCHAIK: What for? Oh, Ted, I wish you'd stop talking like that. *Crosses onto balcony to replace cloth.*

TED, *takes out a pack of Gaulloises and lights one:* Look. Let's get things a bit clear. You go to hundreds of concerts. This is the first time you've picked up a bird and invited her home for fried chicken and vino, isn't it?

TCHAIK, *left of table—ties one shoe:* I didn't pick her up. She was sitting next to me and dropped her program.

TED: On purpose.

TCHAIK, *crosses downstage center:* Don't be silly. She's not the sort.

TED: Everyone's the sort.

TCHAIK: Well, she isn't. I just know. *To front of table, and ties other shoe.*

TED, *crosses to below stool:* Well what's so wrong if she did? She wanted to get to know you. It's just possible, you know, that someone might want to get to know you.

TCHAIK, *uncomfortably:* Don't be daft.

TED, *softer:* You might try believing that, Tchaik. *A tiny pause.*

TCHAIK, *pours himself a glass of water:* In any case, I didn't pick her up. That's a ridiculous expression, anyway. Sort of suggests weight-lifting.

TED, *sits on stool:* What did you do then?

TCHAIK, *crosses to dresser:* Well, I asked her if she liked music. It was a daft question really, because she wouldn't have been at a concert otherwise, would she? It turned out that she was on her own, so I asked her to have a coffee with me after. I could hardly believe it when she said yes. *Takes a drink.*

TED: Why not? Even goddesses get thirsty.

TCHAIK: We went to an Espresso bar in Kensington.

TED: And held hands under the table?

TCHAIK, *crosses center and sits in armchair:* Not exactly. As a matter of fact, I couldn't think of anything to say to her. We just sat there for a little while and then left.

TED: So that's why you asked me here tonight? To help out with the talk?

TCHAIK: Well, you know what to say to women. You've had the practice.

TED: There's no practice needed. Just keep it going, that's all. Bright and not too filthy. The main thing is to edge it subtly towards where you want it to go. You know. In your case you'll be able to start off with music. *He edges stool closer to the chair.* "What a nice concert that was." *Still closer.* "I do like Mozart so much, don't you?" Then if she's got any sense at all she'll say, "Oh, yes, he does things to me!" and you'll say, *(this time the stool ends up right next to the chair)* "What kind of things?"—and you're off to the races then, aren't you? *He rises and crosses center.* I'll give you a tip that usually works a treat. After a couple of hours, if she asks for a cigarette, don't give it to her; light it in your mouth and then hand it to her. *He demonstrates.* It's very intimate.

TCHAIK: I don't smoke.

TED, *crosses upstage center onto balcony:* Well, you'll have to work out your own style, of course.

TCHAIK: What's it matter? She's not coming anyway.

TED, *sarcastic:* Of course not.

TCHAIK: I mean it. Look at the time. It's nearly quarter to. She's thought better of it, I bet you.

TED, *on balcony:* Oh, don't be silly. Most girls think it's chic to be a little late. They think it makes them more desirable. It's only a trick.

TCHAIK: No, that's not her. She doesn't play tricks. That's why all that stuff is so silly—all this plotting. I say this, and she says that. I think things should just happen between people.

TED, *crosses downstage center to right of Tchaik:* Oh, yes. And how many times have they just happened with you?

TCHAIK: Well, that depends on what you want to happen.

TED: You know bloody well what you want to happen. *Crosses to stool, kicks it back to its original position, and sits.*

TCHAIK, *urgently:* I don't. I don't. I don't. This isn't the sort of girl you can make plots about. It would be all wrong. Because she's sort of inaccessible. Pure—but not cold. Very warm.

TED: And you know all this after ten minutes' silence in a coffee bar?

TCHAIK, *rises and puts glass on table:* You can know things like that without talking. She's not a talker—she's a listener.

That can be more profound, you know. And she's got a look about her—not how people are, but how they ought to be. Do you know when I said that about a goddess, do you know who I was thinking of? Her.

TED: Venus?

TCHAIK: She's got exactly the same neck—long and gentle. That's a sign.

TED: What of?

TCHAIK: Spiritual beauty. Like Venus. *Crosses to shelf downstage right for book and back again to center:* That's what the picture really represents. The birth of beauty in the human soul. My Botticelli book says so. Listen. *Reading from a Fontana pocket book:* "Venus, that is to say humanity, is a nymph of excellent comeliness, born of heaven. Her soul and mind are Love and Charity. Her eyes, dignity. Her hands, liberality. Her feet, modesty." All signs, you see. "Venus is the mother of Grace, of Beauty, and of Faith."

TED: And this bird of yours is the mother of all that?

TCHAIK, *sits armchair:* No, of course not. Stop trying to make me into a fool. What I mean is, that look of hers is ideal beauty, TED. It means she's got grace inside her. Really beautiful people are beautiful inside them. Do you see?

TED: You mean like after taking Andrew's Liver Salts?

TCHAIK, *rising and replacing book downstage right:* Yes, that's exactly what I mean.

TED: Oh, Tchaik, now seriously, come off it. That's all a lot of balls, and you know it. There's a lot of dim, greedy little nitty girls about who are as pretty as pictures.

TCHAIK, *puts Mozart record in sleeve:* I don't mean pretty. I mean . . . well, what you called carriage, for instance. What your Lavinia's got. It's not just something you learn, the way to walk and that. It's something inside you. I mean real carriage, the way you see some girls walk, sort of putting the air around them like clothes—you can't practice that. You've got first to love the world. Then it comes out. *Puts sleeve in record jacket. Tiny pause.*

TED, *rising:* You poor nut.

TCHAIK: What do you mean? *Puts record jacket on shelf.*

TED: Nut. Nut.

TCHAIK: Why?

TED: Oh, dear for you.

The doorbell rings.

TCHAIK: God! There she is.

Tchaik rushes to the wardrobe for his blazer. Ted picks up towel, robe, and slippers from the bed. Tchaik crosses to door—Ted to wardrobe—they collide upstage center. Ted throws towel, robe, slippers into the wardrobe. He turns and sees the tags on the blazer, runs to Tchaik and rips them off.

TED: Now listen. Last swallow of coffee and I'm away. Cleaning tag! Nine thirty you'll see me. Nine thirty-one you won't. Work to do at home—get it? *Tchaik exits.* Oh, hey—where's the bottle of Dubonnet? *Tchaik reenters speechless.* It's the one thing I left you to do.

TCHAIK: I know. I forgot.

TED: You nit! Now you've nothing to give her for a cocktail.

The bell rings again.

TCHAIK: What am I going to do?

TED: Well, there's nothing you can do, is there? Just don't mention it, that's all. Say nothing about it. She comes from the suburbs. She probably won't expect anything. Wine at dinner will impress her enough.

TCHAIK: Oh, hell.

TED: Why don't you leave her standing there. She'll go away in five minutes. *He pushes Tchaik out of the door.*

DEATHTRAP

by Ira Levin

ACT II, SCENE 1

Deathtrap is a comedy thriller that twists and turns its way from shock to laugh to shock and back again. Sidney is a mystery playwright living with his wife, Myra, in Connecticut.

Their living room is decorated with theatrical artifacts and real weapons—both ancient and modern. Sidney has taken up with Clifford, a young male playwrighting student, and with Clifford's aid, he contrives and carries out a plan to murder Myra. The plan involves his receiving a great new play in the mail from a young playwright, then leading Myra to believe that he intends to murder the playwright to steal his play, then inviting the playwright (Clifford) to the house. The plot climaxes with a series of violent and startling altercations that, as planned, leave the sickly Myra dead on the floor of a heart attack. The authorities have no reason to expect foul play, and Clifford moves in with Sidney. The next day the two writers are sitting at adjoining desks, pursuing their respective careers side by side. But Sidney, whose one theatrical success was followed by four flops, sits idly by his typewriter and blank pages, while Clifford types away at a feverish pace. Clifford is supposedly writing a serious play about a welfare office but he refuses to show the manuscript to Sidney "till the draft is done." While Clifford is away on an errand, Sidney jimmies open the desk drawer in which Clifford's manuscript is locked away. To his amazement and horror he discovers that the play Clifford is writing is actually an accurate reenactment of Myra's murder, down to the detail of an unexpected visit by a female Dutch psychic. Clifford returns and resumes his typing but Sidney interrupts by reading the opening paragraphs of Clifford's script.

CLIFFORD: That's it? You're not going to act out the eleven pages? Would you like me to explain?

SIDNEY: What's to explain? You're a lunatic with a death wish; Freud covered it thoroughly.

CLIFFORD: I have exactly the same wish you have: a success wish.

SIDNEY: *This*—is going to bring you success?

CLIFFORD: It hit me that night. Remember, I put in that extra speech when you were looking for the key? It can be a terrific thriller.

SIDNEY: In which someone like me and someone like you give someone like Myra a fatal heart attack?

CLIFFORD: Yes. At the end of Act One.

SIDNEY: What, pray tell, is your *definition* of success? Being gang-banged in the shower room at the state penitentiary?

CLIFFORD: I knew you would have reservations about it; that's why my first instinct was to say it wasn't even a thriller. I haven't enjoyed putting you on, Sidney. I'm glad it's out in the open.

SIDNEY: You knew I would have reservations ...

CLIFFORD: Well you do, don't you?

SIDNEY: The house madman is writing a play that'll send both of us to prison—

CLIFFORD: It won't!

SIDNEY: —I'm standing here terrified, petrified, horrified, stupefied, *crapping my pants*—and he calls that "having reservations." I'm not going to use one of *those* on you; I'm going to beat you to death with *Roget's Thesaurus!*

CLIFFORD: There is no possible way for anyone to prove what did or did not cause Myra's heart attack. Look, if I could change things I would, but I can't; it *has* to be a playwright. Who else can pretend to receive a finished work that could make tons of money?

SIDNEY: A novelist! A composer! Why am I discussing this?

CLIFFORD: A sure-fire smash-hit symphony? No. And would a novelist or a composer know where to get a garrotte that squirts blood, and how to stage a convincing murder? And it has to be a playwright *who writes thrillers,* because Arthur Miller probably has old sample cases hanging on his wall. I *suppose* I could make it Wilton instead of Westport ...

SIDNEY: Why make it *anywhere? Why make it?*

CLIFFORD: It's *there,* Sidney!

SIDNEY: That's mountains, not plays! Plays aren't there till some asshole writes them!

CLIFFORD: Stop and think for a minute, will you? Think. About that night. Try to see it all from an audience's viewpoint. *Everything we did to convince Myra that she was seeing a real murder—would have exactly the same effect on them.* Weren't *we* giving a play? Didn't we write it, rehearse it? Wasn't *she* our audience? *He rises. Sidney is listening as one fascinated by a lunatic's raving.* Scene One: Julian tells Doris about this terrific play that's come in the mail. He jokes about killing for it, then calls Willard and invites him over, getting him to bring the original copy. Audience thinks exactly what Doris thinks: Julian might kill Willard. Scene Two: *everything that happened from the moment we came through that door.* All the little ups and downs we put in to make it ring true: the I'm-expecting-a-phone-call bit, everything. Tightened up a little, naturally. And then the strangling, which scares the audience as much as it does Doris.

SIDNEY: No wonder you didn't need an outline . . .

CLIFFORD, *tapping his temple:* It's all up here, every bit of it. Scene Three: "Inga Van Bronk." A few laughs, right? Can't hurt. Then Julian and Doris get ready to go upstairs—it looks as if the act is drawing to a kind of so-so close—and pow, in comes Willard, out of the grave and seeking vengeance. Shock? Surprise? Doris has her heart attack, Julian gets up from the fake beating—and the audience realizes that Julian and Willard are in cahoots, that there isn't any sure-fire thriller, that Willard is moving in. The curtain is Julian burning the manuscripts. Or calling the doctor; I'm not sure which. Now be honest about it: isn't that a sure-fire first act?

SIDNEY: Yes. And what an intermission. Twenty years to life.

CLIFFORD: No one can prove it really happened. They *can't.* How can they?

SIDNEY: And what do you say to the man from the *Times,* when he says, "Don't you work for Sidney Bruhl, and didn't his wife have a heart attack just around the time you came there?"

CLIFFORD, *turning out his hands for the obvious answer:* "No comment."

SIDNEY: Oh my God . . . *(moves upstage in futility)*

CLIFFORD: I know it's going to be a little sticky, but—well, everybody's opening up about everything these days, aren't they? In print, on TV; why not on stage, as long as it can't be proved? I've given it some serious thought, Sidney, and I honestly believe it'll *help* the play, give it an added dimension of—intriguing gossip.

SIDNEY: I'm sure you're right. I can see the little box in *New York Magazine* now: "Tongues are wagging about interesting similarities between events in the new play *Deathtrap* and the private lives of its author Clifford Anderson and his employer Sidney Bruhl, who committed suicide on opening night. When queried, Mr. Anderson said, 'No comment.'" *I* have a comment, Cliff. No. Absolutely, definitely *no.* I have a name and a reputation—tattered, perhaps, but still valid for dinner invitations, house seats, and the conducting of summer seminars. I want to live out my years as "author of *The Murder Game*," not "fag who knocked off his wife." *Turns right.* Why look, a fieldstone fireplace! *Heading for it, folder at the ready:* Let's see if it's practical to the extent that paper—

CLIFFORD, *interrupting him:* DON'T YOU DARE! *Sidney stops.* You burn that—and I go out of here and write it again somewhere else. I'll—get a house-sitting job. *Goes to Sidney and puts out his hand.* Give it to me. Give it, Sidney. *Sidney turns, and hands the folder to Clifford.* I helped you kill for the chance to become what I want to be. You're not going to take it away from me. *He goes to the desk, Sidney watches him.* I had *hoped* that when I showed you the finished draft, you would be impressed enough to—get over your *Angel Street* uptightness and pitch in, but I guess we can forget about *that*.

SIDNEY, *smiles faintly:* A collaboration?

CLIFFORD: It's mostly your idea, isn't it? I'm not pretending it's all my baby. And I know that Scene One is coming out a little—heavy and stilted. I hoped we could be a team, Bruhl and Anderson.

SIDNEY: Rodgers and Heartless.

CLIFFORD: Now you see, I could never come up with something like that.

SIDNEY: I'm sorry, but I really don't feel like collaborating on my public humiliation.

CLIFFORD: Next season's hit. Don't say I didn't ask.

Index

FOR THE BEST IN PAPERBACKS, LOOK FOR THE

In every corner of the world, on every subject under the sun, Penguin represents quality and variety—the very best in publishing today.

For complete information about books available from Penguin—including Pelicans, Puffins, Peregrines, and Penguin Classics—and how to order them, write to us at the appropriate address below. Please note that for copyright reasons the selection of books varies from country to country.

In the United Kingdom: For a complete list of books available from Penguin in the U.K., please write to *Dept E.P., Penguin Books Ltd, Harmondsworth, Middlesex, UB7 0DA*.

In the United States: For a complete list of books available from Penguin in the U.S., please write to *Dept BA, Penguin*, Box 120, Bergenfield, New Jersey 07621-0120.

In Canada: For a complete list of books available from Penguin in Canada, please write to *Penguin Books Canada Ltd, 10 Alcorn Avenue, Suite 300, Toronto, Ontario, Canada M4V 3B2*.

In Australia: For a complete list of books available from Penguin in Australia, please write to the *Marketing Department, Penguin Books Ltd, P.O. Box 257, Ringwood, Victoria 3134*.

In New Zealand: For a complete list of books available from Penguin in New Zealand, please write to the *Marketing Department, Penguin Books (NZ) Ltd, Private Bag, Takapuna, Auckland 9*.

In India: For a complete list of books available from Penguin, please write to *Penguin Overseas Ltd, 706 Eros Apartments, 56 Nehru Place, New Delhi, 110019*.

In Holland: For a complete list of books available from Penguin in Holland, please write to *Penguin Books Nederland B.V., Postbus 195, NL-1380AD Weesp, Netherlands*.

In Germany: For a complete list of books available from Penguin, please write to *Penguin Books Ltd, Friedrichstrasse 10-12, D-6000 Frankfurt Main 1, Federal Republic of Germany*.

In Spain: For a complete list of books available from Penguin in Spain, please write to *Longman, Penguin España, Calle San Nicolas 15, E-28013 Madrid, Spain*.

In Japan: For a complete list of books available from Penguin in Japan, please write to *Longman Penguin Japan Co Ltd, Yamaguchi Building, 2-12-9 Kanda Jimbocho, Chiyoda-Ku, Tokyo 101, Japan*.

FOR THE BEST LITERATURE, LOOK FOR THE

☐ **VOSS**
Patrick White

Set in nineteenth-century Australia, *Voss* is the story of the secret passion between an explorer and a young orphan. From the careful delineation of Victorian society to the stark narrative of adventure in the Australian desert, Patrick White's novel is one of extraordinary power and virtuosity. White won the Nobel Prize for Literature in 1973.

448 pages   ISBN: 0-14-001438-1

☐ **STONES FOR IBARRA**
Harriet Doerr

An American couple, the only foreigners in the Mexican village of Ibarra, have come to reopen a long-dormant copper mine. Their plan is to live out their lives here, connected to the place and to each other. Along the way, they learn much about life, death, and the tide of fate from the Mexican people around them.

214 pages   ISBN: 0-14-007562-3

You can find all these books at your local bookstore, or use this handy coupon for ordering:

Penguin Books By Mail
Dept. BA Box 999
Bergenfield, NJ 07621-0999

Please send me the above title(s). I am enclosing _____
(please add sales tax if appropriate and $1.50 to cover postage and handling). Send check or money order—no CODs. Please allow four weeks for shipping. We cannot ship to post office boxes or addresses outside the USA. *Prices subject to change without notice.*

Ms./Mrs./Mr. _____

Address _____

City/State _____ Zip _____

☐ **A SPORT OF NATURE**
Nadine Gordimer

Hillela, Nadine Gordimer's "sport of nature," is seductive and intuitively gifted at life. Casting herself adrift from her family at seventeen, she lives among political exiles on an East African beach, marries a black revolutionary, and ultimately plays a heroic role in the overthrow of apartheid.

        354 pages   *ISBN: 0-14-008470-3*

☐ **THE COUNTERLIFE**
Philip Roth

By far Philip Roth's most radical work of fiction, *The Counterlife* is a book of conflicting perspectives and points of view about people living out dreams of renewal and escape. Illuminating these lives is the skeptical, enveloping intelligence of the novelist Nathan Zuckerman, who calculates the price and examines the results of his characters' struggles for a change of personal fortune.

        372 pages   *ISBN: 0-14-009769-4*

☐ **THE MONKEY'S WRENCH**
Primo Levi

Through the mesmerizing tales told by two characters—one, a construction worker/philosopher who has built towers and bridges in India and Alaska; the other, a writer/chemist, rigger of words and molecules—Primo Levi celebrates the joys of work and the art of storytelling.

        174 pages   *ISBN: 0-14-010357-0*

☐ **IRONWEED**
William Kennedy

"Riding up the winding road of Saint Agnes Cemetery in the back of the rattling old truck, Francis Phelan became aware that the dead, even more than the living, settled down in neighborhoods." So begins William Kennedy's Pulitzer-Prize winning novel about an ex-ballplayer, part-time gravedigger, and full-time drunk, whose return to the haunts of his youth arouses the ghosts of his past and present.   *228 pages*   *ISBN: 0-14-007020-6*

☐ **THE COMEDIANS**
Graham Greene

Set in Haiti under Duvalier's dictatorship, *The Comedians* is a story about the committed and the uncommitted. Actors with no control over their destiny, they play their parts in the foreground; experience love affairs rather than love; have enthusiasms but not faith; and if they die, they die like Mr. Jones, by accident.

        288 pages   *ISBN: 0-14-002766-1*

FOR THE BEST LITERATURE, LOOK FOR THE

☐ **HERZOG**
Saul Bellow

Winner of the National Book Award, *Herzog* is the imaginative and critically acclaimed story of Moses Herzog: joker, moaner, cuckhold, charmer, and truly an Everyman for our time.

342 pages   ISBN: 0-14-007270-5

☐ **FOOLS OF FORTUNE**
William Trevor

The deeply affecting story of two cousins—one English, one Irish—brought together and then torn apart by the tide of Anglo-Irish hatred, *Fools of Fortune* presents a profound symbol of the tragic entanglements of England and Ireland in this century.   *240 pages   ISBN: 0-14-006982-8*

☐ **THE SONGLINES**
Bruce Chatwin

Venturing into the desolate land of Outback Australia—along timeless paths, and among fortune hunters, redneck Australians, racist policemen, and mysterious Aboriginal holy men—Bruce Chatwin discovers a wondrous vision of man's place in the world.   *296 pages   ISBN: 0-14-009429-6*

☐ **THE GUIDE: A NOVEL**
R. K. Narayan

Raju was once India's most corrupt tourist guide; now, after a peasant mistakes him for a holy man, he gradually begins to play the part. His succeeds so well that God himself intervenes to put Raju's new holiness to the test.

220 pages   ISBN: 0-14-009657-4

FOR THE BEST LITERATURE, LOOK FOR THE

☐ **THE LAST SONG OF MANUEL SENDERO**
Ariel Dorfman

In an unnamed country, in a time that might be now, the son of Manuel Sendero refuses to be born, beginning a revolution where generations of the future wait for a world without victims or oppressors.

464 pages   ISBN: 0-14-008896-2

☐ **THE BOOK OF LAUGHTER AND FORGETTING**
Milan Kundera

In this collection of stories and sketches, Kundera addresses themes including sex and love, poetry and music, sadness and the power of laughter. "*The Book of Laughter and Forgetting* calls itself a novel," writes John Leonard of *The New York Times*, "although it is part fairly tale, part literary criticism, part political tract, part musicology, part autobiography. It can call itself whatever it wants to, because the whole is genius."

240 pages   ISBN: 0-14-009693-0

☐ **TIRRA LIRRA BY THE RIVER**
Jessica Anderson

Winner of the Miles Franklin Award, Australia's most prestigious literary prize, *Tirra Lirra by the River* is the story of a woman's seventy-year search for the place where she truly belongs. Nora Porteous's series of escapes takes her from a small Australia town to the suburbs of Sydney to London, where she seems finally to become the woman she always wanted to be.

142 pages   ISBN: 0-14-006945-3

☐ **LOVE UNKNOWN**
A. N. Wilson

In their sweetly wild youth, Monica, Belinda, and Richeldis shared a bachelor-girl flat and became friends for life. Now, twenty years later, A. N. Wilson charts the intersecting lives of the three women through the perilous waters of love, marriage, and adultery in this wry and moving modern comedy of manners.

202 pages   ISBN: 0-14-010190-X

☐ **THE WELL**
Elizabeth Jolley

Against the stark beauty of the Australian farmlands, Elizabeth Jolley portrays an eccentric, affectionate relationship between the two women—Hester, a lonely spinster, and Katherine, a young orphan. Their pleasant, satisfyingly simple life is nearly perfect until a dark stranger invades their world in a most horrifying way.

176 pages   ISBN: 0-14-008901-2